100
IRREGULAR
PERSIAN VERBS

Fully Conjugated in the Most Common Tenses

Nazanin Mirsadeghi

Bahar Books

www.baharbooks.com

Mirsadeghi, Nazanin
100 Irregular Persian Verbs - Fully Conjugated in the Most Common Tenses(Farsi- English Bi-lingual Edition)/Nazanin Mirsadeghi

ISBN-10: 1939099196
ISBN-13: 978-1939099198

Published by Bahar Books, White Plains, New York

INTRODUCTION

"100 Irregular Persian Verbs" provides you with immediate access to correct irregular verb forms of the Persian language.

Finding the Persian verb conjunctions is not usually an easy task, especially if the verbs are irregular. Using this type of verbs in their correct forms might be a challenge, since the stem of the verbs changes when they conjugate.

This book has been designed to be used as a quick and easy way to find the full conjunction of some essential irregular Persian verbs. In order to use this book effectively, you must be able to read and write in Persian, and be familiar with the grammar and the basic structure of the Persian language. However, in the beginning of the book, some essential materials regarding the Persian alphabet, pronunciation of the Persian letters, the definition of different Persian verb tenses and their uses have been provided.

The book also consists of a brief overview of grammatical rules regarding the Persian verbs and the identification of the present and past stems in regular verbs. In addition, a table of the present and past stems for the 100 irregular verbs presented in this book is included to facilitate the learning process.

Those who are learning the Persian language could use this book as a reference and will find it helpful as they advance their language skills.

Nazanin Mirsadeghi

Pronunciation Guide for the Persian Letters

ă like the "a" in arm	آ – ا *
b like the "b" in boy	بـ – ب
p like the "p" in play	پـ – پ
t like the "t" in tree	تـ – ت
s like the "s" in sun	ثـ – ث
j like the "j" in jam	جـ – ج
č like the "ch" in child	چـ – چ
h like the "h" in hotel	حـ – ح
ǩ like "ch" in the German word *bach*, or Hebrew word *smach*.	خـ – خ
d like the "d" in door	د
z like the "z" in zebra	ذ
r like the "r" in rabbit	ر
z like the "z" in zebra	ز
ž like the "z" in zwago	ژ
s like the "s" in sun	سـ – س
š like the "sh" in shell	شـ – ش
s like the "s" in sun	صـ – ص
z like the "z" in zebra	ضـ – ض
t like the "t" in tree	ط

z like the **"z"** in zebra	ظ
ʿ is a glottal stop, like between the syllables of "uh-oh".	ع – ﻌ – ﻊ
ǧ like the **"r"** in French word *merci*	غ – ﻐ – ﻎ
f like the **"f"** in fall	ف – ﻒ
ǧ like the **"r"** in French word *merci*	ق – ﻖ
k like the **"k"** in kite	ک – ﻚ
g like the **"g"** in game	گ – ﮒ
l like the **"l"** in lost	ل – ﻞ
m like the **"m"** in master	م – ﻤ
n like the **"n"** in night	ن – ﻦ
v like the **"v"** in van	و
o like the **"o"** in ocean	و
On some occasions, it has no sound and becomes silent.	و
u like the **"u"** in sure	* او – و
h like the **"h"** in hotel	ه – ﻬ – ﻪ – ﻩ
e like the **"e"** in element	ﻪ – ﻩ
y like the **"y"** in yellow	ﻳ – ی
i like the **"ee"** in need	* ای – ﻳ – ی – ﺍی

* long vowels

Represents doubled consonants.	ـّ

a like the **"a"** in animal	ـَ أَ **
o like the **"o"** in ocean	ـُ أُ **
e like the **"e"** in element	ـِ اِ **

** short vowels

Persian Letters with the Same Pronunciation

t like the **"t"** in tree	ت – ت
	ط
ǧ like the **"r"** in French word *merci*	ق – ق
	غ – ـغ – ـغ
h like the **"h"** in hotel	ح – ح
	ه – ـه – ـهـ – ـه
s like the **"s"** in sun	ث – ث
	س – س
	ص – ص
z like the **"z"** in zebra	ذ
	ز
	ض
	ظ

Names Given to the Persian Letters

alef	آ – ا
be	ب – بـ
pe	پ – پـ
te	ت – تـ
se	ث – ثـ
jim	ج – جـ
če	چ – چـ
he	ح – حـ
ǩe	خ – خـ
dǎl	د
zǎl	ذ
re	ر
ze	ز
že	ژ
sin	س – سـ
šin	ش – شـ
sǎd	ص – صـ
zǎd	ض – ضـ
tǎ	ط

zǎ	ظ
eyn	ع – ع – ء
ğeyn	غ – ـغـ – ـغ
fe	ف – ف
ğǎf	ق – ق
kǎf	ک – ک
gǎf	گ – گ
lǎm	ل – ا
mim	م – ـه
noon	ن – ز
vǎv	و
he	ه – ـه – ـه – ه
ye	ی – ـی

Persian Pronouns

Plural	Singular
We = ما	**I = من**
/mǎ/	/man/
You = شما	**You = تو**
/šo.mǎ/	/to/
They = آنها	**She – He/ It = او/آن**
/ǎn.hǎ/	/u/ ǎn/

Persian Verb Tenses

Simple Present

مضارع اخباری(حال ساده)

It is used to indicate one of the following:

a) An action at the present time.

Example:

رایان دعوت تو را می پذیرد.

/rǎ.yǎn- daʿ.va.te- to- rǎ- mi.pa.zi.rad/

Ryan *accepts* your invitation.

b) A habitual action.

Example:

شما هر روز برنج می پزید؟

/šo.mǎ- har- ruz- be.renj- mi.pa.zid/

Do you *cook* rice every day?

c) An action in the future.

Example:

برادرم فردا از کانادا برمی گردد.

/ba.rǎ.da.ram- far.dǎ- az- kǎ.nǎ.dǎ- bar.mi.gar.dad/

My brother *will return* from Canada tomorrow.

Present Subjunctive

مضارع التزامی

It is used after a verb that expresses one of the following:

a) A suggestion.

Example:

بهتر است اوّل برای مادرت نامه بنویسی.

/beh.tar- ast- av.val- ba.rǎ.ye- mǎ.da.rat- nǎ.me- be.ne.vi.si/

It's better that (you) *write* a letter to your mother first.

b) A wish.

Example:

ما امیدواریم که تو با ما به پاریس بیایی.

/mǎ- o.mid.vǎ.rim- ke- to- bǎ- mǎ- be- pǎ.ris- bi.yǎ.yi/

We hope that you *come* with us to Paris.

c) A preference.

Example:

لیلا ترجیح می دهد که پسرش فرانسوی بیاموزد.

/ley.lǎ- tar.jih- mi.da.had- ke- pe.sa.raš- fa.rǎn.sa.vi- bi.yǎ.mu.zad/

Leila prefers that her son *learn* French.

d) A doubt.

Example:

شک دارم رایان حقیقت را به دوستانش بگوید.

/šak- dǎ.ram- rǎ.yǎn- ha.ǧi.ǧat- rǎ- be- dus.tǎ.naš- be.gu.yad/

(I) doubt that Ryan *tell* his friends the truth.

e) A necessity.

Example:

من باید لباس ها را بشویم.

/man- bǎ.yad- le.bǎs.hǎ- rǎ- be.šu.yam/

I *have to wash* the clothes.

X

Present Progressive

مضارع مستمر(در جریان)

It is used to describe an action that is an on-going action and that is happening right now. The simple present tense of the verb "داشتن" is always used to conjugate all verbs in the present progressive tense.

Example:

لیلا دارد با برادرت می آید.

/ley.lă- dă.rad- bă- ba.ră.da.rat- mi.ă.yad/

Leila *is coming* with your brother.

Simple Past

ماضی مطلق(گذشته ساده)

It is used to express an action that has happened in the past.

Example:

دوستم کلید خانه اش را به من داد.

/dus.tam- ke.li.de- kă.ne.aš- ră- be- man- dăd/

My friend *gave* me the key to her/his house.

Imperfect Indicative
ماضی استمراری

(The English equivalent: simple past OR past progressive OR "used to" + infinitive)

It is used to express an action that is one of the following:

a) Was continuous in the past.

    Example:

من قبلاً ماشین می فروختم.
/man- ğab.lan- mă.šin- mi.fo.ruǩ.tam/
I *used to sell* cars.

b) Done by someone habitually in the past.

    Example:

وقتی در لندن بودم، هر روز به آن پارک می رفتم.
/vağ.ti- dar- lan.dan- bu.dam- har- ruz- be- ăn- părk- mi.raf.tam/
When (I) was in London, I *went* to that park every day.

Present Perfect
ماضی نقلی

It is used to express an action that has happened in the past but its effect or result continues to the present time.

Example:

لیلا تمام ظرف ها را شسته است.

/ley.lă- ta.mă.me- zarf.hă- ră- šos.te- ast/

Leila *has washed* all the dishes.

Past Perfect
ماضی بعید

It is used to express an action which took place in the past before another past action.

Example:

قبل از اینکه به کانادا بیایم، هیچوقت برف ندیده بودم.

/ğabl- az- in.ke- be- kă.nă.dă- bi.yă.yam- hič.vağt- barf- na.di.de- bu.dam/

(I) *had* never *seen* the snow, before (I) came to Canada.

Past Subjunctive

ماضی التزامی

It is used to express an action that might have happened in the past.

Example:

ممکن است رایان به مادرت گفته باشد.

/mom.ken- ast- rǎ.yǎn- be- mǎ.da.rat- gof.te- bǎ.šad/

Ryan *might have told* your mother.

Past Progressive

ماضی مستمر(در جریان)

It is used to describe an action that was in progress at some point in the past. The simple past tense of the verb "داشتن" is always used to conjugate all verbs in the past progressive tense.

Example:

وقتی آمدی، داشتم بلوزم را می دوختم .

/vağ.ti- ǎ.ma.di- dǎš.tam- bo.lu.zam- rǎ- mi.duǩ.tam/

When (you) came, (I) *was sewing* my shirt.

Simple Future

آینده ساده

It is used to express an action that will take place at some pont in time in the future. The simple present tense of the verb "خواستن" without "می" is always used to conjugate all verbs in the future tense.

Example:

لیلا باز هم قلبت را خواهد شکست.

/ley.lă- băz- ham- ğal.bat- ră- kă.had- še.kast/

Leila *will break* your heart again.

Command

امر

It is used:

a) To express a command.

Example:

همین الآن به خانه برگرد!

/ha.min- al.ăn- be- kă.ne- bar.gard/

***Come back* home right now!**

b) To demand the acceptance of a condition.

Example:

حقیقت را بپذیرید!

/ha.ği.ğat- ră- be.pa.zi.rid/

***Accept* the truth!**

Important Note:

- To facilitate the search for the verbs, they are arranged based on their English translation in alphabetical order.

- The phonetic transcriptions for all Persian verbs and their conjunctions have been provided in different tenses.

- If a verb in a particular tense could be conjugated in more than one form, the additional form has been cited as a foot note.

- If the conjunction of a verb in a particular tense is not commonly used, the tables containing those conjugated forms have been shaded out.

- Brief grammatical overviews and useful tables are included in the beginning and at the end of the book.

100
IRREGULAR
PERSIAN VERBS

Fully Conjugated in the Most Common Tenses

to accept

پَذیرُفتَن

/pa.zi.rof.tan/

Plural	Singular
Simple Present مضارع اخباری(حال ساده)	
(ما) می پذیریم /(mǎ) mi.pa.zi.rim/	(من) می پذیرم /(man) mi.pa.zi.ram/
(شما) می پذیرید /(šo.mǎ) mi.pa.zi.rid/	(تو) می پذیری /(to) mi.pa.zi.ri/
(آنها) می پذیرند /(ǎn.hǎ) mi.pa.zi.rand/	(او/آن) می پذیرد /(u/ ǎn) mi.pa.zi.rad/
Present Subjunctive مضارع التزامی	
(ما) بپذیریم /(mǎ) be.pa.zi.rim/	(من) بپذیرم /(man) be.pa.zi.ram/
(شما) بپذیرید /(šo.mǎ) be.pa.zi.rid/	(تو) بپذیری /(to) be.pa.zi.ri/
(آنها) بپذیرند /(ǎn.hǎ) be.pa.zi.rand/	(او/آن) بپذیرد /(u/ ǎn) be.pa.zi.rad/
Present Progressive مضارع مستمر(در جریان)	
(ما) داریم می پذیریم /(mǎ) dǎ.rim- mi.pa.zi.rim/	(من) دارم می پذیرم /(man) dǎ.ram- mi.pa.zi.ram/
(شما) دارید می پذیرید /(šo.mǎ) dǎ.rid- mi.pa.zi.rid/	(تو) داری می پذیری /(to) dǎ.ri- mi.pa.zi.ri/
(آنها) دارند می پذیرند /(ǎn.hǎ) dǎ.rand- mi.pa.zi.rand/	(او/آن) دارد می پذیرد /(u/ ǎn) dǎ.rad- mi.pa.zi.rad/

Simple Past	
ماضی مطلق (گذشته ساده)	
(ما) پذیرفتیم	(من) پذیرفتم
/(mă) pa.zi.rof.tim/	/(man) pa.zi.rof.tam/
(شما) پذیرفتید	(تو) پذیرفتی
/(šo.mă) pa.zi.rof.tid/	/(to) pa.zi.rof.ti/
(آنها) پذیرفتند	(او/آن) پذیرفت
/(ăn.hă) pa.zi.rof.tand/	/(u/ ăn) pa.zi.roft/

Imperfect Indicative	
ماضی استمراری	
(ما) می پذیرفتیم	(من) می پذیرفتم
/(mă) mi.pa.zi.rof.tim/	/(man) mi.pa.zi.rof.tam/
(شما) می پذیرفتید	(تو) می پذیرفتی
/(šo.mă) mi.pa.zi.rof.tid/	/(to) mi.pa.zi.rof.ti/
(آنها) می پذیرفتند	(او/آن) می پذیرفت
/(ăn.hă) mi.pa.zi.rof.tand/	/(u/ ăn) mi.pa.zi.roft/

Present Perfect	
ماضی نقلی	
(ما) پذیرفته ایم	(من) پذیرفته ام
/(mă) pa.zi.rof.te.im/	/(man) pa.zi.rof.te.am/
(شما) پذیرفته اید	(تو) پذیرفته ای
/(šo.mă) pa.zi.rof.te.id/	/(to) pa.zi.rof.te.i/
(آنها) پذیرفته اند	(او/آن) پذیرفته است
/(ăn.hă) pa.zi.rof.te.and/	/(u/ ăn) pa.zi.rof.te- ast/

Past Perfect	
ماضی بعید	
(ما) پذیرفته بودیم	(من) پذیرفته بودم
/(mă) pa.zi.rof.te- bu.dim/	/(man) pa.zi.rof.te- bu.dam/
(شما) پذیرفته بودید	(تو) پذیرفته بودی
/(šo.mă) pa.zi.rof.te- bu.did/	/(to) pa.zi.rof.te- bu.di/
(آنها) پذیرفته بودند	(او/آن) پذیرفته بود
/(ăn.hă) pa.zi.rof.te- bu.dand/	/(u/ ăn) pa.zi.rof.te- bud/

Past Subjunctive	
ماضی التزامی	
(ما) پذیرفته باشیم /(mǎ) pa.zi.rof.te- bǎ.šim/	(من) پذیرفته باشم /(man) pa.zi.rof.te- bǎ.šam/
(شما) پذیرفته باشید /(šo.mǎ) pa.zi.rof.te- bǎ.šid/	(تو) پذیرفته باشی /(to) pa.zi.rof.te- bǎ.ši/
(آنها) پذیرفته باشند /(ǎn.hǎ) pa.zi.rof.te- bǎ.šand/	(او/آن) پذیرفته باشد /(u/ ǎn) pa.zi.rof.te- bǎ.šad/

Past Progressive	
ماضی مستمر(در جریان)	
(ما) داشتیم می پذیرفتیم /(mǎ) dǎš.tim- mi.pa.zi.rof.tim/	(من) داشتم می پذیرفتم /(man) dǎš.tam- mi.pa.zi.rof.tam/
(شما) داشتید می پذیرفتید /(šo.mǎ) dǎš.tid- mi.pa.zi.rof.tid/	(تو) داشتی می پذیرفتی /(to) dǎš.ti- mi.pa.zi.rof.ti/
(آنها) داشتند می پذیرفتند /(ǎn.hǎ) dǎš.tand- mi.pa.zi.rof.tand/	(او/آن) داشت می پذیرفت /(u/ ǎn) dǎšt- mi.pa.zi.roft/

Simple Future	
مستقبل (آینده ساده)	
(ما) خواهیم پذیرفت /(mǎ) ǩǎ.him- pa.zi.roft/	(من) خواهم پذیرفت /(man) ǩǎ.ham- pa.zi.roft/
(شما) خواهید پذیرفت /(šo.mǎ) ǩǎ.hid- pa.zi.roft/	(تو) خواهی پذیرفت /(to) ǩǎ.hi- pa.zi.roft/
(آنها) خواهند پذیرفت /(ǎn.hǎ) ǩǎ.hand- pa.zi.roft/	(او/آن) خواهد پذیرفت /(u/ ǎn) ǩǎ.had- pa.zi.roft/

Command	
امر	
بپذیرید! /be.pa.zi.rid/	بپذیر! /be.pa.zir/

4

to add

اَفزودَن

/af.zu.dan/

Plural	Singular
Simple Present <div dir="rtl">مضارع اخباری(حال ساده)</div>	
(ما) می افزاییم /(mǎ) mi.af.zǎ.yim/	(من) می افزایم /(man) mi.af.zǎ.yam/
(شما) می افزایید /(šo.mǎ) mi.af.zǎ.yid/	(تو) می افزایی /(to) mi.af.zǎ.yi/
(آنها) می افزایند /(ǎn.hǎ) mi.af.zǎ.yand/	(او/آن) می افزاید /(u/ ǎn) mi.af.zǎ.yad/
Present Subjunctive <div dir="rtl">مضارع التزامی</div>	
(ما) بیفزاییم /(mǎ) bi.yaf.zǎ.yim/	(من) بیفزایم /(man) bi.yaf.zǎ.yam/
(شما) بیفزایید /(šo.mǎ) bi.yaf.zǎ.yid/	(تو) بیفزایی /(to) bi.yaf.zǎ.yi/
(آنها) بیفزایند /(ǎn.hǎ) bi.yaf.zǎ.yand/	(او/آن) بیفزاید /(u/ ǎn) bi.yaf.zǎ.yad/
Present Progressive <div dir="rtl">مضارع مستمر(در جریان)</div>	
(ما) داریم می افزاییم /(mǎ) dǎ.rim- mi.af.zǎ.yim/	(من) دارم می افزایم /(man) dǎ.ram- mi.af.zǎ.yam/
(شما) دارید می افزایید /(šo.mǎ) dǎ.rid- mi.af.zǎ.yid/	(تو) داری می افزایی /(to) dǎ.ri- mi.af.zǎ.yi/
(آنها) دارند می افزایند /(ǎn.hǎ) dǎ.rand- mi.af.zǎ.yand/	(او/آن) دارد می افزاید /(u/ ǎn) dǎ.rad- mi.af.zǎ.yad/

Simple Past
ماضی مطلق (گذشته ساده)

(ما) افزودیم	(من) افزودم
/(mǎ) af.zu.dim/	/(man) af.zu.dam/
(شما) افزودید	(تو) افزودی
/(šo.mǎ) af.zu.did/	/(to) af.zu.di/
(آنها) افزودند	(او/آن) افزود
/(ǎn.hǎ) af.zu.dand/	/(u/ ǎn) af.zud/

Imperfect Indicative
ماضی استمراری

(ما) می افزودیم	(من) می افزودم
/(mǎ) mi.af.zu.dim/	/(man) mi.af.zu.dam/
(شما) می افزودید	(تو) می افزودی
/(šo.mǎ) mi.af.zu.did/	/(to) mi.af.zu.di/
(آنها) می افزودند	(او/آن) می افزود
/(ǎn.hǎ) mi.af.zu.dand/	/(u/ ǎn) mi.af.zud/

Present Perfect
ماضی نقلی

(ما) افزوده ایم	(من) افزوده ام
/(mǎ) af.zu.de.im/	/(man) af.zu.de.am/
(شما) افزوده اید	(تو) افزوده ای
/(šo.mǎ) af.zu.de.id/	/(to) af.zu.de.i/
(آنها) افزوده اند	(او/آن) افزوده است
/(ǎn.hǎ) af.zu.de.and/	/(u/ ǎn) af.zu.de- ast/

Past Perfect
ماضی بعید

(ما) افزوده بودیم	(من) افزوده بودم
/(mǎ) af.zu.de- bu.dim/	/(man) af.zu.de- bu.dam/
(شما) افزوده بودید	(تو) افزوده بودی
/(šo.mǎ) af.zu.de- bu.did/	/(to) af.zu.de- bu.di/
(آنها) افزوده بودند	(او/آن) افزوده بود
/(ǎn.hǎ) af.zu.de- bu.dand/	/(u/ ǎn) af.zu.de- bud/

Past Subjunctive
ماضی التزامی

(ما) افزوده باشیم	(من) افزوده باشم
/(mǎ) af.zu.de- bǎ.šim/	/(man) af.zu.de- bǎ.šam/
(شما) افزوده باشید	(تو) افزوده باشی
/(šo.mǎ) af.zu.de- bǎ.šid/	/(to) af.zu.de- bǎ.ši/
(آنها) افزوده باشند	(او/آن) افزوده باشد
/(ǎn.hǎ) af.zu.de- bǎ.šand/	/(u/ ǎn) af.zu.de- bǎ.šad/

Past Progressive
ماضی مستمر(در جریان)

(ما) داشتیم می افزودیم	(من) داشتم می افزودم
/(mǎ) dǎš.tim- mi.af.zu.dim/	/(man) dǎš.tam- mi.af.zu.dam/
(شما) داشتید می افزودید	(تو) داشتی می افزودی
/(šo.mǎ) dǎš.tid- mi.af.zu.did/	/(to) dǎš.ti- mi.af.zu.di/
(آنها) داشتند می افزودند	(او/آن) داشت می افزود
/(ǎn.hǎ) dǎš.tand- mi.af.zu.dand/	/(u/ ǎn) dǎšt- mi.af.zud/

Simple Future
مستقبل (آینده ساده)

(ما) خواهیم افزود	(من) خواهم افزود
/(mǎ) ǩǎ.him- af.zud/	/(man) ǩǎ.ham- af.zud/
(شما) خواهید افزود	(تو) خواهی افزود
/(šo.mǎ) ǩǎ.hid- af.zud/	/(to) ǩǎ.hi- af.zud/
(آنها) خواهند افزود	(او/آن) خواهد افزود
/(ǎn.hǎ) ǩǎ.hand- af.zud/	/(u/ ǎn) ǩǎ.had- af.zud/

Command
امر

بیفزایید!	بیفزای!
/bi.yaf.zǎ.yid/	/bi.yaf.zǎy/

7

to be

بودَن

/bu.dan/

Plural	Singular
Simple Present	
<div dir="rtl">مضارع اخباری(حال ساده)</div>	
<div dir="rtl">* (ما) هستیم</div> /(mǎ) has.tim/	<div dir="rtl">* (من) هستم</div> /(man) has.tam/
<div dir="rtl">* (شما) هستید</div> /(šo.mǎ) hast.tid/	<div dir="rtl">* (تو) هستی</div> /(to) has.ti/
<div dir="rtl">* (آنها) هستند</div> /(ǎn.hǎ) has.tand/	<div dir="rtl">* (او/آن) هست</div> /(u/ ǎn) hast/
Present Subjunctive	
<div dir="rtl">مضارع التزامی</div>	
<div dir="rtl">(ما) باشیم</div> /(mǎ) bǎ.šim/	<div dir="rtl">(من) باشم</div> /(man) bǎ.šam/
<div dir="rtl">(شما) باشید</div> /(šo.mǎ) bǎ.šid/	<div dir="rtl">(تو) باشی</div> /(to) bǎ.ši/
<div dir="rtl">(آنها) باشند</div> /(ǎn.hǎ) bǎ.šand/	<div dir="rtl">(او/آن) باشد</div> /(u/ ǎn) bǎ.šad/
Present Progressive	
<div dir="rtl">مضارع مستمر(در جریان)</div>	
<div dir="rtl">(ما) داریم می باشیم</div> /(mǎ) dǎ.rim- mi.bǎ.šim/	<div dir="rtl">(من) دارم می باشم</div> /(man) dǎ.ram- mi.bǎ.šam/
<div dir="rtl">(شما) دارید می باشید</div> /(šo.mǎ) dǎ.rid- mi.bǎ.šid/	<div dir="rtl">(تو) داری می باشی</div> /(to) dǎ.ri- mi.bǎ.ši/
<div dir="rtl">(آنها) دارند می باشند</div> /(ǎn.hǎ) dǎ.rand- mi.bǎ.šand/	<div dir="rtl">(او/آن) دارد می باشد</div> /(u/ ǎn) dǎ.rad- mi.bǎ.šad/

8

Simple Past
ماضی مطلق (گذشته ساده)

(ما) بودیم	(من) بودم
/(mǎ) bu.dim/	/(man) bu.dam/
(شما) بودید	(تو) بودی
/(šo.mǎ) bu.did/	/(to) bu.di/
(آنها) بودند	(او/ آن) بود
/(ǎn.hǎ) bu.dand/	/(u/ ǎn) bud/

Imperfect Indicative
ماضی استمراری

(ما) می بودیم	(من) می بودم
/(mǎ) mi.bu.dim/	/(man) mi.bu.dam/
(شما) می بودید	(تو) می بودی
/(šo.mǎ) mi.bu.did/	/(to) mi.bu.di/
(آنها) می بودند	(او/ آن) می بود
/(ǎn.hǎ) mi.bu.dand/	/(u/ ǎn) mi.bud/

Present Perfect
ماضی نقلی

(ما) بوده ایم	(من) بوده ام
/(mǎ) bu.de.im/	/(man) bu.de.am/
(شما) بوده اید	(تو) بوده ای
/(šo.mǎ) bu.de.id/	/(to) bu.de.i/
(آنها) بوده اند	(او/ آن) بوده است
/(ǎn.hǎ) bu.de.and/	/(u/ ǎn) bu.de- ast/

Past Perfect
ماضی بعید

(ما) بوده بودیم	(من) بوده بودم
/(mǎ) bu.de- bu.dim/	/(man) bu.de- bu.dam/
(شما) بوده بودید	(تو) بوده بودی
/(šo.mǎ) bu.de- bu.did/	/(to) bu.de- bu.di/
(آنها) بوده بودند	(او/ آن) بوده بود
/(ǎn.hǎ) bu.de- bu.dand/	/(u/ ǎn) bu.de- bud/

Past Subjunctive
ماضی التزامی

(ما) بوده باشیم	(من) بوده باشم
/(mǎ) bu.de- ba.šim/	/(man) bu.de- ba.šam/
(شما) بوده باشید	(تو) بوده باشی
/(šo.mǎ) bu.de- ba.šid/	/(to) bu.de- ba.ši/
(آنها) بوده باشند	(او/آن) بوده باشد
/(ǎn.hǎ) bu.de- ba.šand/	/(u/ ǎn) bu.de- ba.šad/

Past Progressive
ماضی مستمر(در جریان)

(ما) داشتیم می بودیم	(من) داشتم می بودم
/(mǎ) daš.tim- mi.bu.dim/	/(man) daš.tam- mi.bu.dam/
(شما) داشتید می بودید	(تو) داشتی می بودی
/(šo.mǎ) daš.tid- mi.bu.did/	/(to) daš.ti- mi.bu.di/
(آنها) داشتند می بودند	(او/آن) داشت می بود
/(ǎn.hǎ) daš.tand- mi.bu.dand/	/(u/ ǎn) dašt- mi.bud/

Simple Future
مستقبل (آینده ساده)

(ما) خواهیم بود	(من) خواهم بود
/(mǎ) ǩǎ.him- bud/	/(man) ǩǎ.ham- bud/
(شما) خواهید بود	(تو) خواهی بود
/(šo.mǎ) ǩǎ.hid- bud/	/(to) ǩǎ.hi- bud/
(آنها) خواهند بود	(او/آن) خواهد بود
/(ǎn.hǎ) ǩǎ.hand- bud/	/(u/ ǎn) ǩǎ.had- bud/

Command
امر

باشید!	باش!
/bǎ.šid/	/bǎš/

* also:	(آنها) اَند	(شما) اید	(ما) ایم	(او/آن) اَست	(تو) ای

(من) اَم

to be able to

تَوانِستَن

/ta.vă.nes.tan/

Plural	Singular
Simple Present	
مضارع اخباری(حال ساده)	
(ما) می توانیم	(من) می توانم
/(mă) mi.ta.vă.nim/	/(man) mi.ta.vă.nam/
(شما) می توانید	(تو) می توانی
/(šo.mă) mi.ta.vă.nid/	/(to) mi.ta.vă.ni/
(آنها) می توانند	(او/آن) می تواند
/(ăn.hă) mi.ta.vă.nand/	/(u/ ăn) mi.ta.vă.nad/
Present Subjunctive	
مضارع التزامی	
(ما) بتوانیم	(من) بتوانم
/(mă) be.ta.vă.nim/	(man) be.ta.vă.nam/
(شما) بتوانید	(تو) بتوانی
/(šo.mă) be.ta.vă.nid/	/(to) be.ta.vă.ni/
(آنها) بتوانند	(او/آن) بتواند
/(ăn.hă) be.ta.vă.nand/	/(u/ ăn) be.ta.vă.nad/
Present Progressive	
مضارع مستمر(در جریان)	
(ما) داریم می توانیم	(من) دارم می توانم
/(mă) dă.rim- mi.ta.vă.nim/	/(man) dă.ram- mi.ta.vă.nam/
(شما) دارید می توانید	(تو) داری می توانی
/(šo.mă) dă.rid- mi.ta.vă.nid/	/(to) dă.ri- mi.ta.vă.ni/
(آنها) دارند می توانند	(او/آن) دارد می تواند
/(ăn.hă) dă.rand- mi.ta.vă.nand/	/(u/ ăn) dă.rad- mi.ta.vă.nad/

11

Simple Past	
ماضی مطلق (گذشته ساده)	
(ما) توانستیم	(من) توانستم
/(mă) ta.vă.nes.tim/	/(man) ta.vă.nes.tam/
(شما) توانستید	(تو) توانستی
/(šo.mă) ta.vă.nes.tid/	/(to) ta.vă.nes.ti/
(آنها) توانستند	(او/آن) توانست
/(ăn.hă) ta.vă.nes.tand/	/(u/ ăn) ta.vă.nest/

Imperfect Indicative	
ماضی استمراری	
(ما) می توانستیم	(من) می توانستم
/(mă) mi.ta.vă.nes.tim/	/(man) mi.ta.vă.nes.tam/
(شما) می توانستید	(تو) می توانستی
/(šo.mă) mi.ta.vă.nes.tid/	/(to) mi.ta.vă.nes.ti/
(آنها) می توانستند	(او/آن) می توانست
/(ăn.hă) mi.ta.vă.nes.tand/	/(u/ ăn) mi. ta.vă.nest/

Present Perfect	
ماضی نقلی	
(ما) توانسته ایم	(من) توانسته ام
/(mă) ta.vă.nes.te.im/	(man) ta.vă.nes.te.am/
(شما) توانسته اید	(تو) توانسته ای
/(šo.mă) ta.vă.nes.te.id/	/(to) ta.vă.nes.te.i/
(آنها) توانسته اند	(او/آن) توانسته است
/(ăn.hă) ta.vă.nes.te.and/	/(u/ ăn) ta.vă.nes.te- ast/

Past Perfect	
ماضی بعید	
(ما) توانسته بودیم	(من) توانسته بودم
/(mă) ta.vă.nes.te- bu.dim/	(man) ta.vă.nes.te- bu.dam/
(شما) توانسته بودید	(تو) توانسته بودی
/(šo.mă) ta.vă.nes.te- bu.did/	/(to) ta.vă.nes.te- bu.di/
(آنها) توانسته بودند	(او/آن) توانسته بود
/(ăn.hă) ta.vă.nes.te- bu.dand/	/(u/ ăn) ta.vă.nes.te- bud/

Past Subjunctive	
ماضی التزامی	
(ما) توانسته باشیم	(من) توانسته باشم
/(mǎ) ta.vǎ.nes.te- bǎ.šim/	/(man) ta.vǎ.nes.te- bǎ.šam/
(شما) توانسته باشید	(تو) توانسته باشی
/(šo.mǎ) ta.vǎ.nes.te- bǎ.šid/	/(to) ta.vǎ.nes.te- bǎ.ši/
(آنها) توانسته باشند	(او/آن) توانسته باشد
/(ǎn.hǎ) ta.vǎ.nes.te- bǎ.šand/	/(u/ ǎn) ta.vǎ.nes.te- bǎ.šad/

Past Progressive	
ماضی مستمر(در جریان)	
(ما) داشتیم می توانستیم	(من) داشتم می توانستم
/(mǎ) dǎš.tim- mi.ta.vǎ.nes.tim/	/(man) dǎš.tam- mi.ta.vǎ.nes.tam/
(شما) داشتید می توانستید	(تو) داشتی می توانستی
/(šo.mǎ) dǎš.tid- mi.ta.vǎ.nes.tid/	/(to) dǎš.ti- mi.ta.vǎ.nes.ti/
(آنها) داشتند می توانستند	(او/آن) داشت می توانست
/(ǎn.hǎ) dǎš.tand- mi.ta.vǎ.nes.tand/	/(u/ ǎn) dǎšt- mi.ta.vǎ.nest/

Simple Future	
مستقبل (آینده ساده)	
(ما) خواهیم توانست	(من) خواهم توانست
/(mǎ) kǎ.him- ta.vǎ.nest/	/(man) kǎ.ham- ta.vǎ.nest/
(شما) خواهید توانست	(تو) خواهی توانست
/(šo.mǎ) kǎ.hid- ta.vǎ.nest/	/(to) kǎ.hi- ta.vǎ.nest/
(آنها) خواهند توانست	(او/آن) خواهد توانست
/(ǎn.hǎ) kǎ.hand- ta.vǎ.nest/	/(u/ ǎn) kǎ.had- ta.vǎ.nest/

Command	
امر	
بتوانید!	بتوان!
/be.ta.vǎ.nid/	/be.ta.vǎn/

to become

شُدَن

/šo.dan/

Plural	Singular
Simple Present	
مضارع اخباری(حال ساده)	
(ما) می شویم	(من) می شوم
/(mǎ) mi.ša.vim/	/(man) mi.ša.vam/
(شما) می شوید	(تو) می شوی
/(šo.mǎ) mi.ša.vid/	/(to) mi.ša.vi/
(آنها) می شوند	(او/آن) می شود
/(ǎn.hǎ) mi.ša.vand/	/(u/ ǎn) mi.ša.vad/

Plural	Singular
Present Subjunctive	
مضارع التزامی	
(ما) بشویم	(من) بشوم
/(mǎ) be.ša.vim/	/(man) be.ša.vam/
(شما) بشوید	(تو) بشوی
/(šo.mǎ) be.ša.vid/	/(to) be.ša.vi/
(آنها) بشوند	(او/آن) بشود
/(ǎn.hǎ) be.ša.vand/	/(u/ ǎn) be.ša.vad/

Plural	Singular
Present Progressive	
مضارع مستمر(در جریان)	
(ما) داریم می شویم	(من) دارم می شوم
/(mǎ) dǎ.rim- mi.ša.vim/	/(man) dǎ.ram- mi.ša.vam/
(شما) دارید می شوید	(تو) داری می شوی
/(šo.mǎ) dǎ.rid- mi.ša.vid/	/(to) dǎ.ri- mi.ša.vi/
(آنها) دارند می شوند	(او/آن) دارد می شود
/(ǎn.hǎ) dǎ.rand- mi.ša.vand/	/(u/ ǎn) dǎ.rad- mi.ša.vad/

Simple Past	
ماضی مطلق (گذشته ساده)	
(ما) شدیم	(من) شدم
/(mǎ) šo.dim/	/(man) šo.dam/
(شما) شدید	(تو) شدی
/(šo.mǎ) šo.did/	/(to) šo.di/
(آنها) شدند	(او/آن) شد
/(ǎn.hǎ) šo.dand/	/(u/ ǎn) šod/

Imperfect Indicative	
ماضی استمراری	
(ما) می شدیم	(من) می شدم
/(mǎ) mi.šo.dim/	/(man) mi.šo.dam/
(شما) می شدید	(تو) می شدی
/(šo.mǎ) mi.šo.did/	/(to) mi.šo.di/
(آنها) می شدند	(او/آن) می شد
/(ǎn.hǎ) mi.šo.dand/	/(u/ ǎn) mi.šod/

Present Perfect	
ماضی نقلی	
(ما) شده ایم	(من) شده ام
/(mǎ) šo.de.im/	/(man) šo.de.am/
(شما) شده اید	(تو) شده ای
/(šo.mǎ) šo.de.id/	/(to) šo.de.i/
(آنها) شده اند	(او/آن) شده است
/(ǎn.hǎ) šo.de.and/	/(u/ ǎn) šo.de- ast/

Past Perfect	
ماضی بعید	
(ما) شده بودیم	(من) شده بودم
/(mǎ) šo.de- bu.dim/	/(man) šo.de- bu.dam/
(شما) شده بودید	(تو) شده بودی
/(šo.mǎ) šo.de- bu.did/	/(to) šo.de- bu.di/
(آنها) شده بودند	(او/آن) شده بود
/(ǎn.hǎ) šo.de- bu.dand/	/(u/ ǎn) šo.de- bud/

Past Subjunctive	
ماضی التزامی	
(ما) شده باشیم	(من) شده باشم
/(mǎ) šo.de- bǎ.šim/	/(man) šo.de- bǎ.šam/
(شما) شده باشید	(تو) شده باشی
/(šo.mǎ) šo.de- bǎ.šid/	/(to) šo.de- bǎ.ši/
(آنها) شده باشند	(او/آن) شده باشد
/(ǎn.hǎ) šo.de- bǎ.šand/	/(u/ ǎn) šo.de- bǎ.šad/

Past Progressive	
ماضی مستمر(در جریان)	
(ما) داشتیم می شدیم	(من) داشتم می شدم
/(mǎ) dǎš.tim- mi.šo.dim/	/(man) dǎš.tam- mi.šo.dam/
(شما) داشتید می شدید	(تو) داشتی می شدی
/(šo.mǎ) dǎš.tid- mi.šo.did/	/(to) dǎš.ti- mi.šo.di/
(آنها) داشتند می شدند	(او/آن) داشت می شد
/(ǎn.hǎ) dǎš.tand- mi.šo.dand/	/(u/ ǎn) dǎšt- mi.šod/

Simple Future	
مستقبل (آینده ساده)	
(ما) خواهیم شد	(من) خواهم شد
/(mǎ) ǩǎ.him- šod/	/(man) ǩǎ.ham- šod/
(شما) خواهید شد	(تو) خواهی شد
/(šo.mǎ) ǩǎ.hid- šod/	/(to) ǩǎ.hi- šod/
(آنها) خواهند شد	(او/آن) خواهد شد
/(ǎn.hǎ) ǩǎ.hand- šod/	/(u/ ǎn) ǩǎ.had- šod/

Command	
امر	
بشوید!	بشو!
/be.ša.vid/	/be.šo/

to be disturbed

آشُفتَن

/ă.šof.tan/

Plural	Singular
Simple Present مضارع اخباری(حال ساده)	
(ما) می آشوبیم /(mă) mi.ă.šu.bim/	(من) می آشوبم /(man) mi.ă.šu.bam/
(شما) می آشوبید /(šo.mă) mi.ă.šu.bid/	(تو) می آشوبی /(to) mi.ă.šu.bi/
(آنها) می آشوبند /(ăn.hă) mi.ă.šu.band/	(او/آن) می آشوبد /(u/ ăn) mi.ă.šu.bad/
Present Subjunctive مضارع التزامی	
(ما) بیاشوبیم /(mă) bi.yă.šu.bim/	(من) بیاشوبم /(man) bi.yă.šu.bam/
(شما) بیاشوبید /(šo.mă) bi.yă.šu.bid/	(تو) بیاشوبی /(to) bi.yă.šu.bi/
(آنها) بیاشوبند /(ăn.hă) bi.yă.šu.band/	(او/آن) بیاشوبد /(u/ ăn) bi.yă.šu.bad/
Present Progressive مضارع مستمر(در جریان)	
(ما) داریم می آشوبیم /(mă) dă.rim- mi.ă.šu.bim/	(من) دارم می آشوبم /(man) dă.ram- mi.ă.šu.bam/
(شما) دارید می آشوبید /(šo.mă) dă.rid- mi.ă.šu.bid/	(تو) داری می آشوبی /(to) dă.ri- mi.ă.šu.bi/
(آنها) دارند می آشوبند /(ăn.hă) dă.rand- mi.ă.šu.band/	(او/آن) دارد می آشوبد /(u/ ăn) dă.rad- mi.ă.šu.bad/

17

Simple Past
ماضی مطلق (گذشته ساده)

(ما) آشفتیم	(من) آشفتم
/(mǎ) ǎ.šof.tim/	/(man) ǎ.šof.tam/
(شما) آشفتید	(تو) آشفتی
/(šo.mǎ) ǎ.šof.tid/	/(to) ǎ.šof.ti/
(آنها) آشفتند	(او/آن) آشفت
/(ǎn.hǎ) ǎ.šof.tand/	/(u/ ǎn) ǎ.šoft/

Imperfect Indicative
ماضی استمراری

(ما) می آشفتیم	(من) می آشفتم
/(mǎ) mi.ǎ.šof.tim/	/(man) mi.ǎ.šof.tam/
(شما) می آشفتید	(تو) می آشفتی
/(šo.mǎ) mi.ǎ.šof.tid/	/(to) mi.ǎ.šof.ti/
(آنها) می آشفتند	(او/آن) می آشفت
/(ǎn.hǎ) mi.ǎ.šof.tand/	/(u/ ǎn) mi.ǎ.šoft/

Present Perfect
ماضی نقلی

(ما) آشفته ایم	(من) آشفته ام
/(mǎ) ǎ.šof.te.im/	/(man) ǎ.šof.te.am/
(شما) آشفته اید	(تو) آشفته ای
/(šo.mǎ) ǎ.šof.te.id/	/(to) ǎ.šof.te.i/
(آنها) آشفته اند	(او/آن) آشفته است
/(ǎn.hǎ) ǎ.šof.te.and/	/(u/ ǎn) ǎ.šof.te- ast/

Past Perfect
ماضی بعید

(ما) آشفته بودیم	(من) آشفته بودم
/(mǎ) ǎ.šof.te- bu.dim/	/(man) ǎ.šof.te- bu.dam/
(شما) آشفته بودید	(تو) آشفته بودی
/(šo.mǎ) ǎ.šof.te- bu.did/	/(to) ǎ.šof.te- bu.di/
(آنها) آشفته بودند	(او/آن) آشفته بود
/(ǎn.hǎ) ǎ.šof.te- bu.dand/	/(u/ ǎn) ǎ.šof.te- bud/

18

Past Subjunctive	
ماضی التزامی	
(ما) آشفته باشیم	(من) آشفته باشم
/(mă) ă.šof.te- bă.šim/	/(man) ă.šof.te- bă.šam/
(شما) آشفته باشید	(تو) آشفته باشی
/(šo.mă) ă.šof.te- bă.šid/	/(to) ă.šof.te- bă.ši/
(آنها) آشفته باشند	(او/آن) آشفته باشد
/(ăn.hă) ă.šof.te- bă.šand/	/(u/ ăn) ă.šof.te- bă.šad/

Past Progressive	
ماضی مستمر(در جریان)	
(ما) داشتیم می آشفتیم	(من) داشتم می آشفتم
/(mă) dăš.tim- mi.ă.šof.tim/	/(man) dăš.tam- mi.ă.šof.tam/
(شما) داشتید می آشفتید	(تو) داشتی می آشفتی
/(šo.mă) dăš.tid- mi.ă.šof.tid/	/(to) dăš.ti- mi.ă.šof.ti/
(آنها) داشتند می آشفتند	(او/آن) داشت می آشفت
/(ăn.hă) dăš.tand- mi.ă.šof.tand/	/(u/ ăn) dăšt- mi.ă.šoft/

Simple Future	
مستقبل (آینده ساده)	
(ما) خواهیم آشفت	(من) خواهم آشفت
/(mă) ǩă.him- ă.šoft/	/(man) ǩă.ham- ă.šoft/
(شما) خواهید آشفت	(تو) خواهی آشفت
/(šo.mă) ǩă.hid- ă.šoft/	/(to) ǩă.hi- ă.šoft/
(آنها) خواهند آشفت	(او/آن) خواهد آشفت
/(ăn.hă) ǩă.hand- ă.šoft/	/(u/ ăn) ǩă.had- ă.šoft/

Command	
امر	
بیاشوبید!	بیاشوب!
/bi.yă.šu.bid/	/bi.yă.šub/

to blend

آميخُتَن

/ă.miǩ.tan/

Plural	Singular
Simple Present مضارع اخباری(حال ساده)	
(ما)) می آميزيم /(mă) mi.ă.mi.zim/	(من) می آميزم /(man) mi.ă.mi.zam/
(شما)) می آميزيد /(šo.mă) mi.ă.mi.zid/	(تو)) می آميزی /(to) mi.ă.mi.zi/
(آنها)) می آميزند /(ăn.hă) mi.ă.mi.zand/	(او/آن)) می آميزد /(u/ ăn) mi.ă.mi.zad/
Present Subjunctive مضارع التزامی	
(ما) بياميزيم /(mă) bi.yă.mi.zim/	(من) بياميزم /(man) bi.yă.mi.zam/
(شما) بياميزيد /(šo.mă) bi.yă.mi.zid/	(تو) بياميزی /(to) bi.yă.mi.zi/
(آنها) بياميزند /(ăn.hă) bi.yă.mi.zand/	(او/آن) بياميزد /(u/ ăn) bi.yă.mi.zad/
Present Progressive مضارع مستمر(در جريان)	
(ما) داريم می آميزيم /(mă) dă.rim- mi.ă.mi.zim/	(من) دارم می آميزم /(man) dă.ram- mi.ă.mi.zam/
(شما) داريد می آميزيد /(šo.mă) dă.rid- mi.ă.mi.zid/	(تو) داری می آميزی /(to) dă.ri- mi.ă.mi.zi/
(آنها) دارند می آميزند /(ăn.hă) dă.rand- mi.ă.mi.zand/	(او/آن) دارد می آميزد /(u/ ăn) dă.rad- mi.ă.mi.zad/

Simple Past	
ماضی مطلق (گذشته ساده)	
(ما) آمیختیم	(من) آمیختم
/(mǎ) ǎ.miǩ.tim/	/(man) ǎ.miǩ.tam/
(شما) آمیختید	(تو) آمیختی
/(šo.mǎ) ǎ.miǩ.tid/	/(to) ǎ.miǩ.ti/
(آنها) آمیختند	(او/آن) آمیخت
/(ǎn.hǎ) ǎ.miǩ.tand/	/(u/ ǎn) ǎ.miǩt/

Imperfect Indicative	
ماضی استمراری	
(ما) می آمیختیم	(من) می آمیختم
/(mǎ) mi.ǎ.miǩ.tim/	/(man) mi.ǎ.miǩ.tam/
(شما) می آمیختید	(تو) می آمیختی
/(šo.mǎ) mi.ǎ.miǩ.tid/	/(to) mi.ǎ.miǩ.ti/
(آنها) می آمیختند	(او/آن) می آمیخت
/(ǎn.hǎ) mi.ǎ.miǩ.tand/	/(u/ ǎn) mi.ǎ.miǩt/

Present Perfect	
ماضی نقلی	
(ما) آمیخته ایم	(من) آمیخته ام
/(mǎ) ǎ.miǩ.te.im/	/(man) ǎ.miǩ.te.am/
(شما) آمیخته اید	(تو) آمیخته ای
/(šo.mǎ) ǎ.miǩ.te.id/	/(to) ǎ.miǩ.te.i/
(آنها) آمیخته اند	(او/آن) آمیخته است
/(ǎn.hǎ) ǎ.miǩ.te.and/	/(u/ ǎn) ǎ.miǩ.te- ast/

Past Perfect	
ماضی بعید	
(ما) آمیخته بودیم	(من) آمیخته بودم
/(mǎ) ǎ.miǩ.te- bu.dim/	/(man) ǎ.miǩ.te- bu.dam/
(شما) آمیخته بودید	(تو) آمیخته بودی
/(šo.mǎ) ǎ.miǩ.te- bu.did/	/(to) ǎ.miǩ.te- bu.di/
(آنها) آمیخته بودند	(او/آن) آمیخته بود
/(ǎn.hǎ) ǎ.miǩ.te- bu.dand/	/(u/ ǎn) ǎ.miǩ.te- bud/

Past Subjunctive	
ماضی التزامی	
(ما) آمیخته باشیم /(mă) ă.miǩ.te- bă.šim/	(من) آمیخته باشم /(man) ă.miǩ.te- bă.šam/
(شما) آمیخته باشید /(šo.mă) ă.miǩ.te- bă.šid/	(تو) آمیخته باشی /(to) ă.miǩ.te- bă.ši/
(آنها) آمیخته باشند /(ăn.hă) ă.miǩ.te- bă.šand/	(او/آن) آمیخته باشد /(u/ ăn) ă.miǩ.te- bă.šad/

Past Progressive	
ماضی مستمر(در جریان)	
(ما) داشتیم می آمیختیم /(mă) dăš.tim- mi.ă.miǩ.tim/	(من) داشتم می آمیختم /(man) dăš.tam- mi.ă.miǩ.tam/
(شما) داشتید می آمیختید /(šo.mă) dăš.tid- mi.ă.miǩ.tid/	(تو) داشتی می آمیختی /(to) dăš.ti- mi.ă.miǩ.ti/
(آنها) داشتند می آمیختند /(ăn.hă) dăš.tand- mi.ă.miǩ.tand/	(او/آن) داشت می آمیخت /(u/ ăn) dăšt- mi.ă.miǩt/

Simple Future	
مستقبل (آینده ساده)	
(ما) خواهیم آمیخت /(mă) ǩă.him- ă.miǩt/	(من) خواهم آمیخت /(man) ǩă.ham- ă.miǩt/
(شما) خواهید آمیخت /(šo.mă) ǩă.hid- ă.miǩt/	(تو) خواهی آمیخت /(to) ǩă.hi- ă.miǩt/
(آنها) خواهند آمیخت /(ăn.hă) ǩă.hand- ă.miǩt/	(او/آن) خواهد آمیخت /(u/ ăn) ǩă.had- ă.miǩt/

Command	
امر	
بیامیزید! /bi.yă.mi.zid/	بیامیز! /bi.yă.miz/

to bother

آزُردَن

/ă.zor.dan/

Plural	Singular
Simple Present	
مضارع اخباری(حال ساده)	
(ما) می آزاریم	(من) می آزارم
/(mă) mi.ă.ză.rim/	/(man) mi.ă.ză.ram/
(شما) می آزارید	(تو) می آزاری
/(šo.mă) mi.ă.ză.rid/	/(to) mi.ă.ză.ri/
(آنها) می آزارند	(او/آن) می آزارد
/(ăn.hă) mi.ă.ză.rand/	/(u/ ăn) mi.ă.ză.rad/

Plural	Singular
Present Subjunctive	
مضارع التزامی	
(ما) بیازاریم	(من) بیازارم
/(mă) bi.yă.ză.rim/	/(man) bi.yă.ză.ram/
(شما) بیازارید	(تو) بیازاری
/(šo.mă) bi.yă.ză.rid/	/(to) bi.yă.ză.ri/
(آنها) بیازارند	(او/آن) بیازارد
/(ăn.hă) bi.yă.ză.rand/	/(u/ ăn) bi.yă.ză.rad/

Plural	Singular
Present Progressive	
مضارع مستمر(در جریان)	
(ما) داریم می آزاریم	(من) دارم می آزارم
/(mă) dă.rim- mi.ă.ză.rim/	/(man) dă.ram- mi.ă.ză.ram/
(شما) دارید می آزارید	(تو) داری می آزاری
/(šo.mă) dă.rid- mi.ă.ză.rid/	/(to) dă.ri- mi.ă.ză.ri/
(آنها) دارند می آزارند	(او/آن) دارد می آزارد
/(ăn.hă) dă.rand- mi.ă.ză.rand/	/(u/ ăn) dă.rad- mi.ă.ză.rad/

Simple Past	
ماضی مطلق (گذشته ساده)	
(ما) آزردیم	(من) آزردم
/(mă) ă.zor.dim/	/(man) ă.zor.dam/
(شما) آزردید	(تو) آزردی
/(šo.mă) ă.zor.did/	/(to) ă.zor.di/
(آنها) آزردند	(او/آن) آزرد
/(ăn.hă) ă.zor.dand/	/(u/ ăn) ă.zord/

Imperfect Indicative	
ماضی استمراری	
(ما) می آزردیم	(من) می آزردم
/(mă) mi.ă.zor.dim/	/(man) mi.ă.zor.dam/
(شما) می آزردید	(تو) می آزردی
/(šo.mă) mi.ă.zor.did/	/(to) mi.ă.zor.di/
(آنها) می آزردند	(او/آن) می آزرد
/(ăn.hă) mi.ă.zor.dand/	/(u/ ăn) mi.ă.zord/

Present Perfect	
ماضی نقلی	
(ما) آزرده ایم	(من) آزرده ام
/(mă) ă.zor.de.im/	/(man) ă.zor.de.am/
(شما) آزرده اید	(تو) آزرده ای
/(šo.mă) ă.zor.de.id/	/(to) ă.zor.de.i/
(آنها) آزرده اند	(او/آن) آزرده است
/(ăn.hă) ă.zor.de.and/	/(u/ ăn) ă.zor.de- ast/

Past Perfect	
ماضی بعید	
(ما) آزرده بودیم	(من) آزرده بودم
/(mă) ă.zor.de- bu.dim/	/(man) ă.zor.de- bu.dam/
(شما) آزرده بودید	(تو) آزرده بودی
/(šo.mă) ă.zor.de- bu.did/	/(to) ă.zor.de- bu.di/
(آنها) آزرده بودند	(او/آن) آزرده بود
/(ăn.hă) ă.zor.de- bu.dand/	/(u/ ăn) ă.zor.de- bud/

Past Subjunctive	
ماضی التزامی	
(ما) آزرده باشیم	(من) آزرده باشم
/(mǎ) ǎ.zor.de- bǎ.šim/	/(man) ǎ.zor.de- bǎ.šam/
(شما) آزرده باشید	(تو) آزرده باشی
/(šo.mǎ) ǎ.zor.de- bǎ.šid/	/(to) ǎ.zor.de- bǎ.ši/
(آنها) آزرده باشند	(او/آن) آزرده باشد
/(ǎn.hǎ) ǎ.zor.de- bǎ.šand/	/(u/ ǎn) ǎ.zor.de- bǎ.šad/

Past Progressive	
ماضی مستمر(در جریان)	
(ما) داشتیم می آزردیم	(من) داشتم می آزردم
/(mǎ) dǎš.tim- mi.ǎ.zor.dim/	/(man) dǎš.tam- mi.ǎ.zor.dam/
(شما) داشتید می آزردید	(تو) داشتی می آزردی
/(šo.mǎ) dǎš.tid- mi.ǎ.zor.did/	/(to) dǎš.ti- mi.ǎ.zor.di/
(آنها) داشتند می آزردند	(او/آن) داشت می آزرد
/(ǎn.hǎ) dǎš.tand- mi.ǎ.zor.dand/	/(u/ ǎn) dǎšt- mi.ǎ.zord/

Simple Future	
مستقبل (آینده ساده)	
(ما) خواهیم آزرد	(من) خواهم آزرد
/(mǎ) kǎ.him- ǎ.zord/	/(man) kǎ.ham- ǎ.zord/
(شما) خواهید آزرد	(تو) خواهی آزرد
/(šo.mǎ) kǎ.hid- ǎ.zord/	/(to) kǎ.hi- ǎ.zord/
(آنها) خواهند آزرد	(او/آن) خواهد آزرد
/(ǎn.hǎ) kǎ.hand- ǎ.zord/	/(u/ ǎn) kǎ.had- ǎ.zord/

Command	
امر	
بیازارید!	بیازار!
/ bi.yǎ.zǎ.rid/	/bi.yǎ.zǎr/

to braid

تافتَن

/tăf.tan/

Plural	Singular
Simple Present	
مضارع اخباری(حال ساده)	
(ما) می تابیم	(من) می تابم
/(mă) mi.tă.bim/	/(man) mi.tă.bam/
(شما) می تابید	(تو) می تابی
/(šo.mă) mi.tă.bid/	/(to) mi.tă.bi/
(آنها) می تابند	(او/آن) می تابد
/(ăn.hă) mi.tă.band/	/(u/ ăn) mi.tă.bad/

Plural	Singular
Present Subjunctive	
مضارع التزامی	
(ما) بتابیم	(من) بتابم
/(mă) be.tă.bim/	/(man) be.tă.bam/
(شما) بتابید	(تو) بتابی
/(šo.mă) be.tă.bid/	/(to) be.tă.bi/
(آنها) بتابند	(او/آن) بتابد
/(ăn.hă) be.tă.band/	/(u/ ăn) be.tă.bad/

Plural	Singular
Present Progressive	
مضارع مستمر(در جریان)	
(ما) داریم می تابیم	(من) دارم می تابم
/(mă) dă.rim- mi.tă.bim/	/(man) dă.ram- mi.tă.bam/
(شما) دارید می تابید	(تو) داری می تابی
/(šo.mă) dă.rid- mi.tă.bid/	/(to) dă.ri- mi.tă.bi/
(آنها) دارند می تابند	(او/آن) دارد می تابد
/(ăn.hă) dă.rand- mi.tă.band/	/(u/ ăn) dă.rad- mi.tă.bad/

Simple Past
ماضی مطلق (گذشته ساده)

(ما) تافتیم	(من) تافتم
/(mǎ) tǎf.tim/	/(man) tǎf.tam/
(شما) تافتید	(تو) تافتی
/(šo.mǎ) tǎf.tid/	/(to) tǎf.ti/
(آنها) تافتند	(او/آن) تافت
/(ǎn.hǎ) tǎf.tand/	/(u/ ǎn) tǎft/

Imperfect Indicative
ماضی استمراری

(ما) می تافتیم	(من) می تافتم
/(mǎ) mi.tǎf.tim/	/(man) mi.tǎf.tam/
(شما) می تافتید	(تو) می تافتی
/(šo.mǎ) mi.tǎf.tid/	/(to) mi.tǎf.ti/
(آنها) می تافتند	(او/آن) می تافت
/(ǎn.hǎ) mi.tǎf.tand/	/(u/ ǎn) mi.tǎft/

Present Perfect
ماضی نقلی

(ما) تافته ایم	(من) تافته ام
/(mǎ) tǎf.te.im/	/(man) tǎf.te.am/
(شما) تافته اید	(تو) تافته ای
/(šo.mǎ) tǎf.te.id/	/(to) tǎf.te.i/
(آنها) تافته اند	(او/آن) تافته است
/(ǎn.hǎ) tǎf.te.and/	/(u/ ǎn) tǎf.te- ast/

Past Perfect
ماضی بعید

(ما) تافته بودیم	(من) تافته بودم
/(mǎ) tǎf.te- bu.dim/	/(man) tǎf.te- bu.dam/
(شما) تافته بودید	(تو) تافته بودی
/(šo.mǎ) tǎf.te- bu.did/	/(to) tǎf.te- bu.di/
(آنها) تافته بودند	(او/آن) تافته بود
/(ǎn.hǎ) tǎf.te- bu.dand/	/(u/ ǎn) tǎf.te- bud/

Past Subjunctive
ماضی التزامی

(ما) تافته باشیم	(من) تافته باشم
/(mǎ) tǎf.te- bǎ.šim/	/(man) tǎf.te- bǎ.šam/
(شما) تافته باشید	(تو) تافته باشی
/(šo.mǎ) tǎf.te- bǎ.šid/	/(to) tǎf.te- bǎ.ši/
(آنها) تافته باشند	(او/آن) تافته باشد
/(ǎn.hǎ) tǎf.te- bǎ.šand/	/(u/ ǎn) tǎf.te- bǎ.šad/

Past Progressive
ماضی مستمر(در جریان)

(ما) داشتیم می تافتیم	(من) داشتم می تافتم
/(mǎ) dǎš.tim- mi.tǎf.tim/	/(man) dǎš.tam- mi.tǎf.tam/
(شما) داشتید می تافتید	(تو) داشتی می تافتی
/(šo.mǎ) dǎš.tid- mi.tǎf.tid/	/(to) dǎš.ti- mi.tǎf.ti/
(آنها) داشتند می تافتند	(او/آن) داشت می تافت
/(ǎn.hǎ) dǎš.tand- mi.tǎf.tand/	/(u/ ǎn) dǎšt- mi.tǎft/

Simple Future
مستقبل (آینده ساده)

(ما) خواهیم تافت	(من) خواهم تافت
/(mǎ) ǩǎ.him- tǎft/	/(man) ǩǎ.ham- tǎft/
(شما) خواهید تافت	(تو) خواهی تافت
/(šo.mǎ) ǩǎ.hid- tǎft/	/(to) ǩǎ.hi- tǎft/
(آنها) خواهند تافت	(او/آن) خواهد تافت
/(ǎn.hǎ) ǩǎ.hand- tǎft/	/(u/ ǎn) ǩǎ.had- tǎft/

Command
امر

بتابید!	بتاب!
/be.tǎ.bid/	/be.tǎb/

to break

شِکَستَن

/še.kas.tan/

Plural	*Singular*
Simple Present <div dir="rtl">مضارع اخباری(حال ساده)</div>	
(ما) می شکنیم /(mǎ) mi.še.ka.nim/	(من) می شکنم /(man) mi.še.ka.nam/
(شما) می شکنید /(šo.mǎ) mi.še.ka.nid/	(تو) می شکنی /(to) mi.še.ka.ni/
(آنها) می شکنند /(ǎn.hǎ) mi.še.ka.nand/	(او/آن) می شکند /(u/ ǎn) mi.še.ka.nad/
Present Subjunctive <div dir="rtl">مضارع التزامی</div>	
(ما) بشکنیم /(mǎ) be.še.ka.nim/	(من) بشکنم /(man) be.še.ka.nam/
(شما) بشکنید /(šo.mǎ) be.še.ka.nid/	(تو) بشکنی /(to) be.še.ka.ni/
(آنها) بشکنند /(ǎn.hǎ) be.še.ka.nand/	(او/آن) بشکند /(u/ ǎn) be.še.ka.nad/
Present Progressive <div dir="rtl">مضارع مستمر(در جریان)</div>	
(ما) داریم می شکنیم /(mǎ) dǎ.rim- mi.še.ka.nim/	(من) دارم می شکنم /(man) dǎ.ram- mi.še.ka.nam/
(شما) دارید می شکنید /(šo.mǎ) dǎ.rid- mi.še.ka.nid/	(تو) داری می شکنی /(to) dǎ.ri- mi.še.ka.ni/
(آنها) دارند می شکنند /(ǎn.hǎ) dǎ.rand- mi.še.ka.nand/	(او/آن) دارد می شکند /(u/ ǎn) dǎ.rad- mi.še.ka.nad/

Simple Past
ماضی مطلق (گذشته ساده)

(ما) شکستیم	(من) شکستم
/(mă) še.kas.tim/	/(man) še.kas.tam/
(شما) شکستید	(تو) شکستی
/(šo.mă) še.kas.tid/	/(to) še.kas.ti/
(آنها) شکستند	(او/آن) شکست
/(ăn.hă) še.kas.tand	/(u/ ăn) še.kast/

Imperfect Indicative
ماضی استمراری

(ما) می شکستیم	(من) می شکستم
/(mă) mi.še.kas.tim/	/(man) mi.še.kas.tam/
(شما) می شکستید	(تو) می شکستی
/(šo.mă) mi.še.kas.tid/	/(to) mi.še.kas.ti/
(آنها) می شکستند	(او/آن) می شکست
/(ăn.hă) mi.še.kas.tand/	/(u/ ăn) mi.še.kast/

Present Perfect
ماضی نقلی

(ما) شکسته ایم	(من) شکسته ام
/(mă) še.kas.te.im/	/(man) še.kas.te.am/
(شما) شکسته اید	(تو) شکسته ای
/(šo.mă) še.kas.te.id/	/(to) še.kas.te.i/
(آنها) شکسته اند	(او/آن) شکسته است
/(ăn.hă) še.kas.te.and/	/(u/ ăn) še.kas.te- ast/

Past Perfect
ماضی بعید

(ما) شکسته بودیم	(من) شکسته بودم
/(mă) še.kas.te- bu.dim/	/(man) še.kas.te- bu.dam/
(شما) شکسته بودید	(تو) شکسته بودی
/(šo.mă) še.kas.te- bu.did/	/(to) še.kas.te- bu.di/
(آنها) شکسته بودند	(او/آن) شکسته بود
/(ăn.hă) še.kas.te- bu.dand/	/(u/ ăn) še.kas.te- bud/

Past Subjunctive	
ماضی التزامی	
(ما) شکسته باشیم	(من) شکسته باشم
/(mă) še.kas.te- bă.šim/	/(man) še.kas.te- bă.šam/
(شما) شکسته باشید	(تو) شکسته باشی
/(šo.mă) še.kas.te- bă.šid/	/(to) še.kas.te- bă.ši/
(آنها) شکسته باشند	(او/آن) شکسته باشد
/(ăn.hă) še.kas.te- bă.šand/	/(u/ ăn) še.kas.te- bă.šad/

Past Progressive	
ماضی مستمر(در جریان)	
(ما) داشتیم می شکستیم	(من) داشتم می شکستم
/(mă) dăš.tim- mi.še.kas.tim/	/(man) dăš.tam- mi.še.kas.tam/
(شما) داشتید می شکستید	(تو) داشتی می شکستی
/(šo.mă) dăš.tid- mi.še.kas.tid/	/(to) dăš.ti- mi.še.kas.ti/
(آنها) داشتند می شکستند	(او/آن) داشت می شکست
/(ăn.hă) dăš.tand- mi.še.kas.tand/	/(u/ ăn) dăšt- mi.še.kast/

Simple Future	
مستقبل (آینده ساده)	
(ما) خواهیم شکست	(من) خواهم شکست
/(mă) kă.him- še.kast/	/(man) kă.ham- še.kast/
(شما) خواهید شکست	(تو) خواهی شکست
/(šo.mă) kă.hid- še.kast/	/(to) kă.hi- še.kast/
(آنها) خواهند شکست	(او/آن) خواهد شکست
/(ăn.hă) kă.hand- še.kast/	/(u/ ăn) kă.had- še.kast/

Command	
امر	
بشکنید!	بشکن!
/be.še.ka.nid/	/be.še.kan/

to build

ساخْتَن

/săk̆.tan/

Plural	Singular
Simple Present مضارع اخباری(حال ساده)	
(ما) می سازیم /(mă) mi.să.zim/	(من) می سازم /(man) mi.să.zam/
(شما) می سازید /(šo.mă) mi.să.zid/	(تو) می سازی /(to) mi.să.zi/
(آنها) می سازند /(ăn.hă) mi.să.zand/	(او/آن) می سازد /(u/ ăn) mi.să.zad/

Plural	Singular
Present Subjunctive مضارع التزامی	
(ما) بسازیم /(mă) be.să.zim/	(من) بسازم /(man) be.să.zam/
(شما) بسازید /(šo.mă) be.să.zid/	(تو) بسازی /(to) be.să.zi/
(آنها) بسازند /(ăn.hă) be.să.zand/	(او/آن) بسازد /(u/ ăn) be.să.zad/

Plural	Singular
Present Progressive مضارع مستمر(در جریان)	
(ما) داریم می سازیم /(mă) dă.rim- mi.să.zim/	(من) دارم می سازم /(man) dă.ram- mi.să.zam/
(شما) دارید می سازید /(šo.mă) dă.rid- mi.să.zid/	(تو) داری می سازی /(to) dă.ri- mi.să.zi/
(آنها) دارند می سازند /(ăn.hă) dă.rand- mi.să.zand/	(او/آن) دارد می سازد /(u/ ăn) dă.rad- mi.să.zad/

Simple Past	
ماضی مطلق (گذشته ساده)	
(ما) ساختیم	(من) ساختم
/(mǎ) sǎk̆.tim/	/(man) sǎk̆.tam/
(شما) ساختید	(تو) ساختی
/(šo.mǎ) sǎk̆.tid/	/(to) sǎk̆.ti/
(آنها) ساختند	(او/آن) ساخت
/(ǎn.hǎ) sǎk̆.tand/	/(u/ ǎn) sǎk̆t/

Imperfect Indicative	
ماضی استمراری	
(ما) می ساختیم	(من) می ساختم
/(mǎ) mi.sǎk̆.tim/	/(man) mi.sǎk̆.tam/
(شما) می ساختید	(تو) می ساختی
/(šo.mǎ) mi.sǎk̆.tid/	/(to) mi.sǎk̆.ti/
(آنها) می ساختند	(او/آن) می ساخت
/(ǎn.hǎ) mi.sǎk̆.tand/	/(u/ ǎn) mi.sǎk̆t/

Present Perfect	
ماضی نقلی	
(ما) ساخته ایم	(من) ساخته ام
/(mǎ) sǎk̆.te.im/	/(man) sǎk̆.te.am/
(شما) ساخته اید	(تو) ساخته ای
/(šo.mǎ) sǎk̆.te.id/	/(to) sǎk̆.te.i/
(آنها) ساخته اند	(او/آن) ساخته است
/(ǎn.hǎ) sǎk̆.te.and/	/(u/ ǎn) sǎk̆.te- ast/

Past Perfect	
ماضی بعید	
(ما) ساخته بودیم	(من) ساخته بودم
/(mǎ) sǎk̆.te- bu.dim/	/(man) sǎk̆.te- bu.dam/
(شما) ساخته بودید	(تو) ساخته بودی
/(šo.mǎ) sǎk̆.te- bu.did/	/(to) sǎk̆.te- bu.di/
(آنها) ساخته بودند	(او/آن) ساخته بود
/(ǎn.hǎ) sǎk̆.te- bu.dand/	/(u/ ǎn) sǎk̆.te- bud/

33

	Past Subjunctive
	ماضی التزامی
(ما) ساخته باشیم /(mă) săǩ.te- bă.šim/	(من) ساخته باشم /(man) săǩ.te- bă.šam/
(شما) ساخته باشید /(šo.mă) săǩ.te- bă.šid/	(تو) ساخته باشی /(to) săǩ.te- bă.ši/
(آنها) ساخته باشند /(ăn.hă) săǩ.te- bă.šand/	(او/آن) ساخته باشد /(u/ ăn) săǩ.te- bă.šad/

	Past Progressive
	ماضی مستمر(در جریان)
(ما) داشتیم می ساختیم /(mă) dăš.tim- mi.săǩ.tim/	(من) داشتم می ساختم /(man) dăš.tam- mi.săǩ.tam/
(شما) داشتید می ساختید /(šo.mă) dăš.tid- mi.săǩ.tid/	(تو) داشتی می ساختی /(to) dăš.ti- mi.săǩ.ti/
(آنها) داشتند می ساختند /(ăn.hă) dăš.tand- mi.săǩ.tand/	(او/آن) داشت می ساخت /(u/ ăn) dăšt- mi.săǩt/

	Simple Future
	مستقبل (آینده ساده)
(ما) خواهیم ساخت /(mă) ǩă.him- săǩt/	(من) خواهم ساخت /(man) ǩă.ham- săǩt/
(شما) خواهید ساخت /(šo.mă) ǩă.hid- săǩt/	(تو) خواهی ساخت /(to) ǩă.hi- săǩt/
(آنها) خواهند ساخت /(ăn.hă) ǩă.hand- săǩt/	(او/آن) خواهد ساخت /(u/ ăn) ǩă.had- săǩt/

	Command
	امر
بسازید! /be.să.zid/	بساز! /be.săz/

to burn

سوختَن

/suǩ.tan/

Plural	Singular
Simple Present مضارع اخباری(حال ساده)	
(ما) می سوزیم /(mǎ) mi.su.zim/	(من) می سوزم /(man) mi.su.zam/
(شما) می سوزید /(šo.mǎ) mi.su.zid/	(تو) می سوزی /(to) mi.su.zi/
(آنها) می سوزند /(ǎn.hǎ) mi.su.zand/	(او/آن) می سوزد /(u/ ǎn) mi.su.zad/
Present Subjunctive مضارع التزامی	
(ما) بسوزیم /(mǎ) be.su.zim/	(من) بسوزم /(man) be.su.zam/
(شما) بسوزید /(šo.mǎ) be.su.zid/	(تو) بسوزی /(to) be.su.zi/
(آنها) بسوزند /(ǎn.hǎ) be.su.zand/	(او/آن) بسوزد /(u/ ǎn) be.su.zad/
Present Progressive مضارع مستمر(در جریان)	
(ما) داریم می سوزیم /(mǎ) dǎ.rim- mi.su.zim/	(من) دارم می سوزم /(man) dǎ.ram- mi.su.zam/
(شما) دارید می سوزید /(šo.mǎ) dǎ.rid- mi.su.zid/	(تو) داری می سوزی /(to) dǎ.ri- mi.su.zi/
(آنها) دارند می سوزند /(ǎn.hǎ) dǎ.rand- mi.su.zand/	(او/آن) دارد می سوزد /(u/ ǎn) dǎ.rad- mi.su.zad/

Simple Past
ماضی مطلق (گذشته ساده)

(ما) سوختیم	(من) سوختم
/(mǎ) suǩ.tim/	/(man) suǩ.tam/
(شما) سوختید	(تو) سوختی
/(šo.mǎ) suǩ.tid/	/(to) suǩ.ti/
(آنها) سوختند	(او/آن) سوخت
/(ǎn.hǎ) suǩ.tand/	/(u/ ǎn) suǩt/

Imperfect Indicative
ماضی استمراری

(ما) می سوختیم	(من) می سوختم
/(mǎ) mi.suǩ.tim/	/(man) mi.suǩ.tam/
(شما) می سوختید	(تو) می سوختی
/(šo.mǎ) mi.suǩ.tid/	/(to) mi.suǩ.ti/
(آنها) می سوختند	(او/آن) می سوخت
/(ǎn.hǎ) mi.suǩ.tand/	/(u/ ǎn) mi.suǩt/

Present Perfect
ماضی نقلی

(ما) سوخته ایم	(من) سوخته ام
/(mǎ) suǩ.te.im/	/(man) suǩ.te.am
(شما) سوخته اید	(تو) سوخته ای
/(šo.mǎ) suǩ.te.id/	/(to) suǩ.te.i/
(آنها) سوخته اند	(او/آن) سوخته است
/(ǎn.hǎ) suǩ.te.and/	/(u/ ǎn) suǩ.te- ast/

Past Perfect
ماضی بعید

(ما) سوخته بودیم	(من) سوخته بودم
/(mǎ) suǩ.te- bu.dim/	/(man) suǩ.te- bu.dam/
(شما) سوخته بودید	(تو) سوخته بودی
/(šo.mǎ) suǩ.te- bu.did/	/(to) suǩ.te- bu.di/
(آنها) سوخته بودند	(او/آن) سوخته بود
/(ǎn.hǎ) suǩ.te- bu.dand/	/(u/ ǎn) suǩ.te- bud/

Past Subjunctive	
ماضی التزامی	
(ما) سوخته باشیم	(من) سوخته باشم
/(mǎ) suǩ.te- bǎ.šim/	/(man) suǩ.te- bǎ.šam/
(شما) سوخته باشید	(تو) سوخته باشی
/(šo.mǎ) suǩ.te- bǎ.šid/	/(to) suǩ.te- bǎ.ši/
(آنها) سوخته باشند	(او/آن) سوخته باشد
/(ǎn.hǎ) suǩ.te- bǎ.šand/	/(u/ ǎn) suǩ.te- bǎ.šad/

Past Progressive	
ماضی مستمر(در جریان)	
(ما) داشتیم می سوختیم	(من) داشتم می سوختم
/(mǎ) dǎš.tim- mi.suǩ.tim/	/(man) dǎš.tam- mi.suǩ.tam/
(شما) داشتید می سوختید	(تو) داشتی می سوختی
/(šo.mǎ) dǎš.tid- mi.suǩ.tid/	/(to) dǎš.ti- mi.suǩ.ti/
(آنها) داشتند می سوختند	(او/آن) داشت می سوخت
/(ǎn.hǎ) dǎš.tand- mi.suǩ.tand/	/(u/ ǎn) dǎšt- mi.suǩt/

Simple Future	
مستقبل (آینده ساده)	
(ما) خواهیم سوخت	(من) خواهم سوخت
/(mǎ) ǩǎ.him- suǩt/	/(man) ǩǎ.ham- suǩt/
(شما) خواهید سوخت	(تو) خواهی سوخت
/(šo.mǎ) ǩǎ.hid- suǩt/	/(to) ǩǎ.hi- suǩt/
(آنها) خواهند سوخت	(او/آن) خواهد سوخت
/(ǎn.hǎ) ǩǎ.hand- suǩt/	/(u/ ǎn) ǩǎ.had- suǩt/

Command	
امر	
بسوزید!	بسوز!
/be.su.zid/	/be.suz/

to catch

گِرِفتَن

/ge.ref.tan/

Plural	Singular
Simple Present	
مضارع اخباری(حال ساده)	
(ما) می گیریم	(من) می گیرم
/(mǎ) mi.gi.rim/	/(man) mi.gi.ram/
(شما) می گیرید	(تو) می گیری
/(šo.mǎ) mi.gi.rid/	/(to) mi.gi.ri/
(آنها) می گیرند	(او/آن) می گیرد
/(ǎn.hǎ) mi.gi.rand/	/(u/ ǎn) mi.gi.rad/
Present Subjunctive	
مضارع التزامی	
(ما) بگیریم	(من) بگیرم
/(mǎ) be.gi.rim/	/(man) be.gi.ram/
(شما) بگیرید	(تو) بگیری
/(šo.mǎ) be.gi.rid/	/(to) be.gi.ri/
(آنها) بگیرند	(او/آن) بگیرد
/(ǎn.hǎ) be.gi.rand/	/(u/ ǎn) be.gi.rad/
Present Progressive	
مضارع مستمر(در جریان)	
(ما) داریم می گیریم	(من) دارم می گیرم
/(mǎ) dǎ.rim- mi.gi.rim/	/(man) dǎ.ram- mi.gi.ram/
(شما) دارید می گیرید	(تو) داری می گیری
/(šo.mǎ) dǎ.rid- mi.gi.rid/	/(to) dǎ.ri- mi.gi.ri/
(آنها) دارند می گیرند	(او/آن) دارد می گیرد
/(ǎn.hǎ) dǎ.rand- mi.gi.rand/	/(u/ ǎn) dǎ.rad- mi.gi.rad/

38

Simple Past	
ماضی مطلق (گذشته ساده)	
(ما) گرفتیم	(من) گرفتم
/(mǎ) ge.ref.tim/	/(man) ge.ref.tam/
(شما) گرفتید	(تو) گرفتی
/(šo.mǎ) ge.ref.tid/	/(to) ge.ref.ti/
(آنها) گرفتند	(او/ آن) گرفت
/(ǎn.hǎ) ge.ref.tand/	/(u/ ǎn) ge.reft/

Imperfect Indicative	
ماضی استمراری	
(ما) می گرفتیم	(من) می گرفتم
/(mǎ) mi.ge.ref.tim/	/(man) mi.ge.ref.tam/
(شما) می گرفتید	(تو) می گرفتی
/(šo.mǎ) mi.ge.ref.tid/	/(to) mi.ge.ref.ti/
(آنها) می گرفتند	(او/ آن) می گرفت
/(ǎn.hǎ) mi.ge.ref.tand/	/(u/ ǎn) mi.ge.reft/

Present Perfect	
ماضی نقلی	
(ما) گرفته ایم	(من) گرفته ام
/(mǎ) ge.ref.te.im/	/(man) ge.ref.te.am/
(شما) گرفته اید	(تو) گرفته ای
/(šo.mǎ) ge.ref.te.id/	/(to) ge.ref.te.i/
(آنها) گرفته اند	(او/ آن) گرفته است
/(ǎn.hǎ) ge.ref.te.and/	/(u/ ǎn) ge.ref.te- ast/

Past Perfect	
ماضی بعید	
(ما) گرفته بودیم	(من) گرفته بودم
/(mǎ) ge.ref.te- bu.dim/	/(man) ge.ref.te- bu.dam/
(شما) گرفته بودید	(تو) گرفته بودی
/(šo.mǎ) ge.ref.te- bu.did/	/(to) ge.ref.te- bu.di/
(آنها) گرفته بودند	(او/ آن) گرفته بود
/(ǎn.hǎ) ge.ref.te- bu.dand/	/(u/ ǎn) ge.ref.te- bud/

Past Subjunctive	
ماضی التزامی	
(ما) گرفته باشیم	(من) گرفته باشم
/(mă) ge.ref.te- bă.šim/	/(man) ge.ref.te- bă.šam/
(شما) گرفته باشید	(تو) گرفته باشی
/(šo.mă) ge.ref.te- bă.šid/	/(to) ge.ref.te- bă.ši/
(آنها) گرفته باشند	(او/آن) گرفته باشد
/(ăn.hă) ge.ref.te- bă.šand/	/(u/ ăn) ge.ref.te- bă.šad/

Past Progressive	
ماضی مستمر(در جریان)	
(ما) داشتیم می گرفتیم	(من) داشتم می گرفتم
/(mă) dăš.tim- mi.ge.ref.tim/	/(man) dăš.tam- mi.ge.ref.tam/
(شما) داشتید می گرفتید	(تو) داشتی می گرفتی
/(šo.mă) dăš.tid- mi.ge.ref.tid/	/(to) dăš.ti- mi.ge.ref.ti/
(آنها) داشتند می گرفتند	(او/آن) داشت می گرفت
/(ăn.hă) dăš.tand- mi.ge.ref.tand/	/(u/ ăn) dăšt- mi.ge.reft/

Simple Future	
مستقبل (آینده ساده)	
(ما) خواهیم گرفت	(من) خواهم گرفت
/(mă) kă.him- ge.reft/	/(man) kă.ham- ge.reft/
(شما) خواهید گرفت	(تو) خواهی گرفت
/(šo.mă) kă.hid- ge.reft/	/(to) kă.hi- ge.reft/
(آنها) خواهند گرفت	(او/آن) خواهد گرفت
/(ăn.hă) kă.hand- ge.reft/	/(u/ ăn) kă.had- ge.reft/

Command	
امر	
بگیرید!	بگیر!
/be.gi.rid/	/be.gir/

to choose

گُزیدَن

/go.zi.dan/

Plural	*Singular*
Simple Present مضارع اخباری(حال ساده)	
(ما) می گزینیم /(mǎ) mi.go.zi.nim/	(من) می گزینم /(man) mi.go.zi.nam/
(شما) می گزینید /(šo.mǎ) mi.go.zi.nid/	(تو) می گزینی /(to) mi.go.zi.ni/
(آنها) می گزینند /(ǎn.hǎ) mi.go.zi.nand/	(او/آن) می گزیند /(u/ ǎn) mi.go.zi.nad/
Present Subjunctive مضارع التزامی	
(ما) بگزینیم /(mǎ) be.go.zi.nim/	(من) بگزینم /(man) be.go.zi.nam/
(شما) بگزینید /(šo.mǎ) be.go.zi.nid/	(تو) بگزینی /(to) be.go.zi.ni/
(آنها) بگزینند /(ǎn.hǎ) be.go.zi.nand/	(او/آن) بگزیند /(u/ ǎn) be.go.zi.nad/
Present Progressive مضارع مستمر(در جریان)	
(ما) داریم می گزینیم /(mǎ) dǎ.rim- mi.go.zi.nim/	(من) دارم می گزینم /(man) dǎ.ram- mi.go.zi.nam/
(شما) دارید می گزینید /(šo.mǎ) dǎ.rid- mi.go.zi.nid/	(تو) داری می گزینی /(to) dǎ.ri- mi.go.zi.ni/
(آنها) دارند می گزینند /(ǎn.hǎ) dǎ.rand- mi.go.zi.nand/	(او/آن) دارد می گزیند /(u/ ǎn) dǎ.rad- mi.go.zi.nad/

Simple Past
ماضی مطلق (گذشته ساده)

(ما) گزیدیم	(من) گزیدم
/(mǎ) go.zi.dim/	/(man) go.zi.dam/
(شما) گزیدید	(تو) گزیدی
/(šo.mǎ) go.zi.did/	/(to) go.zi.di/
(آنها) گزیدند	(او/آن) گزید
/(ǎn.hǎ) go.zi.dand/	/(u/ ǎn) go.zid/

Imperfect Indicative
ماضی استمراری

(ما) می گزیدیم	(من) می گزیدم
/(mǎ) mi.go.zi.dim/	/(man) mi.go.zi.dam/
(شما) می گزیدید	(تو) می گزیدی
/(šo.mǎ) mi.go.zi.did/	/(to) mi.go.zi.di/
(آنها) می گزیدند	(او/آن) می گزید
/(ǎn.hǎ) mi.go.zi.dand/	/(u/ ǎn) mi.go.zid/

Present Perfect
ماضی نقلی

(ما) گزیده ایم	(من) گزیده ام
/(mǎ) go.zi.de.im/	/(man) go.zi.de.am/
(شما) گزیده اید	(تو) گزیده ای
/(šo.mǎ) go.zi.de.id/	/(to) go.zi.de.i/
(آنها) گزیده اند	(او/آن) گزیده است
/(ǎn.hǎ) go.zi.de.and/	/(u/ ǎn) go.zi.de- ast/

Past Perfect
ماضی بعید

(ما) گزیده بودیم	(من) گزیده بودم
/(mǎ) go.zi.de- bu.dim/	/(man) go.zi.de- bu.dam/
(شما) گزیده بودید	(تو) گزیده بودی
/(šo.mǎ) go.zi.de- bu.did/	/(to) go.zi.de- bu.di/
(آنها) گزیده بودند	(او/آن) گزیده بود
/(ǎn.hǎ) go.zi.de- bu.dand/	/(u/ ǎn) go.zi.de- bud/

Past Subjunctive
ماضی التزامی

(ما) گزیده باشیم	(من) گزیده باشم
/(mǎ) go.zi.de- bǎ.šim/	/(man) go.zi.de- bǎ.šam/
(شما) گزیده باشید	(تو) گزیده باشی
/(šo.mǎ) go.zi.de- bǎ.šid/	/(to) go.zi.de- bǎ.ši/
(آنها) گزیده باشند	(او/آن) گزیده باشد
/(ǎn.hǎ) go.zi.de- bǎ.šand/	/(u/ ǎn) go.zi.de- bǎ.šad/

Past Progressive
ماضی مستمر(در جریان)

(ما) داشتیم می گزیدیم	(من) داشتم می گزیدم
/(mǎ) dǎš.tim- mi.go.zi.dim/	/(man) dǎš.tam- mi.go.zi.dam/
(شما) داشتید می گزیدید	(تو) داشتی می گزیدی
/(šo.mǎ) dǎš.tid- mi.go.zi.did/	/(to) dǎš.ti- mi.go.zi.di/
(آنها) داشتند می گزیدند	(او/آن) داشت می گزید
/(ǎn.hǎ) dǎš.tand- mi.go.zi.dand/	/(u/ ǎn) dǎšt- mi.go.zid/

Simple Future
مستقبل (آینده ساده)

(ما) خواهیم گزید	(من) خواهم گزید
/(mǎ) ǩǎ.him- go.zid/	/(man) ǩǎ.ham- go.zid/
(شما) خواهید گزید	(تو) خواهی گزید
/(šo.mǎ) ǩǎ.hid- go.zid/	/(to) ǩǎ.hi- go.zid/
(آنها) خواهند گزید	(او/آن) خواهد گزید
/(ǎn.hǎ) ǩǎ.hand- go.zid/	/(u/ ǎn) ǩǎ.had- go.zid/

Command
امر

بگزینید!	بگزین!
/be.go.zi.nid/	/be.go.zin/

43

to close

بَستَن

/bas.tan/

Plural		Singular
Simple Present		
مضارع اخباری(حال ساده)		
(ما) می بندیم		(من) می بندم
/(mă) mi.ban.dim/		/(man) mi.ban.dam/
(شما) می بندید		(تو) می بندی
/(šo.mă) mi.ban.did/		/(to) mi.ban.di/
(آنها) می بندند		(او/آن) می بندد
/(ăn.hă) mi.ban.dand/		/(u/ ăn) mi.ban.dad/
Present Subjunctive		
مضارع التزامی		
(ما) ببندیم		(من) ببندم
/(mă) be.ban.dim/		/(man) be.ban.dam/
(شما) ببندید		(تو) ببندی
/(šo.mă) be.ban.did/		/(to) be.ban.di/
(آنها) ببندند		(او/آن) ببندد
/(ăn.hă) be.ban.dand/		/(u/ ăn) be.ban.dad/
Present Progressive		
مضارع مستمر(در جریان)		
(ما) داریم می بندیم		(من) دارم می بندم
/(mă) dă.rim- mi.ban.dim/		/(man) dă.ram- mi.ban.dam/
(شما) دارید می بندید		(تو) داری می بندی
/(šo.mă) dă.rid- mi.ban.did/		/(to) dă.ri- mi.ban.di/
(آنها) دارند می بندند		(او/آن) دارد می بندد
/(ăn.hă) dă.rand- mi.ban.dand/		/(u/ ăn) dă.rad- mi.ban.dad/

Simple Past	
ماضی مطلق (گذشته ساده)	
(ما) بستیم	(من) بستم
/(mǎ) bas.tim/	/(man) bas.tam/
(شما) بستید	(تو) بستی
/(šo.mǎ) bas.tid/	/(to) bas.ti/
(آنها) بستند	(او/آن) بست
/(ǎn.hǎ) bas.tand/	/(u/ ǎn) bast/

Imperfect Indicative	
ماضی استمراری	
(ما) می بستیم	(من) می بستم
/(mǎ) mi.bas.tim/	/(man) mi.bas.tam/
(شما) می بستید	(تو) می بستی
/(šo.mǎ) mi.bas.tid/	/(to) mi.bas.ti/
(آنها) می بستند	(او/آن) می بست
/(ǎn.hǎ) mi.bas.tand/	/(u/ ǎn) mi.bast/

Present Perfect	
ماضی نقلی	
(ما) بسته ایم	(من) بسته ام
/(mǎ) bas.te.im/	/(man) bas.te.am/
(شما) بسته اید	(تو) بسته ای
/(šo.mǎ) bas.te.id/	/(to) bas.te.i/
(آنها) بسته اند	(او/آن) بسته است
/(ǎn.hǎ) bas.te.and/	/(u/ ǎn) bas.te- ast/

Past Perfect	
ماضی بعید	
(ما) بسته بودیم	(من) بسته بودم
/(mǎ) bas.te- bu.dim/	/(man) bas.te- bu.dam/
(شما) بسته بودید	(تو) بسته بودی
/(šo.mǎ) bas.te- bu.did/	/(to) bas.te- bu.di/
(آنها) بسته بودند	(او/آن) بسته بود
/(ǎn.hǎ) bas.te- bu.dand/	/(u/ ǎn) bas.te- bud/

Past Subjunctive	
ماضی التزامی	
(ما) بسته باشیم	(من) بسته باشم
/(mǎ) bas.te- bǎ.šim/	/(man) bas.te- bǎ.šam/
(شما) بسته باشید	(تو) بسته باشی
/(šo.mǎ) bas.te- bǎ.šid/	/(to) bas.te- bǎ.ši/
(آنها) بسته باشند	(او/آن) بسته باشد
/(ǎn.hǎ) bas.te- bǎ.šand/	/(u/ ǎn) bas.te- bǎ.šad/

Past Progressive	
ماضی مستمر(در جریان)	
(ما) داشتیم می بستیم	(من) داشتم می بستم
/(mǎ) dǎš.tim- mi.bas.tim/	/(man) dǎš.tam- mi.bas.tam/
(شما) داشتید می بستید	(تو) داشتی می بستی
/(šo.mǎ) dǎš.tid- mi.bas.tid/	/(to) dǎš.ti- mi.bas.ti/
(آنها) داشتند می بستند	(او/آن) داشت می بست
/(ǎn.hǎ) dǎš.tand- mi.bas.tand/	/(u/ ǎn) dǎšt- mi.bast/

Simple Future	
مستقبل (آینده ساده)	
(ما) خواهیم بست	(من) خواهم بست
/(mǎ) ǩǎ.him- bast/	/(man) ǩǎ.ham- bast/
(شما) خواهید بست	(تو) خواهی بست
/(šo.mǎ) ǩǎ.hid- bast/	/(to) ǩǎ.hi- bast/
(آنها) خواهند بست	(او/آن) خواهد بست
/(ǎn.hǎ) ǩǎ.hand- bast/	/(u/ ǎn) ǩǎ.had- bast/

Command	
امر	
ببندید!	ببند!
/be.ban.did/	/be.band/

to come

آمَدَن

/ă.ma.dan/

Plural	Singular
Simple Present	
مضارع اخباری(حال ساده)	
(ما) می آییم	(من) می آیم
/(mă) mi.ă.yim/	/(man) mi.ă.yam/
(شما) می آیید	(تو) می آیی
/(šo.mă) mi.ă.yid/	/(to) mi.ă.yi/
(آنها) می آیند	(او/آن) می آید
/(ăn.hă) mi.ă.yand/	/(u/ ăn) mi.ă.yad/

Plural	Singular
Present Subjunctive	
مضارع التزامی	
(ما) بیاییم	(من) بیایم
/(mă) bi.yă.yim/	/(man) bi.yă.yam/
(شما) بیایید	(تو) بیایی
/(šo.mă) bi.yă.yid/	/(to) bi.yă.yi/
(آنها) بیایند	(او/آن) بیاید
/(ăn.hă) bi.yă.yand/	/(u/ ăn) bi.yă.yad/

Plural	Singular
Present Progressive	
مضارع مستمر(در جریان)	
(ما) داریم می آییم	(من) دارم می آیم
/(mă) dă.rim- mi.ă.yim/	/(man) dă.ram- mi.ă.yam/
(شما) دارید می آیید	(تو) داری می آیی
/(šo.mă) dă.rid- mi.ă.yid/	/(to) dă.ri- mi.ă.yi/
(آنها) دارند می آیند	(او/آن) دارد می آید
/(ăn.hă) dă.rand- mi.ă.yand/	/(u/ ăn) dă.rad- mi.ă.yad/

Simple Past
ماضی مطلق (گذشته ساده)

(ما) آمدیم	(من) آمدم
/(mă) ă.ma.dim/	/(man) ă.ma.dam/
(شما) آمدید	(تو) آمدی
/(šo.mă) ă.ma.did/	/(to) ă.ma.di/
(آنها) آمدند	(او/آن) آمد
/(ăn.hă) ă.ma.dand/	/(u/ ăn) ă.mad/

Imperfect Indicative
ماضی استمراری

(ما) می آمدیم	(من) می آمدم
/(mă) mi.ă.ma.dim/	/(man) mi.ă.ma.dam/
(شما) می آمدید	(تو) می آمدی
/(šo.mă) mi.ă.ma.did/	/(to) mi.ă.ma.di/
(آنها) می آمدند	(او/آن) می آمد
/(ăn.hă) mi.ă.ma.dand/	/(u/ ăn) mi.ă.mad/

Present Perfect
ماضی نقلی

(ما) آمده ایم	(من) آمده ام
/(mă) ă.ma.de.im/	/(man) ă.ma.de.am/
(شما) آمده اید	(تو) آمده ای
/(šo.mă) ă.ma.de.id/	/(to) ă.ma.de.i/
(آنها) آمده اند	(او/آن) آمده است
/(ăn.hă) ă.ma.de.and/	/(u/ ăn) ă.ma.de- ast/

Past Perfect
ماضی بعید

(ما) آمده بودیم	(من) آمده بودم
/(mă) ă.ma.de- bu.dim/	/(man) ă.ma.de- bu.dam/
(شما) آمده بودید	(تو) آمده بودی
/(šo.mă) ă.ma.de- bu.did/	/(to) ă.ma.de- bu.di/
(آنها) آمده بودند	(او/آن) آمده بود
/(ăn.hă) ă.ma.de- bu.dand/	/(u/ ăn) ă.ma.de- bud/

Past Subjunctive	
ماضی التزامی	
(ما) آمده باشیم	(من) آمده باشم
/(mǎ) ǎ.ma.de- bǎ.šim/	/(man) ǎ.ma.de- bǎ.šam/
(شما) آمده باشید	(تو) آمده باشی
/(šo.mǎ) ǎ.ma.de- bǎ.šid/	/(to) ǎ.ma.de- bǎ.ši/
(آنها) آمده باشند	(او/ آن) آمده باشد
/(ǎn.hǎ) ǎ.ma.de- bǎ.šand/	/(u/ ǎn) ǎ.ma.de- bǎ.šad/

Past Progressive	
ماضی مستمر(در جریان)	
(ما) داشتیم می آمدیم	(من) داشتم می آمدم
/(mǎ) dǎš.tim- mi.ǎ.ma.dim/	/(man) dǎš.tam- mi.ǎ.ma.dam/
(شما) داشتید می آمدید	(تو) داشتی می آمدی
/(šo.mǎ) dǎš.tid- mi.ǎ.ma.did/	/(to) dǎš.ti- mi.ǎ.ma.di/
(آنها) داشتند می آمدند	(او/ آن) داشت می آمد
/(ǎn.hǎ) dǎš.tand- mi.ǎ.ma.dand/	/(u/ ǎn) dǎšt- mi.ǎ.mad/

Simple Future	
مستقبل (آینده ساده)	
(ما) خواهیم آمد	(من) خواهم آمد
/(mǎ) ǩǎ.him- ǎ.mad/	/(man) ǩǎ.ham- ǎ.mad/
(شما) خواهید آمد	(تو) خواهی آمد
/(šo.mǎ) ǩǎ.hid- ǎ.mad/	/(to) ǩǎ.hi- ǎ.mad/
(آنها) خواهند آمد	(او/ آن) خواهد آمد
/(ǎn.hǎ) ǩǎ.hand- ǎ.mad/	/(u/ ǎn) ǩǎ.had- ǎ.mad/

Command	
امر	
بیایید!	بیا !
/bi.yǎ.yid/	/bi.yǎ/

49

to come apart

گُسیختَن

/go.siǩ.tan/

Plural	Singular
Simple Present مضارع اخباری(حال ساده)	
(ما) می گسلیم /(mǎ) mi.go.sa.lim/	(من) می گسلم /(man) mi.go.sa.lam/
(شما) می گسلید /(šo.mǎ) mi.go.sa.lid/	(تو) می گسلی /(to) mi.go.sa.li/
(آنها) می گسلند /(ǎn.hǎ) mi.go.sa.land/	(او/آن) می گسلد /(u/ ǎn) mi.go.sa.lad/
Present Subjunctive مضارع التزامی	
(ما) بگسلیم /(mǎ) be.go.sa.lim/	(من) بگسلم /(man) be.go.sa.lam/
(شما) بگسلید /(šo.mǎ) be.go.sa.lid/	(تو) بگسلی /(to) be.go.sa.li/
(آنها) بگسلند /(ǎn.hǎ) be.go.sa.land/	(او/آن) بگسلد /(u/ ǎn) be.go.sa.lad/
Present Progressive مضارع مستمر(در جریان)	
(ما) داریم می گسلیم /(mǎ) dǎ.rim- mi.go.sa.lim/	(من) دارم می گسلم /(man) dǎ.ram- mi.go.sa.lam/
(شما) دارید می گسلید /(šo.mǎ) dǎ.rid- mi.go.sa.lid/	(تو) داری می گسلی /(to) dǎ.ri- mi.go.sa.li/
(آنها) دارند می گسلند /(ǎn.hǎ) dǎ.rand- mi.go.sa.land/	(او/آن) دارد می گسلد /(u/ ǎn) dǎ.rad- mi.go.sa.lad/

Simple Past	
ماضی مطلق (گذشته ساده)	
(ما) گسیختیم	(من) گسیختم
/(mă) go.siǩ.tim/	/(man) go.siǩ.tam/
(شما) گسیختید	(تو) گسیختی
/(šo.mă) go.siǩ.tid/	/(to) go.siǩ.ti/
(آنها) گسیختند	(او/ آن) گسیخت
/(ăn.hă) go.siǩ.tand/	/(u/ ăn) go.siǩt/

Imperfect Indicative	
ماضی استمراری	
(ما) می گسیختیم	(من) می گسیختم
/(mă) mi.go.siǩ.tim/	/(man) mi.go.siǩ.tam/
(شما) می گسیختید	(تو) می گسیختی
/(šo.mă) mi.go.siǩ.tid/	/(to) mi.go.siǩ.ti/
(آنها) می گسیختند	(او/ آن) می گسیخت
/(ăn.hă) mi.go.siǩ.tand/	/(u/ ăn) mi.go.siǩt/

Present Perfect	
ماضی نقلی	
(ما) گسیخته ایم	(من) گسیخته ام
/(mă) go.siǩ.te.im/	/(man) go.siǩ.te.am/
(شما) گسیخته اید	(تو) گسیخته ای
/(šo.mă) go.siǩ.te.id/	/(to) go.siǩ.te.i/
(آنها) گسیخته اند	(او/ آن) گسیخته است
/(ăn.hă) go.siǩ.te.and/	/(u/ ăn) go.siǩ.te- ast/

Past Perfect	
ماضی بعید	
(ما) گسیخته بودیم	(من) گسیخته بودم
/(mă) go.siǩ.te- bu.dim/	/(man) go.siǩ.te- bu.dam/
(شما) گسیخته بودید	(تو) گسیخته بودی
/(šo.mă) go.siǩ.te- bu.did/	/(to) go.siǩ.te- bu.di/
(آنها) گسیخته بودند	(او/ آن) گسیخته بود
/(ăn.hă) go.siǩ.te- bu.dand/	/(u/ ăn) go.siǩ.te- bud/

Past Subjunctive	
ماضی التزامی	
(ما) گسیخته باشیم	(من) گسیخته باشم
/(mǎ) go.siǩ.te- bǎ.šim/	/(man) go.siǩ.te- bǎ.šam/
(شما) گسیخته باشید	(تو) گسیخته باشی
/(šo.mǎ) go.siǩ.te- bǎ.šid/	/(to) go.siǩ.te- bǎ.ši/
(آنها) گسیخته باشند	(او/ آن) گسیخته باشد
/(ǎn.hǎ) go.siǩ.te- bǎ.šand/	/(u/ ǎn) go.siǩ.te- bǎ.šad/

Past Progressive	
ماضی مستمر(در جریان)	
(ما) داشتیم می گسیختیم	(من) داشتم می گسیختم
/(mǎ) dǎš.tim-mi.go.siǩ.tim/	/(man) dǎš.tam- mi.go.siǩ.tam/
(شما) داشتید می گسیختید	(تو) داشتی می گسیختی
/(šo.mǎ) dǎš.tid- mi.go.siǩ.tid/	/(to) dǎš.ti- mi.go.siǩ.ti/
(آنها) داشتند می گسیختند	(او/ آن) داشت می گسیخت
/(ǎn.hǎ) dǎš.tand- mi.go.siǩ.tand/	/(u/ ǎn) dǎšt- mi.go.siǩt/

Simple Future	
مستقبل (آینده ساده)	
(ما) خواهیم گسیخت	(من) خواهم گسیخت
/(mǎ) ǩǎ.him- go.siǩt/	/(man) ǩǎ.ham- go.siǩt/
(شما) خواهید گسیخت	(تو) خواهی گسیخت
/(šo.mǎ) ǩǎ.hid- go.siǩt/	/(to) ǩǎ.hi- go.siǩt/
(آنها) خواهند گسیخت	(او/ آن) خواهد گسیخت
/(ǎn.hǎ) ǩǎ.hand- go.siǩt/	/(u/ ǎn) ǩǎ.had- go.siǩt/

Command	
امر	
بگسلید!	بگسل!
/be.go.sa.lid/	/be.go.sal/

to come back

بَرگَشتَن

/bar.gaš.tan/

Plural	Singular
Simple Present	
مضارع اخباری(حال ساده)	
(ما) برمی گردیم /(mǎ) bar.mi gar.dim/	(من) برمی گردم /(man) bar.mi.gar.dam/
(شما) برمی گردید /(šo.mǎ) bar.mi gar.did/	(تو) برمی گردی /(to) bar.mi gar.di/
(آنها) برمی گردند /(ǎn.hǎ) bar.mi gar.dand/	(او/آن) برمی گردد /(u/ ǎn) bar.mi gar.dad/
Present Subjunctive	
مضارع التزامی	
(ما) برگردیم /(mǎ) bar.gar.dim/	(من) برگردم /(man) bar.gar.dam/
(شما) برگردید /(šo.mǎ) bar.gar.did/	(تو) برگردی /(to) bar.gar.di/
(آنها) برگردند /(ǎn.hǎ) bar.gar.dand/	(او/آن) برگردد /(u/ ǎn) bar.gar.dad/
Present Progressive	
مضارع مستمر(در جریان)	
(ما) داریم برمی گردیم /(mǎ) dǎ.rim- bar.mi.gar.dim/	(من) دارم برمی گردم /(man) dǎ.ram- bar.mi.gar.dam/
(شما) دارید برمی گردید /(šo.mǎ) dǎ.rid- bar.mi.gar.did/	(تو) داری برمی گردی /(to) dǎ.ri- bar.mi.gar.di/
(آنها) دارند برمی گردند /(ǎn.hǎ) dǎ.rand- bar.mi.gar.dand/	(او/آن) دارد برمی گردد /(u/ ǎn) dǎ.rad- bar.mi.gar.dad/

Simple Past	
ماضی مطلق (گذشته ساده)	
(ما) برگشتیم	(من) برگشتم
/(mǎ) bar.gaš.tim/	/(man) bar.gaš.tam/
(شما) برگشتید	(تو) برگشتی
/(šo.mǎ) bar.gaš.tid/	/(to) bar.gaš.ti/
(آنها) برگشتند	(او/آن) برگشت
/(ǎn.hǎ) bar.gaš.tand/	/(u/ ǎn) bar.gašt/

Imperfect Indicative	
ماضی استمراری	
(ما) برمی گشتیم	(من) برمی گشتم
/(mǎ) bar.mi.gaš.tim/	/(man) bar.mi.gaš.tam/
(شما) برمی گشتید	(تو) برمی گشتی
/(šo.mǎ) bar.mi.gaš.tid/	/(to) bar.mi.gaš.ti/
(آنها) برمی گشتند	(او/آن) برمی گشت
/(ǎn.hǎ) bar.mi.gaš.tand/	/(u/ ǎn) bar.mi.gašt/

Present Perfect	
ماضی نقلی	
(ما) برگشته ایم	(من) برگشته ام
/(mǎ) bar.gaš.te.im/	/(man) bar.gaš.te.am/
(شما) برگشته اید	(تو) برگشته ای
/(šo.mǎ) bar.gaš.te.id/	/(to) bar.gaš.te.i/
(آنها) برگشته اند	(او/آن) برگشته است
/(ǎn.hǎ) bar.gaš.te.and/	/(u/ ǎn) bar.gaš.te- ast/

Past Perfect	
ماضی بعید	
(ما) برگشته بودیم	(من) برگشته بودم
/(mǎ) bar.gaš.te- bu.dim/	/(man) bar.gaš.te- bu.dam/
(شما) برگشته بودید	(تو) برگشته بودی
/(šo.mǎ) bar.gaš.te- bu.did/	/(to) bar.gaš.te- bu.di/
(آنها) برگشته بودند	(او/آن) برگشته بود
/(ǎn.hǎ) bar.gaš.te- bu.dand/	/(u/ ǎn) bar.gaš.te- bud/

Past Subjunctive
ماضی التزامی

(ما) برگشته باشیم	(من) برگشته باشم
/(mǎ) bar.gaš.te- bǎ.šim/	/(man) bar.gaš.te- bǎ.šam/
(شما) برگشته باشید	(تو) برگشته باشی
/(šo.mǎ) bar.gaš.te- bǎ.šid/	/(to) bar.gaš.te- bǎ.ši/
(آنها) برگشته باشند	(او/آن) برگشته باشد
/(ǎn.hǎ) bar.gaš.te- bǎ.šand/	/(u/ ǎn) bar.gaš.te- bǎ.šad/

Past Progressive
ماضی مستمر(در جریان)

(ما) داشتیم برمی گشتیم	(من) داشتم برمی گشتم
/(mǎ) dǎš.tim- bar.mi.gaš.tim/	/(man) dǎš.tam- bar.mi.gaš.tam/
(شما) داشتید برمی گشتید	(تو) داشتی برمی گشتی
/(šo.mǎ) dǎš.tid- bar.mi.gaš.tid/	/(to) dǎš.ti- bar.mi.gaš.ti/
(آنها) داشتند برمی گشتند	(او/آن) داشت برمی گشت
/(ǎn.hǎ) dǎš.tand- bar.mi.gaš.tand/	/(u/ ǎn) dǎšt- bar.mi.gašt/

Simple Future
مستقبل (آینده ساده)

(ما) برخواهیم گشت	(من) برخواهم گشت
/(mǎ) bar.kǎ.him- gašt/	/(man) bar.kǎ.ham- gašt/
(شما) برخواهید گشت	(تو) برخواهی گشت
/(šo.mǎ) bar.kǎ.hid- gašt/	/(to) bar.kǎ.hi- gašt/
(آنها) برخواهند گشت	(او/آن) برخواهد گشت
/(ǎn.hǎ) bar.kǎ.hand- gašt/	/(u/ ǎn) bar.kǎ.had- gašt/

Command
امر

برگردید!	برگرد!
/bar.gar.did/	/bar.gard/

to compose

سُرودَن

/so.ru.dan/

Plural	Singular
Simple Present	
مضارع اخباری(حال ساده)	
(ما) می سراییم	(من) می سرایم
/(mă) mi.so.ră.yim/	/(man) mi.so.ră.yam/
(شما) می سرایید	(تو) می سرایی
/(šo.mă) mi.so.ră.yid/	/(to) mi.so.ră.yi/
(آنها) می سرایند	(او/آن) می سراید
/(ăn.hă) mi.so.ră.yand/	/(u/ ăn) mi.so.ră.yad/
Present Subjunctive	
مضارع التزامی	
(ما) بسراییم	(من) بسرایم
/(mă) be.so.ră.yim/	/(man) be.so.ră.yam/
(شما) بسرایید	(تو) بسرایی
/(šo.mă) be.so.ră.yid/	/(to) be.so.ră.yi/
(آنها) بسرایند	(او/آن) بسراید
/(ăn.hă) be.so.ră.yand/	/(u/ ăn) be.so.ră.yad/
Present Progressive	
مضارع مستمر(در جریان)	
(ما) داریم می سراییم	(من) دارم می سرایم
/(mă) dă.rim- mi.so.ră.yim/	/(man) dă.ram- mi.so.ră.yam/
(شما) دارید می سرایید	(تو) داری می سرایی
/(šo.mă) dă.rid- mi.so.ră.yid/	/(to) dă.ri- mi.so.ră.yi/
(آنها) دارند می سرایند	(او/آن) دارد می سراید
/(ăn.hă) dă.rand- mi.so.ră.yand/	/(u/ ăn) dă.rad- mi.so.ră.yad/

Simple Past
ماضی مطلق (گذشته ساده)

(ما) سرودیم	(من) سرودم
/(mă) so.ru.dim/	/(man) so.ru.dam/
(شما) سرودید	(تو) سرودی
/(šo.mă) so.ru.did/	/(to) so.ru.di/
(آنها) سرودند	(او/آن) سرود
/(ăn.hă) so.ru.dand/	/(u/ ăn) so.rud/

Imperfect Indicative
ماضی استمراری

(ما) می سرودیم	(من) می سرودم
/(mă) mi.so.ru.dim/	/(man) mi.so.ru.dam/
(شما) می سرودید	(تو) می سرودی
/(šo.mă) mi.so.ru.did/	/(to) mi.so.ru.di/
(آنها) می سرودند	(او/آن) می سرود
/(ăn.hă) mi.so.ru.dand/	/(u/ ăn) mi.so.rud/

Present Perfect
ماضی نقلی

(ما) سروده ایم	(من) سروده ام
/(mă) so.ru.de.im/	/(man) so.ru.de.am/
(شما) سروده اید	(تو) سروده ای
/(šo.mă) so.ru.de.id/	/(to) so.ru.de.i/
(آنها) سروده اند	(او/آن) سروده است
/(ăn.hă) so.ru.de.and/	/(u/ ăn) so.ru.de- ast/

Past Perfect
ماضی بعید

(ما) سروده بودیم	(من) سروده بودم
/(mă) so.ru.de- bu.dim/	/(man) so.ru.de- bu.dam/
(شما) سروده بودید	(تو) سروده بودی
/(šo.mă) so.ru.de- bu.did/	/(to) so.ru.de- bu.di/
(آنها) سروده بودند	(او/آن) سروده بود
/(ăn.hă) so.ru.de- bu.dand/	/(u/ ăn) so.ru.de- bud/

Past Subjunctive	
ماضی التزامی	
(ما) سروده باشیم	(من) سروده باشم
/(mǎ) so.ru.de- bǎ.šim/	/(man) so.ru.de- bǎ.šam/
(شما) سروده باشید	(تو) سروده باشی
/(šo.mǎ) so.ru.de- bǎ.šid/	/(to) so.ru.de- bǎ.ši/
(آنها) سروده باشند	(او/آن) سروده باشد
/(ǎn.hǎ) so.ru.de- bǎ.šand/	/(u/ ǎn) so.ru.de- bǎ.šad/

Past Progressive	
ماضی مستمر(در جریان)	
(ما) داشتیم می سرودیم	(من) داشتم می سرودم
/(mǎ) dǎš.tim- mi.so.ru.dim/	/(man) dǎš.tam- mi.so.ru.dam/
(شما) داشتید می سرودید	(تو) داشتی می سرودی
/(šo.mǎ) dǎš.tid- mi.so.ru.did/	/(to) dǎš.ti- mi.so.ru.di/
(آنها) داشتند می سرودند	(او/آن) داشت می سرود
/(ǎn.hǎ) dǎš.tand- mi.so.ru.dand/	/(u/ ǎn) dǎšt- mi.so.rud/

Simple Future	
مستقبل (آینده ساده)	
(ما) خواهیم سرود	(من) خواهم سرود
/(mǎ) kǎ.him- so.rud/	/(man) kǎ.ham- so.rud/
(شما) خواهید سرود	(تو) خواهی سرود
/(šo.mǎ) kǎ.hid- so.rud/	/(to) kǎ.hi- so.rud/
(آنها) خواهند سرود	(او/آن) خواهد سرود
/(ǎn.hǎ) kǎ.hand- so.rud/	/(u/ ǎn) kǎ.had- so.rud/

Command	
امر	
بسرایید!	بسرای!
/be.so.rǎ.yid/	/be.so.rǎy/

to cook

پُختَن

/poǩ.tan/

Plural	Singular
Simple Present مضارع اخباری(حال ساده)	
(ما) می پزیم /(mǎ) mi.pa.zim/	(من) می پزم /(man) mi.pa.zam/
(شما) می پزید /(šo.mǎ) mi.pa.zid/	(تو) می پزی /(to) mi.pa.zi/
(آنها) می پزند /(ǎn.hǎ) mi.pa.zand/	(او/آن) می پزد /(u/ ǎn) mi.pa.zad/
Present Subjunctive مضارع التزامی	
(ما) بپزیم /(mǎ) be.pa.zim/	(من) بپزم /(man) be.pa.zam/
(شما) بپزید /(šo.mǎ) be.pa.zid/	(تو) بپزی /(to) be.pa.zi/
(آنها) بپزند /(ǎn.hǎ) be.pa.zand/	(او/آن) بپزد /(u/ ǎn) be.pa.zad/
Present Progressive مضارع مستمر(در جریان)	
(ما) داریم می پزیم /(mǎ) dǎ.rim- mi.pa.zim/	(من) دارم می پزم /(man) dǎ.ram- mi.pa.zam/
(شما) دارید می پزید /(šo.mǎ) dǎ.rid- mi.pa.zid/	(تو) داری می پزی /(to) dǎ.ri- mi.pa.zi/
(آنها) دارند می پزند /(ǎn.hǎ) dǎ.rand- mi.pa.zand/	(او/آن) دارد می پزد /(u/ ǎn) dǎ.rad- mi.pa.zad/

59

Simple Past
ماضی مطلق (گذشته ساده)

(ما) پختیم	(من) پختم
/(mă) poǩ.tim/	/(man) poǩ.tam/
(شما) پختید	(تو) پختی
/(šo.mă) poǩ.tid/	/(to) poǩ.ti/
(آنها) پختند	(او/آن) پخت
/(ăn.hă) poǩ.tand/	/(u/ ăn) poǩt/

Imperfect Indicative
ماضی استمراری

(ما) می پختیم	(من) می پختم
/(mă) mi.poǩ.tim/	/(man) mi.poǩ.tam/
(شما) می پختید	(تو) می پختی
/(šo.mă) mi.poǩ.tid/	/(to) mi.poǩ.ti/
(آنها) می پختند	(او/آن) می پخت
/(ăn.hă) mi.poǩ.tand/	/(u/ ăn) mi.poǩt/

Present Perfect
ماضی نقلی

(ما) پخته ایم	(من) پخته ام
/(mă) poǩ.te.im/	/(man) poǩ.te.am/
(شما) پخته اید	(تو) پخته ای
/(šo.mă) poǩ.te.id/	/(to) poǩ.te.i/
(آنها) پخته اند	(او/آن) پخته است
/(ăn.hă) poǩ.te.and/	/(u/ ăn) poǩ.te- ast/

Past Perfect
ماضی بعید

(ما) پخته بودیم	(من) پخته بودم
/(mă) poǩ.te- bu.dim/	/(man) poǩ.te- bu.dam/
(شما) پخته بودید	(تو) پخته بودی
/(šo.mă) poǩ.te- bu.did/	/(to) poǩ.te- bu.di/
(آنها) پخته بودند	(او/آن) پخته بود
/(ăn.hă) poǩ.te- bu.dand/	/(u/ ăn) poǩ.te- bud/

Past Subjunctive
ماضی التزامی

(ما) پخته باشیم	(من) پخته باشم
/(mǎ) poǩ.te- bǎ.šim/	/(man) poǩ.te- bǎ.šam/
(شما) پخته باشید	(تو) پخته باشی
/(šo.mǎ) poǩ.te- bǎ.šid/	/(to) poǩ.te- bǎ.ši/
(آنها) پخته باشند	(او/آن) پخته باشد
/(ǎn.hǎ) poǩ.te- bǎ.šand/	/(u/ ǎn) poǩ.te- bǎ.šad/

Past Progressive
ماضی مستمر(در جریان)

(ما) داشتیم می پختیم	(من) داشتم می پختم
/(mǎ) dǎš.tim- mi.poǩ.tim/	/(man) dǎš.tam- mi.poǩ.tam/
(شما) داشتید می پختید	(تو) داشتی می پختی
/(šo.mǎ) dǎš.tid- mi.poǩ.tid/	/(to) dǎš.ti- mi.poǩ.ti/
(آنها) داشتند می پختند	(او/آن) داشت می پخت
/(ǎn.hǎ) dǎš.tand- mi.poǩ.tand/	/(u/ ǎn) dǎšt- mi.poǩt/

Simple Future
مستقبل (آینده ساده)

(ما) خواهیم پخت	(من) خواهم پخت
/(mǎ) ǩǎ.him- poǩt/	/(man) ǩǎ.ham- poǩt/
(شما) خواهید پخت	(تو) خواهی پخت
/(šo.mǎ) ǩǎ.hid- poǩt/	/(to) ǩǎ.hi- poǩt/
(آنها) خواهند پخت	(او/آن) خواهد پخت
/(ǎn.hǎ) ǩǎ.hand- poǩt/	/(u/ ǎn) ǩǎ.had- poǩt/

Command
امر

بپزید!	بپز!
/be.pa.zid/	/be.paz/

to count

شِمُردَن

/še.mor.dan/

Plural	*Singular*
Simple Present	
مضارع اخباری(حال ساده)	
(ما) می شماریم	(من) می شمارم
/(mǎ) mi.šo.mǎ.rim/	/(man) mi.šo.mǎ.ram/
(شما) می شمارید	(تو) می شماری
/(šo.mǎ) mi.šo.mǎ.rid/	/(to) mi.šo.mǎ.ri/
(آنها) می شمارند	(او/آن) می شمارد
/(ǎn.hǎ) mi.šo.mǎ.rand/	/(u/ ǎn) mi.šo.mǎ.rad/

Present Subjunctive	
مضارع التزامی	
(ما) بشماریم	(من) بشمارم
/(mǎ) be.šo.mǎ.rim/	/(man) be.šo.mǎ.ram/
(شما) بشمارید	(تو) بشماری
/(šo.mǎ) be.šo.mǎ.rid/	/(to) be.šo.mǎ.ri/
(آنها) بشمارند	(او/آن) بشمارد
/(ǎn.hǎ) be.šo.mǎ.rand/	/(u/ ǎn) be.šo.mǎ.rad/

Present Progressive	
مضارع مستمر(در جریان)	
(ما) داریم می شماریم	(من) دارم می شمارم
/(mǎ) dǎ.rim- mi.šo.mǎ.rim/	/(man) dǎ.ram- mi.šo.mǎ.ram/
(شما) دارید می شمارید	(تو) داری می شماری
/(šo.mǎ) dǎ.rid- mi.šo.mǎ.rid/	/(to) dǎ.ri- mi.šo.mǎ.ri/
(آنها) دارند می شمارند	(او/آن) دارد می شمارد
/(ǎn.hǎ) dǎ.rand- mi.šo.mǎ.rand/	/(u/ ǎn) dǎ.rad- mi.šo.mǎ.rad/

Simple Past
ماضی مطلق (گذشته ساده)

(ما) شمردیم	(من) شمردم
/(mǎ) še.mor.dim/	/(man) še.mor.dam/
(شما) شمردید	(تو) شمردی
/(šo.mǎ) še.mor.did/	/(to) še.mor.di/
(آنها) شمردند	(او/آن) شمرد
/(ǎn.hǎ) še.mor.dand/	/(u/ ǎn) še.mord/

Imperfect Indicative
ماضی استمراری

(ما) می شمردیم	(من) می شمردم
/(mǎ) mi.še.mor.dim/	/(man) mi.še.mor.dam/
(شما) می شمردید	(تو) می شمردی
/(šo.mǎ) mi.še.mor.did/	/(to) mi.še.mor.di/
(آنها) می شمردند	(او/آن) می شمرد
/(ǎn.hǎ) mi.še.mor.dand/	/(u/ ǎn) mi.še.mord/

Present Perfect
ماضی نقلی

(ما) شمرده ایم	(من) شمرده ام
/(mǎ) še.mor.de.im/	/(man) še.mor.de.am/
(شما) شمرده اید	(تو) شمرده ای
/(šo.mǎ) še.mor.de.id/	/(to) še.mor.de.i/
(آنها) شمرده اند	(او/آن) شمرده است
/(ǎn.hǎ) še.mor.de.and/	/(u/ ǎn) še.mor.de- ast/

Past Perfect
ماضی بعید

(ما) شمرده بودیم	(من) شمرده بودم
/(mǎ) še.mor.de- bu.dim/	/(man) še.mor.de- bu.dam/
(شما) شمرده بودید	(تو) شمرده بودی
/(šo.mǎ) še.mor.de- bu.did/	/(to) še.mor.de- bu.di/
(آنها) شمرده بودند	(او/آن) شمرده بود
/(ǎn.hǎ) še.mor.de- bu.dand/	/(u/ ǎn) še.mor.de- bud/

Past Subjunctive
ماضی التزامی

(ما) شمرده باشیم	(من) شمرده باشم
/(mǎ) še.mor.de- bǎ.šim/	/(man) še.mor.de- bǎ.šam/
(شما) شمرده باشید	(تو) شمرده باشی
/(šo.mǎ) še.mor.de- bǎ.šid/	/(to) še.mor.de- bǎ.ši/
(آنها) شمرده باشند	(او/آن) شمرده باشد
/(ǎn.hǎ) še.mor.de- bǎ.šand/	/(u/ ǎn) še.mor.de- bǎ.šad/

Past Progressive
ماضی مستمر(در جریان)

(ما) داشتیم می شمردیم	(من) داشتم می شمردم
/(mǎ) dǎš.tim- mi.še.mor.dim/	/(man) dǎš.tam- mi.še.mor.dam/
(شما) داشتید می شمردید	(تو) داشتی می شمردی
/(šo.mǎ) dǎš.tid- mi.še.mor.did/	/(to) dǎš.ti- mi.še.mor.di/
(آنها) داشتند می شمردند	(او/آن) داشت می شمرد
/(ǎn.hǎ) dǎš.tand- mi.še.mor.dand/	/(u/ ǎn) dǎšt- mi.še.mord/

Simple Future
مستقبل (آینده ساده)

(ما) خواهیم شمرد	(من) خواهم شمرد
/(mǎ) kǎ.him- še.mord/	/(man) kǎ.ham- še.mord/
(شما) خواهید شمرد	(تو) خواهی شمرد
/(šo.mǎ) kǎ.hid- še.mord/	/(to) kǎ.hi- še.mord/
(آنها) خواهند شمرد	(او/آن) خواهد شمرد
/(ǎn.hǎ) kǎ.hand- še.mord/	/(u/ ǎn) kǎ.had- še.mord/

Command
امر

بشمارید!	بشمار!
/be.šo.mǎ.rid/	/be.šo.mǎr/

to create

آفَریدَن

/ă.fa.ri.dan/

Plural	Singular
Simple Present مضارع اخباری(حال ساده)	
(ما) می آفرینیم /(mă) mi.ă.fa.ri.nim/	(من) می آفرینم /(man) mi.ă.fa.ri.nam/
(شما) می آفرینید /(šo.mă) mi.ă.fa.ri.nid/	(تو) می آفرینی /(to) mi.ă.fa.ri.ni/
(آنها) می آفرینند /(ăn.hă) mi.ă.fa.ri.nand/	(او/آن) می آفریند /(u/ ăn) mi.ă.fa.ri.nad/

Plural	Singular
Present Subjunctive مضارع التزامی	
(ما) بیافرینیم /(mă) bi.yă.fa.ri.nim/	(من) بیافرینم /(man) bi.yă.fa.ri.nam/
(شما) بیافرینید /(šo.mă) bi.yă.fa.ri.nid/	(تو) بیافرینی /(to) bi.yă.fa.ri.ni/
(آنها) بیافرینند /(ăn.hă) bi.yă.fa.ri.nand/	(او/آن) بیافریند /(u/ ăn) bi.yă.fa.ri.nad/

Plural	Singular
Present Progressive مضارع مستمر(در جریان)	
(ما) داریم می آفرینیم /(mă) dă.rim- mi.ă.fa.ri.nim/	(من) دارم می آفرینم /(man) dă.ram- mi.ă.fa.ri.nam/
(شما) دارید می آفرینید /(šo.mă) dă.rid- mi.ă.fa.ri.nid/	(تو) داری می آفرینی /(to) dă.ri- mi.ă.fa.ri.ni/
(آنها) دارند می آفرینند /(ăn.hă) dă.rand- mi.ă.fa.ri.nand/	(او/آن) دارد می آفریند /(u/ ăn) dă.rad- mi.ă.fa.ri.nad/

Simple Past
ماضی مطلق (گذشته ساده)

(ما) آفریدیم	(من) آفریدم
/(mǎ) ǎ.fa.ri.dim/	/(man) ǎ.fa.ri.dam/
(شما) آفریدید	(تو) آفریدی
/(šo.mǎ) ǎ.fa.ri.did/	/(to) ǎ.fa.ri.di/
(آنها) آفریدند	(او/آن) آفرید
/(ǎn.hǎ) ǎ.fa.ri.dand/	/(u/ ǎn) ǎ.fa.rid/

Imperfect Indicative
ماضی استمراری

(ما) می آفریدیم	(من) می آفریدم
/(mǎ) mi.ǎ.fa.ri.dim/	/(man) mi.ǎ.fa.ri.dam/
(شما) می آفریدید	(تو) می آفریدی
/(šo.mǎ) mi.ǎ.fa.ri.did/	/(to) mi.ǎ.fa.ri.di/
(آنها) می آفریدند	(او/آن) می آفرید
/(ǎn.hǎ) mi.ǎ.fa.ri.dand/	/(u/ ǎn) mi.ǎ.fa.rid/

Present Perfect
ماضی نقلی

(ما) آفریده ایم	(من) آفریده ام
/(mǎ) ǎ.fa.ri.de.im/	/(man) ǎ.fa.ri.de.am/
(شما) آفریده اید	(تو) آفریده ای
/(šo.mǎ) ǎ.fa.ri.de.id/	/(to) ǎ.fa.ri.de.i/
(آنها) آفریده اند	(او/آن) آفریده است
/(ǎn.hǎ) ǎ.fa.ri.de.and/	/(u/ ǎn) ǎ.fa.ri.de- ast/

Past Perfect
ماضی بعید

(ما) آفریده بودیم	(من) آفریده بودم
/(mǎ) ǎ.fa.ri.de- bu.dim/	/(man) ǎ.fa.ri.de- bu.dam/
(شما) آفریده بودید	(تو) آفریده بودی
/(šo.mǎ) ǎ.fa.ri.de- bu.did/	/(to) ǎ.fa.ri.de- bu.di/
(آنها) آفریده بودند	(او/آن) آفریده بود
/(ǎn.hǎ) ǎ.fa.ri.de- bu.dand/	/(u/ ǎn) ǎ.fa.ri.de- bud/

Past Subjunctive	
ماضی التزامی	
(ما) آفریده باشیم	(من) آفریده باشم
/(mă) ă.fa.ri.de- bă.šim/	/(man) ă.fa.ri.de- bă.šam/
(شما) آفریده باشید	(تو) آفریده باشی
/(šo.mă) ă.fa.ri.de- bă.šid/	/(to) ă.fa.ri.de- bă.ši/
(آنها) آفریده باشند	(او/آن) آفریده باشد
/(ăn.hă) ă.fa.ri.de- bă.šand/	/(u/ ăn) ă.fa.ri.de- bă.šad/

Past Progressive	
ماضی مستمر(در جریان)	
(ما) داشتیم می آفریدیم	(من) داشتم می آفریدم
/(mă) dăš.tim- mi.ă.fa.ri.dim/	/(man) dăš.tam- mi.ă.fa.ri.dam/
(شما) داشتید می آفریدید	(تو) داشتی می آفریدی
/(šo.mă) dăš.tid- mi.ă.fa.ri.did/	/(to) dăš.ti- mi.ă.fa.ri.di/
(آنها) داشتند می آفریدند	(او/آن) داشت می آفرید
/(ăn.hă) dăš.tand- mi.ă.fa.ri.dand/	/(u/ ăn) dăšt- mi.ă.fa.rid/

Simple Future	
مستقبل (آینده ساده)	
(ما) خواهیم آفرید	(من) خواهم آفرید
/(mă) kă.him- ă.fa.rid/	/(man) kă.ham- ă.fa.rid/
(شما) خواهید آفرید	(تو) خواهی آفرید
/(šo.mă) kă.hid- ă.fa.rid/	/(to) kă.hi- ă.fa.rid/
(آنها) خواهند آفرید	(او/آن) خواهد آفرید
/(ăn.hă) kă.hand- ă.fa.rid/	/(u/ ăn) kă.had- ă.fa.rid/

Command	
امر	
بیافرینید!	بیافرین!
/bi.yă.fa.ri.nid/	/bi.yă.fa.rin/

to cry

گِریسَتن

/ge.ris.tan/

Plural	Singular
Simple Present	
مضارع اخباری(حال ساده)	
(ما) می گرییم	(من) می گریم
/(mǎ) mi.ger.yim/	/(man) mi.ger.yam/
(شما) می گریید	(تو) می گریی
/(šo.mǎ) mi.ger.yid/	/(to) mi.ger.yi/
(آنها) می گریند	(او/آن) می گرید
/(ǎn.hǎ) mi.ger.yand/	/(u/ ǎn) mi.ger.yad/

Plural	Singular
Present Subjunctive	
مضارع التزامی	
(ما) بگرییم	(من) بگریم
/(mǎ) be.ger.yim/	/(man) be.ger.yam/
(شما) بگریید	(تو) بگریی
/(šo.mǎ) be.ger.yid/	/(to) be.ger.yi/
(آنها) بگریند	(او/آن) بگرید
/(ǎn.hǎ) be.ger.yand/	/(u/ ǎn) be.ger.yad/

Plural	Singular
Present Progressive	
مضارع مستمر(در جریان)	
(ما) داریم می گرییم	(من) دارم می گریم
/(mǎ) dǎ.rim- mi.ger.yim/	/(man) dǎ.ram- mi.ger.yam/
(شما) دارید می گریید	(تو) داری می گریی
/(šo.mǎ) dǎ.rid- mi.ger.yid/	/(to) dǎ.ri- mi.ger.yi/
(آنها) دارند می گریند	(او/آن) دارد می گرید
/(ǎn.hǎ) dǎ.rand- mi.ger.yand/	/(u/ ǎn) dǎ.rad- mi.ger.yad/

Simple Past
ماضی مطلق (گذشته ساده)

(ما) گریستیم	(من) گریستم
/(mǎ) ge.ris.tim/	/(man) ge.ris.tam/
(شما) گریستید	(تو) گریستی
/(šo.mǎ) ge.ris.tid/	/(to) ge.ris.ti/
(آنها) گریستند	(او/آن) گریست
/(ǎn.hǎ) ge.ris.tand/	/(u/ ǎn) ge.rist/

Imperfect Indicative
ماضی استمراری

(ما) می گریستیم	(من) می گریستم
/(mǎ) mi.ge.ris.tim/	/(man) mi.ge.ris.tam/
(شما) می گریستید	(تو) می گریستی
/(šo.mǎ) mi.ge.ris.tid/	/(to) mi.ge.ris.ti/
(آنها) می گریستند	(او/آن) می گریست
/(ǎn.hǎ) mi.ge.ris.tand/	/(u/ ǎn) mi.ge.rist/

Present Perfect
ماضی نقلی

(ما) گریسته ایم	(من) گریسته ام
/(mǎ) ge.ris.te.im/	/(man) ge.ris.te.am/
(شما) گریسته اید	(تو) گریسته ای
/(šo.mǎ) ge.ris.te.id/	/(to) ge.ris.te.i/
(آنها) گریسته اند	(او/آن) گریسته است
/(ǎn.hǎ) ge.ris.te.and/	/(u/ ǎn) ge.ris.te- ast/

Past Perfect
ماضی بعید

(ما) گریسته بودیم	(من) گریسته بودم
/(mǎ) ge.ris.te- bu.dim/	/(man) ge.ris.te- bu.dam/
(شما) گریسته بودید	(تو) گریسته بودی
/(šo.mǎ) ge.ris.te- bu.did/	/(to) ge.ris.te- bu.di/
(آنها) گریسته بودند	(او/آن) گریسته بود
/(ǎn.hǎ) ge.ris.te- bu.dand/	/(u/ ǎn) ge.ris.te- bud/

	Past Subjunctive	
	ماضی التزامی	
(ما) گریسته باشیم	(من) گریسته باشم
/(mǎ) ge.ris.te- bǎ.šim/	/(man) ge.ris.te- bǎ.šam/
(شما) گریسته باشید	(تو) گریسته باشی
/(šo.mǎ) ge.ris.te- bǎ.šid/	/(to) ge.ris.te- bǎ.ši/
(آنها) گریسته باشند	(او/آن) گریسته باشد
/(ǎn.hǎ) ge.ris.te- bǎ.šand/	/(u/ ǎn) ge.ris.te- bǎ.šad/

	Past Progressive	
	ماضی مستمر(در جریان)	
(ما) داشتیم می گریستیم	(من) داشتم می گریستم
/(mǎ) dǎš.tim- mi.ge.ris.tim/	/(man) dǎš.tam- mi.ge.ris.tam/
(شما) داشتید می گریستید	(تو) داشتی می گریستی
/(šo.mǎ) dǎš.tid- mi.ge.ris.tid/	/(to) dǎš.ti- mi.ge.ris.ti/
(آنها) داشتند می گریستند	(او/آن) داشت می گریست
/(ǎn.hǎ) dǎš.tand- mi.ge.ris.tand/	/(u/ ǎn) dǎšt- mi.ge.rist/

	Simple Future	
	مستقبل (آینده ساده)	
(ما) خواهیم گریست	(من) خواهم گریست
/(mǎ) kǎ.him- ge.rist/	/(man) kǎ.ham- ge.rist/
(شما) خواهید گریست	(تو) خواهی گریست
/(šo.mǎ) kǎ.hid- ge.rist/	/(to) kǎ.hi- ge.rist/
(آنها) خواهند گریست	(او/آن) خواهد گریست
/(ǎn.hǎ) kǎ.hand- ge.rist/	/(u/ ǎn) kǎ.had- ge.rist/

	Command	
	امر	
بگریید!	بگری!
/be.ger.yid/	/ be.gery/

to decorate

آراستَن

/ă.răs.tan/

Plural	Singular
Simple Present مضارع اخباری(حال ساده)	
(ما) می آراییم /(mă) mi.ă.ră.yim/	(من) می آرایم /(man) mi.ă.ră.yam/
(شما) می آرایید /(šo.mă) mi.ă.ră.yid/	(تو) می آرایی /(to) mi.ă.ră.yi/
(آنها) می آرایند /(ăn.hă) mi.ă.ră.yand/	(او/آن) می آراید /(u/ ăn) mi.ă.ră.yad/
Present Subjunctive مضارع التزامی	
(ما) بیاراییم /(mă) bi.yă.ră.yim/	(من) بیارایم /(man) bi.yă.ră.yam/
(شما) بیارایید /(šo.mă) bi.yă.ră.yid/	(تو) بیارایی /(to) bi.yă.ră.yi/
(آنها) بیارایند /(ăn.hă) bi.yă.ră.yand/	(او/آن) بیاراید /(u/ ăn) bi.yă.ră.yad/
Present Progressive مضارع مستمر(در جریان)	
(ما) داریم می آراییم /(mă) dă.rim- mi.ă.ră.yim/	(من) دارم می آرایم /(man) dă.ram- mi.ă.ră.yam/
(شما) دارید می آرایید /(šo.mă) dă.rid- mi.ă.ră.yid/	(تو) داری می آرایی /(to) dă.ri- mi.ă.ră.yi/
(آنها) دارند می آرایند /(ăn.hă) dă.rand- mi.ă.ră.yand/	(او/آن) دارد می آراید /(u/ ăn) dă.rad- mi.ă.ră.yad/

Simple Past
ماضی مطلق (گذشته ساده)

(ما) آراستیم	(من) آراستم
/(mǎ) ǎ.rǎs.tim/	/(man) ǎ.rǎs.tam/
(شما) آراستید	(تو) آراستی
/(šo.mǎ) ǎ.rǎs.tid/	/(to) ǎ.rǎs.ti/
(آنها) آراستند	(او/ آن) آراست
/(ǎn.hǎ) ǎ.rǎs.tand/	/(u/ ǎn) ǎ.rǎst/

Imperfect Indicative
ماضی استمراری

(ما) می آراستیم	(من) می آراستم
/(mǎ) mi.ǎ.rǎs.tim/	/(man) mi.ǎ.rǎs.tam/
(شما) می آراستید	(تو) می آراستی
/(šo.mǎ) mi.ǎ.rǎs.tid/	/(to) mi.ǎ.rǎs.ti/
(آنها) می آراستند	(او/ آن) می آراست
/(ǎn.hǎ) mi.ǎ.rǎs.tand/	/(u/ ǎn) mi.ǎ.rǎst/

Present Perfect
ماضی نقلی

(ما) آراسته ایم	(من) آراسته ام
/(mǎ) ǎ.rǎs.te.im/	/(man) ǎ.rǎs.te.am/
(شما) آراسته اید	(تو) آراسته ای
/(šo.mǎ) ǎ.rǎs.te.id/	/(to) ǎ.rǎs.te.i/
(آنها) آراسته اند	(او/ آن) آراسته است
/(ǎn.hǎ) ǎ.rǎs.te.and/	/(u/ ǎn) ǎ.rǎs.te- ast/

Past Perfect
ماضی بعید

(ما) آراسته بودیم	(من) آراسته بودم
/(mǎ) ǎ.rǎs.te- bu.dim/	/(man) ǎ.rǎs.te- bu.dam/
(شما) آراسته بودید	(تو) آراسته بودی
/(šo.mǎ) ǎ.rǎs.te- bu.did/	/(to) ǎ.rǎs.te- bu.di/
(آنها) آراسته بودند	(او/ آن) آراسته بود
/(ǎn.hǎ) ǎ.rǎs.te- bu.dand/	/(u/ ǎn) ǎ.rǎs.te- bud/

Past Subjunctive
ماضی التزامی

(ما) آراسته باشیم	(من) آراسته باشم
/(mǎ) ǎ.rǎs.te- bǎ.šim/	/(man) ǎ.rǎs.te- bǎ.šam/
(شما) آراسته باشید	(تو) آراسته باشی
/(šo.mǎ) ǎ.rǎs.te- bǎ.šid/	/(to) ǎ.rǎs.te- bǎ.ši/
(آنها) آراسته باشند	(او/آن) آراسته باشد
/(ǎn.hǎ) ǎ.rǎs.te- bǎ.šand/	/(u/ ǎn) ǎ.rǎs.te- bǎ.šad/

Past Progressive
ماضی مستمر(در جریان)

(ما) داشتیم می آراستیم	(من) داشتم می آراستم
/(mǎ) dǎš.tim- mi.ǎ.rǎs.tim/	/(man) dǎš.tam- mi.ǎ.rǎs.tam/
(شما) داشتید می آراستید	(تو) داشتی می آراستی
/(šo.mǎ) dǎš.tid- mi.ǎ.rǎs.tid/	/(to) dǎš.ti- mi.ǎ.rǎs.ti/
(آنها) داشتند می آراستند	(او/آن) داشت می آراست
/(ǎn.hǎ) dǎš.tand- mi.ǎ.rǎs.tand/	/(u/ ǎn) dǎšt- mi.ǎ.rǎst/

Simple Future
مستقبل (آینده ساده)

(ما) خواهیم آراست	(من) خواهم آراست
/(mǎ) ǩǎ.him- ǎ.rǎst/	/(man) ǩǎ.ham- ǎ.rǎst/
(شما) خواهید آراست	(تو) خواهی آراست
/(šo.mǎ) ǩǎ.hid- ǎ.rǎst/	/(to) ǩǎ.hi- ǎ.rǎst/
(آنها) خواهند آراست	(او/آن) خواهد آراست
/(ǎn.hǎ) ǩǎ.hand- ǎ.rǎst/	/(u/ ǎn) ǩǎ.had- ǎ.rǎst/

Command
امر

بیارایید!	بیارای!
/bi.yǎ.rǎ.yid/	/bi.yǎ.rǎy/

to deem

پنداشتَن

/pen.dăš.tan/

Plural	Singular
Simple Present مضارع اخباری(حال ساده)	
(ما) می پنداریم /(mă) mi.pen.dă.rim/	(من) می پندارم /(man) mi.pen.dă.ram/
(شما) می پندارید /(šo.mă) mi.pen.dă.rid/	(تو) می پنداری /(to) mi.pen.dă.ri/
(آنها) می پندارند /(ăn.hă) mi.pen.dă.rand/	(او/آن) می پندارد /(u/ ăn) mi.pen.dă.rad/

Plural	Singular
Present Subjunctive مضارع التزامی	
(ما) بپنداریم /(mă) be.pen.dă.rim/	(من) بپندارم /(man) be.pen.dă.ram/
(شما) بپندارید /(šo.mă) be.pen.dă.rid/	(تو) بپنداری /(to) be.pen.dă.ri/
(آنها) بپندارند /(ăn.hă) be.pen.dă.rand/	(او/آن) بپندارد /(u/ ăn) be.pen.dă.rad/

Plural	Singular
Present Progressive مضارع مستمر(در جریان)	
(ما) داریم می پنداریم /(mă) dă.rim- mi.pen.dă.rim/	(من) دارم می پندارم /(man) dă.ram- mi.pen.dă.ram/
(شما) دارید می پندارید /(šo.mă) dă.rid- mi.pen.dă.rid/	(تو) داری می پنداری /(to) dă.ri- mi.pen.dă.ri/
(آنها) دارند می پندارند /(ăn.hă) dă.rand- mi.pen.dă.rand/	(او/آن) دارد می پندارد /(u/ ăn) dă.rad- mi.pen.dă.rad/

74

<table>
<tr><td colspan="2" align="center">**Simple Past**
ماضی مطلق (گذشته ساده)</td></tr>
<tr><td align="center">(ما) پنداشتیم
/(mǎ) pen.dǎš.tim/</td><td align="center">(من) پنداشتم
/(man) pen.dǎš.tam/</td></tr>
<tr><td align="center">(شما) پنداشتید
/(šo.mǎ) pen.dǎš.tid/</td><td align="center">(تو) پنداشتی
/(to) pen.dǎš.ti/</td></tr>
<tr><td align="center">(آنها) پنداشتند
/(ǎn.hǎ) pen.dǎš.tand/</td><td align="center">(او/آن) پنداشت
/(u/ ǎn) pen.dǎšt/</td></tr>
</table>

<table>
<tr><td colspan="2" align="center">**Imperfect Indicative**
ماضی استمراری</td></tr>
<tr><td align="center">(ما) می پنداشتیم
/(mǎ) mi.pen.dǎš.tim/</td><td align="center">(من) می پنداشتم
/(man) mi.pen.dǎš.tam/</td></tr>
<tr><td align="center">(شما) می پنداشتید
/(šo.mǎ) mi.pen.dǎš.tid/</td><td align="center">(تو) می پنداشتی
/(to) mi.pen.dǎš.ti/</td></tr>
<tr><td align="center">(آنها) می پنداشتند
/(ǎn.hǎ) mi.pen.dǎš.tand/</td><td align="center">(او/آن) می پنداشت
/(u/ ǎn) mi.pen.dǎšt/</td></tr>
</table>

<table>
<tr><td colspan="2" align="center">**Present Perfect**
ماضی نقلی</td></tr>
<tr><td align="center">(ما) پنداشته ایم
/(mǎ) pen.dǎš.te.im/</td><td align="center">(من) پنداشته ام
/(man) pen.dǎš.te.am/</td></tr>
<tr><td align="center">(شما) پنداشته اید
/(šo.mǎ) pen.dǎš.te.id/</td><td align="center">(تو) پنداشته ای
/(to) pen.dǎš.te.i/</td></tr>
<tr><td align="center">(آنها) پنداشته اند
/(ǎn.hǎ) pen.dǎš.te.and/</td><td align="center">(او/آن) پنداشته است
/(u/ ǎn) pen.dǎš.te- ast/</td></tr>
</table>

<table>
<tr><td colspan="2" align="center">**Past Perfect**
ماضی بعید</td></tr>
<tr><td align="center">(ما) پنداشته بودیم
/(mǎ) pen.dǎš.te- bu.dim/</td><td align="center">(من) پنداشته بودم
/(man) pen.dǎš.te- bu.dam/</td></tr>
<tr><td align="center">(شما) پنداشته بودید
/(šo.mǎ) pen.dǎš.te- bu.did/</td><td align="center">(تو) پنداشته بودی
/(to) pen.dǎš.te- bu.di/</td></tr>
<tr><td align="center">(آنها) پنداشته بودند
/(ǎn.hǎ) pen.dǎš.te- bu.dand/</td><td align="center">(او/آن) پنداشته بود
/(u/ ǎn) pen.dǎš.te- bud/</td></tr>
</table>

Past Subjunctive	
ماضی التزامی	
(ما) پنداشته باشیم	(من) پنداشته باشم
/(mă) pen.dăš.te- bă.šim/	/(man) pen.dăš.te- bă.šam/
(شما) پنداشته باشید	(تو) پنداشته باشی
/(šo.mă) pen.dăš.te- bă.šid/	/(to) pen.dăš.te- bă.ši/
(آنها) پنداشته باشند	(او/ آن) پنداشته باشد
/(ăn.hă) pen.dăš.te- bă.šand/	/(u/ ăn) pen.dăš.te- bă.šad/

Past Progressive	
ماضی مستمر(در جریان)	
(ما) داشتیم می پنداشتیم	(من) داشتم می پنداشتم
/(mă) dăš.tim- mi.pen.dăš.tim/	/(man) dăš.tam- mi.pen.dăš.tam/
(شما) داشتید می پنداشتید	(تو) داشتی می پنداشتی
/(šo.mă) dăš.tid- mi.pen.dăš.tid/	/(to) dăš.ti- mi.pen.dăš.ti/
(آنها) داشتند می پنداشتند	(او/ آن) داشت می پنداشت
/(ăn.hă) dăš.tand- mi.pen.dăš.tand/	/(u/ ăn) dăšt- mi.pen.dăšt/

Simple Future	
مستقبل (آینده ساده)	
(ما) خواهیم پنداشت	(من) خواهم پنداشت
/(mă) kă.him- pen.dăšt/	/(man) kă.ham- pen.dăšt/
(شما) خواهید پنداشت	(تو) خواهی پنداشت
/(šo.mă) kă.hid- pen.dăšt/	/(to) kă.hi- pen.dăšt/
(آنها) خواهند پنداشت	(او/ آن) خواهد پنداشت
/(ăn.hă) kă.hand- pen.dăšt/	/(u/ ăn) kă.had- pen.dăšt/

Command	
امر	
بپندارید!	بپندار!
/be.pen.dă.rid/	/be.pen.dăr/

76

to die

مُردَن

/mor.dan/

Plural	Singular
Simple Present مضارع اخباری(حال ساده)	
(ما) می میریم /(mǎ) mi.mi.rim/	(من) می میرم /(man) mi.mi.ram/
(شما) می میرید /(šo.mǎ) mi.mi.rid/	(تو) می میری /(to) mi.mi.ri/
(آنها) می میرند /(ǎn.hǎ) mi.mi.rand/	(او/آن) می میرد /(u/ ǎn) mi.mi.rad/
Present Subjunctive مضارع التزامی	
(ما) بمیریم /(mǎ) be.mi.rim/	(من) بمیرم /(man) be.mi.ram/
(شما) بمیرید /(šo.mǎ) be.mi.rid/	(تو) بمیری /(to) be.mi.ri/
(آنها) بمیرند /(ǎn.hǎ) be.mi.rand/	(او/آن) بمیرد /(u/ ǎn) be.mi.rad/
Present Progressive مضارع مستمر(در جریان)	
(ما) داریم می میریم /(mǎ) dǎ.rim- mi.mi.rim/	(من) دارم می میرم /(man) dǎ.ram- mi.mi.ram/
(شما) دارید می میرید /(šo.mǎ) dǎ.rid- mi.mi.rid/	(تو) داری می میری /(to) dǎ.ri- mi.mi.ri/
(آنها) دارند می میرند /(ǎn.hǎ) dǎ.rand- mi.mi.rand/	(او/آن) دارد می میرد /(u/ ǎn) dǎ.rad- mi.mi.rad/

77

Simple Past
ماضی مطلق (گذشته ساده)

(ما) مردیم	(من) مردم
/(mǎ) mor.dim/	/(man) mor.dam/
(شما) مردید	(تو) مردی
/(šo.mǎ) mor.did/	/(to) mor.di/
(آنها) مردند	(او/آن) مرد
/(ǎn.hǎ) mor.dand/	/(u/ ǎn) mord/

Imperfect Indicative
ماضی استمراری

(ما) می مردیم	(من) می مردم
/(mǎ) mi.mor.dim/	/(man) mi.mor.dam/
(شما) می مردید	(تو) می مردی
/(šo.mǎ) mi.mor.did/	/(to) mi.mor.di/
(آنها) می مردند	(او/آن) می مرد
/(ǎn.hǎ) mi.mor.dand/	/(u/ ǎn) mi.mord/

Present Perfect
ماضی نقلی

(ما) مرده ایم	(من) مرده ام
/(mǎ) mor.de.im/	/(man) mor.de.am/
(شما) مرده اید	(تو) مرده ای
/(šo.mǎ) mor.de.id/	/(to) mor.de.i/
(آنها) مرده اند	(او/آن) مرده است
/(ǎn.hǎ) mor.de.and/	/(u/ ǎn) mor.de- ast/

Past Perfect
ماضی بعید

(ما) مرده بودیم	(من) مرده بودم
/(mǎ) mor.de- bu.dim/	/(man) mor.de- bu.dam/
(شما) مرده بودید	(تو) مرده بودی
/(šo.mǎ) mor.de- bu.did/	/(to) mor.de- bu.di/
(آنها) مرده بودند	(او/آن) مرده بود
/(ǎn.hǎ) mor.de- bu.dand/	/(u/ ǎn) mor.de- bud/

<table>
<tr><td colspan="2" align="center">**Past Subjunctive**
ماضی التزامی</td></tr>
<tr><td align="center">(ما) مرده باشیم
/(mǎ) mor.de- bǎ.šim/</td><td align="center">(من) مرده باشم
/(man) mor.de- bǎ.šam/</td></tr>
<tr><td align="center">(شما) مرده باشید
/(šo.mǎ) mor.de- bǎ.šid/</td><td align="center">(تو) مرده باشی
/(to) mor.de- bǎ.ši/</td></tr>
<tr><td align="center">(آنها) مرده باشند
/(ǎn.hǎ) mor.de- bǎ.šand/</td><td align="center">(او/آن) مرده باشد
/(u/ ǎn) mor.de- bǎ.šad/</td></tr>
</table>

<table>
<tr><td colspan="2" align="center">**Past Progressive**
ماضی مستمر(در جریان)</td></tr>
<tr><td align="center">(ما) داشتیم می مردیم
/(mǎ) dǎš.tim- mi.mor.dim/</td><td align="center">(من) داشتم می مردم
/(man) dǎš.tam- mi.mor.dam/</td></tr>
<tr><td align="center">(شما) داشتید می مردید
/(šo.mǎ) dǎš.tid- mi.mor.did/</td><td align="center">(تو) داشتی می مردی
/(to) dǎš.ti- mi.mor.di/</td></tr>
<tr><td align="center">(آنها) داشتند می مردند
/(ǎn.hǎ) dǎš.tand- mi.mor.dand/</td><td align="center">(او/آن) داشت می مرد
/(u/ ǎn) dǎšt- mi.mord/</td></tr>
</table>

<table>
<tr><td colspan="2" align="center">**Simple Future**
مستقبل (آینده ساده)</td></tr>
<tr><td align="center">(ما) خواهیم مرد
/(mǎ) kǎ.him- mord/</td><td align="center">(من) خواهم مرد
/(man) kǎ.ham- mord/</td></tr>
<tr><td align="center">(شما) خواهید مرد
/(šo.mǎ) kǎ.hid- mord/</td><td align="center">(تو) خواهی مرد
/(to) kǎ.hi- mord/</td></tr>
<tr><td align="center">(آنها) خواهند مرد
/(ǎn.hǎ) kǎ.hand- mord/</td><td align="center">(او/آن) خواهد مرد
/(u/ ǎn) kǎ.had- mord/</td></tr>
</table>

<table>
<tr><td colspan="2" align="center">**Command**
امر</td></tr>
<tr><td align="center">بمیرید!
/be.mi.rid/</td><td align="center">بمیر!
/be.mir/</td></tr>
</table>

to do

کَردَن

/kar.dan/

Plural	Singular
Simple Present مضارع اخباری(حال ساده)	
(ما) می کنیم /(mǎ) mi.ko.nim/	(من) می کنم /(man) mi.ko.nam/
(شما) می کنید /(šo.mǎ) mi.ko.nid/	(تو) می کنی /(to) mi.ko.ni/
(آنها) می کنند /(ǎn.hǎ) mi.ko.nand/	(او/آن) می کند /(u/ ǎn) mi.ko.nad/
Present Subjunctive مضارع التزامی	
(ما) بکنیم /(mǎ) be.ko.nim/	(من) بکنم /(man) be.ko.nam/
(شما) بکنید /(šo.mǎ) be.ko.nid/	(تو) بکنی /(to) be.ko.ni/
(آنها) بکنند /(ǎn.hǎ) be.ko.nand/	(او/آن) بکند /(u/ ǎn) be.ko.nad/
Present Progressive مضارع مستمر(در جریان)	
(ما) داریم می کنیم /(mǎ) dǎ.rim- mi.ko.nim/	(من) دارم می کنم /(man) dǎ.ram- mi.ko.nam/
(شما) دارید می کنید /(šo.mǎ) dǎ.rid- mi.ko.nid/	(تو) داری می کنی /(to) dǎ.ri- mi.ko.ni/
(آنها) دارند می کنند /(ǎn.hǎ) dǎ.rand- mi.ko.nand/	(او/آن) دارد می کند /(u/ ǎn) dǎ.rad- mi.ko.nad/

Simple Past
ماضی مطلق (گذشته ساده)

(ما) کردیم	(من) کردم
/(mǎ) kar.dim/	/(man) kar.dam/
(شما) کردید	(تو) کردی
/(šo.mǎ) kar.did/	/(to) kar.di/
(آنها) کردند	(او/آن) کرد
/(ǎn.hǎ) kar.dand/	/(u/ ǎn) kard/

Imperfect Indicative
ماضی استمراری

(ما) می کردیم	(من) می کردم
/(mǎ) mi.kar.dim/	/(man) mi.kar.dam/
(شما) می کردید	(تو) می کردی
/(šo.mǎ) mi.kar.did/	/(to) mi.kar.di/
(آنها) می کردند	(او/آن) می کرد
/(ǎn.hǎ) mi.kar.dand/	/(u/ ǎn) mi.kard/

Present Perfect
ماضی نقلی

(ما) کرده ایم	(من) کرده ام
/(mǎ) kar.de.im/	/(man) kar.de.am/
(شما) کرده اید	(تو) کرده ای
/(šo.mǎ) kar.de.id/	/(to) kar.de.i/
(آنها) کرده اند	(او/آن) کرده است
/(ǎn.hǎ) kar.de.and/	/(u/ ǎn) kar.de- ast/

Past Perfect
ماضی بعید

(ما) کرده بودیم	(من) کرده بودم
/(mǎ) kar.de- bu.dim/	/(man) kar.de- bu.dam/
(شما) کرده بودید	(تو) کرده بودی
/(šo.mǎ) kar.de- bu.did/	/(to) kar.de- bu.di/
(آنها) کرده بودند	(او/آن) کرده بود
/(ǎn.hǎ) kar.de- bu.dand/	/(u/ ǎn) kar.de- bud/

Past Subjunctive	
ماضی التزامی	
(ما) کرده باشیم /(mǎ) kar.de- bǎ.šim/	(من) کرده باشم /(man) kar.de- bǎ.šam/
(شما) کرده باشید /(šo.mǎ) kar.de- bǎ.šid/	(تو) کرده باشی /(to) kar.de- bǎ.ši/
(آنها) کرده باشند /(ǎn.hǎ) kar.de- bǎ.šand/	(او/آن) کرده باشد /(u/ ǎn) kar.de- bǎ.šad/

Past Progressive	
ماضی مستمر(در جریان)	
(ما) داشتیم می کردیم /(mǎ) dǎš.tim- mi.kar.dim/	(من) داشتم می کردم /(man) dǎš.tam- mi.kar.dam/
(شما) داشتید می کردید /(šo.mǎ) dǎš.tid- mi.kar.did/	(تو) داشتی می کردی /(to) dǎš.ti- mi.kar.di/
(آنها) داشتند می کردند /(ǎn.hǎ) dǎš.tand- mi.kar.dand/	(او/آن) داشت می کرد /(u/ ǎn) dǎšt- mi.kard/

Simple Future	
مستقبل (آینده ساده)	
(ما) خواهیم کرد /(mǎ) kǎ.him- kard/	(من) خواهم کرد /(man) kǎ.ham- kard/
(شما) خواهید کرد /(šo.mǎ) kǎ.hid- kard/	(تو) خواهی کرد /(to) kǎ.hi- kard/
(آنها) خواهند کرد /(ǎn.hǎ) kǎ.hand- kard/	(او/آن) خواهد کرد /(u/ ǎn) kǎ.had- kard/

Command	
امر	
بکنید! /be.ko.nid/	بکن! /be.kon/

to drop

اَنداختَن

/an.dǎḵ.tan/

Plural	Singular
Simple Present مضارع اخباری(حال ساده)	
(ما) می اندازیم /(mǎ) mi.an.dǎ.zim/	(من) می اندازم /(man) mi.an.dǎ.zam/
(شما) می اندازید /(šo.mǎ) mi.an.dǎ.zid/	(تو) می اندازی /(to) mi.an.dǎ.zi/
(آنها) می اندازند /(ǎn.hǎ) mi.an.dǎ.zand/	(او/آن) می اندازد /(u/ ǎn) mi.an.dǎ.zad/
Present Subjunctive مضارع التزامی	
(ما) بیندازیم /(mǎ) bi.yan.dǎ.zim/	(من) بیندازم /(man) bi.yan.dǎ.zam/
(شما) بیندازید /(šo.mǎ) bi.yan.dǎ.zid/	(تو) بیندازی /(to) bi.yan.dǎ.zi/
(آنها) بیندازند /(ǎn.hǎ) bi.yan.dǎ.zand/	(او/آن) بیندازد /(u/ ǎn) bi.yan.dǎ.zad/
Present Progressive مضارع مستمر(در جریان)	
(ما) داریم می اندازیم /(mǎ) dǎ.rim- mi.an.dǎ.zim/	(من) دارم می اندازم /(man) dǎ.ram- mi.an.dǎ.zam/
(شما) دارید می اندازید /(šo.mǎ) dǎ.rid- mi.an.dǎ.zid/	(تو) داری می اندازی /(to) dǎ.ri- mi.an.dǎ.zi/
(آنها) دارند می اندازند /(ǎn.hǎ) dǎ.rand- mi.an.dǎ.zand/	(او/آن) دارد می اندازد /(u/ ǎn) dǎ.rad- mi.an.dǎ.zad/

Simple Past
ماضی مطلق (گذشته ساده)

(ما) انداختیم	(من) انداختم
/(mă) an.dăǩ.tim/	/(man) an.dăǩ.tam/
(شما) انداختید	(تو) انداختی
/(šo.mă) an.dăǩ.tid/	/(to) an.dăǩ.ti/
(آنها) انداختند	(او/آن) انداخت
/(ăn.hă) an.dăǩ.tand/	/(u/ ăn) an.dăǩt/

Imperfect Indicative
ماضی استمراری

(ما) می انداختیم	(من) می انداختم
/(mă) mi.an.dăǩ.tim/	/(man) mi.an.dăǩ.tam/
(شما) می انداختید	(تو) می انداختی
/(šo.mă) mi.an.dăǩ.tid/	/(to) mi.an.dăǩ.ti/
(آنها) می انداختند	(او/آن) می انداخت
/(ăn.hă) mi.an.dăǩ.tand/	/(u/ ăn) mi.an.dăǩt/

Present Perfect
ماضی نقلی

(ما) انداخته ایم	(من) انداخته ام
/(mă) an.dăǩ.te.im/	/(man) an.dăǩ.te.am/
(شما) انداخته اید	(تو) انداخته ای
/(šo.mă) an.dăǩ.te.id/	/(to) an.dăǩ.te.i/
(آنها) انداخته اند	(او/آن) انداخته است
/(ăn.hă) an.dăǩ.te.and/	/(u/ ăn) an.dăǩ.te- ast/

Past Perfect
ماضی بعید

(ما) انداخته بودیم	(من) انداخته بودم
/(mă) an.dăǩ.te- bu.dim/	/(man) an.dăǩ.te- bu.dam/
(شما) انداخته بودید	(تو) انداخته بودی
/(šo.mă) an.dăǩ.te- bu.did/	/(to) an.dăǩ.te- bu.di/
(آنها) انداخته بودند	(او/آن) انداخته بود
/(ăn.hă) an.dăǩ.te- bu.dand/	/(u/ ăn) an.dăǩ.te- bud/

Past Subjunctive	
ماضی التزامی	
(ما) انداخته باشیم /(mă) an.dăǩ.te- bă.šim/	(من) انداخته باشم /(man) an.dăǩ.te- bă.šam/
(شما) انداخته باشید /(šo.mă) an.dăǩ.te- bă.šid/	(تو) انداخته باشی /(to) an.dăǩ.te- bă.ši/
(آنها) انداخته باشند /(ăn.hă) an.dăǩ.te- bă.šand/	(او/آن) انداخته باشد /(u/ ăn) an.dăǩ.te- bă.šad/

Past Progressive	
ماضی مستمر(در جریان)	
(ما) داشتیم می انداختیم /(mă) dăš.tim- mi.an.dăǩ.tim/	(من) داشتم می انداختم /(man) dăš.tam- mi.an.dăǩ.tam/
(شما) داشتید می انداختید /(šo.mă) dăš.tid- mi.an.dăǩ.tid/	(تو) داشتی می انداختی /(to) dăš.ti- mi.an.dăǩ.ti/
(آنها) داشتند می انداختند /(ăn.hă) dăš.tand- mi.an.dăǩ.tand/	(او/آن) داشت می انداخت /(u/ ăn) dăšt- mi.an.dăǩt/

Simple Future	
مستقبل (آینده ساده)	
(ما) خواهیم انداخت /(mă) ǩă.him- an.dăǩt/	(من) خواهم انداخت /(man) ǩă.ham- an.dăǩt/
(شما) خواهید انداخت /(šo.mă) ǩă.hid- an.dăǩt/	(تو) خواهی انداخت /(to) ǩă.hi- an.dăǩt/
(آنها) خواهند انداخت /(ăn.hă) ǩă.hand- an.dăǩt/	(او/آن) خواهد انداخت /(u/ ăn) ǩă.had- an.dăǩt/

Command	
امر	
بیندازید! /bi.yan.dă.zid/	بینداز! /bi.yan.dăz/

to entrust

سِپُردَن

/se.por.dan/

Plural	Singular
Simple Present مضارع اخباری(حال ساده)	
(ما) می سپاریم /(mǎ) mi.se.pǎ.rim/	(من) می سپارم /(man) mi.se.pǎ.ram/
(شما) می سپارید /(šo.mǎ) mi.se.pǎ.rid/	(تو) می سپاری /(to) mi.se.pǎ.ri/
(آنها) می سپارند /(ǎn.hǎ) mi.se.pǎ.rand/	(او/آن) می سپارد /(u/ ǎn) mi.se.pǎ.rad/
Present Subjunctive مضارع التزامی	
(ما) بسپاریم /(mǎ) be.se.pǎ.rim/	(من) بسپارم /(man) be.se.pǎ.ram/
(شما) بسپارید /(šo.mǎ) be.se.pǎ.rid/	(تو) بسپاری /(to) be.se.pǎ.ri/
(آنها) بسپارند /(ǎn.hǎ) be.se.pǎ.rand/	(او/آن) بسپارد /(u/ ǎn) be.se.pǎ.rad/
Present Progressive مضارع مستمر(در جریان)	
(ما) داریم می سپاریم /(mǎ) dǎ.rim- mi.se.pǎ.rim/	(من) دارم می سپارم /(man) dǎ.ram- mi.se.pǎ.ram/
(شما) دارید می سپارید /(šo.mǎ) dǎ.rid- mi.se.pǎ.rid/	(تو) داری می سپاری /(to) dǎ.ri- mi.se.pǎ.ri/
(آنها) دارند می سپارند /(ǎn.hǎ) dǎ.rand- mi.se.pǎ.rand/	(او/آن) دارد می سپارد /(u/ ǎn) dǎ.rad- mi.se.pǎ.rad/

Simple Past
ماضی مطلق (گذشته ساده)

(ما) سپردیم	(من) سپردم
/(mă) se.por.dim/	/(man) se.por.dam/
(شما) سپردید	(تو) سپردی
/(šo.mă) se.por.did/	/(to) se.por.di/
(آنها) سپردند	(او/آن) سپرد
/(ăn.hă) se.por.dand/	/(u/ ăn) se.pord/

Imperfect Indicative
ماضی استمراری

(ما) می سپردیم	(من) می سپردم
/(mă) mi.se.por.dim/	/(man) mi.se.por.dam/
(شما) می سپردید	(تو) می سپردی
/(šo.mă) mi.se.por.did/	/(to) mi.se.por.di/
(آنها) می سپردند	(او/آن) می سپرد
/(ăn.hă) mi.se.por.dand/	/(u/ ăn) mi.se.pord/

Present Perfect
ماضی نقلی

(ما) سپرده ایم	(من) سپرده ام
/(mă) se.por.de.im/	/(man) se.por.de.am/
(شما) سپرده اید	(تو) سپرده ای
/(šo.mă) se.por.de.id/	/(to) se.por.de.i/
(آنها) سپرده اند	(او/آن) سپرده است
/(ăn.hă) se.por.de.and/	/(u/ ăn) se.por.de- ast/

Past Perfect
ماضی بعید

(ما) سپرده بودیم	(من) سپرده بودم
/(mă) se.por.de- bu.dim/	/(man) se.por.de- bu.dam/
(شما) سپرده بودید	(تو) سپرده بودی
/(šo.mă) se.por.de- bu.did/	/(to) se.por.de- bu.di/
(آنها) سپرده بودند	(او/آن) سپرده بود
/(ăn.hă) se.por.de- bu.dand/	/(u/ ăn) se.por.de- bud/

Past Subjunctive	
ماضی التزامی	
(ما) سپرده باشیم	(من) سپرده باشم
/(mǎ) se.por.de- bǎ.šim/	/(man) se.por.de- bǎ.šam/
(شما) سپرده باشید	(تو) سپرده باشی
/(šo.mǎ) se.por.de- bǎ.šid/	/(to) se.por.de- bǎ.ši/
(آنها) سپرده باشند	(او/آن) سپرده باشد
/(ǎn.hǎ) se.por.de- bǎ.šand/	/(u/ ǎn) se.por.de- bǎ.šad/

Past Progressive	
ماضی مستمر(در جریان)	
(ما) داشتیم می سپردیم	(من) داشتم می سپردم
/(mǎ) dǎš.tim- mi.se.por.dim/	/(man) dǎš.tam- mi.se.por.dam/
(شما) داشتید می سپردید	(تو) داشتی می سپردی
/(šo.mǎ) dǎš.tid- mi.se.por.did/	/(to) dǎš.ti- mi.se.por.di/
(آنها) داشتند می سپردند	(او/آن) داشت می سپرد
/(ǎn.hǎ) dǎš.tand- mi.se.por.dand/	/(u/ ǎn) dǎšt- mi.se.pord/

Simple Future	
مستقبل (آینده ساده)	
(ما) خواهیم سپرد	(من) خواهم سپرد
/(mǎ) kǎ.him- se.pord/	/(man) kǎ.ham- se.pord/
(شما) خواهید سپرد	(تو) خواهی سپرد
/(šo.mǎ) kǎ.hid- se.pord/	/(to) kǎ.hi- se.pord/
(آنها) خواهند سپرد	(او/آن) خواهد سپرد
/(ǎn.hǎ) kǎ.hand- se.pord/	/(u/ ǎn) kǎ.had- se.pord/

Command	
امر	
بسپارید!	بسپار!
/be.se.pǎ.rid/	/be.se.păr/

to erase

زُدودَن

/zo.du.dan/

Plural	Singular
Simple Present	
مضارع اخباری(حال ساده)	
(ما) می زداییم	(من) می زدایم
/(mǎ) mi.zo.dǎ.yim/	/(man) mi.zo.dǎ.yam/
(شما) می زدایید	(تو) می زدایی
/(šo.mǎ) mi.zo.dǎ.yid/	/(to) mi.zo.dǎ.yi/
(آنها) می زدایند	(او/آن) می زداید
/(ǎn.hǎ) mi.zo.dǎ.yand/	/(u/ ǎn) mi.zo.dǎ.yad/

Plural	Singular
Present Subjunctive	
مضارع التزامی	
(ما) بزداییم	(من) بزدایم
/(mǎ) be.zo.dǎ.yim/	/(man) be.zo.dǎ.yam/
(شما) بزدایید	(تو) بزدایی
/(šo.mǎ) be.zo.dǎ.yid/	/(to) be.zo.dǎ.yi/
(آنها) بزدایند	(او/آن) بزداید
/(ǎn.hǎ) be.zo.dǎ.yand/	/(u/ ǎn) be.zo.dǎ.yad/

Plural	Singular
Present Progressive	
مضارع مستمر(در جریان)	
(ما) داریم می زداییم	(من) دارم می زدایم
/(mǎ) dǎ.rim- mi.zo.dǎ.yim/	/(man) dǎ.ram- mi.zo.dǎ.yam/
(شما) دارید می زدایید	(تو) داری می زدایی
/(šo.mǎ) dǎ.rid- mi.zo.dǎ.yid/	/(to) dǎ.ri- mi.zo.dǎ.yi/
(آنها) دارند می زدایند	(او/آن) دارد می زداید
/(ǎn.hǎ) dǎ.rand- mi.zo.dǎ.yand/	/(u/ ǎn) dǎ.rad- mi.zo.dǎ.yad/

Simple Past	
ماضی مطلق (گذشته ساده)	
(ما) زدودیم	(من) زدودم
/(mǎ) zo.du.dim/	/(man) zo.du.dam/
(شما) زدودید	(تو) زدودی
/(šo.mǎ) zo.du.did/	/(to) zo.du.di/
(آنها) زدودند	(او/آن) زدود
/(ǎn.hǎ) zo.du.dand/	/(u/ ǎn) zo.dud/

Imperfect Indicative	
ماضی استمراری	
(ما) می زدودیم	(من) می زدودم
/(mǎ) mi.zo.du.dim/	/(man) mi.zo.du.dam/
(شما) می زدودید	(تو) می زدودی
/(šo.mǎ) mi.zo.du.did/	/(to) mi.zo.du.di/
(آنها) می زدودند	(او/آن) می زدود
/(ǎn.hǎ) mi.zo.du.dand/	/(u/ ǎn) mi.zo.dud/

Present Perfect	
ماضی نقلی	
(ما) زدوده ایم	(من) زدوده ام
/(mǎ) zo.du.de.im/	/(man) zo.du.de.am/
(شما) زدوده اید	(تو) زدوده ای
/(šo.mǎ) zo.du.de.id/	/(to) zo.du.de.i/
(آنها) زدوده اند	(او/آن) زدوده است
/(ǎn.hǎ) zo.du.de.and/	/(u/ ǎn) zo.du.de- ast/

Past Perfect	
ماضی بعید	
(ما) زدوده بودیم	(من) زدوده بودم
/(mǎ) zo.du.de- bu.dim/	/(man) zo.du.de- bu.dam/
(شما) زدوده بودید	(تو) زدوده بودی
/(šo.mǎ) zo.du.de- bu.did/	/(to) zo.du.de- bu.di/
(آنها) زدوده بودند	(او/آن) زدوده بود
/(ǎn.hǎ) zo.du.de- bu.dand/	/(u/ ǎn) zo.du.de- bud/

Past Subjunctive	
ماضی التزامی	
(ما) زدوده باشیم	(من) زدوده باشم
/(mǎ) zo.du.de- bǎ.šim/	/(man) zo.du.de- bǎ.šam/
(شما) زدوده باشید	(تو) زدوده باشی
/(šo.mǎ) zo.du.de- bǎ.šid/	/(to) zo.du.de- bǎ.ši/
(آنها) زدوده باشند	(او/آن) زدوده باشد
/(ǎn.hǎ) zo.du.de- bǎ.šand/	/(u/ ǎn) zo.du.de- bǎ.šad/

Past Progressive	
ماضی مستمر(در جریان)	
(ما) داشتیم می زدودیم	(من) داشتم می زدودم
/(mǎ) dǎš.tim- mi.zo.du.dim/	/(man) dǎš.tam- mi.zo.du.dam/
(شما) داشتید می زدودید	(تو) داشتی می زدودی
/(šo.mǎ) dǎš.tid- mi.zo.du.did/	/(to) dǎš.ti- mi.zo.du.di/
(آنها) داشتند می زدودند	(او/آن) داشت می زدود
/(ǎn.hǎ) dǎš.tand- mi.zo.du.dand/	/(u/ ǎn) dǎšt- mi.zo.dud/

Simple Future	
مستقبل (آینده ساده)	
(ما) خواهیم زدود	(من) خواهم زدود
/(mǎ) ǩǎ.him- zo.dud/	/(man) ǩǎ.ham- zo.dud/
(شما) خواهید زدود	(تو) خواهی زدود
/(šo.mǎ) ǩǎ.hid- zo.dud/	/(to) ǩǎ.hi- zo.dud/
(آنها) خواهند زدود	(او/آن) خواهد زدود
/(ǎn.hǎ) ǩǎ.hand- zo.dud/	/(u/ ǎn) ǩǎ.had- zo.dud/

Command	
امر	
بزدایید!	بزدای!
/be.zo.dǎ.yid/	/be.zo.dǎy/

to escape

گُریختَن

/go.rik̆.tan/

Plural	Singular
Simple Present <div dir="rtl">مضارع اخباری(حال ساده)</div>	
(ما) می گریزیم /(mǎ) mi.go.ri.zim/	(من) می گریزم /(man) mi.go.ri.zam/
(شما) می گریزید /(šo.mǎ) mi.go.ri.zid/	(تو) می گریزی /(to) mi.go.ri.zi/
(آنها) می گریزند /(ǎn.hǎ) mi.go.ri.zand/	(او/آن) می گریزد /(u/ ǎn) mi.go.ri.zad/
Present Subjunctive <div dir="rtl">مضارع التزامی</div>	
(ما) بگریزیم /(mǎ) be.go.ri.zim/	(من) بگریزم /(man) be.go.ri.zam/
(شما) بگریزید /(šo.mǎ) be.go.ri.zid/	(تو) بگریزی /(to) be.go.ri.zi/
(آنها) بگریزند /(ǎn.hǎ) be.go.ri.zand/	(او/آن) بگریزد /(u/ ǎn) be.go.ri.zad/
Present Progressive <div dir="rtl">مضارع مستمر(در جریان)</div>	
(ما) داریم می گریزیم /(mǎ) dǎ.rim- mi.go.ri.zim/	(من) دارم می گریزم /(man) dǎ.ram- mi.go.ri.zam/
(شما) دارید می گریزید /(šo.mǎ) dǎ.rid- mi.go.ri.zid/	(تو) داری می گریزی /(to) dǎ.ri- mi.go.ri.zi/
(آنها) دارند می گریزند /(ǎn.hǎ) dǎ.rand- mi.go.ri.zand/	(او/آن) دارد می گریزد /(u/ ǎn) dǎ.rad- mi.go.ri.zad/

Simple Past
ماضی مطلق (گذشته ساده)

(ما) گریختیم	(من) گریختم
/(mă) go.riǩ.tim/	/(man) go.riǩ.tam/
(شما) گریختید	(تو) گریختی
/(šo.mă) go.riǩ.tid/	/(to) go.riǩ.ti/
(آنها) گریختند	(او/آن) گریخت
/(ăn.hă) go.riǩ.tand/	/(u/ ăn) go.riǩt/

Imperfect Indicative
ماضی استمراری

(ما) می گریختیم	(من) می گریختم
/(mă) mi.go.riǩ.tim/	/(man) mi.go.riǩ.tam/
(شما) می گریختید	(تو) می گریختی
/(šo.mă) mi.go.riǩ.tid/	/(to) mi.go.riǩ.ti/
(آنها) می گریختند	(او/آن) می گریخت
/(ăn.hă) mi.go.riǩ.tand/	/(u/ ăn) mi.go.riǩt/

Present Perfect
ماضی نقلی

(ما) گریخته ایم	(من) گریخته ام
/(mă) go.riǩ.te.im/	/(man) go.riǩ.te.am/
(شما) گریخته اید	(تو) گریخته ای
/(šo.mă) go.riǩ.te.id/	/(to) go.riǩ.te.i/
(آنها) گریخته اند	(او/آن) گریخته است
/(ăn.hă) go.riǩ.te.and/	/(u/ ăn) go.riǩ.te- ast/

Past Perfect
ماضی بعید

(ما) گریخته بودیم	(من) گریخته بودم
/(mă) go.riǩ.te- bu.dim/	/(man) go.riǩ.te- bu.dam/
(شما) گریخته بودید	(تو) گریخته بودی
/(šo.mă) go.riǩ.te- bu.did/	/(to) go.riǩ.te- bu.di/
(آنها) گریخته بودند	(او/آن) گریخته بود
/(ăn.hă) go.riǩ.te- bu.dand/	/(u/ ăn) go.riǩ.te- bud/

Past Subjunctive	
ماضی التزامی	
(ما) گریخته باشیم	(من) گریخته باشم
/(mă) go.riǩ.te- bă.šim/	/(man) go.riǩ.te- bă.šam/
(شما) گریخته باشید	(تو) گریخته باشی
/(šo.mă) go.riǩ.te- bă.šid/	/(to) go.riǩ.te- bă.ši/
(آنها) گریخته باشند	(او/آن) گریخته باشد
/(ăn.hă) go.riǩ.te- bă.šand/	/(u/ ăn) go.riǩ.te- bă.šad/

Past Progressive	
ماضی مستمر(در جریان)	
(ما) داشتیم می گریختیم	(من) داشتم می گریختم
/(mă) dăš.tim- mi.go.riǩ.tim/	/(man) dăš.tam- mi.go.riǩ.tam/
(شما) داشتید می گریختید	(تو) داشتی می گریختی
/(šo.mă) dăš.tid- mi.go.riǩ.tid/	/(to) dăš.ti- mi.go.riǩ.ti/
(آنها) داشتند می گریختند	(او/آن) داشت می گریخت
/(ăn.hă) dăš.tand- mi.go.riǩ.tand/	/(u/ ăn) dăšt- mi.go.riǩt/

Simple Future	
مستقبل (آینده ساده)	
(ما) خواهیم گریخت	(من) خواهم گریخت
/(mă) ǩă.him- go.riǩt/	/(man) ǩă.ham- go.riǩt/
(شما) خواهید گریخت	(تو) خواهی گریخت
/(šo.mă) ǩă.hid- go.riǩt/	/(to) ǩă.hi- go.riǩt/
(آنها) خواهند گریخت	(او/آن) خواهد گریخت
/(ăn.hă) ǩă.hand- go.riǩt/	/(u/ ăn) ǩă.had- go.riǩt/

Command	
امر	
بگریزید!	بگریز!
/be.go.ri.zid/	/be.go.riz/

to fall

اُفتادَن

/of.tă.dan/

Plural	Singular
Simple Present مضارع اخباری(حال ساده)	
(ما) می افتیم /(mă) mi.of.tim/	(من) می افتم /(man) mi.of.tam/
(شما) می افتید /(šo.mă) mi.of.tid/	(تو) می افتی /(to) mi.of.ti/
(آنها) می افتند /(ăn.hă) mi.of.tand/	(او/آن) می افتد /(u/ ăn) mi.of.tad/
Present Subjunctive مضارع التزامی	
(ما) بیفتیم /(mă) bi.yof.tim/	(من) بیفتم /(man) bi.yof.tam/
(شما) بیفتید /(šo.mă) bi.yof.tid/	(تو) بیفتی /(to) bi.yof.ti/
(آنها) بیفتند /(ăn.hă) bi.yof.tand/	(او/آن) بیفتد /(u/ ăn) bi.yof.tad/
Present Progressive مضارع مستمر(در جریان)	
(ما) داریم می افتیم /(mă) dă.rim- mi.of.tim/	(من) دارم می افتم /(man) dă.ram- mi.of.tam/
(شما) دارید می افتید /(šo.mă) dă.rid- mi.of.tid/	(تو) داری می افتی /(to) dă.ri- mi.of.ti/
(آنها) دارند می افتند /(ăn.hă) dă.rand- mi.of.tand/	(او/آن) دارد می افتد /(u/ ăn) dă.rad- mi.of.tad/

Simple Past
ماضی مطلق (گذشته ساده)

(ما) افتادیم	(من) افتادم
/(mă) of.tă.dim/	/(man) of.tă.dam/
(شما) افتادید	(تو) افتادی
/(šo.mă) of.tă.did/	/(to) of.tă.di/
(آنها) افتادند	(او/آن) افتاد
/(ăn.hă) of.tă.dand/	/(u/ ăn) of.tăd/

Imperfect Indicative
ماضی استمراری

(ما) می افتادیم	(من) می افتادم
/(mă) mi.of.tă.dim/	/(man) mi.of.tă.dam/
(شما) می افتادید	(تو) می افتادی
/(šo.mă) mi.of.tă.did/	/(to) mi.of.tă.di/
(آنها) می افتادند	(او/آن) می افتاد
/(ăn.hă) mi.of.tă.dand/	/(u/ ăn) mi.of.tăd/

Present Perfect
ماضی نقلی

(ما) افتاده ایم	(من) افتاده ام
/(mă) of.tă.de.im/	/(man) of.tă.de.am/
(شما) افتاده اید	(تو) افتاده ای
/(šo.mă) of.tă.de.id/	/(to) of.tă.de.i/
(آنها) افتاده اند	(او/آن) افتاده است
/(ăn.hă) of.tă.de.and/	/(u/ ăn) of.tă.de- ast/

Past Perfect
ماضی بعید

(ما) افتاده بودیم	(من) افتاده بودم
/(mă) of.tă.de- bu.dim/	/(man) of.tă.de- bu.dam/
(شما) افتاده بودید	(تو) افتاده بودی
/(šo.mă) of.tă.de- bu.did/	/(to) of.tă.de- bu.di/
(آنها) افتاده بودند	(او/آن) افتاده بود
/(ăn.hă) of.tă.de- bu.dand/	/(u/ ăn) of.tă.de- bud/

<table>
<tr><td colspan="2" align="center">**Past Subjunctive**
ماضی التزامی</td></tr>
<tr><td align="center">(ما) افتاده باشیم
/(mǎ) of.tǎ.de- bǎ.šim/</td><td align="center">(من) افتاده باشم
/(man) of.tǎ.de- bǎ.šam/</td></tr>
<tr><td align="center">(شما) افتاده باشید
/(šo.mǎ) of.tǎ.de- bǎ.šid/</td><td align="center">(تو) افتاده باشی
/(to) of.tǎ.de- bǎ.ši/</td></tr>
<tr><td align="center">(آنها) افتاده باشند
/(ǎn.hǎ) of.tǎ.de- bǎ.šand/</td><td align="center">(او/آن) افتاده باشد
/(u/ ǎn) of.tǎ.de- bǎ.šad/</td></tr>
</table>

<table>
<tr><td colspan="2" align="center">**Past Progressive**
ماضی مستمر(در جریان)</td></tr>
<tr><td align="center">(ما) داشتیم می افتادیم
/(mǎ) dǎš.tim- mi.of.tǎ.dim/</td><td align="center">(من) داشتم می افتادم
/(man) dǎš.tam- mi.of.tǎ.dam/</td></tr>
<tr><td align="center">(شما) داشتید می افتادید
/(šo.mǎ) dǎš.tid- mi.of.tǎ.did/</td><td align="center">(تو) داشتی می افتادی
/(to) dǎš.ti- mi.of.tǎ.di/</td></tr>
<tr><td align="center">(آنها) داشتند می افتادند
/(ǎn.hǎ) dǎš.tand- mi.of.tǎ.dand/</td><td align="center">(او/آن) داشت می افتاد
/(u/ ǎn) dǎšt- mi.of.tǎd/</td></tr>
</table>

<table>
<tr><td colspan="2" align="center">**Simple Future**
مستقبل (آینده ساده)</td></tr>
<tr><td align="center">(ما) خواهیم افتاد
/(mǎ) ǩǎ.him- of.tǎd/</td><td align="center">(من) خواهم افتاد
/(man) ǩǎ.ham- of.tǎd/</td></tr>
<tr><td align="center">(شما) خواهید افتاد
/(šo.mǎ) ǩǎ.hid- of.tǎd/</td><td align="center">(تو) خواهی افتاد
/(to) ǩǎ.hi- of.tǎd/</td></tr>
<tr><td align="center">(آنها) خواهند افتاد
/(ǎn.hǎ) ǩǎ.hand- of.tǎd/</td><td align="center">(او/آن) خواهد افتاد
/(u/ ǎn) ǩǎ.had- of.tǎd/</td></tr>
</table>

<table>
<tr><td colspan="2" align="center">**Command**
امر</td></tr>
<tr><td align="center">بیفتید!
/bi.yof.tid/</td><td align="center">بیفت!
/bi.yoft/</td></tr>
</table>

to find

یافتَن

/yăf.tan/

Plural	Singular
Simple Present مضارع اخباری(حال ساده)	
(ما) می یابیم /(mă) mi.yă.bim/	(من) می یابم /(man) mi.yă.bam/
(شما) می یابید /(šo.mă) mi.yă.bid/	(تو) می یابی /(to) mi.yă.bi/
(آنها) می یابند /(ăn.hă) mi.yă.band/	(او/آن) می یابد /(u/ ăn) mi.yă.bad/
Present Subjunctive مضارع التزامی	
(ما) بیابیم /(mă) bi.yă.bim/	(من) بیابم /(man) bi.yă.bam/
(شما) بیابید /(šo.mă) bi.yă.bid/	(تو) بیابی /(to) bi.yă.bi/
(آنها) بیابند /(ăn.hă) bi.yă.band/	(او/آن) بیابد /(u/ ăn) bi.yă.bad/
Present Progressive مضارع مستمر(در جریان)	
(ما) داریم می یابیم /(mă) dă.rim- mi.yă.bim/	(من) دارم می یابم /(man) dă.ram- mi.yă.bam/
(شما) دارید می یابید /(šo.mă) dă.rid- mi.yă.bid/	(تو) داری می یابی /(to) dă.ri- mi.yă.bi/
(آنها) دارند می یابند /(ăn.hă) dă.rand- mi.yă.band/	(او/آن) دارد می یابد /(u/ ăn) dă.rad- mi.yă.bad/

Simple Past
ماضی مطلق (گذشته ساده)

(ما) یافتیم	(من) یافتم
/(mǎ) yǎf.tim/	/(man) yǎf.tam/
(شما) یافتید	(تو) یافتی
/(šo.mǎ) yǎf.tid/	/(to) yǎf.ti/
(آنها) یافتند	(او/ آن) یافت
/(ǎn.hǎ) yǎf.tand/	/(u/ ǎn) yǎft/

Imperfect Indicative
ماضی استمراری

(ما) می یافتیم	(من) می یافتم
/(mǎ) mi.yǎf.tim/	/(man) mi.yǎf.tam/
(شما) می یافتید	(تو) می یافتی
/(šo.mǎ) mi.yǎf.tid/	/(to) mi.yǎf.ti/
(آنها) می یافتند	(او/ آن) می یافت
/(ǎn.hǎ) mi.yǎf.tand/	/(u/ ǎn) mi.yǎft/

Present Perfect
ماضی نقلی

(ما) یافته ایم	(من) یافته ام
/(mǎ) yǎf.te.im/	/(man) yǎf.te.am/
(شما) یافته اید	(تو) یافته ای
/(šo.mǎ) yǎf.te.id/	/(to) yǎf.te.i/
(آنها) یافته اند	(او/ آن) یافته است
/(ǎn.hǎ) yǎf.te.and/	/(u/ ǎn) yǎf.te- ast/

Past Perfect
ماضی بعید

(ما) یافته بودیم	(من) یافته بودم
/(mǎ) yǎf.te- bu.dim/	/(man) yǎf.te- bu.dam/
(شما) یافته بودید	(تو) یافته بودی
/(šo.mǎ) yǎf.te- bu.did/	/(to) yǎf.te- bu.di/
(آنها) یافته بودند	(او/ آن) یافته بود
/(ǎn.hǎ) yǎf.te- bu.dand/	/(u/ ǎn) yǎf.te- bud/

Past Subjunctive	
ماضی التزامی	
(ما) یافته باشیم	(من) یافته باشم
/(mǎ) yǎf.te- bǎ.šim/	/(man) yǎf.te- bǎ.šam/
(شما) یافته باشید	(تو) یافته باشی
/(šo.mǎ) yǎf.te- bǎ.šid/	/(to) yǎf.te- bǎ.ši/
(آنها) یافته باشند	(او/آن) یافته باشد
/(ǎn.hǎ) yǎf.te- bǎ.šand/	/(u/ ǎn) yǎf.te- bǎ.šad/

Past Progressive	
ماضی مستمر(در جریان)	
(ما) داشتیم می یافتیم	(من) داشتم می یافتم
/(mǎ) dǎš.tim- mi.yǎf.tim/	/(man) dǎš.tam- mi.yǎf.tam/
(شما) داشتید می یافتید	(تو) داشتی می یافتی
/(šo.mǎ) dǎš.tid- mi.yǎf.tid/	/(to) dǎš.ti- mi.yǎf.ti/
(آنها) داشتند می یافتند	(او/آن) داشت می یافت
/(ǎn.hǎ) dǎš.tand- mi.yǎf.tand/	/(u/ ǎn) dǎšt- mi.yǎft/

Simple Future	
مستقبل (آینده ساده)	
(ما) خواهیم یافت	(من) خواهم یافت
/(mǎ) kǎ.him- yǎft/	/(man) kǎ.ham- yǎft/
(شما) خواهید یافت	(تو) خواهی یافت
/(šo.mǎ) kǎ.hid- yǎft/	/(to) kǎ.hi- yǎft/
(آنها) خواهند یافت	(او/آن) خواهد یافت
/(ǎn.hǎ) kǎ.hand- yǎft/	/(u/ ǎn) kǎ.had- yǎft/

Command	
امر	
بیابید!	بیاب!
/bi.yǎ.bid/	/bi.yǎb/

to forgive

بَخشودَن

/baǩ.šu.dan/

Plural	Singular
Simple Present	
مضارع اخباری(حال ساده)	
(ما) می بخشاییم	(من) می بخشایم
/(mǎ) mi.baǩ.šǎ.yim/	/(man) mi.baǩ.šǎ.yam/
(شما) می بخشایید	(تو) می بخشایی
/(šo.mǎ) mi.baǩ.šǎ.yid/	/(to) mi.baǩ.šǎ.yi/
(آنها) می بخشایند	(او/آن) می بخشاید
/(ǎn.hǎ) mi.baǩ.šǎ.yand/	/(u/ ǎn) mi.baǩ.šǎ.yad/
Present Subjunctive	
مضارع التزامی	
(ما) ببخشاییم	(من) ببخشایم
/(mǎ) be.baǩ.šǎ.yim/	/(man) be.baǩ.šǎ.yam/
(شما) ببخشایید	(تو) ببخشایی
/(šo.mǎ) be.baǩ.šǎ.yid/	/(to) be.baǩ.šǎ.yi/
(آنها) ببخشایند	(او/آن) ببخشاید
/(ǎn.hǎ) be.baǩ.šǎ.yand/	/(u/ ǎn) be.baǩ.šǎ.yad/
Present Progressive	
مضارع مستمر(در جریان)	
(ما) داریم می بخشاییم	(من) دارم می بخشایم
/(mǎ) dǎ.rim- mi.baǩ.šǎ.yim/	/(man) dǎ.ram- mi.baǩ.šǎ.yam/
(شما) دارید می بخشایید	(تو) داری می بخشایی
/(šo.mǎ) dǎ.rid- mi.baǩ.šǎ.yid/	/(to) dǎ.ri- mi.baǩ.šǎ.yi/
(آنها) دارند می بخشایند	(او/آن) دارد می بخشاید
/(ǎn.hǎ) dǎ.rand- mi.baǩ.šǎ.yand/	/(u/ ǎn) dǎ.rad- mi.baǩ.šǎ.yad/

	Simple Past
Simple Past	
ماضی مطلق (گذشته ساده)	
(ما) بخشودیم	(من) بخشودم
/(mǎ) baǩ.šu.dim/	/(man) baǩ.šu.dam/
(شما) بخشودید	(تو) بخشودی
/(šo.mǎ) baǩ.šu.did/	/(to) baǩ.šu.di/
(آنها) بخشودند	(او/آن) بخشود
/(ǎn.hǎ) baǩ.šu.dand/	/(u/ ǎn) baǩ.šud/

	Imperfect Indicative
Imperfect Indicative	
ماضی استمراری	
(ما) می بخشودیم	(من) می بخشودم
/(mǎ) mi.baǩ.šu.dim/	/(man) mi.baǩ.šu.dam/
(شما) می بخشودید	(تو) می بخشودی
/(šo.mǎ) mi.baǩ.šu.did/	/(to) mi.baǩ.šu.di/
(آنها) می بخشودند	(او/آن) می بخشود
/(ǎn.hǎ) mi.baǩ.šu.dand/	/(u/ ǎn) mi.baǩ.šud/

	Present Perfect
Present Perfect	
ماضی نقلی	
(ما) بخشوده ایم	(من) بخشوده ام
/(mǎ) baǩ.šu.de.im/	/(man) baǩ.šu.de.am/
(شما) بخشوده اید	(تو) بخشوده ای
/(šo.mǎ) baǩ.šu.de.id/	/(to) baǩ.šu.de.i/
(آنها) بخشوده اند	(او/آن) بخشوده است
/(ǎn.hǎ) baǩ.šu.de.and/	/(u/ ǎn) baǩ.šu.de- ast/

	Past Perfect
Past Perfect	
ماضی بعید	
(ما) بخشوده بودیم	(من) بخشوده بودم
/(mǎ) baǩ.šu.de- bu.dim/	/(man) baǩ.šu.de- bu.dam/
(شما) بخشوده بودید	(تو) بخشوده بودی
/(šo.mǎ) baǩ.šu.de- bu.did/	/(to) baǩ.šu.de- bu.di/
(آنها) بخشوده بودند	(او/آن) بخشوده بود
/(ǎn.hǎ) baǩ.šu.de- bu.dand/	/(u/ ǎn) baǩ.šu.de- bud/

Past Subjunctive	
ماضی التزامی	
(ما) بخشوده باشیم	(من) بخشوده باشم
/(mă) baǩ.šu.de- bă.šim/	/(man) baǩ.šu.de- bă.šam/
(شما) بخشوده باشید	(تو) بخشوده باشی
/(šo.mă) baǩ.šu.de- bă.šid/	/(to) baǩ.šu.de- bă.ši/
(آنها) بخشوده باشند	(او/آن) بخشوده باشد
/(ăn.hă) baǩ.šu.de- bă.šand/	/(u/ ăn) baǩ.šu.de- bă.šad/

Past Progressive	
ماضی مستمر(در جریان)	
(ما) داشتیم می بخشودیم	(من) داشتم می بخشودم
/(mă) dăš.tim- mi.baǩ.šu.dim/	/(man) dăš.tam- mi.baǩ.šu.dam/
(شما) داشتید می بخشودید	(تو) داشتی می بخشودی
/(šo.mă) dăš.tid- mi.baǩ.šu.did/	/(to) dăš.ti- mi.baǩ.šu.di/
(آنها) داشتند می بخشودند	(او/آن) داشت می بخشود
/(ăn.hă) dăš.tand- mi.baǩ.šu.dand/	/(u/ ăn) dăšt- mi.baǩ.šud/

Simple Future	
مستقبل (آینده ساده)	
(ما) خواهیم بخشود	(من) خواهم بخشود
/(mă) ǩă.him- baǩ.šud/	/(man) ǩă.ham- baǩ.šud/
(شما) خواهید بخشود	(تو) خواهی بخشود
/(šo.mă) ǩă.hid- baǩ.šud/	/(to) ǩă.hi- baǩ.šud/
(آنها) خواهند بخشود	(او/آن) خواهد بخشود
/(ăn.hă) ǩă.hand- baǩ.šud/	/(u/ ăn) ǩă.had- baǩ.šud/

Command	
امر	
ببخشایید!	ببخشای!
/be.baǩ.ša.yid/	/be.baǩ.šay/

to fuse

گُداختَن

/go.dăk̆.tan/

Plural	Singular
Simple Present	
مضارع اخباری(حال ساده)	
(ما) می گدازیم	(من) می گدازم
/(mă) mi.go.dă.zim/	/(man) mi.go.dă.zam/
(شما) می گدازید	(تو) می گدازی
/(šo.mă) mi.go.dă.zid/	/(to) mi.go.dă.zi/
(آنها) می گدازند	(او/آن) می گدازد
/(ăn.hă) mi.go.dă.zand/	/(u/ ăn) mi.go.dă.zad/

Plural	Singular
Present Subjunctive	
مضارع التزامی	
(ما) بگدازیم	(من) بگدازم
/(mă) be.go.dă.zim/	/(man) be.go.dă.zam/
(شما) بگدازید	(تو) بگدازی
/(šo.mă) be.go.dă.zid/	/(to) be.go.dă.zi/
(آنها) بگدازند	(او/آن) بگدازد
/(ăn.hă) be.go.dă.zand/	/(u/ ăn) be.go.dă.zad/

Plural	Singular
Present Progressive	
مضارع مستمر(در جریان)	
(ما) داریم می گدازیم	(من) دارم می گدازم
/(mă) dă.rim-mi.go.dă.zim/	/(man) dă.ram- mi.go.dă.zam/
(شما) دارید می گدازید	(تو) داری می گدازی
/(šo.mă) dă.rid- mi.go.dă.zid/	/(to) dă.ri- mi.go.dă.zi/
(آنها) دارند می گدازند	(او/آن) دارد می گدازد
/(ăn.hă) dă.rand- mi.go.dă.zand/	/(u/ ăn) dă.rad- mi.go.dă.zad/

Simple Past
ماضی مطلق (گذشته ساده)

(ما) گداختیم	(من) گداختم
/(mǎ) go.dǎǩ.tim/	/(man) go.dǎǩ.tam/
(شما) گداختید	(تو) گداختی
/(šo.mǎ) go.dǎǩ.tid/	/(to) go.dǎǩ.ti/
(آنها) گداختند	(او/آن) گداخت
/(ǎn.hǎ) go.dǎǩ.tand/	/(u/ ǎn) go.dǎǩt/

Imperfect Indicative
ماضی استمراری

(ما) می گداختیم	(من) می گداختم
/(mǎ) mi.go.dǎǩ.tim/	/(man) mi.go.dǎǩ.tam/
(شما) می گداختید	(تو) می گداختی
/(šo.mǎ) mi.go.dǎǩ.tid/	/(to) mi.go.dǎǩ.ti/
(آنها) می گداختند	(او/آن) می گداخت
/(ǎn.hǎ) mi.go.dǎǩ.tand/	/(u/ ǎn) mi.go.dǎǩt/

Present Perfect
ماضی نقلی

(ما) گداخته ایم	(من) گداخته ام
/(mǎ) go.dǎǩ.te.im/	/(man) go.dǎǩ.te.am/
(شما) گداخته اید	(تو) گداخته ای
/(šo.mǎ) go.dǎǩ.te.id/	/(to) go.dǎǩ.te.i/
(آنها) گداخته اند	(او/آن) گداخته است
/(ǎn.hǎ) go.dǎǩ.te.and/	/(u/ ǎn) go.dǎǩ.te- ast/

Past Perfect
ماضی بعید

(ما) گداخته بودیم	(من) گداخته بودم
/(mǎ) go.dǎǩ.te- bu.dim/	/(man) go.dǎǩ.te- bu.dam/
(شما) گداخته بودید	(تو) گداخته بودی
/(šo.mǎ) go.dǎǩ.te- bu.did/	/(to) go.dǎǩ.te- bu.di/
(آنها) گداخته بودند	(او/آن) گداخته بود
/(ǎn.hǎ) go.dǎǩ.te- bu.dand/	/(u/ ǎn) go.dǎǩ.te- bud/

Past Subjunctive
ماضی التزامی

(ما) گداخته باشیم	(من) گداخته باشم
/(mă) go.dăǩ.te- bă.šim/	/(man) go.dăǩ.te- bă.šam/
(شما) گداخته باشید	(تو) گداخته باشی
/(šo.mă) go.dăǩ.te- bă.šid/	/(to) go.dăǩ.te- bă.ši/
(آنها) گداخته باشند	(او/آن) گداخته باشد
/(ăn.hă) go.dăǩ.te- bă.šand/	/(u/ ăn) go.dăǩ.te- bă.šad/

Past Progressive
ماضی مستمر(در جریان)

(ما) داشتیم می گداختیم	(من) داشتم می گداختم
/(mă) dăš.tim- mi.go.dăǩ.tim/	/(man) dăš.tam- mi.go.dăǩ.tam/
(شما) داشتید می گداختید	(تو) داشتی می گداختی
/(šo.mă) dăš.tid- mi.go.dăǩ.tid/	/(to) dăš.ti- mi.go.dăǩ.ti/
(آنها) داشتند می گداختند	(او/آن) داشت می گداخت
/(ăn.hă) dăš.tand- mi.go.dăǩ.tand/	/(u/ ăn) dăšt- mi.go.dăǩt/

Simple Future
مستقبل (آینده ساده)

(ما) خواهیم گداخت	(من) خواهم گداخت
/(mă) ǩă.him- go.dăǩt/	/(man) ǩă.ham- go.dăǩt/
(شما) خواهید گداخت	(تو) خواهی گداخت
/(šo.mă) ǩă.hid- go.dăǩt/	/(to) ǩă.hi- go.dăǩt/
(آنها) خواهند گداخت	(او/آن) خواهد گداخت
/(ăn.hă) ǩă.hand- go.dăǩt/	/(u/ ăn) ǩă.had- go.dăǩt/

Command
امر

بگدازید!	بگداز!
/be.go.dă.zid/	/be.go.dăz/

to gallop

تاخِتَن

/tăk̆.tan/

Plural	Singular
Simple Present مضارع اخباری(حال ساده)	
(ما) می تازیم /(mă) mi.tă.zim/	(من) می تازم /(man) mi.tă.zam/
(شما) می تازید /(šo.mă) mi.tă.zid/	(تو) می تازی /(to) mi.tă.zi/
(آنها) می تازند /(ăn.hă) mi.tă.zand/	(او/آن) می تازد /(u/ ăn) mi.tă.zad/
Present Subjunctive مضارع التزامی	
(ما) بتازیم /(mă) be.tă.zim/	(من) بتازم /(man) be.tă.zam/
(شما) بتازید /(šo.mă) be.tă.zid/	(تو) بتازی /(to) be.tă.zi/
(آنها) بتازند /(ăn.hă) be.tă.zand/	(او/آن) بتازد /(u/ ăn) be.tă.zad/
Present Progressive مضارع مستمر(در جریان)	
(ما) داریم می تازیم /(mă) dă.rim- mi.tă.zim/	(من) دارم می تازم /(man) dă.ram- mi.tă.zam/
(شما) دارید می تازید /(šo.mă) dă.rid- mi.tă.zid/	(تو) داری می تازی /(to) dă.ri- mi.tă.zi/
(آنها) دارند می تازند /(ăn.hă) dă.rand- mi.tă.zand/	(او/آن) دارد می تازد /(u/ ăn) dă.rad- mi.tă.zad/

Simple Past	
ماضی مطلق (گذشته ساده)	
(ما) تاختیم	(من) تاختم
/(mǎ) tǎǩ.tim/	/(man) tǎǩ.tam/
(شما) تاختید	(تو) تاختی
/(šo.mǎ) tǎǩ.tid/	/(to) tǎǩ.ti/
(آنها) تاختند	(او/آن) تاخت
/(ǎn.hǎ) tǎǩ.tand/	/(u/ ǎn) tǎǩt/

Imperfect Indicative	
ماضی استمراری	
(ما) می تاختیم	(من) می تاختم
/(mǎ) mi.tǎǩ.tim/	/(man) mi.tǎǩ.tam/
(شما) می تاختید	(تو) می تاختی
/(šo.mǎ) mi.tǎǩ.tid/	/(to) mi.tǎǩ.ti/
(آنها) می تاختند	(او/آن) می تاخت
/(ǎn.hǎ) mi.tǎǩ.tand/	/(u/ ǎn) mi.tǎǩt/

Present Perfect	
ماضی نقلی	
(ما) تاخته ایم	(من) تاخته ام
/(mǎ) tǎǩ.te.im/	/(man) tǎǩ.te.am/
(شما) تاخته اید	(تو) تاخته ای
/(šo.mǎ) tǎǩ.te.id/	/(to) tǎǩ.te.i/
(آنها) تاخته اند	(او/آن) تاخته است
/(ǎn.hǎ) tǎǩ.te.and/	/(u/ ǎn) tǎǩ.te- ast/

Past Perfect	
ماضی بعید	
(ما) تاخته بودیم	(من) تاخته بودم
/(mǎ) tǎǩ.te- bu.dim/	/(man) tǎǩ.te- bu.dam/
(شما) تاخته بودید	(تو) تاخته بودی
/(šo.mǎ) tǎǩ.te- bu.did/	/(to) tǎǩ.te- bu.di/
(آنها) تاخته بودند	(او/آن) تاخته بود
/(ǎn.hǎ) tǎǩ.te- bu.dand/	/(u/ ǎn) tǎǩ.te- bud/

Past Subjunctive	
ماضی التزامی	
(ما) تاخته باشیم	(من) تاخته باشم
/(mă) tăǩ.te- bă.šim/	/(man) tăǩ.te- bă.šam/
(شما) تاخته باشید	(تو) تاخته باشی
/(šo.mă) tăǩ.te- bă.šid/	/(to) tăǩ.te- bă.ši/
(آنها) تاخته باشند	(او/آن) تاخته باشد
/(ăn.hă) tăǩ.te- bă.šand/	/(u/ ăn) tăǩ.te- bă.šad/

Past Progressive	
ماضی مستمر(در جریان)	
(ما) داشتیم می تاختیم	(من) داشتم می تاختم
/(mă) dăš.tim- mi.tăǩ.tim/	/(man) dăš.tam- mi.tăǩ.tam/
(شما) داشتید می تاختید	(تو) داشتی می تاختی
/(šo.mă) dăš.tid- mi.tăǩ.tid/	/(to) dăš.ti- mi.tăǩ.ti/
(آنها) داشتند می تاختند	(او/آن) داشت می تاخت
/(ăn.hă) dăš.tand- mi.tăǩ.tand/	/(u/ ăn) dăšt- mi.tăǩt/

Simple Future	
مستقبل (آینده ساده)	
(ما) خواهیم تاخت	(من) خواهم تاخت
/(mă) ǩă.him- tăǩt/	/(man) ǩă.ham- tăǩt/
(شما) خواهید تاخت	(تو) خواهی تاخت
/(šo.mă) ǩă.hid- tăǩt/	/(to) ǩă.hi- tăǩt/
(آنها) خواهند تاخت	(او/آن) خواهد تاخت
/(ăn.hă) ǩă.hand- tăǩt/	/(u/ ăn) ǩă.had- tăǩt/

Command	
امر	
بتازید!	بتاز!
/be.tă.zid/	/be.tăz/

to get to know

شِناخَتن

/še.năk̆.tan/

Plural	Singular
Simple Present	
مضارع اخباری(حال ساده)	
(ما) می شناسیم	(من) می شناسم
/(mă) mi.še.nă.sim/	/(man) mi.še.nă.sam/
(شما) می شناسید	(تو) می شناسی
/(šo.mă) mi.še.nă.sid/	/(to) mi.še.nă.si/
(آنها) می شناسند	(او/آن) می شناسد
/(ăn.hă) mi.še.nă.sand/	/(u/ ăn) mi.še.nă.sad/
Present Subjunctive	
مضارع التزامی	
(ما) بشناسیم	(من) بشناسم
/(mă) be.še.nă.sim/	/(man) be.še.nă.sam/
(شما) بشناسید	(تو) بشناسی
/(šo.mă) be.še.nă.sid/	/(to) be.še.nă.si/
(آنها) بشناسند	(او/آن) بشناسد
/(ăn.hă) be.še.nă.sand/	/(u/ ăn) be.še.nă.sad/
Present Progressive	
مضارع مستمر(در جریان)	
(ما) داریم می شناسیم	(من) دارم می شناسم
/(mă) dă.rim- mi.še.nă.sim/	/(man) dă.ram- mi.še.nă.sam/
(شما) دارید می شناسید	(تو) داری می شناسی
/(šo.mă) dă.rid- mi.še.nă.sid/	/(to) dă.ri- mi.še.nă.si/
(آنها) دارند می شناسند	(او/آن) دارد می شناسد
/(ăn.hă) dă.rand- mi.še.nă.sand/	/(u/ ăn) dă.rad- mi.še.nă.sad/

110

Simple Past
ماضی مطلق (گذشته ساده)

(ما) شناختیم	(من) شناختم
/(mǎ) še.nǎk̆.tim/	/(man) še.nǎk̆.tam/
(شما) شناختید	(تو) شناختی
/(šo.mǎ) še.nǎk̆.tid/	/(to) še.nǎk̆.ti/
(آنها) شناختند	(او/آن) شناخت
/(ǎn.hǎ) še.nǎk̆.tand/	/(u/ ǎn) še.nǎk̆t/

Imperfect Indicative
ماضی استمراری

(ما) می شناختیم	(من) می شناختم
/(mǎ) mi.še.nǎk̆.tim/	/(man) mi.še.nǎk̆.tam/
(شما) می شناختید	(تو) می شناختی
/(šo.mǎ) mi.še.nǎk̆.tid/	/(to) mi.še.nǎk̆.ti/
(آنها) می شناختند	(او/آن) می شناخت
/(ǎn.hǎ) mi.še.nǎk̆.tand/	/(u/ ǎn) mi.še.nǎk̆t/

Present Perfect
ماضی نقلی

(ما) شناخته ایم	(من) شناخته ام
/(mǎ) še.nǎk̆.te.im/	/(man) še.nǎk̆.te.am/
(شما) شناخته اید	(تو) شناخته ای
/(šo.mǎ) še.nǎk̆.te.id/	/(to) še.nǎk̆.te.i/
(آنها) شناخته اند	(او/آن) شناخته است
/(ǎn.hǎ) še.nǎk̆.te.and/	/(u/ ǎn) še.nǎk̆.te- ast/

Past Perfect
ماضی بعید

(ما) شناخته بودیم	(من) شناخته بودم
/(mǎ) še.nǎk̆.te- bu.dim/	/(man) še.nǎk̆.te- bu.dam/
(شما) شناخته بودید	(تو) شناخته بودی
/(šo.mǎ) še.nǎk̆.te- bu.did/	/(to) še.nǎk̆.te- bu.di/
(آنها) شناخته بودند	(او/آن) شناخته بود
/(ǎn.hǎ) še.nǎk̆.te- bu.dand/	/(u/ ǎn) še.nǎk̆.te- bud/

Past Subjunctive	
ماضی التزامی	
(ما) شناخته باشیم	(من) شناخته باشم
/(mǎ) še.nǎǩ.te- bǎ.šim/	/(man) še.nǎǩ.te- bǎ.šam/
(شما) شناخته باشید	(تو) شناخته باشی
/(šo.mǎ) še.nǎǩ.te- bǎ.šid/	/(to) še.nǎǩ.te- bǎ.ši/
(آنها) شناخته باشند	(او/آن) شناخته باشد
/(ǎn.hǎ) še.nǎǩ.te- bǎ.šand/	/(u/ ǎn) še.nǎǩ.te- bǎ.šad/

Past Progressive	
ماضی مستمر(در جریان)	
(ما) داشتیم می شناختیم	(من) داشتم می شناختم
/(mǎ) dǎš.tim- mi.še.nǎǩ.tim/	/(man) dǎš.tam- mi.še.nǎǩ.tam/
(شما) داشتید می شناختید	(تو) داشتی می شناختی
/(šo.mǎ) dǎš.tid- mi.še.nǎǩ.tid/	/(to) dǎš.ti- mi.še.nǎǩ.ti/
(آنها) داشتند می شناختند	(او/آن) داشت می شناخت
/(ǎn.hǎ) dǎš.tand- mi.še.nǎǩ.tand/	/(u/ ǎn) dǎšt- mi.še.nǎǩt/

Simple Future	
مستقبل (آینده ساده)	
(ما) خواهیم شناخت	(من) خواهم شناخت
/(mǎ) ǩǎ.him- še.nǎǩt/	/(man) ǩǎ.ham- še.nǎǩt/
(شما) خواهید شناخت	(تو) خواهی شناخت
/(šo.mǎ) ǩǎ.hid- še.nǎǩt/	/(to) ǩǎ.hi- še.nǎǩt/
(آنها) خواهند شناخت	(او/آن) خواهد شناخت
/(ǎn.hǎ) ǩǎ.hand- še.nǎǩt/	/(u/ ǎn) ǩǎ.had- še.nǎǩt/

Command	
امر	
بشناسید!	بشناس!
/be.še.nǎ.sid/	/be.še.nǎs/

to give

دادَن

/dă.dan/

Plural	Singular
Simple Present	
مضارع اخباری(حال ساده)	
(ما) می دهیم	(من) می دهم
/(mă) mi.da.him/	/(man) mi.da.ham/
(شما) می دهید	(تو) می دهی
/(šo.mă) mi.da.hid/	/(to) mi.da.hi/
(آنها) می دهند	(او/آن) می دهد
/(ăn.hă) mi.da.hand/	/(u/ ăn) mi.da.had/

Plural	Singular
Present Subjunctive	
مضارع التزامی	
(ما) بدهیم	(من) بدهم
/(mă) be.da.him/	/(man) be.da.ham/
(شما) بدهید	(تو) بدهی
/(šo.mă) be.da.hid/	/(to) be.da.hi/
(آنها) بدهند	(او/آن) بدهد
/(ăn.hă) be.da.hand/	/(u/ ăn) be.da.had/

Plural	Singular
Present Progressive	
مضارع مستمر(در جریان)	
(ما) داریم می دهیم	(من) دارم می دهم
/(mă) dă.rim- mi.da.him/	/(man) dă.ram- mi.da.ham/
(شما) دارید می دهید	(تو) داری می دهی
/(šo.mă) dă.rid- mi.da.hid/	/(to) dă.ri- mi.da.hi/
(آنها) دارند می دهند	(او/آن) دارد می دهد
/(ăn.hă) dă.rand- mi.da.hand/	/(u/ ăn) dă.rad- mi.da.had/

113

Simple Past
ماضی مطلق (گذشته ساده)

(ما) دادیم	(من) دادم
/(mǎ) dǎ.dim/	/(man) dǎ.dam/
(شما) دادید	(تو) دادی
/(šo.mǎ) dǎ.did/	/(to) dǎ.di/
(آنها) دادند	(او/آن) داد
/(ǎn.hǎ) dǎ.dand/	/(u/ ǎn) dǎd/

Imperfect Indicative
ماضی استمراری

(ما) می دادیم	(من) می دادم
/(mǎ) mi.dǎ.dim/	/(man) mi.dǎ.dam/
(شما) می دادید	(تو) می دادی
/(šo.mǎ) mi.dǎ.did/	/(to) mi.dǎ.di/
(آنها) می دادند	(او/آن) می داد
/(ǎn.hǎ) mi.dǎ.dand/	/(u/ ǎn) mi.dǎd/

Present Perfect
ماضی نقلی

(ما) داده ایم	(من) داده ام
/(mǎ) dǎ.de.im/	/(man) dǎ.de.am/
(شما) داده اید	(تو) داده ای
/(šo.mǎ) dǎ.de.id/	/(to) dǎ.de.i/
(آنها) داده اند	(او/آن) داده است
/(ǎn.hǎ) dǎ.de.and/	/(u/ ǎn) dǎ.de- ast/

Past Perfect
ماضی بعید

(ما) داده بودیم	(من) داده بودم
/(mǎ) dǎ.de- bu.dim/	/(man) dǎ.de- bu.dam/
(شما) داده بودید	(تو) داده بودی
/(šo.mǎ) dǎ.de- bu.did/	/(to) dǎ.de- bu.di/
(آنها) داده بودند	(او/آن) داده بود
/(ǎn.hǎ) dǎ.de- bu.dand/	/(u/ ǎn) dǎ.de- bud/

Past Subjunctive
ماضی التزامی

(ما) داده باشیم	(من) داده باشم
/(mă) dă.de- bă.šim/	/(man) dă.de- bă.šam/
(شما) داده باشید	(تو) داده باشی
/(šo.mă) dă.de- bă.šid/	/(to) dă.de- bă.ši/
(آنها) داده باشند	(او/آن) داده باشد
/(ăn.hă) dă.de- bă.šand/	/(u/ ăn) dă.de- bă.šad/

Past Progressive
ماضی مستمر(در جریان)

(ما) داشتیم می دادیم	(من) داشتم می دادم
/(mă) dăš.tim- mi.dă.dim/	/(man) dăš.tam- mi.dă.dam/
(شما) داشتید می دادید	(تو) داشتی می دادی
/(šo.mă) dăš.tid- mi.dă.did/	/(to) dăš.ti- mi.dă.di/
(آنها) داشتند می دادند	(او/آن) داشت می داد
/(ăn.hă) dăš.tand- mi.dă.dand/	/(u/ ăn) dăšt- mi.dăd/

Simple Future
مستقبل (آینده ساده)

(ما) خواهیم داد	(من) خواهم داد
/(mă) kă.him- dăd/	/(man) kă.ham- dăd/
(شما) خواهید داد	(تو) خواهی داد
/(šo.mă) kă.hid- dăd/	/(to) kă.hi- dăd/
(آنها) خواهند داد	(او/آن) خواهد داد
/(ăn.hă) kă.hand- dăd/	/(u/ ăn) kă.had- dăd/

Command
امر

بدهید!	بده!
/be.da.hid/	/be.de/

to go

رَفتَن

/raf.tan/

Plural	*Singular*
Simple Present	
مضارع اخباری(حال ساده)	
(ما) می رویم	(من) می روم
/(mǎ) mi.ra.vim/	/(man) mi.ra.vam/
(شما) می روید	(تو) می روی
/(šo.mǎ) mi.ra.vid/	/(to) mi.ra.vi/
(آنها) می روند	(او/آن) می رود
/(ǎn.hǎ) mi.ra.vand/	/(u/ ǎn) mi.ra.vad/
Present Subjunctive	
مضارع التزامی	
(ما) برویم	(من) بروم
/(mǎ) be.ra.vim/	/(man) be.ra.vam/
(شما) بروید	(تو) بروی
/(šo.mǎ) be.ra.vid/	/(to) be.ra.vi/
(آنها) بروند	(او/آن) برود
/(ǎn.hǎ) be.ra.vand/	/(u/ ǎn) be.ra.vad/
Present Progressive	
مضارع مستمر(در جریان)	
(ما) داریم می رویم	(من) دارم می روم
/(mǎ) dǎ.rim- mi.ra.vim/	/(man) dǎ.ram- mi.ra.vam/
(شما) دارید می روید	(تو) داری می روی
/(šo.mǎ) dǎ.rid- mi.ra.vid/	/(to) dǎ.ri- mi.ra.vi/
(آنها) دارند می روند	(او/آن) دارد می رود
/(ǎn.hǎ) dǎ.rand- mi.ra.vand/	/(u/ ǎn) dǎ.rad- mi.ra.vad/

Simple Past	
ماضی مطلق (گذشته ساده)	
(ما) رفتیم	(من) رفتم
/(mǎ) raf.tim/	/(man) raf.tam/
(شما) رفتید	(تو) رفتی
/(šo.mǎ) raf.tid/	/(to) raf.ti/
(آنها) رفتند	(او/آن) رفت
/(ǎn.hǎ) raf.tand/	/(u/ ǎn) raft/

Imperfect Indicative	
ماضی استمراری	
(ما) می رفتیم	(من) می رفتم
/(mǎ) mi.raf.tim/	/(man) mi.raf.tam/
(شما) می رفتید	(تو) می رفتی
/(šo.mǎ) mi.raf.tid/	/(to) mi.raf.ti/
(آنها) می رفتند	(او/آن) می رفت
/(ǎn.hǎ) mi.raf.tand/	/(u/ ǎn) mi.raft/

Present Perfect	
ماضی نقلی	
(ما) رفته ایم	(من) رفته ام
/(mǎ) raf.te.im/	/(man) raf.te.am/
(شما) رفته اید	(تو) رفته ای
/(šo.mǎ) raf.te.id/	/(to) raf.te.i/
(آنها) رفته اند	(او/آن) رفته است
/(ǎn.hǎ) raf.te.and/	/(u/ ǎn) raf.te- ast/

Past Perfect	
ماضی بعید	
(ما) رفته بودیم	(من) رفته بودم
/(mǎ) raf.te- bu.dim/	/(man) raf.te- bu.dam/
(شما) رفته بودید	(تو) رفته بودی
/(šo.mǎ) raf.te- bu.did/	/(to) raf.te- bu.di/
(آنها) رفته بودند	(او/آن) رفته بود
/(ǎn.hǎ) raf.te- bu.dand/	/(u/ ǎn) raf.te- bud/

117

Past Subjunctive	
ماضی التزامی	
(ما) رفته باشیم	(من) رفته باشم
/(mǎ) raf.te- bǎ.šim/	/(man) raf.te- bǎ.šam/
(شما) رفته باشید	(تو) رفته باشی
/(šo.mǎ) raf.te- bǎ.šid/	/(to) raf.te- bǎ.ši/
(آنها) رفته باشند	(او/آن) رفته باشد
/(ǎn.hǎ) raf.te- bǎ.šand/	/(u/ ǎn) raf.te- bǎ.šad/

Past Progressive	
ماضی مستمر(در جریان)	
(ما) داشتیم می رفتیم	(من) داشتم می رفتم
/(mǎ) dǎš.tim- mi.raf.tim/	/(man) dǎš.tam- mi.raf.tam/
(شما) داشتید می رفتید	(تو) داشتی می رفتی
/(šo.mǎ) dǎš.tid- mi.raf.tid/	/(to) dǎš.ti- mi.raf.ti/
(آنها) داشتند می رفتند	(او/آن) داشت می رفت
/(ǎn.hǎ) dǎš.tand- mi.raf.tand/	/(u/ ǎn) dǎšt- mi.raft/

Simple Future	
مستقبل (آینده ساده)	
(ما) خواهیم رفت	(من) خواهم رفت
/(mǎ) kǎ.him- raft/	/(man) kǎ.ham- raft/
(شما) خواهید رفت	(تو) خواهی رفت
/(šo.mǎ) kǎ.hid- raft/	/(to) kǎ.hi- raft/
(آنها) خواهند رفت	(او/آن) خواهد رفت
/(ǎn.hǎ) kǎ.hand- raft/	/(u/ ǎn) kǎ.had- raft/

Command	
امر	
بروید!	برو!
/be.ra.vid/	/bo.ro/

to groom

پیراستَن

/pi.răs.tan/

Plural	Singular
Simple Present مضارع اخباری(حال ساده)	
(ما) می پیراییم /(mă) mi.pi.ră.yim/	(من) می پیرایم /(man) mi.pi.ră.yam/
(شما) می پیرایید /(šo.mă) mi.pi.ră.yid/	(تو) می پیرایی /(to) mi.pi.ră.yi/
(آنها) می پیرایند /(ăn.hă) mi.pi.ră.yand/	(او/آن) می پیراید /(u/ ăn) mi.pi.ră.yad/
Present Subjunctive مضارع التزامی	
(ما) بپیراییم /(mă) be.pi.ră.yim/	(من) بپیرایم /(man) be.pi.ră.yam/
(شما) بپیرایید /(šo.mă) be.pi.ră.yid/	(تو) بپیرایی /(to) be.pi.ră.yi/
(آنها) بپیرایند /(ăn.hă) be.pi.ră.yand/	(او/آن) بپیراید /(u/ ăn) be.pi.ră.yad/
Present Progressive مضارع مستمر(در جریان)	
(ما) داریم می پیراییم /(mă) dă.rim- mi.pi.ră.yim/	(من) دارم می پیرایم /(man) dă.ram- mi.pi.ră.yam/
(شما) دارید می پیرایید /(šo.mă) dă.rid- mi.pi.ră.yid/	(تو) داری می پیرایی /(to) dă.ri- mi.pi.ră.yi/
(آنها) دارند می پیرایند /(ăn.hă) dă.rand- mi.pi.ră.yand/	(او/آن) دارد می پیراید /(u/ ăn) dă.rad- mi.pi.ră.yad/

	Simple Past	
	ماضی مطلق (گذشته ساده)	
(ما) پیراستیم		(من) پیراستم
/(mǎ) pi.rǎs.tim/		/(man) pi.rǎs.tam/
(شما) پیراستید		(تو) پیراستی
/(šo.mǎ) pi.rǎs.tid/		/(to) pi.rǎs.ti/
(آنها) پیراستند		(او/آن) پیراست
/(ǎn.hǎ) pi.rǎs.tand/		/(u/ ǎn) pi.rǎst/

	Imperfect Indicative	
	ماضی استمراری	
(ما) می پیراستیم		(من) می پیراستم
/(mǎ) mi.pi.rǎs.tim/		/(man) mi.pi.rǎs.tam/
(شما) می پیراستید		(تو) می پیراستی
/(šo.mǎ) mi.pi.rǎs.tid/		/(to) mi.pi.rǎs.ti/
(آنها) می پیراستند		(او/آن) می پیراست
/(ǎn.hǎ) mi.pi.rǎs.tand/		/(u/ ǎn) mi.pi.rǎst/

	Present Perfect	
	ماضی نقلی	
(ما) پیراسته ایم		(من) پیراسته ام
/(mǎ) pi.rǎs.te.im/		/(man) pi.rǎs.te.am/
(شما) پیراسته اید		(تو) پیراسته ای
/(šo.mǎ) pi.rǎs.te.id/		/(to) pi.rǎs.te.i/
(آنها) پیراسته اند		(او/آن) پیراسته است
/(ǎn.hǎ) pi.rǎs.te.and/		/(u/ ǎn) pi.rǎs.te- ast/

	Past Perfect	
	ماضی بعید	
(ما) پیراسته بودیم		(من) پیراسته بودم
/(mǎ) pi.rǎs.te- bu.dim/		/(man) pi.rǎs.te- bu.dam/
(شما) پیراسته بودید		(تو) پیراسته بودی
/(šo.mǎ) pi.rǎs.te- bu.did/		/(to) pi.rǎs.te- bu.di/
(آنها) پیراسته بودند		(او/آن) پیراسته بود
/(ǎn.hǎ) pi.rǎs.te- bu.dand/		/(u/ ǎn) pi.rǎs.te- bud/

Past Subjunctive	
ماضی التزامی	
(ما) پیراسته باشیم	(من) پیراسته باشم
/(mǎ) pi.rǎs.te- bǎ.šim/	/(man) pi.rǎs.te- bǎ.šam/
(شما) پیراسته باشید	(تو) پیراسته باشی
/(šo.mǎ) pi.rǎs.te- bǎ.šid/	/(to) pi.rǎs.te- bǎ.ši/
(آنها) پیراسته باشند	(او/ آن) پیراسته باشد
/(ǎn.hǎ) pi.rǎs.te- bǎ.šand/	/(u/ ǎn) pi.rǎs.te- bǎ.šad/

Past Progressive	
ماضی مستمر(در جریان)	
(ما) داشتیم می پیراستیم	(من) داشتم می پیراستم
/(mǎ) dǎš.tim- mi.pi.rǎs.tim/	/(man) dǎš.tam- mi.pi.rǎs.tam/
(شما) داشتید می پیراستید	(تو) داشتی می پیراستی
/(šo.mǎ) dǎš.tid- mi.pi.rǎs.tid/	/(to) dǎš.ti- mi.pi.rǎs.ti/
(آنها) داشتند می پیراستند	(او/ آن) داشت می پیراست
/(ǎn.hǎ) dǎš.tand- mi.pi.rǎs.tand/	/(u/ ǎn) dǎšt- mi.pi.rǎst/

Simple Future	
مستقبل (آینده ساده)	
(ما) خواهیم پیراست	(من) خواهم پیراست
/(mǎ) ǩǎ.him- pi.rǎst/	/(man) ǩǎ.ham- pi.rǎst/
(شما) خواهید پیراست	(تو) خواهی پیراست
/(šo.mǎ) ǩǎ.hid- pi.rǎst/	/(to) ǩǎ.hi- pi.rǎst/
(آنها) خواهند پیراست	(او/ آن) خواهد پیراست
/(ǎn.hǎ) ǩǎ.hand- pi.rǎst/	/(u/ ǎn) ǩǎ.had- pi.rǎst/

Command	
امر	
بپیرایید!	بپیرای!
/be.pi.rǎ.yid/	/be.pi.rǎy/

to hang

آویختَن

/ă.viǩ.tan/

Plural	Singular
Simple Present	
مضارع اخباری(حال ساده)	
(ما) می آویزیم	(من) می آویزم
/(mă) mi.ă.vi.zim/	/(man) mi.ă.vi.zam/
(شما) می آویزید	(تو) می آویزی
/(šo.mă) mi.ă.vi.zid/	/(to) mi.ă.vi.zi/
(آنها) می آویزند	(او/آن) می آویزد
/(ăn.hă) mi.ă.vi.zand/	/(u/ ăn) mi.ă.vi.zad/

Plural	Singular
Present Subjunctive	
مضارع التزامی	
(ما) بیاویزیم	(من) بیاویزم
/(mă) bi.yă.vi.zim/	/(man) bi.yă.vi.zam/
(شما) بیاویزید	(تو) بیاویزی
/(šo.mă) bi.yă.vi.zid/	/(to) bi.yă.vi.zi/
(آنها) بیاویزند	(او/آن) بیاویزد
/(ăn.hă) bi.yă.vi.zand/	/(u/ ăn) bi.yă.vi.zad/

Plural	Singular
Present Progressive	
مضارع مستمر(در جریان)	
(ما) داریم می آویزیم	(من) دارم می آویزم
/(mă) dă.rim- mi.ă.vi.zim/	/(man) dă.ram- mi.ă.vi.zam/
(شما) دارید می آویزید	(تو) داری می آویزی
/(šo.mă) dă.rid- mi.ă.vi.zid/	/(to) dă.ri- mi.ă.vi.zi/
(آنها) دارند می آویزند	(او/آن) دارد می آویزد
/(ăn.hă) dă.rand- mi.ă.vi.zand/	/(u/ ăn) dă.rad- mi.ă.vi.zad/

Simple Past
ماضی مطلق (گذشته ساده)

(ما) آویختیم	(من) آویختم
/(mǎ) ǎ.viǩ.tim/	/(man) ǎ.viǩ.tam/
(شما) آویختید	(تو) آویختی
/(šo.mǎ) ǎ.viǩ.tid/	/(to) ǎ.viǩ.ti/
(آنها) آویختند	(او/آن) آویخت
/(ǎn.hǎ) ǎ.viǩ.tand/	/(u/ ǎn) ǎ.viǩt/

Imperfect Indicative
ماضی استمراری

(ما) می آویختیم	(من) می آویختم
/(mǎ) mi.ǎ.viǩ.tim/	/(man) mi.ǎ.viǩ.tam/
(شما) می آویختید	(تو) می آویختی
/(šo.mǎ) mi.ǎ.viǩ.tid/	/(to) mi.ǎ.viǩ.ti/
(آنها) می آویختند	(او/آن) می آویخت
/(ǎn.hǎ) mi.ǎ.viǩ.tand/	/(u/ ǎn) mi.ǎ.viǩt/

Present Perfect
ماضی نقلی

(ما) آویخته ایم	(من) آویخته ام
/(mǎ) ǎ.viǩ.te.im/	/(man) ǎ.viǩ.te.am/
(شما) آویخته اید	(تو) آویخته ای
/(šo.mǎ) ǎ.viǩ.te.id/	/(to) ǎ.viǩ.te.i/
(آنها) آویخته اند	(او/آن) آویخته است
/(ǎn.hǎ) ǎ.viǩ.te.and/	/(u/ ǎn) ǎ.viǩ.te- ast/

Past Perfect
ماضی بعید

(ما) آویخته بودیم	(من) آویخته بودم
/(mǎ) ǎ.viǩ.te- bu.dim/	/(man) ǎ.viǩ.te- bu.dam/
(شما) آویخته بودید	(تو) آویخته بودی
/(šo.mǎ) ǎ.viǩ.te- bu.did/	/(to) ǎ.viǩ.te- bu.di/
(آنها) آویخته بودند	(او/آن) آویخته بود
/(ǎn.hǎ) ǎ.viǩ.te- bu.dand/	/(u/ ǎn) ǎ.viǩ.te- bud/

Past Subjunctive	
ماضی التزامی	
(ما) آویخته باشیم	(من) آویخته باشم
/(mǎ) ǎ.viǩ.te- bǎ.šim/	/(man) ǎ.viǩ.te- bǎ.šam/
(شما) آویخته باشید	(تو) آویخته باشی
/(šo.mǎ) ǎ.viǩ.te- bǎ.šid/	/(to) ǎ.viǩ.te- bǎ.ši/
(آنها) آویخته باشند	(او/ آن) آویخته باشد
/(ǎn.hǎ) ǎ.viǩ.te- bǎ.šand/	/(u/ ǎn) ǎ.viǩ.te- bǎ.šad/

Past Progressive	
ماضی مستمر(در جریان)	
(ما) داشتیم می آویختیم	(من) داشتم می آویختم
/(mǎ) dǎš.tim- mi.ǎ.viǩ.tim/	/(man) dǎš.tam- mi.ǎ.viǩ.tam/
(شما) داشتید می آویختید	(تو) داشتی می آویختی
/(šo.mǎ) dǎš.tid- mi.ǎ.viǩ.tid/	/(to) dǎš.ti- mi.ǎ.viǩ.ti/
(آنها) داشتند می آویختند	(او/ آن) داشت می آویخت
/(ǎn.hǎ) dǎš.tand- mi.ǎ.viǩ.tand/	/(u/ ǎn) dǎšt- mi.ǎ.viǩt/

Simple Future	
مستقبل (آینده ساده)	
(ما) خواهیم آویخت	(من) خواهم آویخت
/(mǎ) ǩǎ.him- ǎ.viǩt/	/(man) ǩǎ.ham- ǎ.viǩt/
(شما) خواهید آویخت	(تو) خواهی آویخت
/(šo.mǎ) ǩǎ.hid- ǎ.viǩt/	/(to) ǩǎ.hi- ǎ.viǩt/
(آنها) خواهند آویخت	(او/ آن) خواهد آویخت
/(ǎn.hǎ) ǩǎ.hand- ǎ.viǩt/	/(u/ ǎn) ǩǎ.had- ǎ.viǩt/

Command	
امر	
بیاویزید!	بیاویز!
/bi.yǎ.vi.zid/	/bi.yǎ.viz/

to have

داشتَن

/dăš.tan/

Plural	Singular
Simple Present	
مضارع اخباری(حال ساده)	
(ما) داریم	(من) دارم
/(mă) dă.rim/	/(man) dă.ram/
(شما) دارید	(تو) داری
/(šo.mă) dă.rid/	/(to) dă.ri/
(آنها) دارند	(او/آن) دارد
/(ăn.hă) dă.rand/	/(u/ ăn) dă.rad/
Present Subjunctive	
مضارع التزامی	
(ما) بداریم	(من) بدارم
/(mă) be.dă.rim/	/(man) be.dă.ram/
(شما) بدارید	(تو) بداری
/(šo.mă) be.dă.rid/	/(to) be.dă.ri/
(آنها) بدارند	(او/آن) بدارد
/(ăn.hă) be.dă.rand/	/(u/ ăn) be.dă.rad/
Present Progressive	
مضارع مستمر(در جریان)	
(ما) داریم می داریم	(من) دارم می دارم
/(mă) dă.rim- mi.dă.rim/	/(man) dă.ram- mi.dă.ram/
(شما) دارید می دارید	(تو) داری می داری
/(šo.mă) dă.rid- mi.dă.rid/	/(to) dă.ri- mi.dă.ri/
(آنها) دارند می دارند	(او/آن) دارد می دارد
/(ăn.hă) dă.rand- mi.dă.rand/	/(u/ ăn) dă.rad- mi.dă.rad/

Simple Past	
ماضی مطلق (گذشته ساده)	
(ما) داشتیم	(من) داشتم
/(mǎ) dǎš.tim/	/(man) dǎš.tam/
(شما) داشتید	(تو) داشتی
/(šo.mǎ) dǎš.tid/	/(to) dǎš.ti/
(آنها) داشتند	(او/ آن) داشت
/(ǎn.hǎ) dǎš.tand/	/(u/ ǎn) dǎšt/

Imperfect Indicative	
ماضی استمراری	
(ما) می داشتیم	(من) می داشتم
/(mǎ) mi.dǎš.tim/	/(man) mi.dǎš.tam/
(شما) می داشتید	(تو) می داشتی
/(šo.mǎ) mi.dǎš.tid/	/(to) mi.dǎš.ti/
(آنها) می داشتند	(او/ آن) می داشت
/(ǎn.hǎ) mi.dǎš.tand/	/(u/ ǎn) mi.dǎšt/

Present Perfect	
ماضی نقلی	
(ما) داشته ایم	(من) داشته ام
/(mǎ) dǎš.te.im/	/(man) dǎš.te.am/
(شما) داشته اید	(تو) داشته ای
/(šo.mǎ) dǎš.te.id/	/(to) dǎš.te.i/
(آنها) داشته اند	(او/ آن) داشته است
/(ǎn.hǎ) dǎš.te.and/	/(u/ ǎn) dǎš.te- ast/

Past Perfect	
ماضی بعید	
(ما) داشته بودیم	(من) داشته بودم
/(mǎ) dǎš.te- bu.dim/	/(man) dǎš.te- bu.dam/
(شما) داشته بودید	(تو) داشته بودی
/(šo.mǎ) dǎš.te- bu.did/	/(to) dǎš.te- bu.di/
(آنها) داشته بودند	(او/ آن) داشته بود
/(ǎn.hǎ) dǎš.te- bu.dand/	/(u/ ǎn) dǎš.te- bud/

	Past Subjunctive
	ماضی التزامی
(ما) داشته باشیم	(من) داشته باشم
/(mă) dăš.te- bă.šim/	/(man) dăš.te- bă.šam/
(شما) داشته باشید	(تو) داشته باشی
/(šo.mă) dăš.te- bă.šid/	/(to) dăš.te- bă.ši/
(آنها) داشته باشند	(او/آن) داشته باشد
/(ăn.hă) dăš.te- bă.šand/	/(u/ ăn) dăš.te- bă.šad/

	Past Progressive
	ماضی مستمر(در جریان)
(ما) داشتیم می داشتیم	(من) داشتم می داشتم
/(mă) dăš.tim- mi.dăš.tim/	/(man) dăš.tam- mi.dăš.tam/
(شما) داشتید می داشتید	(تو) داشتی می داشتی
/(šo.mă) dăš.tid- mi.dăš.tid/	/(to) dăš.ti- mi.dăš.ti/
(آنها) داشتند می داشتند	(او/آن) داشت می داشت
/(ăn.hă) dăš.tand- mi.dăš.tand/	/(u/ ăn) dăšt- mi.dăšt/

	Simple Future
	مستقبل (آینده ساده)
(ما) خواهیم داشت	(من) خواهم داشت
/(mă) kă.him- dăšt/	/(man) kă.ham- dăšt/
(شما) خواهید داشت	(تو) خواهی داشت
/(šo.mă) kă.hid- dăšt/	/(to) kă.hi- dăšt/
(آنها) خواهند داشت	(او/آن) خواهد داشت
/(ăn.hă) kă.hand- dăšt/	/(u/ ăn) kă.had- dăšt/

	Command
	امر
بدارید! *	بدار! *
/be.dă.rid/	/be.dăr/

* also: داشته باش! داشته باشید!

to hear

شِنیدَن

/še.ni.dan/

Plural	Singular
Simple Present	
مضارع اخباری(حال ساده)	
(ما) می شنویم /(mă) mi.še.na.vim/	(من) می شنوم /(man) mi.še.na.vam/
(شما) می شنوید /(šo.mă) mi.še.na.vid/	(تو) می شنوی /(to) mi.še.na.vi/
(آنها) می شنوند /(ăn.hă) mi.še.na.vand/	(او/آن) می شنود /(u/ ăn) mi.še.na.vad/
Present Subjunctive	
مضارع التزامی	
(ما) بشنویم /(mă) be.še.na.vim/	(من) بشنوم /(man) be.še.na.vam/
(شما) بشنوید /(šo.mă) be.še.na.vid/	(تو) بشنوی /(to) be.še.na.vi/
(آنها) بشنوند /(ăn.hă) be.še.na.vand/	(او/آن) بشنود /(u/ ăn) be.še.na.vad/
Present Progressive	
مضارع مستمر(در جریان)	
(ما) داریم می شنویم /(mă) dă.rim- mi.še.na.vim/	(من) دارم می شنوم /(man) dă.ram- mi.še.na.vam/
(شما) دارید می شنوید /(šo.mă) dă.rid- mi.še.na.vid/	(تو) داری می شنوی /(to) dă.ri- mi.še.na.vi/
(آنها) دارند می شنوند /(ăn.hă) dă.rand- mi.še.na.vand/	(او/آن) دارد می شنود /(u/ ăn) dă.rad- mi.še.na.vad/

Simple Past
ماضی مطلق (گذشته ساده)

(ما) شنیدیم	(من) شنیدم
/(mǎ) še.ni.dim/	/(man) še.ni.dam/
(شما) شنیدید	(تو) شنیدی
/(šo.mǎ) še.ni.did/	/(to) še.ni.di/
(آنها) شنیدند	(او/آن) شنید
/(ǎn.hǎ) še.ni.dand/	/(u/ ǎn) še.nid/

Imperfect Indicative
ماضی استمراری

(ما) می شنیدیم	(من) می شنیدم
/(mǎ) mi.še.ni.dim/	/(man) mi.še.ni.dam/
(شما) می شنیدید	(تو) می شنیدی
/(šo.mǎ) mi.še.ni.did/	/(to) mi.še.ni.di/
(آنها) می شنیدند	(او/آن) می شنید
/(ǎn.hǎ) mi.še.ni.dand/	/(u/ ǎn) mi.še.nid/

Present Perfect
ماضی نقلی

(ما) شنیده ایم	(من) شنیده ام
/(mǎ) še.ni.de.im/	/(man) še.ni.de.am/
(شما) شنیده اید	(تو) شنیده ای
/(šo.mǎ) še.ni.de.id/	/(to) še.ni.de.i/
(آنها) شنیده اند	(او/آن) شنیده است
/(ǎn.hǎ) še.ni.de.and/	/(u/ ǎn) še.ni.de- ast/

Past Perfect
ماضی بعید

(ما) شنیده بودیم	(من) شنیده بودم
/(mǎ) še.ni.de- bu.dim/	/(man) še.ni.de- bu.dam/
(شما) شنیده بودید	(تو) شنیده بودی
/(šo.mǎ) še.ni.de- bu.did/	/(to) še.ni.de- bu.di/
(آنها) شنیده بودند	(او/آن) شنیده بود
/(ǎn.hǎ) še.ni.de- bu.dand/	/(u/ ǎn) še.ni.de- bud/

Past Subjunctive
ماضی التزامی

(من) شنیده باشم	(ما) شنیده باشیم
/(man) še.ni.de- bă.šam/	/(mă) še.ni.de- bă.šim/
(تو) شنیده باشی	(شما) شنیده باشید
/(to) še.ni.de- bă.ši/	/(šo.mă) še.ni.de- bă.šid/
(او/ آن) شنیده باشد	(آنها) شنیده باشند
/(u/ ăn) še.ni.de- bă.šad/	/(ăn.hă) še.ni.de- bă.šand/

Past Progressive
ماضی مستمر(در جریان)

(من) داشتم می شنیدم	(ما) داشتیم می شنیدیم
/(man) dăš.tam- mi.še.ni.dam/	/(mă) dăš.tim- mi.še.ni.dim/
(تو) داشتی می شنیدی	(شما) داشتید می شنیدید
/(to) dăš.ti- mi.še.ni.di/	/(šo.mă) dăš.tid- mi.še.ni.did/
(او/ آن) داشت می شنید	(آنها) داشتند می شنیدند
/(u/ ăn) dăšt- mi.še.nid/	/(ăn.hă) dăš.tand- mi.še.ni.dand/

Simple Future
مستقبل (آینده ساده)

(من) خواهم شنید	(ما) خواهیم شنید
/(man) kă.ham- še.nid/	/(mă) kă.him- še.nid/
(تو) خواهی شنید	(شما) خواهید شنید
/(to) kă.hi- še.nid/	/(šo.mă) kă.hid- še.nid/
(او/ آن) خواهد شنید	(آنها) خواهند شنید
/(u/ ăn) kă.had- še.nid/	/(ăn.hă) kă.hand- še.nid/

Command
امر

بشنو!	بشنوید!
/be.še.no/	/be.še.na.vid/

to hit

زَدَن

/za.dan/

Plural	Singular
Simple Present مضارع اخباری(حال ساده)	
(ما) می زنیم /(mă) mi.za.nim/	(من) می زنم /(man) mi.za.nam/
(شما) می زنید /(šo.mă) mi.za.nid/	(تو) می زنی /(to) mi.za.ni/
(آنها) می زنند /(ăn.hă) mi.za.nand/	(او/آن) می زند /(u/ ăn) mi.za.nad/

Plural	Singular
Present Subjunctive مضارع التزامی	
(ما) بزنیم /(mă) be.za.nim/	(من) بزنم /(man) be.za.nam/
(شما) بزنید /(šo.mă) be.za.nid/	(تو) بزنی /(to) be.za.ni/
(آنها) بزنند /(ăn.hă) be.za.nand/	(او/آن) بزند /(u/ ăn) be.za.nad/

Plural	Singular
Present Progressive مضارع مستمر(در جریان)	
(ما) داریم می زنیم /(mă) dă.rim- mi.za.nim/	(من) دارم می زنم /(man) dă.ram- mi.za.nam/
(شما) دارید می زنید /(šo.mă) dă.rid- mi.za.nid/	(تو) داری می زنی /(to) dă.ri- mi.za.ni/
(آنها) دارند می زنند /(ăn.hă) dă.rand- mi.za.nand/	(او/آن) دارد می زند /(u/ ăn) dă.rad- mi.za.nad/

Simple Past
ماضی مطلق (گذشته ساده)

(ما) زدیم	(من) زدم
/(mǎ) za.dim/	/(man) za.dam/
(شما) زدید	(تو) زدی
/(šo.mǎ) za.did/	/(to) za.di/
(آنها) زدند	(او/آن) زد
/(ǎn.hǎ) za.dand/	/(u/ ǎn) zad/

Imperfect Indicative
ماضی استمراری

(ما) می زدیم	(من) می زدم
/(mǎ) mi.za.dim/	/(man) mi.za.dam/
(شما) می زدید	(تو) می زدی
/(šo.mǎ) mi.za.did/	/(to) mi.za.di/
(آنها) می زدند	(او/آن) می زد
/(ǎn.hǎ) mi.za.dand/	/(u/ ǎn) mi.zad/

Present Perfect
ماضی نقلی

(ما) زده ایم	(من) زده ام
/(mǎ) za.de.im/	/(man) za.de.am/
(شما) زده اید	(تو) زده ای
/(šo.mǎ) za.de.id/	/(to) za.de.i/
(آنها) زده اند	(او/آن) زده است
/(ǎn.hǎ) za.de.and/	/(u/ ǎn) za.de- ast/

Past Perfect
ماضی بعید

(ما) زده بودیم	(من) زده بودم
/(mǎ) za.de- bu.dim/	/(man) za.de- bu.dam/
(شما) زده بودید	(تو) زده بودی
/(šo.mǎ) za.de- bu.did/	/(to) za.de- bu.di/
(آنها) زده بودند	(او/آن) زده بود
/(ǎn.hǎ) za.de- bu.dand/	/(u/ ǎn) za.de- bud/

Past Subjunctive	
ماضی التزامی	
(ما) زده باشیم	(من) زده باشم
/(mǎ) za.de- bǎ.šim/	/(man) za.de- bǎ.šam/
(شما) زده باشید	(تو) زده باشی
/(šo.mǎ) za.de- bǎ.šid/	/(to) za.de- bǎ.ši/
(آنها) زده باشند	(او/آن) زده باشد
/(ǎn.hǎ) za.de- bǎ.šand/	/(u/ ǎn) za.de- bǎ.šad/

Past Progressive	
ماضی مستمر(در جریان)	
(ما) داشتیم می زدیم	(من) داشتم می زدم
/(mǎ) dǎš.tim- mi.za.dim/	/(man) dǎš.tam- mi.za.dam/
(شما) داشتید می زدید	(تو) داشتی می زدی
/(šo.mǎ) dǎš.tid- mi.za.did/	/(to) dǎš.ti- mi.za.di/
(آنها) داشتند می زدند	(او/آن) داشت می زد
/(ǎn.hǎ) dǎš.tand- mi.za.dand/	/(u/ ǎn) dǎšt- mi.zad/

Simple Future	
مستقبل (آینده ساده)	
(ما) خواهیم زد	(من) خواهم زد
/(mǎ) ǩǎ.him- zad/	/(man) ǩǎ.ham- zad/
(شما) خواهید زد	(تو) خواهی زد
/(šo.mǎ) ǩǎ.hid- zad/	/(to) ǩǎ.hi- zad/
(آنها) خواهند زد	(او/آن) خواهد زد
/(ǎn.hǎ) ǩǎ.hand- zad/	/(u/ ǎn) ǩǎ.had- zad/

Command	
امر	
بزنید!	بزن!
/be.za.nid/	/be.zan/

to hurry

شِتِافتَن

/še.tăf.tan/

Plural	Singular
Simple Present <div dir="rtl">مضارع اخباری(حال ساده)</div>	
(ما) می شتابیم /(mă) mi.še.tă.bim/	(من) می شتابم /(man) mi.še.tă.bam/
(شما) می شتابید /(šo.mă) mi.še.tă.bid/	(تو) می شتابی /(to) mi.še.tă.bi/
(آنها) می شتابند /(ăn.hă) mi.še.tă.band/	(او/آن) می شتابد /(u/ ăn) mi.še.tă.bad/
Present Subjunctive <div dir="rtl">مضارع التزامی</div>	
(ما) بشتابیم /(mă) be.še.tă.bim/	(من) بشتابم /(man) be.še.tă.bam/
(شما) بشتابید /(šo.mă) be.še.tă.bid/	(تو) بشتابی /(to) be.še.tă.bi/
(آنها) بشتابند /(ăn.hă) be.še.tă.band/	(او/آن) بشتابد /(u/ ăn) be.še.tă.bad/
Present Progressive <div dir="rtl">مضارع مستمر(در جریان)</div>	
(ما) داریم می شتابیم /(mă) dă.rim- mi.še.tă.bim/	(من) دارم می شتابم /(man) dă.ram- mi.še.tă.bam/
(شما) دارید می شتابید /(šo.mă) dă.rid- mi.še.tă.bid/	(تو) داری می شتابی /(to) dă.ri- mi.še.tă.bi/
(آنها) دارند می شتابند /(ăn.hă) dă.rand- mi.še.tă.band/	(او/آن) دارد می شتابد /(u/ ăn) dă.rad- mi.še.tă.bad/

Simple Past
ماضی مطلق (گذشته ساده)

(ما) شتافتیم	(من) شتافتم
/(mǎ) še.tǎf.tim/	/(man) še.tǎf.tam/
(شما) شتافتید	(تو) شتافتی
/(šo.mǎ) še.tǎf.tid/	/(to) še.tǎf.ti/
(آنها) شتافتند	(او/ آن) شتافت
/(ǎn.hǎ) še.tǎf.tand/	/(u/ ǎn) še.tǎft/

Imperfect Indicative
ماضی استمراری

(ما) می شتافتیم	(من) می شتافتم
/(mǎ) mi.še.tǎf.tim/	/(man) mi.še.tǎf.tam/
(شما) می شتافتید	(تو) می شتافتی
/(šo.mǎ) mi.še.tǎf.tid/	/(to) mi.še.tǎf.ti/
(آنها) می شتافتند	(او/ آن) می شتافت
/(ǎn.hǎ) mi.še.tǎf.tand/	/(u/ ǎn) mi.še.tǎft/

Present Perfect
ماضی نقلی

(ما) شتافته ایم	(من) شتافته ام
/(mǎ) še.tǎf.te.im/	/(man) še.tǎf.te.am/
(شما) شتافته اید	(تو) شتافته ای
/(šo.mǎ) še.tǎf.te.id/	/(to) še.tǎf.te.i/
(آنها) شتافته اند	(او/ آن) شتافته است
/(ǎn.hǎ) še.tǎf.te.and/	/(u/ ǎn) še.tǎf.te- ast/

Past Perfect
ماضی بعید

(ما) شتافته بودیم	(من) شتافته بودم
/(mǎ) še.tǎf.te- bu.dim/	/(man) še.tǎf.te- bu.dam/
(شما) شتافته بودید	(تو) شتافته بودی
/(šo.mǎ) še.tǎf.te- bu.did/	/(to) še.tǎf.te- bu.di/
(آنها) شتافته بودند	(او/ آن) شتافته بود
/(ǎn.hǎ) še.tǎf.te- bu.dand/	/(u/ ǎn) še.tǎf.te- bud/

135

Past Subjunctive	
ماضی التزامی	
(ما) شتافته باشیم	(من) شتافته باشم
/(mǎ) še.tǎf.te- bǎ.šim/	/(man) še.tǎf.te- bǎ.šam/
(شما) شتافته باشید	(تو) شتافته باشی
/(šo.mǎ) še.tǎf.te- bǎ.šid/	/(to) še.tǎf.te- bǎ.ši/
(آنها) شتافته باشند	(او/آن) شتافته باشد
/(ǎn.hǎ) še.tǎf.te- bǎ.šand/	/(u/ ǎn) še.tǎf.te- bǎ.šad/

Past Progressive	
ماضی مستمر(در جریان)	
(ما) داشتیم می شتافتیم	(من) داشتم می شتافتم
/(mǎ) dǎš.tim- mi.še.tǎf.tim/	/(man) dǎš.tam- mi.še.tǎf.tam/
(شما) داشتید می شتافتید	(تو) داشتی می شتافتی
/(šo.mǎ) dǎš.tid- mi.še.tǎf.tid/	/(to) dǎš.ti- mi.še.tǎf.ti/
(آنها) داشتند می شتافتند	(او/آن) داشت می شتافت
/(ǎn.hǎ) dǎš.tand- mi.še.tǎf.tand/	/(u/ ǎn) dǎšt- mi.še.tǎft/

Simple Future	
مستقبل (آینده ساده)	
(ما) خواهیم شتافت	(من) خواهم شتافت
/(mǎ) ḱǎ.him- še.tǎft/	/(man) ḱǎ.ham- še.tǎft/
(شما) خواهید شتافت	(تو) خواهی شتافت
/(šo.mǎ) ḱǎ.hid- še.tǎft/	/(to) ḱǎ.hi- še.tǎft/
(آنها) خواهند شتافت	(او/آن) خواهد شتافت
/(ǎn.hǎ) ḱǎ.hand- še.tǎft/	/(u/ ǎn) ḱǎ.had- še.tǎft/

Command	
امر	
بشتابید!	بشتاب!
/be.še.tǎ.bid/	/be.še.tǎb/

136

to inscribe

نِگاشتَن

/ne.gǎš.tan/

Plural	Singular
Simple Present مضارع اخباری(حال ساده)	
(ما) می نگاریم /(mǎ) mi.ne.gǎ.rim/	(من) می نگارم /(man) mi.ne.gǎ.ram/
(شما) می نگارید /(šo.mǎ) mi.ne.gǎ.rid/	(تو) می نگاری /(to) mi.ne.gǎ.ri/
(آنها) می نگارند /(ǎn.hǎ) mi.ne.gǎ.rand/	(او/آن) می نگارد /(u/ ǎn) mi.ne.gǎ.rad/
Present Subjunctive مضارع التزامی	
(ما) بنگاریم /(mǎ) be.ne.gǎ.rim/	(من) بنگارم /(man) be.ne.gǎ.ram/
(شما) بنگارید /(šo.mǎ) be.ne.gǎ.rid/	(تو) بنگاری /(to) be.ne.gǎ.ri/
(آنها) بنگارند /(ǎn.hǎ) be.ne.gǎ.rand/	(او/آن) بنگارد /(u/ ǎn) be.ne.gǎ.rad/
Present Progressive مضارع مستمر(در جریان)	
(ما) داریم می نگاریم /(mǎ) dǎ.rim- mi.ne.gǎ.rim/	(من) دارم می نگارم /(man) dǎ.ram- mi.ne.gǎ.ram/
(شما) دارید می نگارید /(šo.mǎ) dǎ.rid- mi.ne.gǎ.rid/	(تو) داری می نگاری /(to) dǎ.ri- mi.ne.gǎ.ri/
(آنها) دارند می نگارند /(ǎn.hǎ) dǎ.rand- mi.ne.gǎ.rand/	(او/آن) دارد می نگارد /(u/ ǎn) dǎ.rad- mi.ne.gǎ.rad/

Simple Past
ماضی مطلق (گذشته ساده)

(ما) نگاشتیم	(من) نگاشتم
/(mǎ) ne.gǎš.tim/	/(man) ne.gǎš.tam/
(شما) نگاشتید	(تو) نگاشتی
/(šo.mǎ) ne.gǎš.tid/	/(to) ne.gǎš.ti/
(آنها) نگاشتند	(او/آن) نگاشت
/(ǎn.hǎ) ne.gǎš.tand/	/(u/ ǎn) ne.gǎšt/

Imperfect Indicative
ماضی استمراری

(ما) می نگاشتیم	(من) می نگاشتم
/(mǎ) mi.ne.gǎš.tim/	/(man) mi.ne.gǎš.tam/
(شما) می نگاشتید	(تو) می نگاشتی
/(šo.mǎ) mi.ne.gǎš.tid/	/(to) mi.ne.gǎš.ti/
(آنها) می نگاشتند	(او/آن) می نگاشت
/(ǎn.hǎ) mi.ne.gǎš.tand/	/(u/ ǎn) mi.ne.gǎšt/

Present Perfect
ماضی نقلی

(ما) نگاشته ایم	(من) نگاشته ام
/(mǎ) ne.gǎš.te.im/	/(man) ne.gǎš.te.am/
(شما) نگاشته اید	(تو) نگاشته ای
/(šo.mǎ) ne.gǎš.te.id/	/(to) ne.gǎš.te.i/
(آنها) نگاشته اند	(او/آن) نگاشته است
/(ǎn.hǎ) ne.gǎš.te.and/	/(u/ ǎn) ne.gǎš.te- ast/

Past Perfect
ماضی بعید

(ما) نگاشته بودیم	(من) نگاشته بودم
/(mǎ) ne.gǎš.te- bu.dim/	/(man) ne.gǎš.te- bu.dam/
(شما) نگاشته بودید	(تو) نگاشته بودی
/(šo.mǎ) ne.gǎš.te- bu.did/	/(to) ne.gǎš.te- bu.di/
(آنها) نگاشته بودند	(او/آن) نگاشته بود
/(ǎn.hǎ) ne.gǎš.te- bu.dand/	/(u/ ǎn) ne.gǎš.te- bud/

138

Past Subjunctive	
ماضی التزامی	
(ما) نگاشته باشیم	(من) نگاشته باشم
/(mǎ) ne.gǎš.te- bǎ.šim/	/(man) ne.gǎš.te- bǎ.šam/
(شما) نگاشته باشید	(تو) نگاشته باشی
/(šo.mǎ) ne.gǎš.te- bǎ.šid/	/(to) ne.gǎš.te- bǎ.ši/
(آنها) نگاشته باشند	(او/آن) نگاشته باشد
/(ǎn.hǎ) ne.gǎš.te- bǎ.šand/	/(u/ ǎn) ne.gǎš.te- bǎ.šad/

Past Progressive	
ماضی مستمر (در جریان)	
(ما) داشتیم می نگاشتیم	(من) داشتم می نگاشتم
/(mǎ) dǎš.tim- mi.ne.gǎš.tim/	/(man) dǎš.tam- mi.ne.gǎš.tam/
(شما) داشتید می نگاشتید	(تو) داشتی می نگاشتی
/(šo.mǎ) dǎš.tid- mi.ne.gǎš.tid/	/(to) dǎš.ti- mi.ne.gǎš.ti/
(آنها) داشتند می نگاشتند	(او/آن) داشت می نگاشت
/(ǎn.hǎ) dǎš.tand- mi.ne.gǎš.tand/	/(u/ ǎn) dǎšt- mi.ne.gǎšt/

Simple Future	
مستقبل (آینده ساده)	
(ما) خواهیم نگاشت	(من) خواهم نگاشت
/(mǎ) ǩǎ.him- ne.gǎšt/	/(man) ǩǎ.ham- ne.gǎšt/
(شما) خواهید نگاشت	(تو) خواهی نگاشت
/(šo.mǎ) ǩǎ.hid- ne.gǎšt/	/(to) ǩǎ.hi- ne.gǎšt/
(آنها) خواهند نگاشت	(او/آن) خواهد نگاشت
/(ǎn.hǎ) ǩǎ.hand- ne.gǎšt/	/(u/ ǎn) ǩǎ.had- ne.gǎšt/

Command	
امر	
بنگارید!	بنگار!
/be.ne.gǎ.rid/	/be.ne.gǎr/

139

to join

پیوَستَن

/pey.vas.tan/

Plural	Singular
Simple Present <div dir="rtl">مضارع اخباری(حال ساده)</div>	
(ما) می پیوندیم /(mǎ) mi.pey.van.dim/	(من) می پیوندم /(man) mi.pey.van.dam/
(شما) می پیوندید /(šo.mǎ) mi.pey.van.did/	(تو) می پیوندی /(to) mi.pey.van.di/
(آنها) می پیوندند /(ǎn.hǎ) mi.pey.van.dand/	(او/آن) می پیوندد /(u/ ǎn) mi.pey.van.dad/
Present Subjunctive <div dir="rtl">مضارع التزامی</div>	
(ما) بپیوندیم /(mǎ) be.pey.van.dim/	(من) بپیوندم /(man) be.pey.van.dam/
(شما) بپیوندید /(šo.mǎ) be.pey.van.did/	(تو) بپیوندی /(to) be.pey.van.di/
(آنها) بپیوندند /(ǎn.hǎ) be.pey.van.dand/	(او/آن) بپیوندد /(u/ ǎn) be.pey.van.dad/
Present Progressive <div dir="rtl">مضارع مستمر(در جریان)</div>	
(ما) داریم می پیوندیم /(mǎ) dǎ.rim- mi.pey.van.dim/	(من) دارم می پیوندم /(man) dǎ.ram- mi.pey.van.dam/
(شما) دارید می پیوندید /(šo.mǎ) dǎ.rid- mi.pey.van.did/	(تو) داری می پیوندی /(to) dǎ.ri- mi.pey.van.di/
(آنها) دارند می پیوندند /(ǎn.hǎ) dǎ.rand- mi.pey.van.dand/	(او/آن) دارد می پیوندد /(u/ ǎn) dǎ.rad- mi.pey.van.dad/

<table>
<tr><td colspan="2" align="center">**Simple Past**
ماضی مطلق (گذشته ساده)</td></tr>
<tr>
<td align="center">(ما) پیوستیم
/(mǎ) pey.vas.tim/</td>
<td align="center">(من) پیوستم
/(man) pey.vas.tam/</td>
</tr>
<tr>
<td align="center">(شما) پیوستید
/(šo.mǎ) pey.vas.tid/</td>
<td align="center">(تو) پیوستی
/(to) pey.vas.ti/</td>
</tr>
<tr>
<td align="center">(آنها) پیوستند
/(ǎn.hǎ) pey.vas.tand/</td>
<td align="center">(او/آن) پیوست
/(u/ ǎn) pey.vast/</td>
</tr>
</table>

<table>
<tr><td colspan="2" align="center">**Imperfect Indicative**
ماضی استمراری</td></tr>
<tr>
<td align="center">(ما) می پیوستیم
/(mǎ) mi.pey.vas.tim/</td>
<td align="center">(من) می پیوستم
/(man) mi.pey.vas.tam/</td>
</tr>
<tr>
<td align="center">(شما) می پیوستید
/(šo.mǎ) mi.pey.vas.tid/</td>
<td align="center">(تو) می پیوستی
/(to) mi.pey.vas.ti/</td>
</tr>
<tr>
<td align="center">(آنها) می پیوستند
/(ǎn.hǎ) mi.pey.vas.tand/</td>
<td align="center">(او/آن) می پیوست
/(u/ ǎn) mi.pey.vast/</td>
</tr>
</table>

<table>
<tr><td colspan="2" align="center">**Present Perfect**
ماضی نقلی</td></tr>
<tr>
<td align="center">(ما) پیوسته ایم
/(mǎ) pey.vas.te.im/</td>
<td align="center">(من) پیوسته ام
/(man) pey.vas.te.am/</td>
</tr>
<tr>
<td align="center">(شما) پیوسته اید
/(šo.mǎ) pey.vas.te.id/</td>
<td align="center">(تو) پیوسته ای
/(to) pey.vas.te.i/</td>
</tr>
<tr>
<td align="center">(آنها) پیوسته اند
/(ǎn.hǎ) pey.vas.te.and/</td>
<td align="center">(او/آن) پیوسته است
/(u/ ǎn) pey.vas.te- ast/</td>
</tr>
</table>

<table>
<tr><td colspan="2" align="center">**Past Perfect**
ماضی بعید</td></tr>
<tr>
<td align="center">(ما) پیوسته بودیم
/(mǎ) pey.vas.te- bu.dim/</td>
<td align="center">(من) پیوسته بودم
/(man) pey.vas.te- bu.dam/</td>
</tr>
<tr>
<td align="center">(شما) پیوسته بودید
/(šo.mǎ) pey.vas.te- bu.did/</td>
<td align="center">(تو) پیوسته بودی
/(to) pey.vas.te- bu.di/</td>
</tr>
<tr>
<td align="center">(آنها) پیوسته بودند
/(ǎn.hǎ) pey.vas.te- bu.dand/</td>
<td align="center">(او/آن) پیوسته بود
/(u/ ǎn) pey.vas.te- bud/</td>
</tr>
</table>

141

Past Subjunctive
ماضی التزامی

(ما) پیوسته باشیم	(من) پیوسته باشم
/(mă) pey.vas.te- bă.šim/	/(man) pey.vas.te- bă.šam/
(شما) پیوسته باشید	(تو) پیوسته باشی
/(šo.mă) pey.vas.te- bă.šid/	/(to) pey.vas.te- bă.ši/
(آنها) پیوسته باشند	(او/آن) پیوسته باشد
/(ăn.hă) pey.vas.te- bă.šand/	/(u/ ăn) pey.vas.te- bă.šad/

Past Progressive
ماضی مستمر(در جریان)

(ما) داشتیم می پیوستیم	(من) داشتم می پیوستم
/(mă) dăš.tim- mi.pey.vas.tim/	/(man) dăš.tam- mi.pey.vas.tam/
(شما) داشتید می پیوستید	(تو) داشتی می پیوستی
/(šo.mă) dăš.tid- mi.pey.vas.tid/	/(to) dăš.ti- mi.pey.vas.ti/
(آنها) داشتند می پیوستند	(او/آن) داشت می پیوست
/(ăn.hă) dăš.tand- mi.pey.vas.tand/	/(u/ ăn) dăšt- mi.pey.vast/

Simple Future
مستقبل (آینده ساده)

(ما) خواهیم پیوست	(من) خواهم پیوست
/(mă) kă.him- pey.vast/	/(man) kă.ham- pey.vast/
(شما) خواهید پیوست	(تو) خواهی پیوست
/(šo.mă) kă.hid- pey.vast/	/(to) kă.hi- pey.vast/
(آنها) خواهند پیوست	(او/آن) خواهد پیوست
/(ăn.hă) kă.hand- pey.vast/	/(u/ ăn) kă.had- pey.vast/

Command
امر

بپیوندید!	بپیوند!
/be.pey.van.did/	/be.pey.vand/

to kindle

اَفروختَن

/af.ruǩ.tan/

Plural	Singular
Simple Present مضارع اخباری(حال ساده)	
(ما) می افروزیم /(mǎ) mi.af.ru.zim/	(من) می افروزم /(man) mi.af.ru.zam/
(شما) می افروزید /(šo.mǎ) mi.af.ru.zid/	(تو) می افروزی /(to) mi.af.ru.zi/
(آنها) می افروزند /(ǎn.hǎ) mi.af.ru.zand/	(او/آن) می افروزد /(u/ ǎn) mi.af.ru.zad/

Plural	Singular
Present Subjunctive مضارع التزامی	
(ما) بیفروزیم /(mǎ) bi.yaf.ru.zim/	(من) بیفروزم /(man) bi.yaf.ru.zam/
(شما) بیفروزید /(šo.mǎ) bi.yaf.ru.zid/	(تو) بیفروزی /(to) bi.yaf.ru.zi/
(آنها) بیفروزند /(ǎn.hǎ) bi.yaf.ru.zand/	(او/آن) بیفروزد /(u/ ǎn) bi.yaf.ru.zad/

Plural	Singular
Present Progressive مضارع مستمر(در جریان)	
(ما) داریم می افروزیم /(mǎ) dǎ.rim- mi.af.ru.zim/	(من) دارم می افروزم /(man) dǎ.ram- mi.af.ru.zam/
(شما) دارید می افروزید /(šo.mǎ) dǎ.rid- mi.af.ru.zid/	(تو) داری می افروزی /(to) dǎ.ri- mi.af.ru.zi/
(آنها) دارند می افروزند /(ǎn.hǎ) dǎ.rand- mi.af.ru.zand/	(او/آن) دارد می افروزد /(u/ ǎn) dǎ.rad- mi.af.ru.zad/

Simple Past
ماضی مطلق (گذشته ساده)

(ما) افروختیم	(من) افروختم
/(mǎ) af.ruǩ.tim/	/(man) af.ruǩ.tam/
(شما) افروختید	(تو) افروختی
/(šo.mǎ) af.ruǩ.tid/	/(to) af.ruǩ.ti/
(آنها) افروختند	(او/آن) افروخت
/(ǎn.hǎ) af.ruǩ.tand/	/(u/ ǎn) af.ruǩt/

Imperfect Indicative
ماضی استمراری

(ما) می افروختیم	(من) می افروختم
/(mǎ) mi.af.ruǩ.tim/	/(man) mi.af.ruǩ.tam/
(شما) می افروختید	(تو) می افروختی
/(šo.mǎ) mi.af.ruǩ.tid/	/(to) mi.af.ruǩ.ti/
(آنها) می افروختند	(او/آن) می افروخت
/(ǎn.hǎ) mi.af.ruǩ.tand/	/(u/ ǎn) mi.af.ruǩt/

Present Perfect
ماضی نقلی

(ما) افروخته ایم	(من) افروخته ام
/(mǎ) af.ruǩ.te.im/	/(man) af.ruǩ.te.am/
(شما) افروخته اید	(تو) افروخته ای
/(šo.mǎ) af.ruǩ.te.id/	/(to) af.ruǩ.te.i/
(آنها) افروخته اند	(او/آن) افروخته است
/(ǎn.hǎ) af.ruǩ.te.and/	/(u/ ǎn) af.ruǩ.te- ast/

Past Perfect
ماضی بعید

(ما) افروخته بودیم	(من) افروخته بودم
/(mǎ) af.ruǩ.te- bu.dim/	/(man) af.ruǩ.te- bu.dam/
(شما) افروخته بودید	(تو) افروخته بودی
/(šo.mǎ) af.ruǩ.te- bu.did/	/(to) af.ruǩ.te- bu.di/
(آنها) افروخته بودند	(او/آن) افروخته بود
/(ǎn.hǎ) af.ruǩ.te- bu.dand/	/(u/ ǎn) af.ruǩ.te- bud/

144

Past Subjunctive	
ماضی التزامی	
(ما) افروخته باشیم	(من) افروخته باشم
/(mǎ) af.ruǩ.te- bǎ.šim/	/(man) af.ruǩ.te- bǎ.šam/
(شما) افروخته باشید	(تو) افروخته باشی
/(šo.mǎ) af.ruǩ.te- bǎ.šid/	/(to) af.ruǩ.te- bǎ.ši/
(آنها) افروخته باشند	(او/آن) افروخته باشد
/(ǎn.hǎ) af.ruǩ.te- bǎ.šand/	/(u/ ǎn) af.ruǩ.te- bǎ.šad/

Past Progressive	
ماضی مستمر(در جریان)	
(ما) داشتیم می افروختیم	(من) داشتم می افروختم
/(mǎ) dǎš.tim- mi.af.ruǩ.tim/	/(man) dǎš.tam- mi.af.ruǩ.tam/
(شما) داشتید می افروختید	(تو) داشتی می افروختی
/(šo.mǎ) dǎš.tid- mi.af.ruǩ.tid/	/(to) dǎš.ti- mi.af.ruǩ.ti/
(آنها) داشتند می افروختند	(او/آن) داشت می افروخت
/(ǎn.hǎ) dǎš.tand- mi.af.ruǩ.tand/	/(u/ ǎn) dǎšt- mi.af.ruǩt/

Simple Future	
مستقبل (آینده ساده)	
(ما) خواهیم افروخت	(من) خواهم افروخت
/(mǎ) ǩǎ.him- af.ruǩt/	/(man) ǩǎ.ham- af.ruǩt/
(شما) خواهید افروخت	(تو) خواهی افروخت
/(šo.mǎ) ǩǎ.hid- af.ruǩt/	/(to) ǩǎ.hi- af.ruǩt/
(آنها) خواهند افروخت	(او/آن) خواهد افروخت
/(ǎn.hǎ) ǩǎ.hand- af.ruǩt/	/(u/ ǎn) ǩǎ.had- af.ruǩt/

Command	
امر	
بیفروزید!	بیفروز!
/bi.yaf.ru.zid/	/bi.yaf.ruz/

145

to know

دانِستَن

/dǎ.nes.tan/

Plural	Singular
Simple Present مضارع اخباری(حال ساده)	
(ما) می دانیم /(mǎ) mi.dǎ.nim/	(من) می دانم /(man) mi.dǎ.nam/
(شما) می دانید /(šo.mǎ) mi.dǎ.nid/	(تو) می دانی /(to) mi.dǎ.ni/
(آنها) می دانند /(ǎn.hǎ) mi.dǎ.nand/	(او/آن) می داند /(u/ ǎn) mi.dǎ.nad/
Present Subjunctive مضارع التزامی	
(ما) بدانیم /(mǎ) be.dǎ.nim/	(من) بدانم /(man) be.dǎ.nam/
(شما) بدانید /(šo.mǎ) be.dǎ.nid/	(تو) بدانی /(to) be.dǎ.ni/
(آنها) بدانند /(ǎn.hǎ) be.dǎ.nand/	(او/آن) بداند /(u/ ǎn) be.dǎ.nad/
Present Progressive مضارع مستمر(در جریان)	
(ما) داریم می دانیم /(mǎ) dǎ.rim- mi.dǎ.nim/	(من) دارم می دانم /(man) dǎ.ram- mi.dǎ.nam/
(شما) دارید می دانید /(šo.mǎ) dǎ.rid- mi.dǎ.nid/	(تو) داری می دانی /(to) dǎ.ri- mi.dǎ.ni/
(آنها) دارند می دانند /(ǎn.hǎ) dǎ.rand- mi.dǎ.nand/	(او/آن) دارد می داند /(u/ ǎn) dǎ.rad- mi.dǎ.nad/

146

<table>
<tr><td colspan="2" align="center">Simple Past
ماضی مطلق (گذشته ساده)</td></tr>
<tr><td align="center">(ما) دانستیم
/(mǎ) dǎ.nes.tim/</td><td align="center">(من) دانستم
/(man) dǎ.nes.tam/</td></tr>
<tr><td align="center">(شما) دانستید
/(šo.mǎ) dǎ.nes.tid/</td><td align="center">(تو) دانستی
/(to) dǎ.nes.ti/</td></tr>
<tr><td align="center">(آنها) دانستند
/(ǎn.hǎ) dǎ.nes.tand/</td><td align="center">(او/آن) دانست
/(u/ ǎn) dǎ.nest/</td></tr>
</table>

<table>
<tr><td colspan="2" align="center">Imperfect Indicative
ماضی استمراری</td></tr>
<tr><td align="center">(ما) می دانستیم
/(mǎ) mi.dǎ.nes.tim/</td><td align="center">(من) می دانستم
/(man) mi.dǎ.nes.tam/</td></tr>
<tr><td align="center">(شما) می دانستید
/(šo.mǎ) mi.dǎ.nes.tid/</td><td align="center">(تو) می دانستی
/(to) mi.dǎ.nes.ti/</td></tr>
<tr><td align="center">(آنها) می دانستند
/(ǎn.hǎ) mi.dǎ.nes.tand/</td><td align="center">(او/آن) می دانست
/(u/ ǎn) mi.dǎ.nest/</td></tr>
</table>

<table>
<tr><td colspan="2" align="center">Present Perfect
ماضی نقلی</td></tr>
<tr><td align="center">(ما) دانسته ایم
/(mǎ) dǎ.nes.te.im/</td><td align="center">(من) دانسته ام
/(man) dǎ.nes.te.am/</td></tr>
<tr><td align="center">(شما) دانسته اید
/(šo.mǎ) dǎ.nes.te.id/</td><td align="center">(تو) دانسته ای
/(to) dǎ.nes.te.i/</td></tr>
<tr><td align="center">(آنها) دانسته اند
/(ǎn.hǎ) dǎ.nes.te.and/</td><td align="center">(او/آن) دانسته است
/(u/ ǎn) dǎ.nes.te- ast/</td></tr>
</table>

<table>
<tr><td colspan="2" align="center">Past Perfect
ماضی بعید</td></tr>
<tr><td align="center">(ما) دانسته بودیم
/(mǎ) dǎ.nes.te- bu.dim/</td><td align="center">(من) دانسته بودم
/(man) dǎ.nes.te- bu.dam/</td></tr>
<tr><td align="center">(شما) دانسته بودید
/(šo.mǎ) dǎ.nes.te- bu.did/</td><td align="center">(تو) دانسته بودی
/(to) dǎ.nes.te- bu.di/</td></tr>
<tr><td align="center">(آنها) دانسته بودند
/(ǎn.hǎ) dǎ.nes.te- bu.dand/</td><td align="center">(او/آن) دانسته بود
/(u/ ǎn) dǎ.nes.te- bud/</td></tr>
</table>

Past Subjunctive	
ماضی التزامی	
(ما) دانسته باشیم	(من) دانسته باشم
/(mǎ) dǎ.nes.te- bǎ.šim/	/(man) dǎ.nes.te- bǎ.šam/
(شما) دانسته باشید	(تو) دانسته باشی
/(šo.mǎ) dǎ.nes.te- bǎ.šid/	/(to) dǎ.nes.te- bǎ.ši/
(آنها) دانسته باشند	(او/آن) دانسته باشد
/(ǎn.hǎ) dǎ.nes.te- bǎ.šand/	/(u/ ǎn) dǎ.nes.te- bǎ.šad/

Past Progressive	
ماضی مستمر(در جریان)	
(ما) داشتیم می دانستیم	(من) داشتم می دانستم
/(mǎ) dǎš.tim- mi.dǎ.nes.tim/	/(man) dǎš.tam- mi.dǎ.nes.tam/
(شما) داشتید می دانستید	(تو) داشتی می دانستی
/(šo.mǎ) dǎš.tid- mi.dǎ.nes.tid/	/(to) dǎš.ti- mi.dǎ.nes.ti/
(آنها) داشتند می دانستند	(او/آن) داشت می دانست
/(ǎn.hǎ) dǎš.tand- mi.dǎ.nes.tand/	/(u/ ǎn) dǎšt- mi.dǎ.nest/

Simple Future	
مستقبل (آینده ساده)	
(ما) خواهیم دانست	(من) خواهم دانست
/(mǎ) kǎ.him- dǎ.nest/	/(man) kǎ.ham- dǎ.nest/
(شما) خواهید دانست	(تو) خواهی دانست
/(šo.mǎ) kǎ.hid- dǎ.nest/	/(to) kǎ.hi- dǎ.nest/
(آنها) خواهند دانست	(او/آن) خواهد دانست
/(ǎn.hǎ) kǎ.hand- dǎ.nest/	/(u/ ǎn) kǎ.had- dǎ.nest/

Command	
امر	
بدانید!	بدان!
/be.dǎ.nid/	/be.dǎn/

to leap

جَستَن

/jas.tan/

Plural	Singular
Simple Present مضارع اخباری(حال ساده)	
(ما) می جهیم /(mǎ) mi.ja.him/	(من) می جهم /(man) mi.ja.ham/
(شما) می جهید /(šo.mǎ) mi.ja.hid/	(تو) می جهی /(to) mi.ja.hi/
(آنها) می جهند /(ǎn.hǎ) mi.ja.hand/	(او/آن) می جهد /(u/ ǎn) mi.ja.had/
Present Subjunctive مضارع التزامی	
(ما) بجهیم /(mǎ) be.ja.him/	(من) بجهم /(man) be.ja.ham/
(شما) بجهید /(šo.mǎ) be.ja.hid/	(تو) بجهی /(to) be.ja.hi/
(آنها) بجهند /(ǎn.hǎ) be.ja.hand/	(او/آن) بجهد /(u/ ǎn) be.ja.had/
Present Progressive مضارع مستمر(در جریان)	
(ما) داریم می جهیم /(mǎ) dǎ.rim- mi.ja.him/	(من) دارم می جهم /(man) dǎ.ram- mi.ja.ham/
(شما) دارید می جهید /(šo.mǎ) dǎ.rid- mi.ja.hid/	(تو) داری می جهی /(to) dǎ.ri- mi.ja.hi/
(آنها) دارند می جهند /(ǎn.hǎ) dǎ.rand- mi.ja.hand/	(او/آن) دارد می جهد /(u/ ǎn) dǎ.rad- mi.ja.had/

Simple Past
ماضی مطلق (گذشته ساده)

(ما) جستیم	(من) جستم
/(mǎ) jas.tim/	/(man) jas.tam/
(شما) جستید	(تو) جستی
/(šo.mǎ) jas.tid/	/(to) jas.ti/
(آنها) جستند	(او/آن) جست
/(ǎn.hǎ) jas.tand/	/(u/ ǎn) jast/

Imperfect Indicative
ماضی استمراری

(ما) می جستیم	(من) می جستم
/(mǎ) mi.jas.tim/	/(man) mi.jas.tam/
(شما) می جستید	(تو) می جستی
/(šo.mǎ) mi.jas.tid/	/(to) mi.jas.ti/
(آنها) می جستند	(او/آن) می جست
/(ǎn.hǎ) mi.jas.tand/	/(u/ ǎn) mi.jast/

Present Perfect
ماضی نقلی

(ما) جسته ایم	(من) جسته ام
/(mǎ) jas.te.im/	/(man) jas.te.am/
(شما) جسته اید	(تو) جسته ای
/(šo.mǎ) jas.te.id/	/(to) jas.te.i/
(آنها) جسته اند	(او/آن) جسته است
/(ǎn.hǎ) jas.te.and/	/(u/ ǎn) jas.te- ast/

Past Perfect
ماضی بعید

(ما) جسته بودیم	(من) جسته بودم
/(mǎ) jas.te- bu.dim/	/(man) jas.te- bu.dam/
(شما) جسته بودید	(تو) جسته بودی
/(šo.mǎ) jas.te- bu.did/	/(to) jas.te- bu.di/
(آنها) جسته بودند	(او/آن) جسته بود
/(ǎn.hǎ) jas.te- bu.dand/	/(u/ ǎn) jas.te- bud/

Past Subjunctive
ماضی التزامی

(ما) جسته باشیم	(من) جسته باشم
/(mǎ) jas.te- bǎ.šim/	/(man) jas.te- bǎ.šam/
(شما) جسته باشید	(تو) جسته باشی
/(šo.mǎ) jas.te- bǎ.šid/	/(to) jas.te- bǎ.ši/
(آنها) جسته باشند	(او/آن) جسته باشد
/(ǎn.hǎ) jas.te- bǎ.šand/	/(u/ ǎn) jas.te- bǎ.šad/

Past Progressive
ماضی مستمر(در جریان)

(ما) داشتیم می جستیم	(من) داشتم می جستم
/(mǎ) dǎš.tim- mi.jas.tim/	/(man) dǎš.tam- mi.jas.tam/
(شما) داشتید می جستید	(تو) داشتی می جستی
/(šo.mǎ) dǎš.tid- mi.jas.tid/	/(to) dǎš.ti- mi.jas.ti/
(آنها) داشتند می جستند	(او/آن) داشت می جست
/(ǎn.hǎ) dǎš.tand- mi.jas.tand/	/(u/ ǎn) dǎšt- mi.jast/

Simple Future
مستقبل (آینده ساده)

(ما) خواهیم جست	(من) خواهم جست
/(mǎ) kǎ.him- jast/	/(man) kǎ.ham- jast/
(شما) خواهید جست	(تو) خواهی جست
/(šo.mǎ) kǎ.hid- jast/	/(to) kǎ.hi- jast/
(آنها) خواهند جست	(او/آن) خواهد جست
/(ǎn.hǎ) kǎ.hand- jast/	/(u/ ǎn) kǎ.had- jast/

Command
امر

بجهید!	بجه!
/be.ja.hid/	/be.jah/

151

to learn, to teach

آموخَتَن

/ă.muǩ.tan/

Plural	Singular
Simple Present مضارع اخباری(حال ساده)	
(ما) می آموزیم /(mă) mi.ă.mu.zim/	(من) می آموزم /(man) mi.ă.mu.zam/
(شما) می آموزید /(šo.mă) mi.ă.mu.zid/	(تو) می آموزی /(to) mi.ă.mu.zi/
(آنها) می آموزند /(ăn.hă) mi.ă.mu.zand/	(او/آن) می آموزد /(u/ ăn) mi.ă.mu.zad/
Present Subjunctive مضارع التزامی	
(ما) بیاموزیم /(mă) bi.yă.mu.zim/	(من) بیاموزم /(man) bi.yă.mu.zam/
(شما) بیاموزید /(šo.mă) bi.yă.mu.zid/	(تو) بیاموزی /(to) bi.yă.mu.zi/
(آنها) بیاموزند /(ăn.hă) bi.yă.mu.zand/	(او/آن) بیاموزد /(u/ ăn) bi.yă.mu.zad/
Present Progressive مضارع مستمر(در جریان)	
(ما) داریم می آموزیم /(mă) dă.rim- mi.ă.mu.zim/	(من) دارم می آموزم /(man) dă.ram- mi.ă.mu.zam/
(شما) دارید می آموزید /(šo.mă) dă.rid- mi.ă.mu.zid/	(تو) داری می آموزی /(to) dă.ri- mi.ă.mu.zi/
(آنها) دارند می آموزند /(ăn.hă) dă.rand- mi.ă.mu.zand/	(او/آن) دارد می آموزد /(u/ ăn) dă.rad- mi.ă.mu.zad/

Simple Past	
ماضی مطلق (گذشته ساده)	
(ما) آموختیم	(من) آموختم
/(mă) ă.muǩ.tim/	/(man) ă.muǩ.tam/
(شما) آموختید	(تو) آموختی
/(šo.mă) ă.muǩ.tid/	/(to) ă.muǩ.ti/
(آنها) آموختند	(او/آن) آموخت
/(ăn.hă) ă.muǩ.tand/	/(u/ ăn) ă.muǩt/

Imperfect Indicative	
ماضی استمراری	
(ما) می آموختیم	(من) می آموختم
/(mă) mi.ă.muǩ.tim/	/(man) mi.ă.muǩ.tam/
(شما) می آموختید	(تو) می آموختی
/(šo.mă) mi.ă.muǩ.tid/	/(to) mi.ă.muǩ.ti/
(آنها) می آموختند	(او/آن) می آموخت
/(ăn.hă) mi.ă.muǩ.tand/	/(u/ ăn) mi.ă.muǩt/

Present Perfect	
ماضی نقلی	
(ما) آموخته ایم	(من) آموخته ام
/(mă) ă.muǩ.te.im/	/(man) ă.muǩ.te.am/
(شما) آموخته اید	(تو) آموخته ای
/(šo.mă) ă.muǩ.te.id/	/(to) ă.muǩ.te.i/
(آنها) آموخته اند	(او/آن) آموخته است
/(ăn.hă) ă.muǩ.te.and/	/(u/ ăn) ă.muǩ.te- ast/

Past Perfect	
ماضی بعید	
(ما) آموخته بودیم	(من) آموخته بودم
/(mă) ă.muǩ.te- bu.dim/	/(man) ă.muǩ.te- bu.dam/
(شما) آموخته بودید	(تو) آموخته بودی
/(šo.mă) ă.muǩ.te- bu.did/	/(to) ă.muǩ.te- bu.di/
(آنها) آموخته بودند	(او/آن) آموخته بود
/(ăn.hă) ă.muǩ.te- bu.dand/	/(u/ ăn) ă.muǩ.te- bud/

153

Past Subjunctive	
ماضی التزامی	
(ما) آموخته باشیم	(من) آموخته باشم
/(mǎ) ǎ.muǩ.te- bǎ.šim/	/(man) ǎ.muǩ.te- bǎ.šam/
(شما) آموخته باشید	(تو) آموخته باشی
/(šo.mǎ) ǎ.muǩ.te- bǎ.šid/	/(to) ǎ.muǩ.te- bǎ.ši/
(آنها) آموخته باشند	(او/آن) آموخته باشد
/(ǎn.hǎ) ǎ.muǩ.te- bǎ.šand/	/(u/ ǎn) ǎ.muǩ.te- bǎ.šad/

Past Progressive	
ماضی مستمر(در جریان)	
(ما) داشتیم می آموختیم	(من) داشتم می آموختم
/(mǎ) dǎš.tim- mi.ǎ.muǩ.tim/	/(man) dǎš.tam- mi.ǎ.muǩ.tam/
(شما) داشتید می آموختید	(تو) داشتی می آموختی
/(šo.mǎ) dǎš.tid- mi.ǎ.muǩ.tid/	/(to) dǎš.ti- mi.ǎ.muǩ.ti/
(آنها) داشتند می آموختند	(او/آن) داشت می آموخت
/(ǎn.hǎ) dǎš.tand- mi.ǎ.muǩ.tand/	/(u/ ǎn) dǎšt- mi.ǎ.muǩt/

Simple Future	
مستقبل (آینده ساده)	
(ما) خواهیم آموخت	(من) خواهم آموخت
/(mǎ) ǩǎ.him- ǎ.muǩt/	/(man) ǩǎ.ham- ǎ.muǩt/
(شما) خواهید آموخت	(تو) خواهی آموخت
/(šo.mǎ) ǩǎ.hid- ǎ.muǩt/	/(to) ǩǎ.hi- ǎ.muǩt/
(آنها) خواهند آموخت	(او/آن) خواهد آموخت
/(ǎn.hǎ) ǩǎ.hand- ǎ.muǩt/	/(u/ ǎn) ǩǎ.had- ǎ.muǩt/

Command	
امر	
بیاموزید!	بیاموز!
/bi.yǎ.mu.zid/	/bi.yǎ.muz/

to live

زیستَن

/zis.tan/

Plural	Singular
Simple Present مضارع اخباری(حال ساده)	
(ما) می زییم /(mǎ) mi.zi.yim/	(من) می زیم /(man) mi.zi.yam/
(شما) می زیید /(šo.mǎ) mi.zi.yid/	(تو) می زیی /(to) mi.zi.yi/
(آنها) می زیند /(ǎn.hǎ) mi.zi.yand/	(او/آن) می زید /(u/ ǎn) mi.zi.yad/
Present Subjunctive مضارع التزامی	
(ما) بزییم /(mǎ) be.zi.yim/	(من) بزیم /(man) be.zi.yam/
(شما) بزیید /(šo.mǎ) be.zi.yid/	(تو) بزیی /(to) be.zi.yi/
(آنها) بزیند /(ǎn.hǎ) be.zi.yand/	(او/آن) بزید /(u/ ǎn) be.zi.yad/
Present Progressive مضارع مستمر(در جریان)	
(ما) داریم می زییم /(mǎ) dǎ.rim- mi.zi.yim/	(من) دارم می زیم /(man) dǎ.ram- mi.zi.yam/
(شما) دارید می زیید /(šo.mǎ) dǎ.rid- mi.zi.yid/	(تو) داری می زیی /(to) dǎ.ri- mi.zi.yi/
(آنها) دارند می زیند /(ǎn.hǎ) dǎ.rand- mi.zi.yand/	(او/آن) دارد می زید /(u/ ǎn) dǎ.rad- mi.zi.yad/

155

<table>
<tr><td colspan="2" align="center">Simple Past
ماضی مطلق (گذشته ساده)</td></tr>
<tr>
<td align="center">(ما) زیستیم
/(mă) zis.tim/</td>
<td align="center">(من) زیستم
/(man) zis.tam/</td>
</tr>
<tr>
<td align="center">(شما) زیستید
/(šo.mă) zis.tid/</td>
<td align="center">(تو) زیستی
/(to) zis.ti/</td>
</tr>
<tr>
<td align="center">(آنها) زیستند
/(ăn.hă) zis.tand/</td>
<td align="center">(او/آن) زیست
/(u/ ăn) zist/</td>
</tr>
</table>

<table>
<tr><td colspan="2" align="center">Imperfect Indicative
ماضی استمراری</td></tr>
<tr>
<td align="center">(ما) می زیستیم
/(mă) mi.zis.tim/</td>
<td align="center">(من) می زیستم
/(man) mi.zis.tam/</td>
</tr>
<tr>
<td align="center">(شما) می زیستید
/(šo.mă) mi.zis.tid/</td>
<td align="center">(تو) می زیستی
/(to) mi.zis.ti/</td>
</tr>
<tr>
<td align="center">(آنها) می زیستند
/(ăn.hă) mi.zis.tand/</td>
<td align="center">(او/آن) می زیست
/(u/ ăn) mi.zist/</td>
</tr>
</table>

<table>
<tr><td colspan="2" align="center">Present Perfect
ماضی نقلی</td></tr>
<tr>
<td align="center">(ما) زیسته ایم
/(mă) zis.te.im/</td>
<td align="center">(من) زیسته ام
/(man) zis.te.am/</td>
</tr>
<tr>
<td align="center">(شما) زیسته اید
/(šo.mă) zis.te.id/</td>
<td align="center">(تو) زیسته ای
/(to) zis.te.i/</td>
</tr>
<tr>
<td align="center">(آنها) زیسته اند
/(ăn.hă) zis.te.and/</td>
<td align="center">(او/آن) زیسته است
/(u/ ăn) zis.te- ast/</td>
</tr>
</table>

<table>
<tr><td colspan="2" align="center">Past Perfect
ماضی بعید</td></tr>
<tr>
<td align="center">(ما) زیسته بودیم
/(mă) zis.te- bu.dim/</td>
<td align="center">(من) زیسته بودم
/(man) zis.te- bu.dam/</td>
</tr>
<tr>
<td align="center">(شما) زیسته بودید
/(šo.mă) zis.te- bu.did/</td>
<td align="center">(تو) زیسته بودی
/(to) zis.te- bu.di/</td>
</tr>
<tr>
<td align="center">(آنها) زیسته بودند
/(ăn.hă) zis.te- bu.dand/</td>
<td align="center">(او/آن) زیسته بود
/(u/ ăn) zis.te- bud/</td>
</tr>
</table>

<table>
<tr><td colspan="2" align="center">**Past Subjunctive**
ماضی التزامی</td></tr>
<tr>
<td align="center">(ما) زیسته باشیم
/(mă) zis.te- bă.šim/</td>
<td align="center">(من) زیسته باشم
/(man) zis.te- bă.šam/</td>
</tr>
<tr>
<td align="center">(شما) زیسته باشید
/(šo.mă) zis.te- bă.šid/</td>
<td align="center">(تو) زیسته باشی
/(to) zis.te- bă.ši/</td>
</tr>
<tr>
<td align="center">(آنها) زیسته باشند
/(ăn.hă) zis.te- bă.šand/</td>
<td align="center">(او/آن) زیسته باشد
/(u/ ăn) zis.te- bă.šad/</td>
</tr>
</table>

<table>
<tr><td colspan="2" align="center">**Past Progressive**
ماضی مستمر(در جریان)</td></tr>
<tr>
<td align="center">(ما) داشتیم می زیستیم
/(mă) dăš.tim- mi.zis.tim/</td>
<td align="center">(من) داشتم می زیستم
/(man) dăš.tam- mi.zis.tam/</td>
</tr>
<tr>
<td align="center">(شما) داشتید می زیستید
/(šo.mă) dăš.tid- mi.zis.tid/</td>
<td align="center">(تو) داشتی می زیستی
/(to) dăš.ti- mi.zis.ti/</td>
</tr>
<tr>
<td align="center">(آنها) داشتند می زیستند
/(ăn.hă) dăš.tand- mi.zis.tand/</td>
<td align="center">(او/آن) داشت می زیست
/(u/ ăn) dăšt- mi.zist/</td>
</tr>
</table>

<table>
<tr><td colspan="2" align="center">**Simple Future**
مستقبل (آینده ساده)</td></tr>
<tr>
<td align="center">(ما) خواهیم زیست
/(mă) ќă.him- zist/</td>
<td align="center">(من) خواهم زیست
/(man) ќă.ham- zist/</td>
</tr>
<tr>
<td align="center">(شما) خواهید زیست
/(šo.mă) ќă.hid- zist/</td>
<td align="center">(تو) خواهی زیست
/(to) ќă.hi- zist/</td>
</tr>
<tr>
<td align="center">(آنها) خواهند زیست
/(ăn.hă) ќă.hand- zist/</td>
<td align="center">(او/آن) خواهد زیست
/(u/ ăn) ќă.had- zist/</td>
</tr>
</table>

<table>
<tr><td colspan="2" align="center">**Command**
امر</td></tr>
<tr>
<td align="center">بزیید!
/be.zi.yid/</td>
<td align="center">بزی!
/be.zi/</td>
</tr>
</table>

157

to look

نِگَریستَن

/ne.ga.ris.tan/

Plural	Singular
Simple Present	
مضارع اخباری(حال ساده)	
(ما) می نگریم	(من) می نگرم
/(mǎ) mi.ne.ga.rim/	/(man) mi.ne.ga.ram/
(شما) می نگرید	(تو) می نگری
/(šo.mǎ) mi.ne.ga.rid/	/(to) mi.ne.ga.ri/
(آنها) می نگرند	(او/آن) می نگرد
/(ǎn.hǎ) mi.ne.ga.rand/	/(u/ ǎn) mi.ne.ga.rad/

Plural	Singular
Present Subjunctive	
مضارع التزامی	
(ما) بنگریم	(من) بنگرم
/(mǎ) be.ne.ga.rim/	/(man) be.ne.ga.ram/
(شما) بنگرید	(تو) بنگری
/(šo.mǎ) be.ne.ga.rid/	/(to) be.ne.ga.ri/
(آنها) بنگرند	(او/آن) بنگرد
/(ǎn.hǎ) be.ne.ga.rand/	/(u/ ǎn) be.ne.ga.rad/

Plural	Singular
Present Progressive	
مضارع مستمر(در جریان)	
(ما) داریم می نگریم	(من) دارم می نگرم
/(mǎ) dǎ.rim- mi.ne.ga.rim/	/(man) dǎ.ram- mi.ne.ga.ram/
(شما) دارید می نگرید	(تو) داری می نگری
/(šo.mǎ) dǎ.rid- mi.ne.ga.rid/	/(to) dǎ.ri- mi.ne.ga.ri/
(آنها) دارند می نگرند	(او/آن) دارد می نگرد
/(ǎn.hǎ) dǎ.rand- mi.ne.ga.rand/	/(u/ ǎn) dǎ.rad- mi.ne.ga.rad/

Simple Past
ماضی مطلق (گذشته ساده)

(ما) نگریستیم	(من) نگریستم
/(mǎ) ne.ga.ris.tim/	/(man) ne.ga.ris.tam/
(شما) نگریستید	(تو) نگریستی
/(šo.mǎ) ne.ga.ris.tid/	/(to) ne.ga.ris.ti/
(آنها) نگریستند	(او/آن) نگریست
/(ǎn.hǎ) ne.ga.ris.tand/	/(u/ ǎn) ne.ga.rist/

Imperfect Indicative
ماضی استمراری

(ما) می نگریستیم	(من) می نگریستم
/(mǎ) mi.ne.ga.ris.tim/	/(man) mi.ne.ga.ris.tam/
(شما) می نگریستید	(تو) می نگریستی
/(šo.mǎ) mi.ne.ga.ris.tid/	/(to) mi.ne.ga.ris.ti/
(آنها) می نگریستند	(او/آن) می نگریست
/(ǎn.hǎ) mi.ne.ga.ris.tand/	/(u/ ǎn) mi.ne.ga.rist/

Present Perfect
ماضی نقلی

(ما) نگریسته ایم	(من) نگریسته ام
/(mǎ) ne.ga.ris.te.im/	/(man) ne.ga.ris.te.am/
(شما) نگریسته اید	(تو) نگریسته ای
/(šo.mǎ) ne.ga.ris.te.id/	/(to) ne.ga.ris.te.i/
(آنها) نگریسته اند	(او/آن) نگریسته است
/(ǎn.hǎ) ne.ga.ris.te.and/	/(u/ ǎn) ne.ga.ris.te- ast/

Past Perfect
ماضی بعید

(ما) نگریسته بودیم	(من) نگریسته بودم
/(mǎ) ne.ga.ris.te- bu.dim/	/(man) ne.ga.ris.te- bu.dam/
(شما) نگریسته بودید	(تو) نگریسته بودی
/(šo.mǎ) ne.ga.ris.te- bu.did/	/(to) ne.ga.ris.te- bu.di/
(آنها) نگریسته بودند	(او/آن) نگریسته بود
/(ǎn.hǎ) ne.ga.ris.te- bu.dand/	/(u/ ǎn) ne.ga.ris.te- bud/

Past Subjunctive	
ماضی التزامی	
(ما) نگریسته باشیم	(من) نگریسته باشم
/(mă) ne.ga.ris.te- bă.šim/	/(man) ne.ga.ris.te- bă.šam/
(شما) نگریسته باشید	(تو) نگریسته باشی
/(šo.mă) ne.ga.ris.te- bă.šid/	/(to) ne.ga.ris.te- bă.ši/
(آنها) نگریسته باشند	(او/آن) نگریسته باشد
/(ăn.hă) ne.ga.ris.te- bă.šand/	/(u/ ăn) ne.ga.ris.te- bă.šad/

Past Progressive	
ماضی مستمر(در جریان)	
(ما) داشتیم می نگریستیم	(من) داشتم می نگریستم
/(mă) dăš.tim- mi.ne.ga.ris.tim/	/(man) dăš.tam- mi.ne.ga.ris.tam/
(شما) داشتید می نگریستید	(تو) داشتی می نگریستی
/(šo.mă) dăš.tid- mi.ne.ga.ris.tid/	/(to) dăš.ti- mi.ne.ga.ris.ti/
(آنها) داشتند می نگریستند	(او/آن) داشت می نگریست
/(ăn.hă) dăš.tand- mi.ne.ga.ris.tand/	/(u/ ăn) dăšt- mi.ne.ga.rist/

Simple Future	
مستقبل (آینده ساده)	
(ما) خواهیم نگریست	(من) خواهم نگریست
/(mă) kă.him- ne.ga.rist/	/(man) kă.ham- ne.ga.rist/
(شما) خواهید نگریست	(تو) خواهی نگریست
/(šo.mă) kă.hid- ne.ga.rist/	/(to) kă.hi- ne.ga.rist/
(آنها) خواهند نگریست	(او/آن) خواهد نگریست
/(ăn.hă) kă.hand- ne.ga.rist/	/(u/ ăn) kă.had- ne.ga.rist/

Command	
امر	
بنگرید!	بنگر!
/be.ne.ga.rid/	/be.ne.gar/

to lose

باخْتَن

/băk.tan/

Plural	Singular
Simple Present	
مضارع اخباری(حال ساده)	
(ما) می بازیم	(من) می بازم
/(mă) mi.bă.zim/	/(man) mi.bă.zam/
(شما) می بازید	(تو) می بازی
/(šo.mă) mi.bă.zid/	/(to) mi.bă.zi/
(آنها) می بازند	(او/آن) می بازد
/(ăn.hă) mi.bă.zand/	/(u/ ăn) mi.bă.zad/
Present Subjunctive	
مضارع التزامی	
(ما) ببازیم	(من) ببازم
/(mă) be.bă.zim/	/(man) be.bă.zam/
(شما) ببازید	(تو) ببازی
/(šo.mă) be.bă.zid/	/(to) be.bă.zi/
(آنها) ببازند	(او/آن) ببازد
/(ăn.hă) be.bă.zand/	/(u/ ăn) be.bă.zad/
Present Progressive	
مضارع مستمر(در جریان)	
(ما) داریم می بازیم	(من) دارم می بازم
/(mă) dă.rim- mi.bă.zim/	/(man) dă.ram- mi.bă.zam/
(شما) دارید می بازید	(تو) داری می بازی
/(šo.mă) dă.rid- mi.bă.zid/	/(to) dă.ri- mi.bă.zi/
(آنها) دارند می بازند	(او/آن) دارد می بازد
/(ăn.hă) dă.rand- mi.bă.zand/	/(u/ ăn) dă.rad- mi.bă.zad/

Simple Past	
ماضی مطلق (گذشته ساده)	
(ما) باختیم	(من) باختم
/(mă) băǩ.tim/	/(man) băǩ.tam/
(شما) باختید	(تو) باختی
/(šo.mă) băǩ.tid/	/(to) băǩ.ti/
(آنها) باختند	(او/آن) باخت
/(ăn.hă) băǩ.tand/	/(u/ ăn) băǩt/

Imperfect Indicative	
ماضی استمراری	
(ما) می باختیم	(من) می باختم
/(mă) mi.băǩ.tim/	/(man) mi.băǩ.tam/
(شما) می باختید	(تو) می باختی
/(šo.mă) mi.băǩ.tid/	/(to) mi.băǩ.ti/
(آنها) می باختند	(او/آن) می باخت
/(ăn.hă) mi.băǩ.tand/	/(u/ ăn) mi.băǩt/

Present Perfect	
ماضی نقلی	
(ما) باخته ایم	(من) باخته ام
/(mă) băǩ.te.im/	/(man) băǩ.te.am/
(شما) باخته اید	(تو) باخته ای
/(šo.mă) băǩ.te.id/	/(to) băǩ.te.i/
(آنها) باخته اند	(او/آن) باخته است
/(ăn.hă) băǩ.te.and/	/(u/ ăn) băǩ.te- ast/

Past Perfect	
ماضی بعید	
(ما) باخته بودیم	(من) باخته بودم
/(mă) băǩ.te- bu.dim/	/(man) băǩ.te- bu.dam/
(شما) باخته بودید	(تو) باخته بودی
/(šo.mă) băǩ.te- bu.did/	/(to) băǩ.te- bu.di/
(آنها) باخته بودند	(او/آن) باخته بود
/(ăn.hă) băǩ.te- bu.dand/	/(u/ ăn) băǩ.te- bud/

162

<table>
<tr><td colspan="2" align="center">**Past Subjunctive**
ماضی التزامی</td></tr>
<tr><td align="center">(ما) باخته باشیم
/(mă) băǩ.te- bă.šim/</td><td align="center">(من) باخته باشم
/(man) băǩ.te- bă.šam/</td></tr>
<tr><td align="center">(شما) باخته باشید
/(šo.mă) băǩ.te- bă.šid/</td><td align="center">(تو) باخته باشی
/(to) băǩ.te- bă.ši/</td></tr>
<tr><td align="center">(آنها) باخته باشند
/(ăn.hă) băǩ.te- bă.šand/</td><td align="center">(او/آن) باخته باشد
/(u/ ăn) băǩ.te- bă.šad/</td></tr>
</table>

<table>
<tr><td colspan="2" align="center">**Past Progressive**
ماضی مستمر(در جریان)</td></tr>
<tr><td align="center">(ما) داشتیم می باختیم
/(mă) dăš.tim- mi.băǩ.tim/</td><td align="center">(من) داشتم می باختم
/(man) dăš.tam- mi.băǩ.tam/</td></tr>
<tr><td align="center">(شما) داشتید می باختید
/(šo.mă) dăš.tid- mi.băǩ.tid/</td><td align="center">(تو) داشتی می باختی
/(to) dăš.ti- mi.băǩ.ti/</td></tr>
<tr><td align="center">(آنها) داشتند می باختند
/(ăn.hă) dăš.tand- mi.băǩ.tand/</td><td align="center">(او/آن) داشت می باخت
/(u/ ăn) dăšt- mi.băǩt/</td></tr>
</table>

<table>
<tr><td colspan="2" align="center">**Simple Future**
مستقبل (آینده ساده)</td></tr>
<tr><td align="center">(ما) خواهیم باخت
/(mă) ǩă.him- băǩt/</td><td align="center">(من) خواهم باخت
/(man) ǩă.ham- băǩt/</td></tr>
<tr><td align="center">(شما) خواهید باخت
/(šo.mă) ǩă.hid- băǩt/</td><td align="center">(تو) خواهی باخت
/(to) ǩă.hi- băǩt/</td></tr>
<tr><td align="center">(آنها) خواهند باخت
/(ăn.hă) ǩă.hand- băǩt/</td><td align="center">(او/آن) خواهد باخت
/(u/ ăn) ǩă.had- băǩt/</td></tr>
</table>

<table>
<tr><td colspan="2" align="center">**Command**
امر</td></tr>
<tr><td align="center">ببازید!
/be.bă.zid/</td><td align="center">بباز!
/be.băz/</td></tr>
</table>

163

to open

گُشودَن

/go.šu.dan/

Plural	Singular
Simple Present	
مضارع اخباری(حال ساده)	
(ما) می گشاییم	(من) می گشایم
/(mǎ) mi.go.šǎ.yim/	/(man) mi.go.šǎ.yam/
(شما) می گشایید	(تو) می گشایی
/(šo.mǎ) mi.go.šǎ.yid/	/(to) mi.go.šǎ.yi/
(آنها) می گشایند	(او/آن) می گشاید
/(ǎn.hǎ) mi.go.šǎ.yand/	/(u/ ǎn) mi.go.šǎ.yad/

Plural	Singular
Present Subjunctive	
مضارع التزامی	
(ما) بگشاییم	(من) بگشایم
/(mǎ) be.go.šǎ.yim/	/(man) be.go.šǎ.yam/
(شما) بگشایید	(تو) بگشایی
/(šo.mǎ) be.go.šǎ.yid/	/(to) be.go.šǎ.yi/
(آنها) بگشایند	(او/آن) بگشاید
/(ǎn.hǎ) be.go.šǎ.yand/	/(u/ ǎn) be.go.šǎ.yad/

Plural	Singular
Present Progressive	
مضارع مستمر(در جریان)	
(ما) داریم می گشاییم	(من) دارم می گشایم
/(mǎ) dǎ.rim- mi.go.šǎ.yim/	/(man) dǎ.ram- mi.go.šǎ.yam/
(شما) دارید می گشایید	(تو) داری می گشایی
/(šo.mǎ) dǎ.rid- mi.go.šǎ.yid/	/(to) dǎ.ri- mi.go.šǎ.yi/
(آنها) دارند می گشایند	(او/آن) دارد می گشاید
/(ǎn.hǎ) dǎ.rand- mi.go.šǎ.yand/	/(u/ ǎn) dǎ.rad- mi.go.šǎ.yad/

164

Simple Past	
ماضی مطلق (گذشته ساده)	
(ما) گشودیم	(من) گشودم
/(mǎ) go.šu.dim/	/(man) go.šu.dam/
(شما) گشودید	(تو) گشودی
/(šo.mǎ) go.šu.did/	/(to) go.šu.di/
(آنها) گشودند	(او/آن) گشود
/(ǎn.hǎ) go.šu.dand/	/(u/ ǎn) go.šud/

Imperfect Indicative	
ماضی استمراری	
(ما) می گشودیم	(من) می گشودم
/(mǎ) mi.go.šu.dim/	/(man) mi.go.šu.dam/
(شما) می گشودید	(تو) می گشودی
/(šo.mǎ) mi.go.šu.did/	/(to) mi.go.šu.di/
(آنها) می گشودند	(او/آن) می گشود
/(ǎn.hǎ) mi.go.šu.dand/	/(u/ ǎn) mi.go.šud/

Present Perfect	
ماضی نقلی	
(ما) گشوده ایم	(من) گشوده ام
/(mǎ) go.šu.de.im/	/(man) go.šu.de.am/
(شما) گشوده اید	(تو) گشوده ای
/(šo.mǎ) go.šu.de.id/	/(to) go.šu.de.i/
(آنها) گشوده اند	(او/آن) گشوده است
/(ǎn.hǎ) go.šu.de.and/	/(u/ ǎn) go.šu.de- ast/

Past Perfect	
ماضی بعید	
(ما) گشوده بودیم	(من) گشوده بودم
/(mǎ) go.šu.de- bu.dim/	/(man) go.šu.de- bu.dam/
(شما) گشوده بودید	(تو) گشوده بودی
/(šo.mǎ) go.šu.de- bu.did/	/(to) go.šu.de- bu.di/
(آنها) گشوده بودند	(او/آن) گشوده بود
/(ǎn.hǎ) go.šu.de- bu.dand/	/(u/ ǎn) go.šu.de- bud/

Past Subjunctive
ماضی التزامی

(ما) گشوده باشیم	(من) گشوده باشم
/(mǎ) go.šu.de- bǎ.šim/	/(man) go.šu.de- bǎ.šam/
(شما) گشوده باشید	(تو) گشوده باشی
/(šo.mǎ) go.šu.de- bǎ.šid/	/(to) go.šu.de- bǎ.ši/
(آنها) گشوده باشند	(او/آن) گشوده باشد
/(ǎn.hǎ) go.šu.de- bǎ.šand/	/(u/ ǎn) go.šu.de- bǎ.šad/

Past Progressive
ماضی مستمر(در جریان)

(ما) داشتیم می گشودیم	(من) داشتم می گشودم
/(mǎ) dǎš.tim- mi.go.šu.dim/	/(man) dǎš.tam- mi.go.šu.dam/
(شما) داشتید می گشودید	(تو) داشتی می گشودی
/(šo.mǎ) dǎš.tid- mi.go.šu.did/	/(to) dǎš.ti- mi.go.šu.di/
(آنها) داشتند می گشودند	(او/آن) داشت می گشود
/(ǎn.hǎ) dǎš.tand- mi.go.šu.dand/	/(u/ ǎn) dǎšt- mi.go.šud/

Simple Future
مستقبل (آینده ساده)

(ما) خواهیم گشود	(من) خواهم گشود
/(mǎ) ǩǎ.him- go.šud/	/(man) ǩǎ.ham- go.šud/
(شما) خواهید گشود	(تو) خواهی گشود
/(šo.mǎ) ǩǎ.hid- go.šud/	/(to) ǩǎ.hi- go.šud/
(آنها) خواهند گشود	(او/آن) خواهد گشود
/(ǎn.hǎ) ǩǎ.hand- go.šud/	/(u/ ǎn) ǩǎ.had- go.šud/

Command
امر

بگشایید!	بگشای!
/be.go.šǎ.yid/	/be.go.šǎy/

166

to order

فَرمودَن

/far.mu.dan/

Plural	Singular
Simple Present مضارع اخباری(حال ساده)	
(ما) می فرماییم /(mǎ) mi.far.mǎ.yim/	(من) می فرمایم /(man) mi.far.mǎ.yam/
(شما) می فرمایید /(šo.mǎ) mi.far.mǎ.yid/	(تو) می فرمایی /(to) mi.far.mǎ.yi/
(آنها) می فرمایند /(ǎn.hǎ) mi.far.mǎ.yand/	(او/آن) می فرماید /(u/ ǎn) mi.far.mǎ.yad/
Present Subjunctive مضارع التزامی	
(ما) بفرماییم /(mǎ) be.far.mǎ.yim/	(من) بفرمایم /(man) be.far.mǎ.yam/
(شما) بفرمایید /(šo.mǎ) be.far.mǎ.yid/	(تو) بفرمایی /(to) be.far.mǎ.yi/
(آنها) بفرمایند /(ǎn.hǎ) be.far.mǎ.yand/	(او/آن) بفرماید /(u/ ǎn) be.far.mǎ.yad/
Present Progressive مضارع مستمر(در جریان)	
(ما) داریم می فرماییم /(mǎ) dǎ.rim- mi.far.mǎ.yim/	(من) دارم می فرمایم /(man) dǎ.ram- mi.far.mǎ.yam/
(شما) دارید می فرمایید /(šo.mǎ) dǎ.rid- mi.far.mǎ.yid/	(تو) داری می فرمایی /(to) dǎ.ri- mi.far.mǎ.yi/
(آنها) دارند می فرمایند /(ǎn.hǎ) dǎ.rand- mi.far.mǎ.yand/	(او/آن) دارد می فرماید /(u/ ǎn) dǎ.rad- mi.far.mǎ.yad/

Simple Past
ماضی مطلق (گذشته ساده)

(ما) فرمودیم	(من) فرمودم
/(mǎ) far.mu.dim/	/(man) far.mu.dam/
(شما) فرمودید	(تو) فرمودی
/(šo.mǎ) far.mu.did/	/(to) far.mu.di/
(آنها) فرمودند	(او/آن) فرمود
/(ǎn.hǎ) far.mu.dand/	/(u/ ǎn) far.mud/

Imperfect Indicative
ماضی استمراری

(ما) می فرمودیم	(من) می فرمودم
/(mǎ) mi.far.mu.dim/	/(man) mi.far.mu.dam/
(شما) می فرمودید	(تو) می فرمودی
/(šo.mǎ) mi.far.mu.did/	/(to) mi.far.mu.di/
(آنها) می فرمودند	(او/آن) می فرمود
/(ǎn.hǎ) mi.far.mu.dand/	/(u/ ǎn) mi.far.mud/

Present Perfect
ماضی نقلی

(ما) فرموده ایم	(من) فرموده ام
/(mǎ) far.mu.de.im/	/(man) far.mu.de.am/
(شما) فرموده اید	(تو) فرموده ای
/(šo.mǎ) far.mu.de.id/	/(to) far.mu.de.i/
(آنها) فرموده اند	(او/آن) فرموده است
/(ǎn.hǎ) far.mu.de.and/	/(u/ ǎn) far.mu.de- ast/

Past Perfect
ماضی بعید

(ما) فرموده بودیم	(من) فرموده بودم
/(mǎ) far.mu.de- bu.dim/	/(man) far.mu.de- bu.dam/
(شما) فرموده بودید	(تو) فرموده بودی
/(šo.mǎ) far.mu.de- bu.did/	/(to) far.mu.de- bu.di/
(آنها) فرموده بودند	(او/آن) فرموده بود
/(ǎn.hǎ) far.mu.de- bu.dand/	/(u/ ǎn) far.mu.de- bud/

<table>
<tr><td colspan="2" align="center">**Past Subjunctive**
ماضی التزامی</td></tr>
<tr><td align="center">(ما) فرموده باشیم
/(mǎ) far.mu.de- bǎ.šim/</td><td align="center">(من) فرموده باشم
/(man) far.mu.de- bǎ.šam/</td></tr>
<tr><td align="center">(شما) فرموده باشید
/(šo.mǎ) far.mu.de- bǎ.šid/</td><td align="center">(تو) فرموده باشی
/(to) far.mu.de- bǎ.ši/</td></tr>
<tr><td align="center">(آنها) فرموده باشند
/(ǎn.hǎ) far.mu.de- bǎ.šand/</td><td align="center">(او/ آن) فرموده باشد
/(u/ ǎn) far.mu.de- bǎ.šad/</td></tr>
</table>

<table>
<tr><td colspan="2" align="center">**Past Progressive**
ماضی مستمر(در جریان)</td></tr>
<tr><td align="center">(ما) داشتیم می فرمودیم
/(mǎ) dǎš.tim- mi.far.mu.dim/</td><td align="center">(من) داشتم می فرمودم
/(man) dǎš.tam- mi.far.mu.dam/</td></tr>
<tr><td align="center">(شما) داشتید می فرمودید
/(šo.mǎ) dǎš.tid- mi.far.mu.did/</td><td align="center">(تو) داشتی می فرمودی
/(to) dǎš.ti- mi.far.mu.di/</td></tr>
<tr><td align="center">(آنها) داشتند می فرمودند
/(ǎn.hǎ) dǎš.tand- mi.far.mu.dand/</td><td align="center">(او/آن) داشت می فرمود
/(u/ ǎn) dǎšt- mi.far.mud/</td></tr>
</table>

<table>
<tr><td colspan="2" align="center">**Simple Future**
مستقبل (آینده ساده)</td></tr>
<tr><td align="center">(ما) خواهیم فرمود
/(mǎ) kǎ.him- far.mud/</td><td align="center">(من) خواهم فرمود
/(man) kǎ.ham- far.mud/</td></tr>
<tr><td align="center">(شما) خواهید فرمود
/(šo.mǎ) kǎ.hid- far.mud/</td><td align="center">(تو) خواهی فرمود
/(to) kǎ.hi- far.mud/</td></tr>
<tr><td align="center">(آنها) خواهند فرمود
/(ǎn.hǎ) kǎ.hand- far.mud/</td><td align="center">(او/آن) خواهد فرمود
/(u/ ǎn) kǎ.had- far.mud/</td></tr>
</table>

<table>
<tr><td colspan="2" align="center">**Command**
امر</td></tr>
<tr><td align="center">بفرمایید!
/be.far.mǎ.yid/</td><td align="center">بفرمای!
/be.far.mǎy/</td></tr>
</table>

to overthrow

بَرَانداختَن

/bar.an.dǎǩ.tan/

Plural	Singular
Simple Present	
مضارع اخباری(حال ساده)	
(ما) بر می اندازیم	(من) بر می اندازم
/(mǎ) bar.mi.an.dǎ.zim/	/(man) bar.mi.an.dǎ.zam/
(شما) بر می اندازید	(تو) بر می اندازی
/(šo.mǎ) bar.mi.an.dǎ.zid/	/(to) bar.mi.an.dǎ.zi/
(آنها) بر می اندازند	(او/آن) بر می اندازد
/(ǎn.hǎ) bar.mi.an.dǎ.zand/	/(u/ ǎn) bar.mi.an.dǎ.zad/

Plural	Singular
Present Subjunctive	
مضارع التزامی	
(ما) بر بیندازیم	(من) بر بیندازم
/(mǎ) bar.bi.yan.dǎ.zim/	/(man) bar.bi.yan.dǎ.zam/
(شما) بر بیندازید	(تو) بر بیندازی
/(šo.mǎ) bar.bi.yan.dǎ.zid/	/(to) bar.bi.yan.dǎ.zi/
(آنها) بر بیندازند	(او/آن) بر بیندازد
/(ǎn.hǎ) bar.bi.yan.dǎ.zand/	/(u/ ǎn) bar.bi.yan.dǎ.zad/

Plural	Singular
Present Progressive	
مضارع مستمر(در جریان)	
(ما) داریم بر می اندازیم	(من) دارم بر می اندازم
/(mǎ) dǎ.rim- bar.mi.an.dǎ.zim/	/(man) dǎ.ram- bar.mi.an.dǎ.zam/
(شما) دارید بر می اندازید	(تو) داری بر می اندازی
/(šo.mǎ) dǎ.rid- bar.mi.an.dǎ.zid/	/(to) dǎ.ri- bar.mi.an.dǎ.zi/
(آنها) دارند بر می اندازند	(او/آن) دارد بر می اندازد
/(ǎn.hǎ) dǎ.rand- bar.mi.an.dǎ.zand/	/(u/ ǎn) dǎ.rad- bar.mi.an.dǎ.zad/

Simple Past	
ماضی مطلق (گذشته ساده)	
(ما) بر انداختیم	(من) بر انداختم
/(mă) bar.an.dăǩ.tim/	/(man) bar.an.dăǩ.tam/
(شما) بر انداختید	(تو) بر انداختی
/(šo.mă) bar.an.dăǩ.tid/	/(to) bar.an.dăǩ.ti/
(آنها) بر انداختند	(او/آن) بر انداخت
/(ăn.hă) bar.an.dăǩ.tand/	/(u/ ăn) bar.an.dăǩt/

Imperfect Indicative	
ماضی استمراری	
(ما) بر می انداختیم	(من) بر می انداختم
/(mă) bar.mi.an.dăǩ.tim/	/(man) bar.mi.an.dăǩ.tam/
(شما) بر می انداختید	(تو) بر می انداختی
/(šo.mă) bar.mi.an.dăǩ.tid/	/(to) bar.mi.an.dăǩ.ti/
(آنها) بر می انداختند	(او/آن) بر می انداخت
/(ăn.hă) bar.mi.an.dăǩ.tand/	/(u/ ăn) bar.mi.an.dăǩt/

Present Perfect	
ماضی نقلی	
(ما) بر انداخته ایم	(من) بر انداخته ام
/(mă) bar.an.dăǩ.te.im/	/(man) bar.an.dăǩ.te.am/
(شما) بر انداخته اید	(تو) بر انداخته ای
/(šo.mă) bar.an.dăǩ.te.id/	/(to) bar.an.dăǩ.te.i/
(آنها) بر انداخته اند	(او/آن) بر انداخته است
/(ăn.hă) bar.an.dăǩ.te.and/	/(u/ ăn) bar.an.dăǩ.te- ast/

Past Perfect	
ماضی بعید	
(ما) بر انداخته بودیم	(من) بر انداخته بودم
/(mă) bar.an.dăǩ.te- bu.dim/	/(man) bar.an.dăǩ.te- bu.dam/
(شما) بر انداخته بودید	(تو) بر انداخته بودی
/(šo.mă) bar.an.dăǩ.te- bu.did/	/(to) bar.an.dăǩ.te- bu.di/
(آنها) بر انداخته بودند	(او/آن) بر انداخته بود
/(ăn.hă) bar.an.dăǩ.te- bu.dand/	/(u/ ăn) bar.an.dăǩ.te- bud/

Past Subjunctive
ماضی التزامی

(ما) بر انداخته باشیم	(من) بر انداخته باشم
/(mǎ) bar.an.dǎǩ.te- bǎ.šim/	/(man) bar.an.dǎǩ.te- bǎ.šam/
(شما) بر انداخته باشید	(تو) بر انداخته باشی
/(šo.mǎ) bar.an.dǎǩ.te- bǎ.šid/	/(to) bar.an.dǎǩ.te- bǎ.ši/
(آنها) بر انداخته باشند	(او/آن) بر انداخته باشد
/(ǎn.hǎ) bar.an.dǎǩ.te- bǎ.šand/	/(u/ ǎn) bar.an.dǎǩ.te- bǎ.šad/

Past Progressive
ماضی مستمر(در جریان)

(ما) داشتیم بر می انداختیم	(من) داشتم بر می انداختم
/(mǎ) dǎš.tim- bar.mi.an.dǎǩ.tim/	/(man) dǎš.tam- bar.mi.an.dǎǩ.tam/
(شما) داشتید بر می انداختید	(تو) داشتی بر می انداختی
/(šo.mǎ) dǎš.tid- bar.mi.an.dǎǩ.tid/	/(to) dǎš.ti- bar.mi.an.dǎǩ.ti/
(آنها) داشتند برمی انداختند	(او/آن) داشت بر می انداخت
/(ǎn.hǎ) dǎš.tand- bar.mi.an.dǎǩ.tand/	/(u/ ǎn) dǎšt- bar.mi.an.dǎǩt/

Simple Future
مستقبل (آینده ساده)

(ما) بر خواهیم انداخت	(من) بر خواهم انداخت
/(mǎ) bar.ǩǎ.him- an.dǎǩt/	/(man) bar.ǩǎ.ham- an.dǎǩt/
(شما) بر خواهید انداخت	(تو) بر خواهی انداخت
/(šo.mǎ) bar.ǩǎ.hid- an.dǎǩt/	/(to) bar.ǩǎ.hi- an.dǎǩt/
(آنها) بر خواهند انداخت	(او/آن) بر خواهد انداخت
/(ǎn.hǎ) bar.ǩǎ.hand- an.dǎǩt/	/(u/ ǎn) bar.ǩǎ.had- an.dǎǩt/

Command
امر

براندازید!	برانداز!
/bar.an.dǎ.zid/	/bar.an.dǎz/

172

to pass

گُذَشتَن

/go.zaš.tan/

Plural	Singular
Simple Present <div dir="rtl">مضارع اخباری(حال ساده)</div>	
<div dir="rtl">(ما) می گذریم</div> /(mǎ) mi.go.za.rim/	<div dir="rtl">(من) می گذرم</div> /(man) mi.go.za.ram/
<div dir="rtl">(شما) می گذرید</div> /(šo.mǎ) mi.go.za.ri/	<div dir="rtl">(تو) می گذری</div> /(to) mi.go.za.ri/
<div dir="rtl">(آنها) می گذرند</div> /(ǎn.hǎ) mi.go.za.rad/	<div dir="rtl">(او/آن) می گذرد</div> /(u/ ǎn) mi.go.za.rad/
Present Subjunctive <div dir="rtl">مضارع التزامی</div>	
<div dir="rtl">(ما) بگذریم</div> /(mǎ) be.go.za.rim/	<div dir="rtl">(من) بگذرم</div> /(man) be.go.za.ram/
<div dir="rtl">(شما) بگذرید</div> /(šo.mǎ) be.go.za.rid/	<div dir="rtl">(تو) بگذری</div> /(to) be.go.za.ri/
<div dir="rtl">(آنها) بگذرند</div> /(ǎn.hǎ) be.go.za.rand/	<div dir="rtl">(او/آن) بگذرد</div> /(u/ ǎn) be.go.za.rad/
Present Progressive <div dir="rtl">مضارع مستمر(در جریان)</div>	
<div dir="rtl">(ما) داریم می گذریم</div> /(mǎ) dǎ.rim- mi.go.za.rim/	<div dir="rtl">(من) دارم می گذرم</div> /(man) dǎ.ram- mi.go.za.ram/
<div dir="rtl">(شما) دارید می گذرید</div> /(šo.mǎ) dǎ.rid- mi.go.za.rid/	<div dir="rtl">(تو) داری می گذری</div> /(to) dǎ.ri- mi.go.za.ri/
<div dir="rtl">(آنها) دارند می گذرند</div> /(ǎn.hǎ) dǎ.rand- mi.go.za.rand/	<div dir="rtl">(او/آن) دارد می گذرد</div> /(u/ ǎn) dǎ.rad- mi.go.za.rad/

Simple Past	
ماضی مطلق (گذشته ساده)	
(ما) گذشتیم	(من) گذشتم
/(mă) go.zaš.tim/	/(man) go.zaš.tam/
(شما) گذشتید	(تو) گذشتی
/(šo.mă) go.zaš.tid/	/(to) go.zaš.ti/
(آنها) گذشتند	(او/ آن) گذشت
/(ăn.hă) go.zaš.tand/	/(u/ ăn) go.zašt/

Imperfect Indicative	
ماضی استمراری	
(ما) می گذشتیم	(من) می گذشتم
/(mă) mi.go.zaš.tim/	/(man) mi.go.zaš.tam/
(شما) می گذشتید	(تو) می گذشتی
/(šo.mă) mi.go.zaš.tid/	/(to) mi.go.zaš.ti/
(آنها) می گذشتند	(او/ آن) می گذشت
/(ăn.hă) mi.go.zaš.tand/	/(u/ ăn) mi.go.zašt/

Present Perfect	
ماضی نقلی	
(ما) گذشته ایم	(من) گذشته ام
/(mă) go.zaš.te.im/	/(man) go.zaš.te.am/
(شما) گذشته اید	(تو) گذشته ای
/(šo.mă) go.zaš.te.id/	/(to) go.zaš.te.i/
(آنها) گذشته اند	(او/ آن) گذشته است
/(ăn.hă) go.zaš.te.and/	/(u/ ăn) go.zaš.te- ast/

Past Perfect	
ماضی بعید	
(ما) گذشته بودیم	(من) گذشته بودم
/(mă) go.zaš.te- bu.dim/	/(man) go.zaš.te- bu.dam/
(شما) گذشته بودید	(تو) گذشته بودی
/(šo.mă) go.zaš.te- bu.did/	/(to) go.zaš.te- bu.di/
(آنها) گذشته بودند	(او/ آن) گذشته بود
/(ăn.hă) go.zaš.te- bu.dand/	/(u/ ăn) go.zaš.te- bud/

174

Past Subjunctive	
ماضی التزامی	
(ما) گذشته باشیم	(من) گذشته باشم
/(mă) go.zaš.te- bă.šim/	/(man) go.zaš.te- bă.šam/
(شما) گذشته باشید	(تو) گذشته باشی
/(šo.mă) go.zaš.te- bă.šid/	/(to) go.zaš.te- bă.ši/
(آنها) گذشته باشند	(او/آن) گذشته باشد
/(ăn.hă) go.zaš.te- bă.šand/	/(u/ ăn) go.zaš.te- bă.šad/

Past Progressive	
ماضی مستمر(در جریان)	
(ما) داشتیم می گذشتیم	(من) داشتم می گذشتم
/(mă) dăš.tim- mi.go.zaš.tim/	/(man) dăš.tam- mi.go.zaš.tam/
(شما) داشتید می گذشتید	(تو) داشتی می گذشتی
/(šo.mă) dăš.tid- mi.go.zaš.tid/	/(to) dăš.ti- mi.go.zaš.ti/
(آنها) داشتند می گذشتند	(او/آن) داشت می گذشت
/(ăn.hă) dăš.tand- mi.go.zaš.tand/	/(u/ ăn) dăšt- mi.go.zašt/

Simple Future	
مستقبل (آینده ساده)	
(ما) خواهیم گذشت	(من) خواهم گذشت
/(mă) kă.him- go.zašt/	/(man) kă.ham- go.zašt/
(شما) خواهید گذشت	(تو) خواهی گذشت
/(šo.mă) kă.hid- go.zašt/	/(to) kă.hi- go.zašt/
(آنها) خواهند گذشت	(او/آن) خواهد گذشت
/(ăn.hă) kă.hand- go.zašt/	/(u/ ăn) kă.had- go.zašt/

Command	
امر	
بگذرید!	بگذر!
/be.go.za.rid/	/be.go.zar/

to pay

پَرداخْتَن

/par.dăẋ.tan/

Plural	Singular
Simple Present مضارع اخباری(حال ساده)	
(ما) می پردازیم /(mă) mi.par.dă.zim/	(من) می پردازم /(man) mi.par.dă.zam/
(شما) می پردازید /(šo.mă) mi.par.dă.zid/	(تو) می پردازی /(to) mi.par.dă.zi/
(آنها) می پردازند /(ăn.hă) mi.par.dă.zand/	(او/آن) می پردازد /(u/ ăn) mi.par.dă.zad/
Present Subjunctive مضارع التزامی	
(ما) بپردازیم /(mă) be.par.dă.zim/	(من) بپردازم /(man) be.par.dă.zam/
(شما) بپردازید /(šo.mă) be.par.dă.zid/	(تو) بپردازی /(to) be.par.dă.zi/
(آنها) بپردازند /(ăn.hă) be.par.dă.zand/	(او/آن) بپردازد /(u/ ăn) be.par.dă.zad/
Present Progressive مضارع مستمر(در جریان)	
(ما) داریم می پردازیم /(mă) dă.rim- mi.par.dă.zim/	(من) دارم می پردازم /(man) dă.ram- mi.par.dă.zam/
(شما) دارید می پردازید /(šo.mă) dă.rid- mi.par.dă.zid/	(تو) داری می پردازی /(to) dă.ri- mi.par.dă.zi/
(آنها) دارند می پردازند /(ăn.hă) dă.rand- mi.par.dă.zand/	(او/آن) دارد می پردازد /(u/ ăn) dă.rad- mi.par.dă.zad/

176

Simple Past	
ماضی مطلق (گذشته ساده)	
(ما) پرداختیم	(من) پرداختم
/(mǎ) par.dǎǩ.tim/	/(man) par.dǎǩ.tam/
(شما) پرداختید	(تو) پرداختی
/(šo.mǎ) par.dǎǩ.tid/	/(to) par.dǎǩ.ti/
(آنها) پرداختند	(او/آن) پرداخت
/(ǎn.hǎ) par.dǎǩ.tand/	/(u/ ǎn) par.dǎǩt/

Imperfect Indicative	
ماضی استمراری	
(ما) می پرداختیم	(من) می پرداختم
/(mǎ) mi.par.dǎǩ.tim/	/(man) mi.par.dǎǩ.tam/
(شما) می پرداختید	(تو) می پرداختی
/(šo.mǎ) mi.par.dǎǩ.tid/	/(to) mi.par.dǎǩ.ti/
(آنها) می پرداختند	(او/آن) می پرداخت
/(ǎn.hǎ) mi.par.dǎǩ.tand/	/(u/ ǎn) mi.par.dǎǩt/

Present Perfect	
ماضی نقلی	
(ما) پرداخته ایم	(من) پرداخته ام
/(mǎ) par.dǎǩ.te.im/	/(man) par.dǎǩ.te.am/
(شما) پرداخته اید	(تو) پرداخته ای
/(šo.mǎ) par.dǎǩ.te.id/	/(to) par.dǎǩ.te.i/
(آنها) پرداخته اند	(او/آن) پرداخته است
/(ǎn.hǎ) par.dǎǩ.te.and/	/(u/ ǎn) par.dǎǩ.te- ast/

Past Perfect	
ماضی بعید	
(ما) پرداخته بودیم	(من) پرداخته بودم
/(mǎ) par.dǎǩ.te- bu.dim/	/(man) par.dǎǩ.te- bu.dam/
(شما) پرداخته بودید	(تو) پرداخته بودی
/(šo.mǎ) par.dǎǩ.te- bu.did/	/(to) par.dǎǩ.te- bu.di/
(آنها) پرداخته بودند	(او/آن) پرداخته بود
/(ǎn.hǎ) par.dǎǩ.te- bu.dand/	/(u/ ǎn) par.dǎǩ.te- bud/

Past Subjunctive	
ماضی التزامی	
(ما) پرداخته باشیم /(mă) par.dăǩ.te- bă.šim/	(من) پرداخته باشم /(man) par.dăǩ.te- bă.šam/
(شما) پرداخته باشید /(šo.mă) par.dăǩ.te- bă.šid/	(تو) پرداخته باشی /(to) par.dăǩ.te- bă.ši/
(آنها) پرداخته باشند /(ăn.hă) par.dăǩ.te- bă.šand/	(او/آن) پرداخته باشد /(u/ ăn) par.dăǩ.te- bă.šad/

Past Progressive	
ماضی مستمر(در جریان)	
(ما) داشتیم می پرداختیم /(mă) dăš.tim- mi.par.dăǩ.tim/	(من) داشتم می پرداختم /(man) dăš.tam- mi.par.dăǩ.tam/
(شما) داشتید می پرداختید /(šo.mă) dăš.tid- mi.par.dăǩ.tid/	(تو) داشتی می پرداختی /(to) dăš.ti- mi.par.dăǩ.ti/
(آنها) داشتند می پرداختند /(ăn.hă) dăš.tand- mi.par.dăǩ.tand/	(او/آن) داشت می پرداخت /(u/ ăn) dăšt- mi.par.dăǩt/

Simple Future	
مستقبل (آینده ساده)	
(ما) خواهیم پرداخت /(mă) ǩă.him- par.dăǩt/	(من) خواهم پرداخت /(man) ǩă.ham- par.dăǩt/
(شما) خواهید پرداخت /(šo.mă) ǩă.hid- par.dăǩt/	(تو) خواهی پرداخت /(to) ǩă.hi- par.dăǩt/
(آنها) خواهند پرداخت /(ăn.hă) ǩă.hand- par.dăǩt/	(او/آن) خواهد پرداخت /(u/ ăn) ǩă.had- par.dăǩt/

Command	
امر	
بپردازید! /be.par.dă.zid/	بپرداز! /be.par.dăz/

178

to pick a flower, to cut with scissors

چیدَن

/chi.dan/

Plural	Singular
Simple Present مضارع اخباری(حال ساده)	
(ما) می چینیم /(mǎ) mi.chi.nim/	(من) می چینم /(man) mi.chi.nam/
(شما) می چینید /(šo.mǎ) mi.chi.nid/	(تو) می چینی /(to) mi.chi.ni/
(آنها) می چینند /(ǎn.hǎ) mi.chi.nand/	(او/آن) می چیند /(u/ ǎn) mi.chi.nad/
Present Subjunctive مضارع التزامی	
(ما) بچینیم /(mǎ) be.chi.nim/	(من) بچینم /(man) be.chi.nam/
(شما) بچینید /(šo.mǎ) be.chi.nid/	(تو) بچینی /(to) be.chi.ni/
(آنها) بچینند /(ǎn.hǎ) be.chi.nand/	(او/آن) بچیند /(u/ ǎn) be.chi.nad/
Present Progressive مضارع مستمر(در جریان)	
(ما) داریم می چینیم /(mǎ) dǎ.rim- mi.chi.nim/	(من) دارم می چینم /(man) dǎ.ram- mi.chi.nam/
(شما) دارید می چینید /(šo.mǎ) dǎ.rid- mi.chi.nid/	(تو) داری می چینی /(to) dǎ.ri- mi.chi.ni/
(آنها) دارند می چینند /(ǎn.hǎ) dǎ.rand- mi.chi.nand/	(او/آن) دارد می چیند /(u/ ǎn) dǎ.rad- mi.chi.nad/

Simple Past
ماضی مطلق (گذشته ساده)

(ما) چیدیم	(من) چیدم
/(mă) chi.dim/	/(man) chi.dam/
(شما) چیدید	(تو) چیدی
/(šo.mă) chi.did/	/(to) chi.di/
(آنها) چیدند	(او/ آن) چید
/(ăn.hă) chi.dand/	/(u/ ăn) chid/

Imperfect Indicative
ماضی استمراری

(ما) می چیدیم	(من) می چیدم
/(mă) mi.chi.dim/	/(man) mi.chi.dam/
(شما) می چیدید	(تو) می چیدی
/(šo.mă) mi.chi.did/	/(to) mi.chi.di/
(آنها) می چیدند	(او/ آن) می چید
/(ăn.hă) mi.chi.dand/	/(u/ ăn) mi.chid/

Present Perfect
ماضی نقلی

(ما) چیده ایم	(من) چیده ام
/(mă) chi.de.im/	/(man) chi.de.am/
(شما) چیده اید	(تو) چیده ای
/(šo.mă) chi.de.id/	/(to) chi.de.i/
(آنها) چیده اند	(او/ آن) چیده است
/(ăn.hă) chi.de.and/	/(u/ ăn) chi.de- ast/

Past Perfect
ماضی بعید

(ما) چیده بودیم	(من) چیده بودم
/(mă) chi.de- bu.dim/	/(man) chi.de- bu.dam/
(شما) چیده بودید	(تو) چیده بودی
/(šo.mă) chi.de- bu.did/	/(to) chi.de- bu.di/
(آنها) چیده بودند	(او/ آن) چیده بود
/(ăn.hă) chi.de- bu.dand/	/(u/ ăn) chi.de- bud/

<table>
<tr><td colspan="2" align="center">**Past Subjunctive**
ماضی التزامی</td></tr>
<tr>
<td align="center">(ما) چیده باشیم
/(mă) chi.de- bă.šim/</td>
<td align="center">(من) چیده باشم
/(man) chi.de- bă.šam/</td>
</tr>
<tr>
<td align="center">(شما) چیده باشید
/(šo.mă) chi.de- bă.šid/</td>
<td align="center">(تو) چیده باشی
/(to) chi.de- bă.ši/</td>
</tr>
<tr>
<td align="center">(آنها) چیده باشند
/(ăn.hă) chi.de- bă.šand/</td>
<td align="center">(او/آن) چیده باشد
/(u/ ăn) chi.de- bă.šad/</td>
</tr>
</table>

<table>
<tr><td colspan="2" align="center">**Past Progressive**
ماضی مستمر(در جریان)</td></tr>
<tr>
<td align="center">(ما) داشتیم می چیدیم
/(mă) dăš.tim- mi.chi.dim/</td>
<td align="center">(من) داشتم می چیدم
/(man) dăš.tam- mi.chi.dam/</td>
</tr>
<tr>
<td align="center">(شما) داشتید می چیدید
/(šo.mă) dăš.tid- mi.chi.did/</td>
<td align="center">(تو) داشتی می چیدی
/(to) dăš.ti- mi.chi.di/</td>
</tr>
<tr>
<td align="center">(آنها) داشتند می چیدند
/(ăn.hă) dăš.tand- mi.chi.dand/</td>
<td align="center">(او/آن) داشت می چید
/(u/ ăn) dăšt- mi.chid/</td>
</tr>
</table>

<table>
<tr><td colspan="2" align="center">**Simple Future**
مستقبل (آینده ساده)</td></tr>
<tr>
<td align="center">(ما) خواهیم چید
/(mă) ǩă.him- chid/</td>
<td align="center">(من) خواهم چید
/(man) ǩă.ham- chid/</td>
</tr>
<tr>
<td align="center">(شما) خواهید چید
/(šo.mă) ǩă.hid- chid/</td>
<td align="center">(تو) خواهی چید
/(to) ǩă.hi- chid/</td>
</tr>
<tr>
<td align="center">(آنها) خواهند چید
/(ăn.hă) ǩă.hand- chid/</td>
<td align="center">(او/آن) خواهد چید
/(u/ ăn) ǩă.had- chid/</td>
</tr>
</table>

<table>
<tr><td colspan="2" align="center">**Command**
امر</td></tr>
<tr>
<td align="center">بچینید!
/be.chi.nid/</td>
<td align="center">بچین!
/be.chin/</td>
</tr>
</table>

to pick up

بَرداشتَن

/bar.dăš.tan/

Plural	Singular
Simple Present	
مضارع اخباری(حال ساده)	
(ما) برمی داریم	(من) برمی دارم
/(mă) bar.mi.dă.rim/	/(man) bar.mi.dă.ram/
(شما) برمی دارید	(تو) برمی داری
/(šo.mă) bar.mi.dă.rid/	/(to) bar.mi.dă.ri/
(آنها) برمی دارند	(او/آن) برمی دارد
/(ăn.hă) bar.mi.dă.rand/	/(u/ ăn) bar.mi.dă.rad/

Plural	Singular
Present Subjunctive	
مضارع التزامی	
(ما) برداریم	(من) بردارم
/(mă) bar.dă.rim/	/(man) bar.dă.ram/
(شما) بردارید	(تو) برداری
/(šo.mă) bar.dă.rid/	/(to) bar.dă.ri/
(آنها) بردارند	(او/آن) بردارد
/(ăn.hă) bar.dă.rand/	/(u/ ăn) bar.dă.rad/

Plural	Singular
Present Progressive	
مضارع مستمر(در جریان)	
(ما) داریم بر می داریم	(من) دارم بر می دارم
/(mă) dă.rim- bar.mi.dă.rim/	/(man) dă.ram- bar.mi.dă.ram/
(شما) دارید بر می دارید	(تو) داری بر می داری
/(šo.mă) dă.rid- bar.mi.dă.rid/	/(to) dă.ri- bar.mi.dă.ri/
(آنها) دارند بر می دارند	(او/آن) دارد بر می دارد
/(ăn.hă) dă.rand- bar.mi.dă.rand/	/(u/ ăn) dă.rad- bar.mi.dă.rad/

Simple Past	
ماضی مطلق (گذشته ساده)	
(ما) برداشتیم	(من) برداشتم
/(mǎ) bar.dǎš.tim/	/(man) bar.dǎš.tam/
(شما) برداشتید	(تو) برداشتی
/(šo.mǎ) bar.dǎš.tid/	/(to) bar.dǎš.ti/
(آنها) برداشتند	(او/آن) برداشت
/(ǎn.hǎ) bar.dǎš.tand/	/(u/ ǎn) bar.dǎšt/

Imperfect Indicative	
ماضی استمراری	
(ما) برمی داشتیم	(من) برمی داشتم
/(mǎ) bar.mi.dǎš.tim/	/(man) bar.mi.dǎš.tam/
(شما) برمی داشتید	(تو) برمی داشتی
/(šo.mǎ) bar.mi.dǎš.tid/	/(to) bar.mi.dǎš.ti/
(آنها) برمی داشتند	(او/آن) برمی داشت
/(ǎn.hǎ) bar.mi.dǎš.tand/	/(u/ ǎn) bar.mi.dǎšt/

Present Perfect	
ماضی نقلی	
(ما) برداشته ایم	(من) برداشته ام
/(mǎ) bar.dǎš.te.im/	/(man) bar.dǎš.te.am/
(شما) برداشته اید	(تو) برداشته ای
/(šo.mǎ) bar.dǎš.te.id/	/(to) bar.dǎš.te.i/
(آنها) برداشته اند	(او/آن) برداشته است
/(ǎn.hǎ) bar.dǎš.te.and/	/(u/ ǎn) bar.dǎš.te- ast/

Past Perfect	
ماضی بعید	
(ما) برداشته بودیم	(من) برداشته بودم
/(mǎ) bar.dǎš.te- bu.dim/	/(man) bar.dǎš.te- bu.dam/
(شما) برداشته بودید	(تو) برداشته بودی
/(šo.mǎ) bar.dǎš.te- bu.did/	/(to) bar.dǎš.te- bu.di/
(آنها) برداشته بودند	(او/آن) برداشته بود
/(ǎn.hǎ) bar.dǎš.te- bu.dand/	/(u/ ǎn) bar.dǎš.te- bud/

Past Subjunctive	
ماضی التزامی	
(ما) برداشته باشیم	(من) برداشته باشم
/(mǎ) bar.dǎš.te- bǎ.šim/	/(man) bar.dǎš.te- bǎ.šam/
(شما) برداشته باشید	(تو) برداشته باشی
/(šo.mǎ) bar.dǎš.te- bǎ.šid/	/(to) bar.dǎš.te- bǎ.ši/
(آنها) برداشته باشند	(او/ آن) برداشته باشد
/(ǎn.hǎ) bar.dǎš.te- bǎ.šand/	/(u/ ǎn) bar.dǎš.te- bǎ.šad/

Past Progressive	
ماضی مستمر(در جریان)	
(ما) داشتیم برمی داشتیم	(من) داشتم برمی داشتم
/(mǎ) dǎš.tim- bar.mi.dǎš.tim/	/(man) dǎš.tam- bar.mi.dǎš.tam/
(شما) داشتید برمی داشتید	(تو) داشتی برمی داشتی
/(šo.mǎ) dǎš.tid- bar.mi.dǎš.tid/	/(to) dǎš.ti- bar.mi.dǎš.ti/
(آنها) داشتند برمی داشتند	(او/ آن) داشت برمی داشت
/(ǎn.hǎ) dǎš.tand- bar.mi.dǎš.tand/	/(u/ ǎn) dǎšt- bar.mi.dǎšt/

Simple Future	
مستقبل (آینده ساده)	
(ما) برخواهیم داشت	(من) برخواهم داشت
/(mǎ) bar.ǩǎ.him- dǎšt/	/(man) bar.ǩǎ.ham- dǎšt/
(شما) برخواهید داشت	(تو) برخواهی داشت
/(šo.mǎ) bar.ǩǎ.hid- dǎšt/	/(to) bar.ǩǎ.hi- dǎšt/
(آنها) برخواهند داشت	(او/ آن) برخواهد داشت
/(ǎn.hǎ) bar.ǩǎ.hand- dǎšt/	/(u/ ǎn) bar.ǩǎ.had- dǎšt/

Command	
امر	
بردارید!	بردار!
/bar.dǎ.rid/	/bar.dǎr/

184

to pile

آنباشتَن

/an.băš.tan/

Plural	Singular
Simple Present <div dir="rtl">مضارع اخباری(حال ساده)</div>	
<div dir="rtl">(ما) می انباریم</div> /(mă) mi.an.bă.rim/	<div dir="rtl">(من) می انبارم</div> /(man) mi.an.bă.ram/
<div dir="rtl">(شما) می انبارید</div> /(šo.mă) mi.an.bă.rid/	<div dir="rtl">(تو) می انباری</div> /(to) mi.an.bă.ri/
<div dir="rtl">(آنها) می انبارند</div> /(ăn.hă) mi.an.bă.rand/	<div dir="rtl">(او/آن) می انبارد</div> /(u/ ăn) mi.an.bă.rad/

Plural	Singular
Present Subjunctive <div dir="rtl">مضارع التزامی</div>	
<div dir="rtl">(ما) بینباریم</div> /(mă) bi.yan.bă.rim/	<div dir="rtl">(من) بینبارم</div> /(man) bi.yan.bă.ram/
<div dir="rtl">(شما) بینبارید</div> /(šo.mă) bi.yan.bă.rid/	<div dir="rtl">(تو) بینباری</div> /(to) bi.yan.bă.ri/
<div dir="rtl">(آنها) بینبارند</div> /(ăn.hă) bi.yan.bă.rand/	<div dir="rtl">(او/آن) بینبارد</div> /(u/ ăn) bi.yan.bă.rad/

Plural	Singular
Present Progressive <div dir="rtl">مضارع مستمر(در جریان)</div>	
<div dir="rtl">(ما) داریم می انباریم</div> /(mă) dă.rim- mi.an.bă.rim/	<div dir="rtl">(من) دارم می انبارم</div> /(man) dă.ram- mi.an.bă.ram/
<div dir="rtl">(شما) دارید می انبارید</div> /(šo.mă) dă.rid- mi.an.bă.rid/	<div dir="rtl">(تو) داری می انباری</div> /(to) dă.ri- mi.an.bă.ri/
<div dir="rtl">(آنها) دارند می انبارند</div> /(ăn.hă) dă.rand- mi.an.bă.rand/	<div dir="rtl">(او/آن) دارد می انبارد</div> /(u/ ăn) dă.rad- mi.an.bă.rad/

<table>
<tr><td colspan="2" align="center">**Simple Past**
ماضی مطلق (گذشته ساده)</td></tr>
<tr><td align="center">(ما) انباشتیم
/(mă) an.băš.tim/</td><td align="center">(من) انباشتم
/(man) an.băš.tam/</td></tr>
<tr><td align="center">(شما) انباشتید
/(šo.mă) an.băš.tid/</td><td align="center">(تو) انباشتی
/(to) an.băš.ti/</td></tr>
<tr><td align="center">(آنها) انباشتند
/(ăn.hă) an.băš.tand/</td><td align="center">(او/آن) انباشت
/(u/ ăn) an.băšt/</td></tr>
</table>

<table>
<tr><td colspan="2" align="center">**Imperfect Indicative**
ماضی استمراری</td></tr>
<tr><td align="center">(ما) می انباشتیم
/(mă) mi.an.băš.tim/</td><td align="center">(من) می انباشتم
/(man) mi.an.băš.tam/</td></tr>
<tr><td align="center">(شما) می انباشتید
/(šo.mă) mi.an.băš.tid/</td><td align="center">(تو) می انباشتی
/(to) mi.an.băš.ti/</td></tr>
<tr><td align="center">(آنها) می انباشتند
/(ăn.hă) mi.an.băš.tand/</td><td align="center">(او/آن) می انباشت
/(u/ ăn) mi.an.băšt/</td></tr>
</table>

<table>
<tr><td colspan="2" align="center">**Present Perfect**
ماضی نقلی</td></tr>
<tr><td align="center">(ما) انباشته ایم
/(mă) an.băš.te.im/</td><td align="center">(من) انباشته ام
/(man) an.băš.te.am/</td></tr>
<tr><td align="center">(شما) انباشته اید
/(šo.mă) an.băš.te.id/</td><td align="center">(تو) انباشته ای
/(to) an.băš.te.i/</td></tr>
<tr><td align="center">(آنها) انباشته اند
/(ăn.hă) an.băš.te.and/</td><td align="center">(او/آن) انباشته است
/(u/ ăn) an.băš.te- ast/</td></tr>
</table>

<table>
<tr><td colspan="2" align="center">**Past Perfect**
ماضی بعید</td></tr>
<tr><td align="center">(ما) انباشته بودیم
/(mă) an.băš.te- bu.dim/</td><td align="center">(من) انباشته بودم
/(man) an.băš.te- bu.dam/</td></tr>
<tr><td align="center">(شما) انباشته بودید
/(šo.mă) an.băš.te- bu.did/</td><td align="center">(تو) انباشته بودی
/(to) an.băš.te- bu.di/</td></tr>
<tr><td align="center">(آنها) انباشته بودند
/(ăn.hă) an.băš.te- bu.dand/</td><td align="center">(او/آن) انباشته بود
/(u/ ăn) an.băš.te- bud/</td></tr>
</table>

Past Subjunctive	
ماضی التزامی	
(ما) انباشته باشیم	(من) انباشته باشم
/(mǎ) an.bǎš.te- bǎ.šim/	/(man) an.bǎš.te- bǎ.šam/
(شما) انباشته باشید	(تو) انباشته باشی
/(šo.mǎ) an.bǎš.te- bǎ.šid/	/(to) an.bǎš.te- bǎ.ši/
(آنها) انباشته باشند	(او/آن) انباشته باشد
/(ǎn.hǎ) an.bǎš.te- bǎ.šand/	/(u/ ǎn) an.bǎš.te- bǎ.šad/

Past Progressive	
ماضی مستمر(در جریان)	
(ما) داشتیم می انباشتیم	(من) داشتم می انباشتم
/(mǎ) dǎš.tim- mi.an.bǎš.tim/	/(man) dǎš.tam- mi.an.bǎš.tam/
(شما) داشتید می انباشتید	(تو) داشتی می انباشتی
/(šo.mǎ) dǎš.tid- mi.an.bǎš.tid/	/(to) dǎš.ti- mi.an.bǎš.ti/
(آنها) داشتند می انباشتند	(او/آن) داشت می انباشت
/(ǎn.hǎ) dǎš.tand- mi.an.bǎš.tand/	/(u/ ǎn) dǎšt- mi.an.bǎšt/

Simple Future	
مستقبل (آینده ساده)	
(ما) خواهیم انباشت	(من) خواهم انباشت
/(mǎ) ǩǎ.him- an.bǎšt/	/(man) ǩǎ.ham- an.bǎšt/
(شما) خواهید انباشت	(تو) خواهی انباشت
/(šo.mǎ) ǩǎ.hid- an.bǎšt/	/(to) ǩǎ.hi- an.bǎšt/
(آنها) خواهند انباشت	(او/آن) خواهد انباشت
/(ǎn.hǎ) ǩǎ.hand- an.bǎšt/	/(u/ ǎn) ǩǎ.had- an.bǎšt/

Command	
امر	
بینبارید!	بینبار!
/be.yan.bǎ.rid/	/be.yan.bǎr/

to place

نَهادَن

/na.hǎ.dan/

Plural	Singular
Simple Present مضارع اخباری(حال ساده)	
(ما) می نهیم /(mǎ) mi.na.him/	(من) می نهم /(man) mi.na.ham/
(شما) می نهید /(šo.mǎ) mi.na.hid/	(تو) می نهی /(to) mi.na.hi/
(آنها) می نهند /(ǎn.hǎ) mi.na.hand/	(او/آن) می نهد /(u/ ǎn) mi.na.had/
Present Subjunctive مضارع التزامی	
(ما) بنهیم /(mǎ) be.na.him/	(من) بنهم /(man) be.na.ham/
(شما) بنهید /(šo.mǎ) be.na.hid/	(تو) بنهی /(to) be.na.hi/
(آنها) بنهند /(ǎn.hǎ) be.na.hand/	(او/آن) بنهد /(u/ ǎn) be.na.had/
Present Progressive مضارع مستمر(در جریان)	
(ما) داریم می نهیم /(mǎ) dǎ.rim- mi.na.him/	(من) دارم می نهم /(man) dǎ.ram- mi.na.ham/
(شما) دارید می نهید /(šo.mǎ) dǎ.rid- mi.na.hid/	(تو) داری می نهی /(to) dǎ.ri- mi.na.hi/
(آنها) دارند می نهند /(ǎn.hǎ) dǎ.rand- mi.na.hand/	(او/آن) دارد می نهد /(u/ ǎn) dǎ.rad- mi.na.had/

	Simple Past
	ماضی مطلق (گذشته ساده)
(ما) نهادیم	(من) نهادم
/(mă) na.hă.dim/	/(man) na.hă.dam/
(شما) نهادید	(تو) نهادی
/(šo.mă) na.hă.did/	/(to) na.hă.di/
(آنها) نهادند	(او/آن) نهاد
/(ăn.hă) na.hă.dand/	/(u/ ăn) na.hăd/

	Imperfect Indicative
	ماضی استمراری
(ما) می نهادیم	(من) می نهادم
/(mă) mi.na.hă.dim/	/(man) mi.na.hă.dam/
(شما) می نهادید	(تو) می نهادی
/(šo.mă) mi.na.hă.did/	/(to) mi.na.hă.di/
(آنها) می نهادند	(او/آن) می نهاد
/(ăn.hă) mi.na.hă.dand/	/(u/ ăn) mi.na.hăd/

	Present Perfect
	ماضی نقلی
(ما) نهاده ایم	(من) نهاده ام
/(mă) na.hă.de.im/	/(man) na.hă.de.am/
(شما) نهاده اید	(تو) نهاده ای
/(šo.mă) na.hă.de.id/	/(to) na.hă.de.i/
(آنها) نهاده اند	(او/آن) نهاده است
/(ăn.hă) na.hă.de.and/	/(u/ ăn) na.hă.de- ast/

	Past Perfect
	ماضی بعید
(ما) نهاده بودیم	(من) نهاده بودم
/(mă) na.hă.de- bu.dim/	/(man) na.hă.de- bu.dam/
(شما) نهاده بودید	(تو) نهاده بودی
/(šo.mă) na.hă.de- bu.did/	/(to) na.hă.de- bu.di/
(آنها) نهاده بودند	(او/آن) نهاده بود
/(ăn.hă) na.hă.de- bu.dand/	/(u/ ăn) na.hă.de- bud/

189

Past Subjunctive	
ماضی التزامی	
(ما) نهاده باشیم /(mă) na.hă.de- bă.šim/	(من) نهاده باشم /(man) na.hă.de- bă.šam/
(شما) نهاده باشید /(šo.mă) na.hă.de- bă.šid/	(تو) نهاده باشی /(to) na.hă.de- bă.ši/
(آنها) نهاده باشند /(ăn.hă) na.hă.de- bă.šand/	(او/آن) نهاده باشد /(u/ ăn) na.hă.de- bă.šad/

Past Progressive	
ماضی مستمر(در جریان)	
(ما) داشتیم می نهادیم /(mă) dăš.tim- mi.na.hă.dim/	(من) داشتم می نهادم /(man) dăš.tam- mi.na.hă.dam/
(شما) داشتید می نهادید /(šo.mă) dăš.tid- mi.na.hă.did/	(تو) داشتی می نهادی /(to) dăš.ti- mi.na.hă.di/
(آنها) داشتند می نهادند /(ăn.hă) dăš.tand- mi.na.hă.dand/	(او/آن) داشت می نهاد /(u/ ăn) dăšt- mi.na.hăd/

Simple Future	
مستقبل (آینده ساده)	
(ما) خواهیم نهاد /(mă) ǩă.him- na.hăd/	(من) خواهم نهاد /(man) ǩă.ham- na.hăd/
(شما) خواهید نهاد /(šo.mă) ǩă.hid- na.hăd/	(تو) خواهی نهاد /(to) ǩă.hi- na.hăd/
(آنها) خواهند نهاد /(ăn.hă) ǩă.hand- na.hăd/	(او/آن) خواهد نهاد /(u/ ăn) ǩă.had- na.hăd/

Command	
امر	
بنهید! /be.na.hid/	بنه! /be.neh/

to plant

کاشتَن

/kăš.tan/

Plural	Singular
Simple Present مضارع اخباری(حال ساده)	
(ما) می کاریم /(mă) mi.kă.rim/	(من) می کارم /(man) mi.kă.ram/
(شما) می کارید /(šo.mă) mi.kă.rid/	(تو) می کاری /(to) mi.kă.ri/
(آنها) می کارند /(ăn.hă) mi.kă.rand/	(او/آن) می کارد /(u/ ăn) mi.kă.rad/

Plural	Singular
Present Subjunctive مضارع التزامی	
(ما) بکاریم /(mă) be.kă.rim/	(من) بکارم /(man) be.kă.ram/
(شما) بکارید /(šo.mă) be.kă.rid/	(تو) بکاری /(to) be.kă.ri/
(آنها) بکارند /(ăn.hă) be.kă.rand/	(او/آن) بکارد /(u/ ăn) be.kă.rad/

Plural	Singular
Present Progressive مضارع مستمر(در جریان)	
(ما) داریم می کاریم /(mă) dă.rim- mi.kă.rim/	(من) دارم می کارم /(man) dă.ram- mi.kă.ram/
(شما) دارید می کارید /(šo.mă) dă.rid- mi.kă.rid/	(تو) داری می کاری /(to) dă.ri- mi.kă.ri/
(آنها) دارند می کارند /(ăn.hă) dă.rand- mi.kă.rand/	(او/آن) دارد می کارد /(u/ ăn) dă.rad- mi.kă.rad/

191

Simple Past
ماضی مطلق (گذشته ساده)

(ما) کاشتیم	(من) کاشتم
/(mă) kăš.tim/	/(man) kăš.tam/
(شما) کاشتید	(تو) کاشتی
/(šo.mă) kăš.tid/	/(to) kăš.ti/
(آنها) کاشتند	(او/آن) کاشت
/(ăn.hă) kăš.tand/	/(u/ ăn) kăšt/

Imperfect Indicative
ماضی استمراری

(ما) می کاشتیم	(من) می کاشتم
/(mă) mi.kăš.tim/	/(man) mi.kăš.tam/
(شما) می کاشتید	(تو) می کاشتی
/(šo.mă) mi.kăš.tid/	/(to) mi.kăš.ti/
(آنها) می کاشتند	(او/آن) می کاشت
/(ăn.hă) mi.kăš.tand/	/(u/ ăn) mi.kăšt/

Present Perfect
ماضی نقلی

(ما) کاشته ایم	(من) کاشته ام
/(mă) kăš.te.im/	/(man) kăš.te.am/
(شما) کاشته اید	(تو) کاشته ای
/(šo.mă) kăš.te.id/	/(to) kăš.te.i/
(آنها) کاشته اند	(او/آن) کاشته است
/(ăn.hă) kăš.te.and/	/(u/ ăn) kăš.te- ast/

Past Perfect
ماضی بعید

(ما) کاشته بودیم	(من) کاشته بودم
/(mă) kăš.te- bu.dim/	/(man) kăš.te- bu.dam/
(شما) کاشته بودید	(تو) کاشته بودی
/(šo.mă) kăš.te- bu.did/	/(to) kăš.te- bu.di/
(آنها) کاشته بودند	(او/آن) کاشته بود
/(ăn.hă) kăš.te- bu.dand/	/(u/ ăn) kăš.te- bud/

Past Subjunctive	
ماضی التزامی	
(ما) کاشته باشیم	(من) کاشته باشم
/(mă) kăš.te- bă.šim/	/(man) kăš.te- bă.šam/
(شما) کاشته باشید	(تو) کاشته باشی
/(šo.mă) kăš.te- bă.šid/	/(to) kăš.te- bă.ši/
(آنها) کاشته باشند	(او/آن) کاشته باشد
/(ăn.hă) kăš.te- bă.šand/	/(u/ ăn) kăš.te- bă.šad/

Past Progressive	
ماضی مستمر(در جریان)	
(ما) داشتیم می کاشتیم	(من) داشتم می کاشتم
/(mă) dăš.tim- mi.kăš.tim/	/(man) dăš.tam- mi.kăš.tam/
(شما) داشتید می کاشتید	(تو) داشتی می کاشتی
/(šo.mă) dăš.tid- mi.kăš.tid/	/(to) dăš.ti- mi.kăš.ti/
(آنها) داشتند می کاشتند	(او/آن) داشت می کاشت
/(ăn.hă) dăš.tand- mi.kăš.tand/	/(u/ ăn) dăšt- mi.kăšt/

Simple Future	
مستقبل (آینده ساده)	
(ما) خواهیم کاشت	(من) خواهم کاشت
/(mă) ǩă.him- kăšt/	/(man) ǩă.ham- kăšt/
(شما) خواهید کاشت	(تو) خواهی کاشت
/(šo.mă) ǩă.hid- kăšt/	/(to) ǩă.hi- kăšt/
(آنها) خواهند کاشت	(او/آن) خواهد کاشت
/(ăn.hă) ǩă.hand- kăšt/	/(u/ ăn) ǩă.had- kăšt/

Command	
امر	
بکارید!	بکار!
/be.kă.rid/	/be.kăr/

to play a musical instrument

نَواختَن

/na.văǩ.tan/

Plural	Singular
Simple Present مضارع اخباری(حال ساده)	
(ما) می نوازیم /(mă) mi.na.vă.zim/	(من) می نوازم /(man) mi.na.vă.zam/
(شما) می نوازید /(šo.mă) mi.na.vă.zid/	(تو) می نوازی /(to) mi.na.vă.zi/
(آنها) می نوازند /(ăn.hă) mi.na.vă.zand/	(او/آن) می نوازد /(u/ ăn) mi.na.vă.zad/
Present Subjunctive مضارع التزامی	
(ما) بنوازیم /(mă) be.na.vă.zim/	(من) بنوازم /(man) be.na.vă.zam/
(شما) بنوازید /(šo.mă) be.na.vă.zid/	(تو) بنوازی /(to) be.na.vă.zi/
(آنها) بنوازند /(ăn.hă) be.na.vă.zand/	(او/آن) بنوازد /(u/ ăn) be.na.vă.zad/
Present Progressive مضارع مستمر(در جریان)	
(ما) داریم می نوازیم /(mă) dă.rim- mi.na.vă.zim/	(من) دارم می نوازم /(man) dă.ram- mi.na.vă.zam/
(شما) دارید می نوازید /(šo.mă) dă.rid- mi.na.vă.zid/	(تو) داری می نوازی /(to) dă.ri- mi.na.vă.zi/
(آنها) دارند می نوازند /(ăn.hă) dă.rand- mi.na.vă.zand/	(او/آن) دارد می نوازد /(u/ ăn) dă.rad- mi.na.vă.zad/

194

Simple Past
ماضی مطلق (گذشته ساده)

(ما) نواختیم	(من) نواختم
/(mǎ) na.vǎǩ.tim/	/(man) na.vǎǩ.tam/
(شما) نواختید	(تو) نواختی
/(šo.mǎ) na.vǎǩ.tid/	/(to) na.vǎǩ.ti/
(آنها) نواختند	(او/آن) نواخت
/(ǎn.hǎ) na.vǎǩ.tand/	/(u/ ǎn) na.vǎǩt/

Imperfect Indicative
ماضی استمراری

(ما) می نواختیم	(من) می نواختم
/(mǎ) mi.na.vǎǩ.tim/	/(man) mi.na.vǎǩ.tam/
(شما) می نواختید	(تو) می نواختی
/(šo.mǎ) mi.na.vǎǩ.tid/	/(to) mi.na.vǎǩ.ti/
(آنها) می نواختند	(او/آن) می نواخت
/(ǎn.hǎ) mi.na.vǎǩ.tand/	/(u/ ǎn) mi.na.vǎǩt/

Present Perfect
ماضی نقلی

(ما) نواخته ایم	(من) نواخته ام
/(mǎ) na.vǎǩ.te.im/	/(man) na.vǎǩ.te.am/
(شما) نواخته اید	(تو) نواخته ای
/(šo.mǎ) na.vǎǩ.te.id/	/(to) na.vǎǩ.te.i/
(آنها) نواخته اند	(او/آن) نواخته است
/(ǎn.hǎ) na.vǎǩ.te.and/	/(u/ ǎn) na.vǎǩ.te- ast/

Past Perfect
ماضی بعید

(ما) نواخته بودیم	(من) نواخته بودم
/(mǎ) na.vǎǩ.te- bu.dim/	/(man) na.vǎǩ.te- bu.dam/
(شما) نواخته بودید	(تو) نواخته بودی
/(šo.mǎ) na.vǎǩ.te- bu.did/	/(to) na.vǎǩ.te- bu.di/
(آنها) نواخته بودند	(او/آن) نواخته بود
/(ǎn.hǎ) na.vǎǩ.te- bu.dand/	/(u/ ǎn) na.vǎǩ.te- bud/

<table>
<tr><td colspan="2" align="center">Past Subjunctive
ماضی التزامی</td></tr>
<tr>
<td align="center">(ما) نواخته باشیم
/(mă) na.văǩ.te- bă.šim/</td>
<td align="center">(من) نواخته باشم
/(man) na.văǩ.te- bă.šam/</td>
</tr>
<tr>
<td align="center">(شما) نواخته باشید
/(šo.mă) na.văǩ.te- bă.šid/</td>
<td align="center">(تو) نواخته باشی
/(to) na.văǩ.te- bă.ši/</td>
</tr>
<tr>
<td align="center">(آنها) نواخته باشند
/(ăn.hă) na.văǩ.te- bă.šand/</td>
<td align="center">(او/آن) نواخته باشد
/(u/ ăn) na.văǩ.te- bă.šad/</td>
</tr>
</table>

<table>
<tr><td colspan="2" align="center">Past Progressive
ماضی مستمر(در جریان)</td></tr>
<tr>
<td align="center">(ما) داشتیم می نواختیم
/(mă) dăš.tim- mi.na.văǩ.tim/</td>
<td align="center">(من) داشتم می نواختم
/(man) dăš.tam- mi.na.văǩ.tam/</td>
</tr>
<tr>
<td align="center">(شما) داشتید می نواختید
/(šo.mă) dăš.tid- mi.na.văǩ.tid/</td>
<td align="center">(تو) داشتی می نواختی
/(to) dăš.ti- mi.na.văǩ.ti/</td>
</tr>
<tr>
<td align="center">(آنها) داشتند می نواختند
/(ăn.hă) dăš.tand- mi.na.văǩ.tand/</td>
<td align="center">(او/آن) داشت می نواخت
/(u/ ăn) dăšt- mi.na.văkt/</td>
</tr>
</table>

<table>
<tr><td colspan="2" align="center">Simple Future
مستقبل (آینده ساده)</td></tr>
<tr>
<td align="center">(ما) خواهیم نواخت
/(mă) ǩă.him- na.văkt/</td>
<td align="center">(من) خواهم نواخت
/(man) ǩă.ham- na.văkt/</td>
</tr>
<tr>
<td align="center">(شما) خواهید نواخت
/(šo.mă) ǩă.hid- na.văkt/</td>
<td align="center">(تو) خواهی نواخت
/(to) ǩă.hi- na.văkt/</td>
</tr>
<tr>
<td align="center">(آنها) خواهند نواخت
/(ăn.hă) ǩă.hand- na.văkt/</td>
<td align="center">(او/آن) خواهد نواخت
/(u/ ăn) ǩă.had- na.văkt/</td>
</tr>
</table>

<table>
<tr><td colspan="2" align="center">Command
امر</td></tr>
<tr>
<td align="center">بنوازید!
/be.na.vă.zid/</td>
<td align="center">بنواز!
/be.na.văz/</td>
</tr>
</table>

to pollute

آلودَن

/ă.lu.dan/

Plural	Singular
Simple Present مضارع اخباری(حال ساده)	
(ما) می آلاییم /(mă) mi.ă.lă.yim/	(من) می آلایم /(man) mi.ă.lă.yam/
(شما) می آلایید /(šo.mă) mi.ă.lă.yid/	(تو) می آلایی /(to) mi.ă.lă.yi/
(آنها) می آلایند /(ăn.hă) mi.ă.lă.yand/	(او/آن) می آلاید /(u/ ăn) mi.ă.lă.yad/
Present Subjunctive مضارع التزامی	
(ما) بیالاییم /(mă) bi.yă.lă.yim/	(من) بیالایم /(man) bi.yă.lă.yam/
(شما) بیالایید /(šo.mă) bi.yă.lă.yid/	(تو) بیالایی /(to) bi.yă.lă.yi/
(آنها) بیالایند /(ăn.hă) bi.yă.lă.yand/	(او/آن) بیالاید /(u/ ăn) bi.yă.lă.yad/
Present Progressive مضارع مستمر(در جریان)	
(ما) داریم می آلاییم /(mă) dă.rim- mi.ă.lă.yim/	(من) دارم می آلایم /(man) dă.ram- mi.ă.lă.yam/
(شما) دارید می آلایید /(šo.mă) dă.rid- mi.ă.lă.yid/	(تو) داری می آلایی /(to) dă.ri- mi.ă.lă.yi/
(آنها) دارند می آلایند /(ăn.hă) dă.rand- mi.ă.lă.yand/	(او/آن) دارد می آلاید /(u/ ăn) dă.rad- mi.ă.lă.yad/

Simple Past
ماضی مطلق (گذشته ساده)

(ما) آلودیم	(من) آلودم
/(mǎ) ǎ.lu.dim/	/(man) ǎ.lu.dam/
(شما) آلودید	(تو) آلودی
/(šo.mǎ) ǎ.lu.did/	/(to) ǎ.lu.di/
(آنها) آلودند	(او/آن) آلود
/(ǎn.hǎ) ǎ.lu.dand/	/(u/ ǎn) ǎ.lud/

Imperfect Indicative
ماضی استمراری

(ما) می آلودیم	(من) می آلودم
/(mǎ) mi.ǎ.lu.dim/	/(man) mi.ǎ.lu.dam/
(شما) می آلودید	(تو) می آلودی
/(šo.mǎ) mi.ǎ.lu.did/	/(to) mi.ǎ.lu.di/
(آنها) می آلودند	(او/آن) می آلود
/(ǎn.hǎ) mi.ǎ.lu.dand/	/(u/ ǎn) mi.ǎ.lud/

Present Perfect
ماضی نقلی

(ما) آلوده ایم	(من) آلوده ام
/(mǎ) ǎ.lu.de.im/	/(man) ǎ.lu.de.am/
(شما) آلوده اید	(تو) آلوده ای
/(šo.mǎ) ǎ.lu.de.id/	/(to) ǎ.lu.de.i/
(آنها) آلوده اند	(او/آن) آلوده است
/(ǎn.hǎ) ǎ.lu.de.and/	/(u/ ǎn) ǎ.lu.de- ast/

Past Perfect
ماضی بعید

(ما) آلوده بودیم	(من) آلوده بودم
/(mǎ) ǎ.lu.de- bu.dim/	/(man) ǎ.lu.de- bu.dam/
(شما) آلوده بودید	(تو) آلوده بودی
/(šo.mǎ) ǎ.lu.de- bu.did/	/(to) ǎ.lu.de- bu.di/
(آنها) آلوده بودند	(او/آن) آلوده بود
/(ǎn.hǎ) ǎ.lu.de- bu.dand/	/(u/ ǎn) ǎ.lu.de- bud/

Past Subjunctive	
ماضی التزامی	
(ما) آلوده باشیم	(من) آلوده باشم
/(mă) ă.lu.de- bă.šim/	/(man) ă.lu.de- bă.šam/
(شما) آلوده باشید	(تو) آلوده باشی
/(šo.mă) ă.lu.de- bă.šid/	/(to) ă.lu.de- bă.ši/
(آنها) آلوده باشند	(او/آن) آلوده باشد
/(ăn.hă) ă.lu.de- bă.šand/	/(u/ ăn) ă.lu.de- bă.šad/

Past Progressive	
ماضی مستمر(در جریان)	
(ما) داشتیم می آلودیم	(من) داشتم می آلودم
/(mă) dăš.tim- mi.ă.lu.dim/	/(man) dăš.tam- mi.ă.lu.dam/
(شما) داشتید می آلودید	(تو) داشتی می آلودی
/(šo.mă) dăš.tid- mi.ă.lu.did/	/(to) dăš.ti- mi.ă.lu.di/
(آنها) داشتند می آلودند	(او/آن) داشت می آلود
/(ăn.hă) dăš.tand- mi.ă.lu.dand/	/(u/ ăn) dăšt- mi.ă.lud/

Simple Future	
مستقبل (آینده ساده)	
(ما) خواهیم آلود	(من) خواهم آلود
/(mă) kă.him- ă.lud/	/(man) kă.ham- ă.lud/
(شما) خواهید آلود	(تو) خواهی آلود
/(šo.mă) kă.hid- ă.lud/	/(to) kă.hi- ă.lud/
(آنها) خواهند آلود	(او/آن) خواهد آلود
/(ăn.hă) kă.hand- ă.lud/	/(u/ ăn) kă.had- ă.lud/

Command	
امر	
بیالایید!	بیالای!
/bi.yă.lă.yid/	/bi.yă.lăy/

to pour, to spill

ریختَن

/riǩ.tan/

Plural	Singular
Simple Present مضارع اخباری(حال ساده)	
(ما) می ریزیم /(mǎ) mi.ri.zim/	(من) می ریزم /(man) mi.ri.zam/
(شما) می ریزید /(šo.mǎ) mi.ri.zid/	(تو) می ریزی /(to) mi.ri.zi/
(آنها) می ریزند /(ǎn.hǎ) mi.ri.zand/	(او/آن) می ریزد /(u/ ǎn) mi.ri.zad/
Present Subjunctive مضارع التزامی	
(ما) بریزیم /(mǎ) be.ri.zim/	(من) بریزم /(man) be.ri.zam/
(شما) بریزید /(šo.mǎ) be.ri.zid/	(تو) بریزی /(to) be.ri.zi/
(آنها) بریزند /(ǎn.hǎ) be.ri.zand/	(او/آن) بریزد /(u/ ǎn) be.ri.zad/
Present Progressive مضارع مستمر(در جریان)	
(ما) داریم می ریزیم /(mǎ) dǎ.rim- mi.ri.zim/	(من) دارم می ریزم /(man) dǎ.ram- mi.ri.zam/
(شما) دارید می ریزید /(šo.mǎ) dǎ.rid- mi.ri.zid/	(تو) داری می ریزی /(to) dǎ.ri- mi.ri.zi/
(آنها) دارند می ریزند /(ǎn.hǎ) dǎ.rand- mi.ri.zand/	(او/آن) دارد می ریزد /(u/ ǎn) dǎ.rad- mi.ri.zad/

	Simple Past
	ماضی مطلق (گذشته ساده)
(ما) ریختیم /(mǎ) riǩ.tim/	(من) ریختم /(man) riǩ.tam/
(شما) ریختید /(šo.mǎ) riǩ.tid/	(تو) ریختی /(to) riǩ.ti/
(آنها) ریختند /(ǎn.hǎ) riǩ.tand/	(او/آن) ریخت /(u/ ǎn) riǩt/

	Imperfect Indicative
	ماضی استمراری
(ما) می ریختیم /(mǎ) mi.riǩ.tim/	(من) می ریختم /(man) mi.riǩ.tam/
(شما) می ریختید /(šo.mǎ) mi.riǩ.tid/	(تو) می ریختی /(to) mi.riǩ.ti/
(آنها) می ریختند /(ǎn.hǎ) mi.riǩ.tand/	(او/آن) می ریخت /(u/ ǎn) mi.riǩt/

	Present Perfect
	ماضی نقلی
(ما) ریخته ایم /(mǎ) riǩ.te.im/	(من) ریخته ام /(man) riǩ.te.am/
(شما) ریخته اید /(šo.mǎ) riǩ.te.id/	(تو) ریخته ای /(to) riǩ.te.i/
(آنها) ریخته اند /(ǎn.hǎ) riǩ.te.and/	(او/آن) ریخته است /(u/ ǎn) riǩ.te- ast/

	Past Perfect
	ماضی بعید
(ما) ریخته بودیم /(mǎ) riǩ.te- bu.dim/	(من) ریخته بودم /(man) riǩ.te- bu.dam/
(شما) ریخته بودید /(šo.mǎ) riǩ.te- bu.did/	(تو) ریخته بودی /(to) riǩ.te- bu.di/
(آنها) ریخته بودند /(ǎn.hǎ) riǩ.te- bu.dand/	(او/آن) ریخته بود /(u/ ǎn) riǩ.te- bud/

Past Subjunctive	
ماضی التزامی	
(ما) ریخته باشیم	(من) ریخته باشم
/(mă) riǩ.te- bă.šim/	/(man) riǩ.te- bă.šam/
(شما) ریخته باشید	(تو) ریخته باشی
/(šo.mă) riǩ.te- bă.šid/	/(to) riǩ.te- bă.ši/
(آنها) ریخته باشند	(او/آن) ریخته باشد
/(ăn.hă) riǩ.te- bă.šand/	/(u/ ăn) riǩ.te- bă.šad/

Past Progressive	
ماضی مستمر(در جریان)	
(ما) داشتیم می ریختیم	(من) داشتم می ریختم
/(mă) dăš.tim- mi.riǩ.tim/	/(man) dăš.tam- mi.riǩ.tam/
(شما) داشتید می ریختید	(تو) داشتی می ریختی
/(šo.mă) dăš.tid- mi.riǩ.tid/	/(to) dăš.ti- mi.riǩ.ti/
(آنها) داشتند می ریختند	(او/آن) داشت می ریخت
/(ăn.hă) dăš.tand- mi.riǩ.tand/	/(u/ ăn) dăšt- mi.riǩt/

Simple Future	
مستقبل (آینده ساده)	
(ما) خواهیم ریخت	(من) خواهم ریخت
/(mă) ǩă.him- riǩt/	/(man) ǩă.ham- riǩt/
(شما) خواهید ریخت	(تو) خواهی ریخت
/(šo.mă) ǩă.hid- riǩt/	/(to) ǩă.hi- riǩt/
(آنها) خواهند ریخت	(او/آن) خواهد ریخت
/(ăn.hă) ǩă.hand- riǩt/	/(u/ ăn) ǩă.had- riǩt/

Command	
امر	
بریزید!	بریز!
/be.ri.zid/	/be.riz/

to praise

سُتودَن

/so.tu.dan/

Plural	Singular
Simple Present مضارع اخباری(حال ساده)	
(ما) می ستاییم /(mǎ) mi.se.tǎ.yim/	(من) می ستایم /(man) mi.se.tǎ.yam/
(شما) می ستایید /(šo.mǎ) mi.se.tǎ.yid/	(تو) می ستایی /(to) mi.se.tǎ.yi/
(آنها) می ستایند /(ǎn.hǎ) mi.se.tǎ.yand/	(او/آن) می ستاید /(u/ ǎn) mi.se.tǎ.yad/

Plural	Singular
Present Subjunctive مضارع التزامی	
(ما) بستاییم /(mǎ) be.se.tǎ.yim/	(من) بستایم /(man) be.se.tǎ.yam/
(شما) بستایید /(šo.mǎ) be.se.tǎ.yid/	(تو) بستایی /(to) be.se.tǎ.yi/
(آنها) بستایند /(ǎn.hǎ) be.se.tǎ.yand/	(او/آن) بستاید /(u/ ǎn) be.se.tǎ.yad/

Plural	Singular
Present Progressive مضارع مستمر(در جریان)	
(ما) داریم می ستاییم /(mǎ) dǎ.rim- mi.se.tǎ.yim/	(من) دارم می ستایم /(man) dǎ.ram- mi.se.tǎ.yam/
(شما) دارید می ستایید /(šo.mǎ) dǎ.rid- mi.se.tǎ.yid/	(تو) داری می ستایی /(to) dǎ.ri- mi.se.tǎ.yi/
(آنها) دارند می ستایند /(ǎn.hǎ) dǎ.rand- mi.se.tǎ.yand/	(او/آن) دارد می ستاید /(u/ ǎn) dǎ.rad- mi.se.tǎ.yad/

Simple Past
ماضی مطلق (گذشته ساده)

(ما) ستودیم	(من) ستودم
/(mǎ) so.tu.dim/	/(man) so.tu.dam/
(شما) ستودید	(تو) ستودی
/(šo.mǎ) so.tu.did/	/(to) so.tu.di/
(آنها) ستودند	(او/آن) ستود
/(ǎn.hǎ) so.tu.dand/	/(u/ ǎn) so.tud/

Imperfect Indicative
ماضی استمراری

(ما) می ستودیم	(من) می ستودم
/(mǎ) mi.so.tu.dim/	/(man) mi.so.tu.dam/
(شما) می ستودید	(تو) می ستودی
/(šo.mǎ) mi.so.tu.did/	/(to) mi.so.tu.di/
(آنها) می ستودند	(او/آن) می ستود
/(ǎn.hǎ) mi.so.tu.dand/	/(u/ ǎn) mi.so.tud/

Present Perfect
ماضی نقلی

(ما) ستوده ایم	(من) ستوده ام
/(mǎ) so.tu.de.im/	/(man) so.tu.de.am/
(شما) ستوده اید	(تو) ستوده ای
/(šo.mǎ) so.tu.de.id/	/(to) so.tu.de.i/
(آنها) ستوده اند	(او/آن) ستوده است
/(ǎn.hǎ) so.tu.de.and/	/(u/ ǎn) so.tu.de- ast/

Past Perfect
ماضی بعید

(ما) ستوده بودیم	(من) ستوده بودم
/(mǎ) so.tu.de- bu.dim/	/(man) so.tu.de- bu.dam/
(شما) ستوده بودید	(تو) ستوده بودی
/(šo.mǎ) so.tu.de- bu.did/	/(to) so.tu.de- bu.di/
(آنها) ستوده بودند	(او/آن) ستوده بود
/(ǎn.hǎ) so.tu.de- bu.dand/	/(u/ ǎn) so.tu.de- bud/

Past Subjunctive	
ماضی التزامی	
(ما) ستوده باشیم	(من) ستوده باشم
/(mǎ) so.tu.de- bǎ.šim/	/(man) so.tu.de- bǎ.šam/
(شما) ستوده باشید	(تو) ستوده باشی
/(šo.mǎ) so.tu.de- bǎ.šid/	/(to) so.tu.de- bǎ.ši/
(آنها) ستوده باشند	(او/آن) ستوده باشد
/(ǎn.hǎ) so.tu.de- bǎ.šand/	/(u/ ǎn) so.tu.de- bǎ.šad/

Past Progressive	
ماضی مستمر(در جریان)	
(ما) داشتیم می ستودیم	(من) داشتم می ستودم
/(mǎ) dǎš.tim- mi.so.tu.dim/	/(man) dǎš.tam- mi.so.tu.dam/
(شما) داشتید می ستودید	(تو) داشتی می ستودی
/(šo.mǎ) dǎš.tid- mi.so.tu.did/	/(to) dǎš.ti- mi.so.tu.di/
(آنها) داشتند می ستودند	(او/آن) داشت می ستود
/(ǎn.hǎ) dǎš.tand- mi.so.tu.dand/	/(u/ ǎn) dǎšt- mi.so.tud/

Simple Future	
مستقبل (آینده ساده)	
(ما) خواهیم ستود	(من) خواهم ستود
/(mǎ) ǩǎ.him- so.tud/	/(man) ǩǎ.ham- so.tud/
(شما) خواهید ستود	(تو) خواهی ستود
/(šo.mǎ) ǩǎ.hid- so.tud/	/(to) ǩǎ.hi- so.tud/
(آنها) خواهند ستود	(او/آن) خواهد ستود
/(ǎn.hǎ) ǩǎ.hand- so.tud/	/(u/ ǎn) ǩǎ.had- so.tud/

Command	
امر	
بستایید!	بستای!
/be.se.tǎ.yid/	/be.se.tǎy/

205

to prevent

باز داشتَن

/băz.dăš.tan/

Plural	*Singular*
Simple Present مضارع اخباری(حال ساده)	
(ما) باز می داریم /(mă) băz.mi.dă.rim/	(من) باز می دارم /(man) băz.mi.dă.ram/
(شما) باز می دارید /(šo.mă) băz.mi.dă.rid/	(تو) باز می داری /(to) băz.mi.dă.ri/
(آنها) باز می دارند /(ăn.hă) băz.mi.dă.rand/	(او/آن) باز می دارد /(u/ ăn) băz.mi.dă.rad/
Present Subjunctive مضارع التزامی	
(ما) باز بداریم /(mă) băz.be.dă.rim/	(من) باز بدارم /(man) băz.be.dă.ram/
(شما) باز بدارید /(šo.mă) băz.be.dă.rid/	(تو) باز بداری /(to) băz.be.dă.ri/
(آنها) باز بدارند /(ăn.hă) băz.be.dă.rand/	(او/آن) باز بدارد /(u/ ăn) băz.be.dă.rad/
Present Progressive مضارع مستمر(در جریان)	
(ما) داریم باز می داریم /(mă) dă.rim- băz.mi.dă.rim/	(من) دارم باز می دارم /(man) dă.ram- băz.mi.dă.ram/
(شما) دارید باز می دارید /(šo.mă) dă.rid- băz.mi.dă.rid/	(تو) داری باز می داری /(to) dă.ri- băz.mi.dă.ri/
(آنها) دارند باز می دارند /(ăn.hă) dă.rand- băz.mi.dă.rand/	(او/آن) دارد باز می دارد /(u/ ăn) dă.rad- băz.mi.dă.rad/

Simple Past
ماضی مطلق (گذشته ساده)

(ما) باز داشتیم	(من) باز داشتم
/(mǎ) bǎz.dǎš.tim/	/(man) bǎz.dǎš.tam/
(شما) باز داشتید	(تو) باز داشتی
/(šo.mǎ) bǎz.dǎš.tid/	/(to) bǎz.dǎš.ti/
(آنها) باز داشتند	(او/آن) باز داشت
/(ǎn.hǎ) bǎz.dǎš.tand/	/(u/ ǎn) bǎz.dǎšt/

Imperfect Indicative
ماضی استمراری

(ما) باز می داشتیم	(من) باز می داشتم
/(mǎ) bǎz.mi.dǎš.tim/	/(man) bǎz.mi.dǎš.tam/
(شما) باز می داشتید	(تو) باز می داشتی
/(šo.mǎ) bǎz.mi.dǎš.tid/	/(to) bǎz.mi.dǎš.ti/
(آنها) باز می داشتند	(او/آن) باز می داشت
/(ǎn.hǎ) bǎz.mi.dǎš.tand/	/(u/ ǎn) bǎz.mi.dǎšt/

Present Perfect
ماضی نقلی

(ما) باز داشته ایم	(من) باز داشته ام
/(mǎ) bǎz.dǎš.te.im/	/(man) bǎz.dǎš.te.am/
(شما) باز داشته اید	(تو) باز داشته ای
/(šo.mǎ) bǎz.dǎš.te.id/	/(to) bǎz.dǎš.te.i/
(آنها) باز داشته اند	(او/آن) باز داشته است
/(ǎn.hǎ) bǎz.dǎš.te.and/	/(u/ ǎn) bǎz.dǎš.te- ast/

Past Perfect
ماضی بعید

(ما) باز داشته بودیم	(من) باز داشته بودم
/(mǎ) bǎz.dǎš.te- bu.dim/	/(man) bǎz.dǎš.te- bu.dam/
(شما) باز داشته بودید	(تو) باز داشته بودی
/(šo.mǎ) bǎz.dǎš.te- bu.did/	/(to) bǎz.dǎš.te- bu.di/
(آنها) باز داشته بودند	(او/آن) باز داشته بود
/(ǎn.hǎ) bǎz.dǎš.te- bu.dand/	/(u/ ǎn) bǎz.dǎš.te- bud/

Past Subjunctive	
ماضی التزامی	
(ما) باز داشته باشیم	(من) باز داشته باشم
/(mă) băz.dăš.te- bă.šim/	/(man) băz.dăš.te- bă.šam/
(شما) باز داشته باشید	(تو) باز داشته باشی
/(šo.mă) băz.dăš.te- bă.šid/	/(to) băz.dăš.te- bă.ši/
(آنها) باز داشته باشند	(او/آن) باز داشته باشد
/(ăn.hă) băz.dăš.te- bă.šand/	/(u/ ăn) băz.dăš.te- bă.šad/

Past Progressive	
ماضی مستمر(در جریان)	
(ما) داشتیم باز می داشتیم	(من) داشتم باز می داشتم
/(mă) dăš.tim- băz.mi.dăš.tim/	/(man) dăš.tam- băz.mi.dăš.tam/
(شما) داشتید باز می داشتید	(تو) داشتی باز می داشتی
/(šo.mă) dăš.tid- băz.mi.dăš.tid/	/(to) dăš.ti- băz.mi.dăš.ti/
(آنها) داشتند باز می داشتند	(او/آن) داشت باز می داشت
/(ăn.hă) dăš.tand- băz.mi.dăš.tand/	/(u/ ăn) dăšt- băz.mi.dăšt/

Simple Future	
مستقبل (آینده ساده)	
(ما) باز خواهیم داشت	(من) باز خواهم داشت
/(mă) băz.k̆ă.him- dăšt/	/(man) băz.k̆ă.ham- dăšt/
(شما) باز خواهید داشت	(تو) باز خواهی داشت
/(šo.mă) băz.k̆ă.hid- dăšt/	/(to) băz.k̆ă.hi- dăšt/
(آنها) باز خواهند داشت	(او/آن) باز خواهد داشت
/(ăn.hă) băz.k̆ă.hand- dăšt/	/(u/ ăn) băz.k̆ă.had- dăšt/

Command	
امر	
باز بدارید!	باز بدار!
/băz.be.dă.rid/	/băz.be.dăr/

to put

گُذاشتَن

/go.zǎš.tan/

Plural	Singular
Simple Present	
مضارع اخباری(حال ساده)	
(ما) می گذاریم	(من) می گذارم
/(mǎ) mi.go.zǎ.rim/	/(man) mi.go.zǎ.ram/
(شما) می گذارید	(تو) می گذاری
/(šo.mǎ) mi.go.zǎ.rid/	/(to) mi.go.zǎ.ri/
(آنها) می گذارند	(او/آن) می گذارد
/(ǎn.hǎ) mi.go.zǎ.rand/	/(u/ ǎn) mi.go.zǎ.rad/

Plural	Singular
Present Subjunctive	
مضارع التزامی	
(ما) بگذاریم	(من) بگذارم
/(mǎ) be.go.zǎ.rim/	/(man) be.go.zǎ.ram/
(شما) بگذارید	(تو) بگذاری
/(šo.mǎ) be.go.zǎ.rid/	/(to) be.go.zǎ.ri/
(آنها) بگذارند	(او/آن) بگذارد
/(ǎn.hǎ) be.go.zǎ.rand/	/(u/ ǎn) be.go.zǎ.rad/

Plural	Singular
Present Progressive	
مضارع مستمر(در جریان)	
(ما) داریم می گذاریم	(من) دارم می گذارم
/(mǎ) dǎ.rim- mi.go.zǎ.rim/	/(man) dǎ.ram- mi.go.zǎ.ram/
(شما) دارید می گذارید	(تو) داری می گذاری
/(šo.mǎ) dǎ.rid- mi.go.zǎ.rid/	/(to) dǎ.ri- mi.go.zǎ.ri/
(آنها) دارند می گذارند	(او/آن) دارد می گذارد
/(ǎn.hǎ) dǎ.rand- mi.go.zǎ.rand/	/(u/ ǎn) dǎ.rad- mi.go.zǎ.rad/

Simple Past	
ماضی مطلق (گذشته ساده)	
(ما) گذاشتیم	(من) گذاشتم
/(mǎ) go.zǎš.tim/	/(man) go.zǎš.tam/
(شما) گذاشتید	(تو) گذاشتی
/(šo.mǎ) go.zǎš.tid/	/(to) go.zǎš.ti/
(آنها) گذاشتند	(او/ آن) گذاشت
/(ǎn.hǎ) go.zǎš.tand/	/(u/ ǎn) go.zǎšt/

Imperfect Indicative	
ماضی استمراری	
(ما) می گذاشتیم	(من) می گذاشتم
/(mǎ) mi.go.zǎš.tim/	/(man) mi.go.zǎš.tam/
(شما) می گذاشتید	(تو) می گذاشتی
/(šo.mǎ) mi.go.zǎš.tid/	/(to) mi.go.zǎš.ti/
(آنها) می گذاشتند	(او/ آن) می گذاشت
/(ǎn.hǎ) mi.go.zǎš.tand/	/(u/ ǎn) mi.go.zǎšt/

Present Perfect	
ماضی نقلی	
(ما) گذاشته ایم	(من) گذاشته ام
/(mǎ) go.zǎš.te.im/	/(man) go.zǎš.te.am/
(شما) گذاشته اید	(تو) گذاشته ای
/(šo.mǎ) go.zǎš.te.id/	/(to) go.zǎš.te.i/
(آنها) گذاشته اند	(او/ آن) گذاشته است
/(ǎn.hǎ) go.zǎš.te.and/	/(u/ ǎn) go.zǎš.te- ast/

Past Perfect	
ماضی بعید	
(ما) گذاشته بودیم	(من) گذاشته بودم
/(mǎ) go.zǎš.te- bu.dim/	/(man) go.zǎš.te- bu.dam/
(شما) گذاشته بودید	(تو) گذاشته بودی
/(šo.mǎ) go.zǎš.te- bu.did/	/(to) go.zǎš.te- bu.di/
(آنها) گذاشته بودند	(او/ آن) گذاشته بود
/(ǎn.hǎ) go.zǎš.te- bu.dand/	/(u/ ǎn) go.zǎš.te- bud/

Past Subjunctive	
ماضی التزامی	
(ما) گذاشته باشیم	(من) گذاشته باشم
/(mǎ) go.zǎš.te- bǎ.šim/	/(man) go.zǎš.te- bǎ.šam/
(شما) گذاشته باشید	(تو) گذاشته باشی
/(šo.mǎ) go.zǎš.te- bǎ.šid/	/(to) go.zǎš.te- bǎ.ši/
(آنها) گذاشته باشند	(او/آن) گذاشته باشد
/(ǎn.hǎ) go.zǎš.te- bǎ.šand/	/(u/ ǎn) go.zǎš.te- bǎ.šad/

Past Progressive	
ماضی مستمر(در جریان)	
(ما) داشتیم می گذاشتیم	(من) داشتم می گذاشتم
/(mǎ) dǎš.tim- mi.go.zǎš.tim/	/(man) dǎš.tam- mi.go.zǎš.tam/
(شما) داشتید می گذاشتید	(تو) داشتی می گذاشتی
/(šo.mǎ) dǎš.tid- mi.go.zǎš.tid/	/(to) dǎš.ti- mi.go.zǎš.ti/
(آنها) داشتند می گذاشتند	(او/آن) داشت می گذاشت
/(ǎn.hǎ) dǎš.tand- mi.go.zǎš.tand/	/(u/ ǎn) dǎšt- mi.go.zǎšt/

Simple Future	
مستقبل (آینده ساده)	
(ما) خواهیم گذاشت	(من) خواهم گذاشت
/(mǎ) ǩǎ.him- go.zǎšt/	/(man) ǩǎ.ham- go.zǎšt/
(شما) خواهید گذاشت	(تو) خواهی گذاشت
/(šo.mǎ) ǩǎ.hid- go.zǎšt/	/(to) ǩǎ.hi- go.zǎšt/
(آنها) خواهند گذاشت	(او/آن) خواهد گذاشت
/(ǎn.hǎ) ǩǎ.hand- go.zǎšt/	/(u/ ǎn) ǩǎ.had- go.zǎšt/

Command	
امر	
بگذارید!	بگذار!
/be.go.zǎ.rid/	/be.go.zǎr/

211

to raise a flag

اَفراشتَن

/af.răš.tan/

Plural	Singular
Simple Present مضارع اخباری(حال ساده)	
(ما) می افرازیم /(mă) mi.af.ră.zim/	(من) می افرازم /(man) mi.af.ră.zam/
(شما) می افرازید /(šo.mă) mi.af.ră.zid/	(تو) می افرازی /(to) mi.af.ră.zi/
(آنها) می افرازند /(ăn.hă) mi.af.ră.zand/	(او/آن) می افرازد /(u/ ăn) mi.af.ră.zad/
Present Subjunctive مضارع التزامی	
(ما) بیفرازیم /(mă) bi.yaf.ră.zim/	(من) بیفرازم /(man) bi.yaf.ră.zam/
(شما) بیفرازید /(šo.mă) bi.yaf.ră.zid/	(تو) بیفرازی /(to) bi.yaf.ră.zi/
(آنها) بیفرازند /(ăn.hă) bi.yaf.ră.zand/	(او/آن) بیفرازد /(u/ ăn) bi.yaf.ră.zad/
Present Progressive مضارع مستمر(در جریان)	
(ما) داریم می افرازیم /(mă) dă.rim- mi.af.ră.zim/	(من) دارم می افرازم /(man) dă.ram- mi.af.ră.zam/
(شما) دارید می افرازید /(šo.mă) dă.rid- mi.af.ră.zid/	(تو) داری می افرازی /(to) dă.ri- mi.af.ră.zi/
(آنها) دارند می افرازند /(ăn.hă) dă.rand- mi.af.ră.zand/	(او/آن) دارد می افرازد /(u/ ăn) dă.rad- mi.af.ră.zad/

Simple Past
ماضی مطلق (گذشته ساده)

(ما) افراشتیم	(من) افراشتم
/(mǎ) af.rǎš.tim/	/(man) af.rǎš.tam/
(شما) افراشتید	(تو) افراشتی
/(šo.mǎ) af.rǎš.tid/	/(to) af.rǎš.ti/
(آنها) افراشتند	(او/ آن) افراشت
/(ǎn.hǎ) af.rǎš.tand/	/(u/ ǎn) af.rǎšt/

Imperfect Indicative
ماضی استمراری

(ما) می افراشتیم	(من) می افراشتم
/(mǎ) mi.af.rǎš.tim/	/(man) mi.af.rǎš.tam/
(شما) می افراشتید	(تو) می افراشتی
/(šo.mǎ) mi.af.rǎš.tid/	/(to) mi.af.rǎš.ti/
(آنها) می افراشتند	(او/آن) می افراشت
/(ǎn.hǎ) mi.af.rǎš.tand/	/(u/ ǎn) mi.af.rǎšt/

Present Perfect
ماضی نقلی

(ما) افراشته ایم	(من) افراشته ام
/(mǎ) af.rǎš.te.im/	/(man) af.rǎš.te.am/
(شما) افراشته اید	(تو) افراشته ای
/(šo.mǎ) af.rǎš.te.id/	/(to) af.rǎš.te.i/
(آنها) افراشته اند	(او/آن) افراشته است
/(ǎn.hǎ) af.rǎš.te.and/	/(u/ ǎn) af.rǎš.te- ast/

Past Perfect
ماضی بعید

(ما) افراشته بودیم	(من) افراشته بودم
/(mǎ) af.rǎš.te- bu.dim/	/(man) af.rǎš.te- bu.dam/
(شما) افراشته بودید	(تو) افراشته بودی
/(šo.mǎ) af.rǎš.te- bu.did/	/(to) af.rǎš.te- bu.di/
(آنها) افراشته بودند	(او/آن) افراشته بود
/(ǎn.hǎ) af.rǎš.te- bu.dand/	/(u/ ǎn) af.rǎš.te- bud/

<table>
<tr><td colspan="2" align="center">**Past Subjunctive**
ماضی التزامی</td></tr>
<tr>
<td align="center">(ما) افراشته باشیم
/(mǎ) af.rǎš.te- bǎ.šim/</td>
<td align="center">(من) افراشته باشم
/(man) af.rǎš.te- bǎ.šam/</td>
</tr>
<tr>
<td align="center">(شما) افراشته باشید
/(šo.mǎ) af.rǎš.te- bǎ.šid/</td>
<td align="center">(تو) افراشته باشی
/(to) af.rǎš.te- bǎ.ši/</td>
</tr>
<tr>
<td align="center">(آنها) افراشته باشند
/(ǎn.hǎ) af.rǎš.te- bǎ.šand/</td>
<td align="center">(او/آن) افراشته باشد
/(u/ ǎn) af.rǎš.te- bǎ.šad/</td>
</tr>
</table>

<table>
<tr><td colspan="2" align="center">**Past Progressive**
ماضی مستمر(در جریان)</td></tr>
<tr>
<td align="center">(ما) داشتیم می افراشتیم
/(mǎ) dǎš.tim- mi.af.rǎš.tim/</td>
<td align="center">(من) داشتم می افراشتم
/(man) dǎš.tam- mi.af.rǎš.tam/</td>
</tr>
<tr>
<td align="center">(شما) داشتید می افراشتید
/(šo.mǎ) dǎš.tid- mi.af.rǎš.tid/</td>
<td align="center">(تو) داشتی می افراشتی
/(to) dǎš.ti- mi.af.rǎš.ti/</td>
</tr>
<tr>
<td align="center">(آنها) داشتند می افراشتند
/(ǎn.hǎ) dǎš.tand- mi.af.rǎš.tand/</td>
<td align="center">(او/آن) داشت می افراشت
/(u/ ǎn) dǎšt- mi.af.rǎšt/</td>
</tr>
</table>

<table>
<tr><td colspan="2" align="center">**Simple Future**
مستقبل (آینده ساده)</td></tr>
<tr>
<td align="center">(ما) خواهیم افراشت
/(mǎ) ǩǎ.him- af.rǎšt/</td>
<td align="center">(من) خواهم افراشت
/(man) ǩǎ.ham- af.rǎšt/</td>
</tr>
<tr>
<td align="center">(شما) خواهید افراشت
/(šo.mǎ) ǩǎ.hid- af.rǎšt/</td>
<td align="center">(تو) خواهی افراشت
/(to) ǩǎ.hi- af.rǎšt/</td>
</tr>
<tr>
<td align="center">(آنها) خواهند افراشت
/(ǎn.hǎ) ǩǎ.hand- af.rǎšt/</td>
<td align="center">(او/آن) خواهد افراشت
/(u/ ǎn) ǩǎ.had- af.rǎšt/</td>
</tr>
</table>

<table>
<tr><td colspan="2" align="center">**Command**
امر</td></tr>
<tr>
<td align="center">بیفرازید!
/bi.yaf.rǎ.zid/</td>
<td align="center">بیفراز!
/bi.yaf.rǎz/</td>
</tr>
</table>

to refine

پالودَن

/pă.lu.dan/

Plural	Singular
Simple Present مضارع اخباری(حال ساده)	
(ما) می پالاییم /(mă) mi.pă.lă.yim/	(من) می پالایم /(man) mi.pă.lă.yam/
(شما) می پالایید /(šo.mă) mi.pă.lă.yid/	(تو) می پالایی /(to) mi.pă.lă.yi/
(آنها) می پالایند /(ăn.hă) mi.pă.lă.yand/	(او/آن) می پالاید /(u/ ăn) mi.pă.lă.yad/
Present Subjunctive مضارع التزامی	
(ما) بپالاییم /(mă) be.pă.lă.yim/	(من) بپالایم /(man) be.pă.lă.yam/
(شما) بپالایید /(šo.mă) be.pă.lă.yid/	(تو) بپالایی /(to) be.pă.lă.yi/
(آنها) بپالایند /(ăn.hă) be.pă.lă.yand/	(او/آن) بپالاید /(u/ ăn) be.pă.lă.yad/
Present Progressive مضارع مستمر(در جریان)	
(ما) داریم می پالاییم /(mă) dă.rim- mi.pă.lă.yim/	(من) دارم می پالایم /(man) dă.ram- mi.pă.lă.yam/
(شما) دارید می پالایید /(šo.mă) dă.rid- mi.pă.lă.yid/	(تو) داری می پالایی /(to) dă.ri- mi.pă.lă.yi/
(آنها) دارند می پالایند /(ăn.hă) dă.rand- mi.pă.lă.yand/	(او/آن) دارد می پالاید /(u/ ăn) dă.rad- mi.pă.lă.yad/

Simple Past
ماضی مطلق (گذشته ساده)

(ما) پالودیم	(من) پالودم
/(mă) pă.lu.dim/	/(man) pă.lu.dam/
(شما) پالودید	(تو) پالودی
/(šo.mă) pă.lu.did/	/(to) pă.lu.di/
(آنها) پالودند	(او/آن) پالود
/(ăn.hă) pă.lu.dand/	/(u/ ăn) pă.lud/

Imperfect Indicative
ماضی استمراری

(ما) می پالودیم	(من) می پالودم
/(mă) mi.pă.lu.dim/	/(man) mi.pă.lu.dam/
(شما) می پالودید	(تو) می پالودی
/(šo.mă) mi.pă.lu.did/	/(to) mi.pă.lu.di/
(آنها) می پالودند	(او/آن) می پالود
/(ăn.hă) mi.pă.lu.dand/	/(u/ ăn) mi.pă.lud/

Present Perfect
ماضی نقلی

(ما) پالوده ایم	(من) پالوده ام
/(mă) pă.lu.de.im/	/(man) pă.lu.de.am/
(شما) پالوده اید	(تو) پالوده ای
/(šo.mă) pă.lu.de.id/	/(to) pă.lu.de.i/
(آنها) پالوده اند	(او/آن) پالوده است
/(ăn.hă) pă.lu.de.and/	/(u/ ăn) pă.lu.de- ast/

Past Perfect
ماضی بعید

(ما) پالوده بودیم	(من) پالوده بودم
/(mă) pă.lu.de- bu.dim/	/(man) pă.lu.de- bu.dam/
(شما) پالوده بودید	(تو) پالوده بودی
/(šo.mă) pă.lu.de- bu.did/	/(to) pă.lu.de- bu.di/
(آنها) پالوده بودند	(او/آن) پالوده بود
/(ăn.hă) pă.lu.de- bu.dand/	/(u/ ăn) pă.lu.de- bud/

216

<table>
<tr><td colspan="2" align="center">**Past Subjunctive**
ماضی التزامی</td></tr>
<tr>
<td align="center">(ما) پالوده باشیم
/(mǎ) pǎ.lu.de- bǎ.šim/</td>
<td align="center">(من) پالوده باشم
/(man) pǎ.lu.de- bǎ.šam/</td>
</tr>
<tr>
<td align="center">(شما) پالوده باشید
/(šo.mǎ) pǎ.lu.de- bǎ.šid/</td>
<td align="center">(تو) پالوده باشی
/(to) pǎ.lu.de- bǎ.ši/</td>
</tr>
<tr>
<td align="center">(آنها) پالوده باشند
/(ǎn.hǎ) pǎ.lu.de- bǎ.šand/</td>
<td align="center">(او/آن) پالوده باشد
/(u/ ǎn) pǎ.lu.de- bǎ.šad/</td>
</tr>
</table>

<table>
<tr><td colspan="2" align="center">**Past Progressive**
ماضی مستمر(در جریان)</td></tr>
<tr>
<td align="center">(ما) داشتیم می پالودیم
/(mǎ) dǎš.tim- mi.pǎ.lu.dim/</td>
<td align="center">(من) داشتم می پالودم
/(man) dǎš.tam- mi.pǎ.lu.dam/</td>
</tr>
<tr>
<td align="center">(شما) داشتید می پالودید
/(šo.mǎ) dǎš.tid- mi.pǎ.lu.did/</td>
<td align="center">(تو) داشتی می پالودی
/(to) dǎš.ti- mi.pǎ.lu.di/</td>
</tr>
<tr>
<td align="center">(آنها) داشتند می پالودند
/(ǎn.hǎ) dǎš.tand- mi.pǎ.lu.dand/</td>
<td align="center">(او/آن) داشت می پالود
/(u/ ǎn) dǎšt- mi.pǎ.lud/</td>
</tr>
</table>

<table>
<tr><td colspan="2" align="center">**Simple Future**
مستقبل (آینده ساده)</td></tr>
<tr>
<td align="center">(ما) خواهیم پالود
/(mǎ) ǩǎ.him- pǎ.lud/</td>
<td align="center">(من) خواهم پالود
/(man) ǩǎ.ham- pǎ.lud/</td>
</tr>
<tr>
<td align="center">(شما) خواهید پالود
/(šo.mǎ) ǩǎ.hid- pǎ.lud/</td>
<td align="center">(تو) خواهی پالود
/(to) ǩǎ.hi- pǎ.lud/</td>
</tr>
<tr>
<td align="center">(آنها) خواهند پالود
/(ǎn.hǎ) ǩǎ.hand- pǎ.lud/</td>
<td align="center">(او/آن) خواهد پالود
/(u/ ǎn) ǩǎ.had- pǎ.lud/</td>
</tr>
</table>

<table>
<tr><td colspan="2" align="center">**Command**
امر</td></tr>
<tr>
<td align="center">بپالایید!
/be.pǎ.lǎ.yid/</td>
<td align="center">بپالای!
/be.pǎ.lǎy/</td>
</tr>
</table>

217

to retell

بازگُفتَن

/băz.gof.tan/

Plural	Singular
Simple Present <div dir="rtl">مضارع اخباری(حال ساده)</div>	
<div dir="rtl">(ما) باز می گوییم</div> /(mă) băz.mi.gu.yim/	<div dir="rtl">(من) باز می گویم</div> /(man) băz.mi.gu.yam/
<div dir="rtl">(شما) باز می گویید</div> /(šo.mă) băz.mi.gu.yid/	<div dir="rtl">(تو) باز می گویی</div> /(to) băz.mi.gu.yi/
<div dir="rtl">(آنها) باز می گویند</div> /(ăn.hă) băz.mi.gu.yand/	<div dir="rtl">(او/آن) باز می گوید</div> /(u/ ăn) băz.mi.gu.yad/
Present Subjunctive <div dir="rtl">مضارع التزامی</div>	
<div dir="rtl">(ما) باز بگوییم</div> /(mă) băz.be.gu.yim/	<div dir="rtl">(من) باز بگویم</div> /(man) băz.be.gu.yam/
<div dir="rtl">(شما) باز بگویید</div> /(šo.mă) băz.be.gu.yid/	<div dir="rtl">(تو) باز بگویی</div> /(to) băz.be.gu.yi/
<div dir="rtl">(آنها) باز بگویند</div> /(ăn.hă) băz.be.gu.yand/	<div dir="rtl">(او/آن) باز بگوید</div> /(u/ ăn) băz.be.gu.yad/
Present Progressive <div dir="rtl">مضارع مستمر(در جریان)</div>	
<div dir="rtl">(ما) داریم باز می گوییم</div> /(mă) dă.rim- băz.mi.gu.yim/	<div dir="rtl">(من) دارم باز می گویم</div> /(man) dă.ram- băz.mi.gu.yam/
<div dir="rtl">(شما) دارید باز می گویید</div> /(šo.mă) dă.rid- băz.mi.gu.yid/	<div dir="rtl">(تو) داری باز می گویی</div> /(to) dă.ri- băz.mi.gu.yi/
<div dir="rtl">(آنها) دارند باز می گویند</div> /(ăn.hă) dă.rand- băz.mi.gu.yand/	<div dir="rtl">(او/آن) دارد باز می گوید</div> /(u/ ăn) dă.rad- băz.mi.gu.yad/

Simple Past
ماضی مطلق (گذشته ساده)

(ما) باز گفتیم	(من) باز گفتم
/(mă) băz.gof.tim/	/(man) băz.gof.tam/
(شما) باز گفتید	(تو) باز گفتی
/(šo.mă) băz.gof.tid/	/(to) băz.gof.ti/
(آنها) باز گفتند	(او/آن) باز گفت
/(ăn.hă) băz.gof.tand/	/(u/ ăn) băz.goft/

Imperfect Indicative
ماضی استمراری

(ما) باز می گفتیم	(من) باز می گفتم
/(mă) băz.mi.gof.tim/	/(man) băz.mi.gof.tam/
(شما) باز می گفتید	(تو) باز می گفتی
/(šo.mă) băz.mi.gof.tid/	/(to) băz.mi.gof.ti/
(آنها) باز می گفتند	(او/آن) باز می گفت
/(ăn.hă) băz.mi.gof.tand/	/(u/ ăn) băz.mi.goft/

Present Perfect
ماضی نقلی

(ما) باز گفته ایم	(من) باز گفته ام
/(mă) băz.gof.te.im/	/(man) băz.gof.te.am/
(شما) باز گفته اید	(تو) باز گفته ای
/(šo.mă) băz.gof.te.id/	/(to) băz.gof.te.i/
(آنها) باز گفته اند	(او/آن) باز گفته است
/(ăn.hă) băz.gof.te.and/	/(u/ ăn) băz.gof.te- ast/

Past Perfect
ماضی بعید

(ما) باز گفته بودیم	(من) باز گفته بودم
/(mă) băz.gof.te- bu.dim/	/(man) băz.gof.te- bu.dam/
(شما) باز گفته بودید	(تو) باز گفته بودی
/(šo.mă) băz.gof.te- bu.did/	/(to) băz.gof.te- bu.di/
(آنها) باز گفته بودند	(او/آن) باز گفته بود
/(ăn.hă) băz.gof.te- bu.dand/	/(u/ ăn) băz.gof.te- bud/

<table>
<tr><td colspan="2" align="center">Past Subjunctive
ماضی التزامی</td></tr>
<tr>
<td align="center">(ما) باز گفته باشیم
/(mă) băz.gof.te- bă.šim/</td>
<td align="center">(من) باز گفته باشم
/(man) băz.gof.te- bă.šam/</td>
</tr>
<tr>
<td align="center">(شما) باز گفته باشید
/(šo.mă) băz.gof.te- bă.šid/</td>
<td align="center">(تو) باز گفته باشی
/(to) băz.gof.te- bă.ši/</td>
</tr>
<tr>
<td align="center">(آنها) باز گفته باشند
/(ăn.hă) băz.gof.te- bă.šand/</td>
<td align="center">(او/آن) باز گفته باشد
/(u/ ăn) băz.gof.te- bă.šad/</td>
</tr>
</table>

<table>
<tr><td colspan="2" align="center">Past Progressive
ماضی مستمر(در جریان)</td></tr>
<tr>
<td align="center">(ما) داشتیم باز می گفتیم
/(mă) dăš.tim- băz.mi.gof.tim/</td>
<td align="center">(من) داشتم باز می گفتم
/(man) dăš.tam- băz.mi.gof.tam/</td>
</tr>
<tr>
<td align="center">(شما) داشتید باز می گفتید
/(šo.mă) dăš.tid- băz.mi.gof.tid/</td>
<td align="center">(تو) داشتی باز می گفتی
/(to) dăš.ti- băz.mi.gof.ti/</td>
</tr>
<tr>
<td align="center">(آنها) داشتند باز می گفتند
/(ăn.hă) dăš.tand- băz.mi.gof.tand/</td>
<td align="center">(او/آن) داشت باز می گفت
/(u/ ăn) dăšt- băz.mi.goft/</td>
</tr>
</table>

<table>
<tr><td colspan="2" align="center">Simple Future
مستقبل (آینده ساده)</td></tr>
<tr>
<td align="center">(ما) باز خواهیم گفت
/(mă) băz.ǩă.him- goft/</td>
<td align="center">(من) باز خواهم گفت
/(man) băz.ǩă.ham- goft/</td>
</tr>
<tr>
<td align="center">(شما) باز خواهید گفت
/(šo.mă) băz.ǩă.hid- goft/</td>
<td align="center">(تو) باز خواهی گفت
/(to) băz.ǩă.hi- goft/</td>
</tr>
<tr>
<td align="center">(آنها) باز خواهند گفت
/(ăn.hă) băz.ǩă.hand- goft/</td>
<td align="center">(او/آن) باز خواهد گفت
/(u/ ăn) băz.ǩă.had- goft/</td>
</tr>
</table>

<table>
<tr><td colspan="2" align="center">Command
امر</td></tr>
<tr>
<td align="center">باز بگویید!
/băz.be.gu.yid/</td>
<td align="center">باز بگوی!
/ băz.be.guy/</td>
</tr>
</table>

to rest

آسودَن

/ă.su.dan/

Plural	Singular
Simple Present مضارع اخباری(حال ساده)	
(ما) می آساییم /(mă) mi.ă.să.yim/	(من) می آسایم /(man) mi.ă.să.yam/
(شما) می آسایید /(šo.mă) mi.ă.să.yid/	(تو) می آسایی /(to) mi.ă.să.yi/
(آنها) می آسایند /(ăn.hă) mi.ă.să.yand/	(او/آن) می آساید /(u/ ăn) mi.ă.să.yad/
Present Subjunctive مضارع التزامی	
(ما) بیاساییم /(mă) bi.yă.să.yim/	(من) بیاسایم /(man) bi.yă.să.yam/
(شما) بیاسایید /(šo.mă) bi.yă.să.yid/	(تو) بیاسایی /(to) bi.yă.să.yi/
(آنها) بیاسایند /(ăn.hă) bi.yă.să.yand/	(او/آن) بیاساید /(u/ ăn) bi.yă.să.yad/
Present Progressive مضارع مستمر(در جریان)	
(ما) داریم می آساییم /(mă) dă.rim- mi.ă.să.yim/	(من) دارم می آسایم /(man) dă.ram- mi.ă.să.yam/
(شما) دارید می آسایید /(šo.mă) dă.rid- mi.ă.să.yid/	(تو) داری می آسایی /(to) dă.ri- mi.ă.să.yi/
(آنها) دارند می آسایند /(ăn.hă) dă.rand- mi.ă.să.yand/	(او/آن) دارد می آساید /(u/ ăn) dă.rad- mi.ă.să.yad/

Simple Past	
ماضی مطلق (گذشته ساده)	
(ما) آسودیم	(من) آسودم
/(mǎ) ǎ.su.dim/	/(man) ǎ.su.dam/
(شما) آسودید	(تو) آسودی
/(šo.mǎ) ǎ.su.did/	/(to) ǎ.su.di/
(آنها) آسودند	(او/آن) آسود
/(ǎn.hǎ) ǎ.su.dand/	/(u/ ǎn) ǎ.sud/

Imperfect Indicative	
ماضی استمراری	
(ما) می آسودیم	(من) می آسودم
/(mǎ) mi.ǎ.su.dim/	/(man) mi.ǎ.su.dam/
(شما) می آسودید	(تو) می آسودی
/(šo.mǎ) mi.ǎ.su.did/	/(to) mi.ǎ.su.di/
(آنها) می آسودند	(او/آن) می آسود
/(ǎn.hǎ) mi.ǎ.su.dand/	/(u/ ǎn) mi.ǎ.sud/

Present Perfect	
ماضی نقلی	
(ما) آسوده ایم	(من) آسوده ام
/(mǎ) ǎ.su.de.im/	/(man) ǎ.su.de.am/
(شما) آسوده اید	(تو) آسوده ای
/(šo.mǎ) ǎ.su.de.id/	/(to) ǎ.su.de.i/
(آنها) آسوده اند	(او/آن) آسوده است
/(ǎn.hǎ) ǎ.su.de.and/	/(u/ ǎn) ǎ.su.de- ast/

Past Perfect	
ماضی بعید	
(ما) آسوده بودیم	(من) آسوده بودم
/(mǎ) ǎ.su.de- bu.dim/	/(man) ǎ.su.de- bu.dam/
(شما) آسوده بودید	(تو) آسوده بودی
/(šo.mǎ) ǎ.su.de- bu.did/	/(to) ǎ.su.de- bu.di/
(آنها) آسوده بودند	(او/آن) آسوده بود
/(ǎn.hǎ) ǎ.su.de- bu.dand/	/(u/ ǎn) ǎ.su.de- bud/

<table>
<tr><td colspan="2" align="center">Past Subjunctive
ماضی التزامی</td></tr>
<tr>
<td align="center">(ما) آسوده باشیم
/(mă) ă.su.de- bă.šim/</td>
<td align="center">(من) آسوده باشم
/(man) ă.su.de- bă.šam/</td>
</tr>
<tr>
<td align="center">(شما) آسوده باشید
/(šo.mă) ă.su.de- bă.šid/</td>
<td align="center">(تو) آسوده باشی
/(to) ă.su.de- bă.ši/</td>
</tr>
<tr>
<td align="center">(آنها) آسوده باشند
/(ăn.hă) ă.su.de- bă.šand/</td>
<td align="center">(او/آن) آسوده باشد
/(u/ ăn) ă.su.de- bă.šad/</td>
</tr>
</table>

<table>
<tr><td colspan="2" align="center">Past Progressive
ماضی مستمر(در جریان)</td></tr>
<tr>
<td align="center">(ما) داشتیم می آسودیم
/(mă) dăš.tim- mi.ă.su.dim/</td>
<td align="center">(من) داشتم می آسودم
/(man) dăš.tam- mi.ă.su.dam/</td>
</tr>
<tr>
<td align="center">(شما) داشتید می آسودید
/(šo.mă) dăš.tid- mi.ă.su.did/</td>
<td align="center">(تو) داشتی می آسودی
/(to) dăš.ti- mi.ă.su.di/</td>
</tr>
<tr>
<td align="center">(آنها) داشتند می آسودند
/(ăn.hă) dăš.tand- mi.ă.su.dand/</td>
<td align="center">(او/آن) داشت می آسود
/(u/ ăn) dăšt- mi.ă.sud/</td>
</tr>
</table>

<table>
<tr><td colspan="2" align="center">Simple Future
مستقبل (آینده ساده)</td></tr>
<tr>
<td align="center">(ما) خواهیم آسود
/(mă) kă.him- ă.sud/</td>
<td align="center">(من) خواهم آسود
/(man) kă.ham- ă.sud/</td>
</tr>
<tr>
<td align="center">(شما) خواهید آسود
/(šo.mă) kă.hid- ă.sud/</td>
<td align="center">(تو) خواهی آسود
/(to) kă.hi- ă.sud/</td>
</tr>
<tr>
<td align="center">(آنها) خواهند آسود
/(ăn.hă) kă.hand- ă.sud/</td>
<td align="center">(او/آن) خواهد آسود
/(u/ ăn) kă.had- ă.sud/</td>
</tr>
</table>

<table>
<tr><td colspan="2" align="center">Command
امر</td></tr>
<tr>
<td align="center">بیاسایید!
/bi.yă.să.yid/</td>
<td align="center">بیاسای!
/bi.yă.săy/</td>
</tr>
</table>

to rise

بَرخاستَن

/bar.kǎs.tan/

Plural	Singular
Simple Present مضارع اخباری(حال ساده)	
(ما) بر می خیزیم /(mǎ) bar.mi.ǩi.zim/	(من) بر می خیزم /(man) bar.mi.ǩi.zam/
(شما) بر می خیزید /(šo.mǎ) bar.mi.ǩi.zid/	(تو) بر می خیزی /(to) bar.mi.ǩi.zi/
(آنها) بر می خیزند /(ǎn.hǎ) bar.mi.ǩi.zand/	(او/آن) بر می خیزد /(u/ ǎn) bar.mi.ǩi.zad/
Present Subjunctive مضارع التزامی	
(ما) بر بخیزیم /(mǎ) bar.be.ǩi.zim/	(من) بر بخیزم /(man) bar.be.ǩi.zam/
(شما) بر بخیزید /(šo.mǎ) bar.be.ǩi.zid/	(تو) بر بخیزی /(to) bar.be.ǩi.zi/
(آنها) بر بخیزند /(ǎn.hǎ) bar.be.ǩi.zand/	(او/آن) بر بخیزد /(u/ ǎn) bar.be.ǩi.zad/
Present Progressive مضارع مستمر(در جریان)	
(ما) داریم بر می خیزیم /(mǎ) dǎ.rim- bar.mi.ǩi.zim/	(من) دارم بر می خیزم /(man) dǎ.ram- bar.mi.ǩi.zam/
(شما) دارید بر می خیزید /(šo.mǎ) dǎ.rid- bar.mi.ǩi.zid/	(تو) داری بر می خیزی /(to) dǎ.ri- bar.mi.ǩi.zi/
(آنها) دارند بر می خیزند /(ǎn.hǎ) dǎ.rand- bar.mi.ǩi.zand/	(او/آن) دارد بر می خیزد /(u/ ǎn) dǎ.rad- bar.mi.ǩi.zad/

Simple Past	
ماضی مطلق (گذشته ساده)	
(ما) برخاستیم	(من) برخاستم
/(mǎ) bar.ǩǎs.tim/	/(man) bar.ǩǎs.tam/
(شما) برخاستید	(تو) برخاستی
/(šo.mǎ) bar.ǩǎs.tid/	/(to) bar.ǩǎs.ti/
(آنها) برخاستند	(او/ آن) برخاست
/(ǎn.hǎ) bar.ǩǎs.tand/	/(u/ ǎn) bar.ǩǎst/

Imperfect Indicative	
ماضی استمراری	
(ما) بر می خاستیم	(من) بر می خاستم
/(mǎ) bar.mi.ǩǎs.tim/	/(man) bar.mi.ǩǎs.tam/
(شما) بر می خاستید	(تو) بر می خاستی
/(šo.mǎ) bar.mi.ǩǎs.tid/	/(to) bar.mi.ǩǎs.ti/
(آنها) بر می خاستند	(او/آن) بر می خاست
/(ǎn.hǎ) bar.mi.ǩǎs.tand/	/(u/ ǎn) bar.mi.ǩǎst/

Present Perfect	
ماضی نقلی	
(ما) برخاسته ایم	(من) برخاسته ام
/(mǎ) bar.ǩǎs.te.im/	/(man) bar.ǩǎs.te.am/
(شما) برخاسته اید	(تو) برخاسته ای
/(šo.mǎ) bar.ǩǎs.te.id/	/(to) bar.ǩǎs.te.i/
(آنها) برخاسته اند	(او/آن) برخاسته است
/(ǎn.hǎ) bar.ǩǎs.te.and/	/(u/ ǎn) bar.ǩǎs.te- ast/

Past Perfect	
ماضی بعید	
(ما) برخاسته بودیم	(من) برخاسته بودم
/(mǎ) bar.ǩǎs.te- bu.dim/	/(man) bar.ǩǎs.te- bu.dam/
(شما) برخاسته بودید	(تو) برخاسته بودی
/(šo.mǎ) bar.ǩǎs.te- bu.did/	/(to) bar.ǩǎs.te- bu.di/
(آنها) برخاسته بودند	(او/آن) برخاسته بود
/(ǎn.hǎ) bar.ǩǎs.te- bu.dand/	/(u/ ǎn) bar.ǩǎs.te- bud/

225

<table>
<tr><td colspan="2" align="center">Past Subjunctive
ماضی التزامی</td></tr>
<tr>
<td align="center">(ما) برخاسته باشیم
/(mă) bar.kăs.te- bă.šim/</td>
<td align="center">(من) برخاسته باشم
/(man) bar.kăs.te- bă.šam/</td>
</tr>
<tr>
<td align="center">(شما) برخاسته باشید
/(šo.mă) bar.kăs.te- bă.šid/</td>
<td align="center">(تو) برخاسته باشی
/(to) bar.kăs.te- bă.ši/</td>
</tr>
<tr>
<td align="center">(آنها) برخاسته باشند
/(ăn.hă) bar.kăs.te- bă.šand/</td>
<td align="center">(او/آن) برخاسته باشد
/(u/ ăn) bar.kăs.te- bă.šad/</td>
</tr>
</table>

<table>
<tr><td colspan="2" align="center">Past Progressive
ماضی مستمر(در جریان)</td></tr>
<tr>
<td align="center">(ما) داشتیم بر می خاستیم
/(mă) dăš.tim- bar.mi.kăs.tim/</td>
<td align="center">(من) داشتم بر می خاستم
/(man) dăš.tam- bar.mi.kăs.tam/</td>
</tr>
<tr>
<td align="center">(شما) داشتید بر می خاستید
/(šo.mă) dăš.tid- bar.mi.kăs.tid/</td>
<td align="center">(تو) داشتی بر می خاستی
/(to) dăš.ti- bar.mi.kăs.ti/</td>
</tr>
<tr>
<td align="center">(آنها) داشتند بر می خاستند
/(ăn.hă) dăš.tand- bar.mi.kăs.tand/</td>
<td align="center">(او/آن) داشت بر می خاست
/(u/ ăn) dăšt- bar.mi.kăst/</td>
</tr>
</table>

<table>
<tr><td colspan="2" align="center">Simple Future
مستقبل (آینده ساده)</td></tr>
<tr>
<td align="center">(ما) برخواهیم خاست
/(mă) bar.kă.him- kăst/</td>
<td align="center">(من) برخواهم خاست
/(man) bar.kă.ham- kăst/</td>
</tr>
<tr>
<td align="center">(شما) برخواهید خاست
/(šo.mă) bar.kă.hid- kăst/</td>
<td align="center">(تو) برخواهی خاست
/(to) bar.kă.hi- kăst/</td>
</tr>
<tr>
<td align="center">(آنها) برخواهند خاست
/(ăn.hă) bar.kă.hand- kăst/</td>
<td align="center">(او/آن) برخواهد خاست
/(u/ ăn) bar.kă.had- kăst/</td>
</tr>
</table>

<table>
<tr><td colspan="2" align="center">Command
امر</td></tr>
<tr>
<td align="center">برخیزید!
/bar.ki.zid/</td>
<td align="center">برخیز!
/bar.kiz/</td>
</tr>
</table>

to save, to store

اَندوختَن

/an.duǩ.tan/

Plural	Singular
Simple Present مضارع اخباری(حال ساده)	
(ما) می اندوزیم /(mǎ) mi.an.du.zim/	(من) می اندوزم /(man) mi.an.du.zam/
(شما) می اندوزید /(šo.mǎ) mi.an.du.zid/	(تو) می اندوزی /(to) mi.an.du.zi/
(آنها) می اندوزند /(ǎn.hǎ) mi.an.du.zand/	(او/آن) می اندوزد /(u/ ǎn) mi.an.du.zad/
Present Subjunctive مضارع التزامی	
(ما) بیندوزیم /(mǎ) bi.yan.du.zim/	(من) بیندوزم /(man) bi.yan.du.zam/
(شما) بیندوزید /(šo.mǎ) bi.yan.du.zid/	(تو) بیندوزی /(to) bi.yan.du.zi/
(آنها) بیندوزند /(ǎn.hǎ) bi.yan.du.zand/	(او/آن) بیندوزد /(u/ ǎn) bi.yan.du.zad/
Present Progressive مضارع مستمر(در جریان)	
(ما) داریم می اندوزیم /(mǎ) dǎ.rim- mi.an.du.zim/	(من) دارم می اندوزم /(man) dǎ.ram- mi.an.du.zam/
(شما) دارید می اندوزید /(šo.mǎ) dǎ.rid- mi.an.du.zid/	(تو) داری می اندوزی /(to) dǎ.ri- mi.an.du.zi/
(آنها) دارند می اندوزند /(ǎn.hǎ) dǎ.rand- mi.an.du.zand/	(او/آن) دارد می اندوزد /(u/ ǎn) dǎ.rad- mi.an.du.zad/

Simple Past		
ماضی مطلق (گذشته ساده)		
(ما) اندوختیم	(من) اندوختم	
/(mǎ) an.duǩ.tim/	/(man) an.duǩ.tam/	
(شما) اندوختید	(تو) اندوختی	
/(šo.mǎ) an.duǩ.tid/	/(to) an.duǩ.ti/	
(آنها) اندوختند	(او/آن) اندوخت	
/(ǎn.hǎ) an.duǩ.tand/	/(u/ ǎn) an.duǩt/	

Imperfect Indicative		
ماضی استمراری		
(ما) می اندوختیم	(من) می اندوختم	
/(mǎ) mi.an.duǩ.tim/	/(man) mi.an.duǩ.tam/	
(شما) می اندوختید	(تو) می اندوختی	
/(šo.mǎ) mi.an.duǩ.tid/	/(to) mi.an.duǩ.ti/	
(آنها) می اندوختند	(او/آن) می اندوخت	
/(ǎn.hǎ) mi.an.duǩ.tand/	/(u/ ǎn) mi.an.duǩt/	

Present Perfect		
ماضی نقلی		
(ما) اندوخته ایم	(من) اندوخته ام	
/(mǎ) an.duǩ.te.im/	/(man) an.duǩ.te.am/	
(شما) اندوخته اید	(تو) اندوخته ای	
/(šo.mǎ) an.duǩ.te.id/	/(to) an.duǩ.te.i/	
(آنها) اندوخته اند	(او/آن) اندوخته است	
/(ǎn.hǎ) an.duǩ.te.and/	/(u/ ǎn) an.duǩ.te- ast/	

Past Perfect		
ماضی بعید		
(ما) اندوخته بودیم	(من) اندوخته بودم	
/(mǎ) an.duǩ.te- bu.dim/	/(man) an.duǩ.te- bu.dam/	
(شما) اندوخته بودید	(تو) اندوخته بودی	
/(šo.mǎ) an.duǩ.te- bu.did/	/(to) an.duǩ.te- bu.di/	
(آنها) اندوخته بودند	(او/آن) اندوخته بود	
/(ǎn.hǎ) an.duǩ.te- bu.dand/	/(u/ ǎn) an.duǩ.te- bud/	

Past Subjunctive	
ماضی التزامی	
(ما) اندوخته باشیم	(من) اندوخته باشم
/(mă) an.duǩ.te- bă.šim/	/(man) an.duǩ.te- bă.šam/
(شما) اندوخته باشید	(تو) اندوخته باشی
/(šo.mă) an.duǩ.te- bă.šid/	/(to) an.duǩ.te- bă.ši/
(آنها) اندوخته باشند	(او/آن) اندوخته باشد
/(ăn.hă) an.duǩ.te- bă.šand/	/(u/ ăn) an.duǩ.te- bă.šad/

Past Progressive	
ماضی مستمر(در جریان)	
(ما) داشتیم می اندوختیم	(من) داشتم می اندوختم
/(mă) dăš.tim- mi.an.duǩ.tim/	/(man) dăš.tam- mi.an.duǩ.tam/
(شما) داشتید می اندوختید	(تو) داشتی می اندوختی
/(šo.mă) dăš.tid- mi.an.duǩ.tid/	/(to) dăš.ti- mi.an.duǩ.ti/
(آنها) داشتند می اندوختند	(او/آن) داشت می اندوخت
/(ăn.hă) dăš.tand- mi.an.duǩ.tand/	/(u/ ăn) dăšt- mi.an.duǩt/

Simple Future	
مستقبل (آینده ساده)	
(ما) خواهیم اندوخت	(من) خواهم اندوخت
/(mă) ǩă.him- an.duǩt/	/(man) ǩă.ham- an.duǩt/
(شما) خواهید اندوخت	(تو) خواهی اندوخت
/(šo.mă) ǩă.hid- an.duǩt/	/(to) ǩă.hi- an.duǩt/
(آنها) خواهند اندوخت	(او/آن) خواهد اندوخت
/(ăn.hă) ǩă.hand- an.duǩt/	/(u/ ăn) ǩă.had- an.duǩt/

Command	
امر	
بیندوزید!	بیندوز!
/bi.yan.du.zid/	/bi.yan.duz/

to search

گَشتَن

/gaš.tan/

Plural	Singular
Simple Present مضارع اخباری(حال ساده)	
(ما) می گردیم /(mǎ) mi.gar.dim/	(من) می گردم /(man) mi.gar.dam/
(شما) می گردید /(šo.mǎ) mi.gar.did/	(تو) می گردی /(to) mi.gar.di/
(آنها) می گردند /(ǎn.hǎ) mi.gar.dand/	(او/آن) می گردد /(u/ ǎn) mi.gar.dad/
Present Subjunctive مضارع التزامی	
(ما) بگردیم /(mǎ) be.gar.dim/	(من) بگردم /(man) be.gar.dam/
(شما) بگردید /(šo.mǎ) be.gar.did/	(تو) بگردی /(to) be.gar.di/
(آنها) بگردند /(ǎn.hǎ) be.gar.dand/	(او/آن) بگردد /(u/ ǎn) be.gar.dad/
Present Progressive مضارع مستمر(در جریان)	
(ما) داریم می گردیم /(mǎ) dǎ.rim- mi.gar.dim/	(من) دارم می گردم /(man) dǎ.ram- mi.gar.dam/
(شما) دارید می گردید /(šo.mǎ) dǎ.rid- mi.gar.did/	(تو) داری می گردی /(to) dǎ.ri- mi.gar.di/
(آنها) دارند می گردند /(ǎn.hǎ) dǎ.rand- mi.gar.dand/	(او/آن) دارد می گردد /(u/ ǎn) dǎ.rad- mi.gar.dad/

Simple Past
ماضی مطلق (گذشته ساده)

(ما) گشتیم	(من) گشتم
/(mǎ) gaš.tim/	/(man) gaš.tam/
(شما) گشتید	(تو) گشتی
/(šo.mǎ) gaš.tid/	/(to) gaš.ti/
(آنها) گشتند	(او/ آن) گشت
/(ǎn.hǎ) gaš.tand/	/(u/ ǎn) gašt/

Imperfect Indicative
ماضی استمراری

(ما) می گشتیم	(من) می گشتم
/(mǎ) mi.gaš.tim/	/(man) mi.gaš.tam/
(شما) می گشتید	(تو) می گشتی
/(šo.mǎ) mi.gaš.tid/	/(to) mi.gaš.ti/
(آنها) می گشتند	(او/ آن) می گشت
/(ǎn.hǎ) mi.gaš.tand/	/(u/ ǎn) mi.gašt/

Present Perfect
ماضی نقلی

(ما) گشته ایم	(من) گشته ام
/(mǎ) gaš.te.im/	/(man) gaš.te.am/
(شما) گشته اید	(تو) گشته ای
/(šo.mǎ) gaš.te.id/	/(to) gaš.te.i/
(آنها) گشته اند	(او/ آن) گشته است
/(ǎn.hǎ) gaš.te.and/	/(u/ ǎn) gaš.te- ast/

Past Perfect
ماضی بعید

(ما) گشته بودیم	(من) گشته بودم
/(mǎ) gaš.te- bu.dim/	/(man) gaš.te- bu.dam/
(شما) گشته بودید	(تو) گشته بودی
/(šo.mǎ) gaš.te- bu.did/	/(to) gaš.te- bu.di/
(آنها) گشته بودند	(او/ آن) گشته بود
/(ǎn.hǎ) gaš.te- bu.dand/	/(u/ ǎn) gaš.te- bud/

Past Subjunctive	
ماضی التزامی	
(ما) گشته باشیم	(من) گشته باشم
/(mǎ) gaš.te- bǎ.šim/	/(man) gaš.te- bǎ.šam/
(شما) گشته باشید	(تو) گشته باشی
/(šo.mǎ) gaš.te- bǎ.šid/	/(to) gaš.te- bǎ.ši/
(آنها) گشته باشند	(او/آن) گشته باشد
/(ǎn.hǎ) gaš.te- bǎ.šand/	/(u/ ǎn) gaš.te- bǎ.šad/

Past Progressive	
ماضی مستمر(در جریان)	
(ما) داشتیم می گشتیم	(من) داشتم می گشتم
/(mǎ) dǎš.tim- mi.gaš.tim/	/(man) dǎš.tam- mi.gaš.tam/
(شما) داشتید می گشتید	(تو) داشتی می گشتی
/(šo.mǎ) dǎš.tid- mi.gaš.tid/	/(to) dǎš.ti- mi.gaš.ti/
(آنها) داشتند می گشتند	(او/آن) داشت می گشت
/(ǎn.hǎ) dǎš.tand- mi.gaš.tand/	/(u/ ǎn) dǎšt- mi.gašt/

Simple Future	
مستقبل (آینده ساده)	
(ما) خواهیم گشت	(من) خواهم گشت
/(mǎ) ǩǎ.him- gašt/	/(man) ǩǎ.ham- gašt/
(شما) خواهید گشت	(تو) خواهی گشت
/(šo.mǎ) ǩǎ.hid- gašt/	/(to) ǩǎ.hi- gašt/
(آنها) خواهند گشت	(او/آن) خواهد گشت
/(ǎn.hǎ) ǩǎ.hand- gašt/	/(u/ ǎn) ǩǎ.had- gašt/

Command	
امر	
بگردید!	بگرد!
/be.gar.did/	/be.gard/

to seduce

فَریفتَن

/fa.rif.tan/

Plural	Singular
Simple Present مضارع اخباری(حال ساده)	
(ما) می فریبیم /(mǎ) mi.fa.ri.bim/	(من) می فریبم /(man) mi.fa.ri.bam/
(شما) می فریبید /(šo.mǎ) mi.fa.ri.bid/	(تو) می فریبی /(to) mi.fa.ri.bi/
(آنها) می فریبند /(ǎn.hǎ) mi.fa.ri.band/	(او/آن) می فریبد /(u/ ǎn) mi.fa.ri.bad/
Present Subjunctive مضارع التزامی	
(ما) بفریبیم /(mǎ) be.fa.ri.bim/	(من) بفریبم /(man) be.fa.ri.bam/
(شما) بفریبید /(šo.mǎ) be.fa.ri.bid/	(تو) بفریبی /(to) be.fa.ri.bi/
(آنها) بفریبند /(ǎn.hǎ) be.fa.ri.band/	(او/آن) بفریبد /(u/ ǎn) be.fa.ri.bad/
Present Progressive مضارع مستمر(در جریان)	
(ما) داریم می فریبیم /(mǎ) dǎ.rim- mi.fa.ri.bim/	(من) دارم می فریبم /(man) dǎ.ram- mi.fa.ri.bam/
(شما) دارید می فریبید /(šo.mǎ) dǎ.rid- mi.fa.ri.bid/	(تو) داری می فریبی /(to) dǎ.ri- mi.fa.ri.bi/
(آنها) دارند می فریبند /(ǎn.hǎ) dǎ.rand- mi.fa.ri.band/	(او/آن) دارد می فریبد /(u/ ǎn) dǎ.rad- mi.fa.ri.bad/

233

Simple Past

ماضی مطلق (گذشته ساده)

(ما) فریفتیم	(من) فریفتم
/(mǎ) fa.rif.tim/	/(man) fa.rif.tam/
(شما) فریفتید	(تو) فریفتی
/(šo.mǎ) fa.rif.tid/	/(to) fa.rif.ti/
(آنها) فریفتند	(او/آن) فریفت
/(ǎn.hǎ) fa.rif.tand/	/(u/ ǎn) fa.rift/

Imperfect Indicative

ماضی استمراری

(ما) می فریفتیم	(من) می فریفتم
/(mǎ) mi.fa.rif.tim/	/(man) mi.fa.rif.tam/
(شما) می فریفتید	(تو) می فریفتی
/(šo.mǎ) mi.fa.rif.tid/	/(to) mi.fa.rif.ti/
(آنها) می فریفتند	(او/آن) می فریفت
/(ǎn.hǎ) mi.fa.rif.tand/	/(u/ ǎn) mi.fa.rift/

Present Perfect

ماضی نقلی

(ما) فریفته ایم	(من) فریفته ام
/(mǎ) fa.rif.te.im/	/(man) fa.rif.te.am/
(شما) فریفته اید	(تو) فریفته ای
/(šo.mǎ) fa.rif.te.id/	/(to) fa.rif.te.i/
(آنها) فریفته اند	(او/آن) فریفته است
/(ǎn.hǎ) fa.rif.te.and/	/(u/ ǎn) fa.rif.te- ast/

Past Perfect

ماضی بعید

(ما) فریفته بودیم	(من) فریفته بودم
/(mǎ) fa.rif.te- bu.dim/	/(man) fa.rif.te- bu.dam/
(شما) فریفته بودید	(تو) فریفته بودی
/(šo.mǎ) fa.rif.te- bu.did/	/(to) fa.rif.te- bu.di/
(آنها) فریفته بودند	(او/آن) فریفته بود
/(ǎn.hǎ) fa.rif.te- bu.dand/	/(u/ ǎn) fa.rif.te- bud/

Past Subjunctive	
ماضی التزامی	
(ما) فریفته باشیم	(من) فریفته باشم
/(mǎ) fa.rif.te- bǎ.šim/	/(man) fa.rif.te- bǎ.šam/
(شما) فریفته باشید	(تو) فریفته باشی
/(šo.mǎ) fa.rif.te- bǎ.šid/	/(to) fa.rif.te- bǎ.ši/
(آنها) فریفته باشند	(او/آن) فریفته باشد
/(ǎn.hǎ) fa.rif.te- bǎ.šand/	/(u/ ǎn) fa.rif.te- bǎ.šad/

Past Progressive	
ماضی مستمر(در جریان)	
(ما) داشتیم می فریفتیم	(من) داشتم می فریفتم
/(mǎ) dǎš.tim- mi.fa.rif.tim/	/(man) dǎš.tam- mi.fa.rif.tam/
(شما) داشتید می فریفتید	(تو) داشتی می فریفتی
/(šo.mǎ) dǎš.tid- mi.fa.rif.tid/	/(to) dǎš.ti- mi.fa.rif.ti/
(آنها) داشتند می فریفتند	(او/آن) داشت می فریفت
/(ǎn.hǎ) dǎš.tand- mi.fa.rif.tand/	/(u/ ǎn) dǎšt- mi.fa.rift/

Simple Future	
مستقبل (آینده ساده)	
(ما) خواهیم فریفت	(من) خواهم فریفت
/(mǎ) ǩǎ.him- fa.rift/	/(man) ǩǎ.ham- fa.rift/
(شما) خواهید فریفت	(تو) خواهی فریفت
/(šo.mǎ) ǩǎ.hid- fa.rift/	/(to) ǩǎ.hi- fa.rift/
(آنها) خواهند فریفت	(او/آن) خواهد فریفت
/(ǎn.hǎ) ǩǎ.hand- fa.rift/	/(u/ ǎn) ǩǎ.had- fa.rift/

Command	
امر	
بفریبید!	بفریب!
/be.fa.ri.bid/	/be.fa.rib/

to see

دیدَن

/di.dan/

Plural	Singular
Simple Present <div dir="rtl">مضارع اخباری(حال ساده)</div>	
<div dir="rtl">(ما) می بینیم</div> /(mǎ) mi.bi.nim/	<div dir="rtl">(من) می بینم</div> /(man) mi.bi.nam/
<div dir="rtl">(شما) می بینید</div> /(šo.mǎ) mi.bi.nid/	<div dir="rtl">(تو) می بینی</div> /(to) mi.bi.ni/
<div dir="rtl">(آنها) می بینند</div> /(ǎn.hǎ) mi.bi.nand/	<div dir="rtl">(او/آن) می بیند</div> /(u/ ǎn) mi.bi.nad/
Present Subjunctive <div dir="rtl">مضارع التزامی</div>	
<div dir="rtl">(ما) ببینیم</div> /(mǎ) be.bi.nim/	<div dir="rtl">(من) ببینم</div> /(man) be.bi.nam/
<div dir="rtl">(شما) ببینید</div> /(šo.mǎ) be.bi.nid/	<div dir="rtl">(تو) ببینی</div> /(to) be.bi.ni/
<div dir="rtl">(آنها) ببینند</div> /(ǎn.hǎ) be.bi.nand/	<div dir="rtl">(او/آن) ببیند</div> /(u/ ǎn) be.bi.nad/
Present Progressive <div dir="rtl">مضارع مستمر(در جریان)</div>	
<div dir="rtl">(ما) داریم می بینیم</div> /(mǎ) dǎ.rim- mi.bi.nim/	<div dir="rtl">(من) دارم می بینم</div> /(man) dǎ.ram- mi.bi.nam/
<div dir="rtl">(شما) دارید می بینید</div> /(šo.mǎ) dǎ.rid- mi.bi.nid/	<div dir="rtl">(تو) داری می بینی</div> /(to) dǎ.ri- mi.bi.ni/
<div dir="rtl">(آنها) دارند می بینند</div> /(ǎn.hǎ) dǎ.rand- mi.bi.nand/	<div dir="rtl">(او/آن) دارد می بیند</div> /(u/ ǎn) dǎ.rad- mi.bi.nad/

<table>
<tr><td colspan="2" align="center">**Simple Past**
ماضی مطلق (گذشته ساده)</td></tr>
<tr>
<td align="center">(ما) دیدیم
/(mǎ) di.dim/</td>
<td align="center">(من) دیدم
/(man) di.dam/</td>
</tr>
<tr>
<td align="center">(شما) دیدید
/(šo.mǎ) di.did/</td>
<td align="center">(تو) دیدی
/(to) di.di/</td>
</tr>
<tr>
<td align="center">(آنها) دیدند
/(ǎn.hǎ) di.dand/</td>
<td align="center">(او/آن) دید
/(u/ ǎn) did/</td>
</tr>
</table>

<table>
<tr><td colspan="2" align="center">**Imperfect Indicative**
ماضی استمراری</td></tr>
<tr>
<td align="center">(ما) می دیدیم
/(mǎ) mi.di.dim/</td>
<td align="center">(من) می دیدم
/(man) mi.di.dam/</td>
</tr>
<tr>
<td align="center">(شما) می دیدید
/(šo.mǎ) mi.di.did/</td>
<td align="center">(تو) می دیدی
/(to) mi.di.di/</td>
</tr>
<tr>
<td align="center">(آنها) می دیدند
/(ǎn.hǎ) mi.di.dand/</td>
<td align="center">(او/آن) می دید
/(u/ ǎn) mi.did/</td>
</tr>
</table>

<table>
<tr><td colspan="2" align="center">**Present Perfect**
ماضی نقلی</td></tr>
<tr>
<td align="center">(ما) دیده ایم
/(mǎ) de.de.im/</td>
<td align="center">(من) دیده ام
/(man) di.de.am/</td>
</tr>
<tr>
<td align="center">(شما) دیده اید
/(šo.mǎ) di.de.id/</td>
<td align="center">(تو) دیده ای
/(to) di.de.i/</td>
</tr>
<tr>
<td align="center">(آنها) دیده اند
/(ǎn.hǎ) di.de.and/</td>
<td align="center">(او/آن) دیده است
/(u/ ǎn) di.de- ast/</td>
</tr>
</table>

<table>
<tr><td colspan="2" align="center">**Past Perfect**
ماضی بعید</td></tr>
<tr>
<td align="center">(ما) دیده بودیم
/(mǎ) di.de- bu.dim/</td>
<td align="center">(من) دیده بودم
/(man) di.de- bu.dam/</td>
</tr>
<tr>
<td align="center">(شما) دیده بودید
/(šo.mǎ) di.de- bu.did/</td>
<td align="center">(تو) دیده بودی
/(to) di.de- bu.di/</td>
</tr>
<tr>
<td align="center">(آنها) دیده بودند
/(ǎn.hǎ) di.de- bu.dand/</td>
<td align="center">(او/آن) دیده بود
/(u/ ǎn) di.de- bud/</td>
</tr>
</table>

Past Subjunctive	
ماضی التزامی	
(ما) دیده باشیم	(من) دیده باشم
/(mǎ) di.de- bǎ.šim/	/(man) di.de- bǎ.šam/
(شما) دیده باشید	(تو) دیده باشی
/(šo.mǎ) di.de- bǎ.šid/	/(to) di.de- bǎ.ši/
(آنها) دیده باشند	(او/آن) دیده باشد
/(ǎn.hǎ) di.de- bǎ.šand/	/(u/ ǎn) di.de- bǎ.šad/

Past Progressive	
ماضی مستمر(در جریان)	
(ما) داشتیم می دیدیم	(من) داشتم می دیدم
/(mǎ) dǎš.tim- mi.di.dim/	/(man) dǎš.tam- mi.di.dam/
(شما) داشتید می دیدید	(تو) داشتی می دیدی
/(šo.mǎ) dǎš.tid- mi.di.did/	/(to) dǎš.ti- mi.di.di/
(آنها) داشتند می دیدند	(او/آن) داشت می دید
/(ǎn.hǎ) dǎš.tand- mi.di.dand/	/(u/ ǎn) dǎšt- mi.did/

Simple Future	
مستقبل (آینده ساده)	
(ما) خواهیم دید	(من) خواهم دید
/(mǎ) ǩǎ.him- did/	/(man) ǩǎ.ham- did/
(شما) خواهید دید	(تو) خواهی دید
/(šo.mǎ) ǩǎ.hid- did/	/(to) ǩǎ.hi- did/
(آنها) خواهند دید	(او/آن) خواهد دید
/(ǎn.hǎ) ǩǎ.hand- did/	/(u/ ǎn) ǩǎ.had- did/

Command	
امر	
ببینید!	ببین!
/be.bi.nid/	/be.bin/

to seek

جُستَن

/jos.tan/

Plural	*Singular*
Simple Present مضارع اخباری(حال ساده)	
(ما) می جوییم /(mǎ) mi.ju.yim/	(من) می جویم /(man) mi.ju.yam/
(شما) می جویید /(šo.mǎ) mi.ju.yid/	(تو) می جویی /(to) mi.ju.yi/
(آنها) می جویند /(ǎn.hǎ) mi.ju.yand/	(او/آن) می جوید /(u/ ǎn) mi.ju.yad/
Present Subjunctive مضارع التزامی	
(ما) بجوییم /(mǎ) be.ju.yim/	(من) بجویم /(man) be.ju.yam/
(شما) بجویید /(šo.mǎ) be.ju.yid/	(تو) بجویی /(to) be.ju.yi/
(آنها) بجویند /(ǎn.hǎ) be.ju.yand/	(او/آن) بجوید /(u/ ǎn) be.ju.yad/
Present Progressive مضارع مستمر(در جریان)	
(ما) داریم می جوییم /(mǎ) dǎ.rim- mi.ju.yim/	(من) دارم می جویم /(man) dǎ.ram- mi.ju.yam/
(شما) دارید می جویید /(šo.mǎ) dǎ.rid- mi.ju.yid/	(تو) داری می جویی /(to) dǎ.ri- mi.ju.yi/
(آنها) دارند می جویند /(ǎn.hǎ) dǎ.rand- mi.ju.yand/	(او/آن) دارد می جوید /(u/ ǎn) dǎ.rad- mi.ju.yad/

Simple Past
ماضی مطلق (گذشته ساده)

(ما) جستیم	(من) جستم
/(mǎ) jos.tim/	/(man) jos.tam/
(شما) جستید	(تو) جستی
/(šo.mǎ) jos.tid/	/(to) jos.ti/
(آنها) جستند	(او/ آن) جست
/(ǎn.hǎ) jos.tand/	/(u/ ǎn) jost/

Imperfect Indicative
ماضی استمراری

(ما) می جستیم	(من) می جستم
/(mǎ) mi.jos.tim/	/(man) mi.jos.tam/
(شما) می جستید	(تو) می جستی
/(šo.mǎ) mi.jos.tid/	/(to) mi.jos.ti/
(آنها) می جستند	(او/ آن) می جست
/(ǎn.hǎ) mi.jos.tand/	/(u/ ǎn) mi.jost/

Present Perfect
ماضی نقلی

(ما) جسته ایم	(من) جسته ام
/(mǎ) jos.te.im/	/(man) jos.te.am/
(شما) جسته اید	(تو) جسته ای
/(šo.mǎ) jos.te.id/	/(to) jos.te.i/
(آنها) جسته اند	(او/ آن) جسته است
/(ǎn.hǎ) jos.te.and/	/(u/ ǎn) jos.te- ast/

Past Perfect
ماضی بعید

(ما) جسته بودیم	(من) جسته بودم
/(mǎ) jos.te- bu.dim/	/(man) jos.te- bu.dam/
(شما) جسته بودید	(تو) جسته بودی
/(šo.mǎ) jos.te- bu.did/	/(to) jos.te- bu.di/
(آنها) جسته بودند	(او/ آن) جسته بود
/(ǎn.hǎ) jos.te- bu.dand/	/(u/ ǎn) jos.te- bud/

<table>
<tr><td colspan="2" align="center">Past Subjunctive
ماضی التزامی</td></tr>
<tr>
<td align="center">(ما) جسته باشیم
/(mǎ) jos.te- bǎ.šim/</td>
<td align="center">(من) جسته باشم
/(man) jos.te- bǎ.šam/</td>
</tr>
<tr>
<td align="center">(شما) جسته باشید
/(šo.mǎ) jos.te- bǎ.šid/</td>
<td align="center">(تو) جسته باشی
/(to) jos.te- bǎ.ši/</td>
</tr>
<tr>
<td align="center">(آنها) جسته باشند
/(ǎn.hǎ) jos.te- bǎ.šand/</td>
<td align="center">(او/آن) جسته باشد
/(u/ ǎn) jos.te- bǎ.šad/</td>
</tr>
</table>

<table>
<tr><td colspan="2" align="center">Past Progressive
ماضی مستمر(در جریان)</td></tr>
<tr>
<td align="center">(ما) داشتیم می جستیم
/(mǎ) dǎš.tim- mi.jos.tim/</td>
<td align="center">(من) داشتم می جستم
/(man) dǎš.tam- mi.jos.tam/</td>
</tr>
<tr>
<td align="center">(شما) داشتید می جستید
/(šo.mǎ) dǎš.tid- mi.jos.tid/</td>
<td align="center">(تو) داشتی می جستی
/(to) dǎš.ti- mi.jos.ti/</td>
</tr>
<tr>
<td align="center">(آنها) داشتند می جستند
/(ǎn.hǎ) dǎš.tand- mi.jos.tand/</td>
<td align="center">(او/آن) داشت می جست
/(u/ ǎn) dǎšt- mi.jost/</td>
</tr>
</table>

<table>
<tr><td colspan="2" align="center">Simple Future
مستقبل (آینده ساده)</td></tr>
<tr>
<td align="center">(ما) خواهیم جست
/(mǎ) ǩǎ.him- jost/</td>
<td align="center">(من) خواهم جست
/(man) ǩǎ.ham- jost/</td>
</tr>
<tr>
<td align="center">(شما) خواهید جست
/(šo.mǎ) ǩǎ.hid- jost/</td>
<td align="center">(تو) خواهی جست
/(to) ǩǎ.hi- jost/</td>
</tr>
<tr>
<td align="center">(آنها) خواهند جست
/(ǎn.hǎ) ǩǎ.hand- jost/</td>
<td align="center">(او/آن) خواهد جست
/(u/ ǎn) ǩǎ.had- jost/</td>
</tr>
</table>

<table>
<tr><td colspan="2" align="center">Command
امر</td></tr>
<tr>
<td align="center">بجویید!
/be.ju.yid/</td>
<td align="center">بجوی!
/be.juy/</td>
</tr>
</table>

to select

بَرگُزیدَن

/bar.go.zi.dan/

Plural	Singular
Simple Present	
مضارع اخباری(حال ساده)	
(ما) بر می گزینیم	(من) بر می گزینم
/(mǎ) bar.mi.go.zi.nim/	/(man) bar.mi.go.zi.nam/
(شما) بر می گزینید	(تو) بر می گزینی
/(šo.mǎ) bar.mi.go.zi.nid/	/(to) bar.mi.go.zi.ni/
(آنها) بر می گزینند	(او/آن) بر می گزیند
/(ǎn.hǎ) bar.mi.go.zi.nand/	/(u/ ǎn) bar.mi.go.zi.nad/

Plural	Singular
Present Subjunctive	
مضارع التزامی	
(ما) بر بگزینیم	(من) بر بگزینم
/(mǎ) bar.be.go.zi.nim/	/(man) bar.be.go.zi.nam/
(شما) بر بگزینید	(تو) بر بگزینی
/(šo.mǎ) bar.be.go.zi.nid/	/(to) bar.be.go.zi.ni/
(آنها) بر بگزینند	(او/آن) بر بگزیند
/(ǎn.hǎ) bar.be.go.zi.nand/	/(u/ ǎn) bar.be.go.zi.nad/

Plural	Singular
Present Progressive	
مضارع مستمر(در جریان)	
(ما) داریم بر می گزینیم	(من) دارم بر می گزینم
/(mǎ) dǎ.rim- bar.mi.go.zi.nim/	/(man) dǎ.ram- bar.mi.go.zi.nam/
(شما) دارید بر می گزینید	(تو) داری بر می گزینی
/(šo.mǎ) dǎ.rid- bar.mi.go.zi.nid/	/(to) dǎ.ri- bar.mi.go.zi.ni/
(آنها) دارند بر می گزینند	(او/آن) دارد بر می گزیند
/(ǎn.hǎ) dǎ.rand- bar.mi.go.zi.nand/	/(u/ ǎn) dǎ.rad- bar.mi.go.zi.nad/

Simple Past	
ماضی مطلق (گذشته ساده)	
(ما) برگزیدیم	(من) برگزیدم
/(mǎ) bar.go.zi.dim/	/(man) bar.go.zi.dam/
(شما) برگزیدید	(تو) برگزیدی
/(šo.mǎ) bar.go.zi.did/	/(to) bar.go.zi.di/
(آنها) برگزیدند	(او/آن) برگزید
/(ǎn.hǎ) bar.go.zi.dand/	/(u/ ǎn) bar.go.zid/

Imperfect Indicative	
ماضی استمراری	
(ما) بر می گزیدیم	(من) بر می گزیدم
/(mǎ) bar.mi.go.zi.dim/	/(man) bar.mi.go.zi.dam/
(شما) بر می گزیدید	(تو) بر می گزیدی
/(šo.mǎ) bar.mi.go.zi.did/	/(to) bar.mi.go.zi.di/
(آنها) بر می گزیدند	(او/آن) بر می گزید
/(ǎn.hǎ) bar.mi.go.zi.dand/	/(u/ ǎn) bar.mi.go.zid/

Present Perfect	
ماضی نقلی	
(ما) برگزیده ایم	(من) برگزیده ام
/(mǎ) bar.go.zi.de.im/	/(man) bar.go.zi.de.am/
(شما) برگزیده اید	(تو) برگزیده ای
/(šo.mǎ) bar.go.zi.de.id/	/(to) bar.go.zi.de.i/
(آنها) برگزیده اند	(او/آن) برگزیده است
/(ǎn.hǎ) bar.go.zi.de.and/	/(u/ ǎn) bar.go.zi.de- ast/

Past Perfect	
ماضی بعید	
(ما) برگزیده بودیم	(من) برگزیده بودم
/(mǎ) bar.go.zi.de- bu.dim/	/(man) bar.go.zi.de- bu.dam/
(شما) برگزیده بودید	(تو) برگزیده بودی
/(šo.mǎ) bar.go.zi.de- bu.did/	/(to) bar.go.zi.de- bu.di/
(آنها) برگزیده بودند	(او/آن) برگزیده بود
/(ǎn.hǎ) bar.go.zi.de- bu.dand/	/(u/ ǎn) bar.go.zi.de- bud/

Past Subjunctive	
ماضی التزامی	
(ما) برگزیده باشیم	(من) برگزیده باشم
/(mǎ) bar.go.zi.de- bǎ.šim/	/(man) bar.go.zi.de- bǎ.šam/
(شما) برگزیده باشید	(تو) برگزیده باشی
/(šo.mǎ) bar.go.zi.de- bǎ.šid/	/(to) bar.go.zi.de- bǎ.ši/
(آنها) برگزیده باشند	(او/آن) برگزیده باشد
/(ǎn.hǎ) bar.go.zi.de- bǎ.šand/	/(u/ ǎn) bar.go.zi.de- bǎ.šad/

Past Progressive	
ماضی مستمر(در جریان)	
(ما) داشتیم بر می گزیدیم	(من) داشتم بر می گزیدم
/(mǎ) dǎš.tim- bar.mi.go.zi.dim/	/(man) dǎš.tam- bar.mi.go.zi.dam/
(شما) داشتید بر می گزیدید	(تو) داشتی بر می گزیدی
/(šo.mǎ) dǎš.tid- bar.mi.go.zi.did/	/(to) dǎš.ti- bar.mi.go.zi.di/
(آنها) داشتند بر می گزیدند	(او/آن) داشت بر می گزید
/(ǎn.hǎ) dǎš.tand- bar.mi.go.zi.dand/	/(u/ ǎn) dǎšt- bar.mi.go.zid/

Simple Future	
مستقبل (آینده ساده)	
(ما) برخواهیم گزید	(من) برخواهم گزید
/(mǎ) bar.kǎ.him- go.zid/	/(man) bar.kǎ.ham- go.zid/
(شما) برخواهید گزید	(تو) برخواهی گزید
/(šo.mǎ) bar.kǎ.hid- go.zid/	/(to) bar.kǎ.hi- go.zid/
(آنها) برخواهند گزید	(او/آن) برخواهد گزید
/(ǎn.hǎ) bar.kǎ.hand- go.zid/	/(u/ ǎn) bar.kǎ.had- go.zid/

Command	
امر	
* بر بگزینید!	* بر بگزین!
/bar.be.go.zi.nid/	/bar.be.go.zin/

* also: برگزینید!   برگزین!

to sell

فُروختَن

/fo.ruǩ.tan/

Plural	Singular
Simple Present	
مضارع اخباری(حال ساده)	
(ما) می فروشیم	(من) می فروشم
/(mǎ) mi.fo.ru.šim/	/(man) mi.fo.ru.šam/
(شما) می فروشید	(تو) می فروشی
/(šo.mǎ) mi.fo.ru.šid/	/(to) mi.fo.ru.ši/
(آنها) می فروشند	(او/آن) می فروشد
/(ǎn.hǎ) mi.fo.ru.šand/	/(u/ ǎn) mi.fo.ru.šad/

Plural	Singular
Present Subjunctive	
مضارع التزامی	
(ما) بفروشیم	(من) بفروشم
/(mǎ) be.fo.ru.šim/	/(man) be.fo.ru.šam/
(شما) بفروشید	(تو) بفروشی
/(šo.mǎ) be.fo.ru.šid/	/(to) be.fo.ru.ši/
(آنها) بفروشند	(او/آن) بفروشد
/(ǎn.hǎ) be.fo.ru.šand/	/(u/ ǎn) be.fo.ru.šad/

Plural	Singular
Present Progressive	
مضارع مستمر(در جریان)	
(ما) داریم می فروشیم	(من) دارم می فروشم
/(mǎ) dǎ.rim- mi.fo.ru.šim/	/(man) dǎ.ram- mi.fo.ru.šam/
(شما) دارید می فروشید	(تو) داری می فروشی
/(šo.mǎ) dǎ.rid- mi.fo.ru.šid/	/(to) dǎ.ri- mi.fo.ru.ši/
(آنها) دارند می فروشند	(او/آن) دارد می فروشد
/(ǎn.hǎ) dǎ.rand- mi.fo.ru.šand/	/(u/ ǎn) dǎ.rad- mi.fo.ru.šad/

Simple Past	
ماضی مطلق (گذشته ساده)	
(ما) فروختیم	(من) فروختم
/(mǎ) fo.ruǩ.tim/	/(man) fo.ruǩ.tam/
(شما) فروختید	(تو) فروختی
/(šo.mǎ) fo.ruǩ.tid/	/(to) fo.ruǩ.ti/
(آنها) فروختند	(او/آن) فروخت
/(ǎn.hǎ) fo.ruǩ.tand/	/(u/ ǎn) fo.ruǩt/

Imperfect Indicative	
ماضی استمراری	
(ما) می فروختیم	(من) می فروختم
/(mǎ) mi.fo.ruǩ.tim/	/(man) mi.fo.ruǩ.tam/
(شما) می فروختید	(تو) می فروختی
/(šo.mǎ) mi.fo.ruǩ.tid/	/(to) mi.fo.ruǩ.ti/
(آنها) می فروختند	(او/آن) می فروخت
/(ǎn.hǎ) mi.fo.ruǩ.tand/	/(u/ ǎn) mi.fo.ruǩt/

Present Perfect	
ماضی نقلی	
(ما) فروخته ایم	(من) فروخته ام
/(mǎ) fo.ruǩ.te.im/	/(man) fo.ruǩ.te.am/
(شما) فروخته اید	(تو) فروخته ای
/(šo.mǎ) fo.ruǩ.te.id/	/(to) fo.ruǩ.te.i/
(آنها) فروخته اند	(او/آن) فروخته است
/(ǎn.hǎ) fo.ruǩ.te.and/	/(u/ ǎn) fo.ruǩ.te- ast/

Past Perfect	
ماضی بعید	
(ما) فروخته بودیم	(من) فروخته بودم
/(mǎ) fo.ruǩ.te- bu.dim/	/(man) fo.ruǩ.te- bu.dam/
(شما) فروخته بودید	(تو) فروخته بودی
/(šo.mǎ) fo.ruǩ.te- bu.did/	/(to) fo.ruǩ.te- bu.di/
(آنها) فروخته بودند	(او/آن) فروخته بود
/(ǎn.hǎ) fo.ruǩ.te- bu.dand/	/(u/ ǎn) fo.ruǩ.te- bud/

Past Subjunctive
ماضی التزامی

(ما) فروخته باشیم	(من) فروخته باشم
/(mă) fo.ruǩ.te- bă.šim/	/(man) fo.ruǩ.te- bă.šam/
(شما) فروخته باشید	(تو) فروخته باشی
/(šo.mă) fo.ruǩ.te- bă.šid/	/(to) fo.ruǩ.te- bă.ši/
(آنها) فروخته باشند	(او/آن) فروخته باشد
/(ăn.hă) fo.ruǩ.te- bă.šand/	/(u/ ăn) fo.ruǩ.te- bă.šad/

Past Progressive
ماضی مستمر(در جریان)

(ما) داشتیم می فروختیم	(من) داشتم می فروختم
/(mă) dăš.tim- mi.fo.ruǩ.tim/	/(man) dăš.tam- mi.fo.ruǩ.tam/
(شما) داشتید می فروختید	(تو) داشتی می فروختی
/(šo.mă) dăš.tid- mi.fo.ruǩ.tid/	/(to) dăš.ti- mi.fo.ruǩ.ti/
(آنها) داشتند می فروختند	(او/آن) داشت می فروخت
/(ăn.hă) dăš.tand- mi.fo.ruǩ.tand/	/(u/ ăn) dăšt- mi.fo.ruǩt/

Simple Future
مستقبل (آینده ساده)

(ما) خواهیم فروخت	(من) خواهم فروخت
/(mă) ǩă.him- fo.ruǩt/	/(man) ǩă.ham- fo.ruǩt/
(شما) خواهید فروخت	(تو) خواهی فروخت
/(šo.mă) ǩă.hid- fo.ruǩt/	/(to) ǩă.hi- fo.ruǩt/
(آنها) خواهند فروخت	(او/آن) خواهد فروخت
/(ăn.hă) ǩă.hand- fo.ruǩt/	/(u/ ăn) ǩă.had- fo.ruǩt/

Command
امر

بفروشید!	بفروش!
/be.fo.ru.šid/	/be.fo.ruš/

247

to send

فِرِستادَن

/fe.res.tă.dan/

Plural	Singular
Simple Present	
مضارع اخباری(حال ساده)	
(ما) می فرستیم	(من) می فرستم
/(mă) mi.fe.res.tim/	/(man) mi.fe.res.tam/
(شما) می فرستید	(تو) می فرستی
/(šo.mă) mi.fe.res.tid/	/(to) mi.fe.res.ti/
(آنها) می فرستند	(او/آن) می فرستد
/(ăn.hă) mi.fe.res.tand/	/(u/ ăn) mi.fe.res.tad/
Present Subjunctive	
مضارع التزامی	
(ما) بفرستیم	(من) بفرستم
/(mă) be.fe.res.tim/	/(man) be.fe.res.tam/
(شما) بفرستید	(تو) بفرستی
/(šo.mă) be.fe.res.tid/	/(to) be.fe.res.ti/
(آنها) بفرستند	(او/آن) بفرستد
/(ăn.hă) be.fe.res.tand/	/(u/ ăn) be.fe.res.tad/
Present Progressive	
مضارع مستمر(در جریان)	
(ما) داریم می فرستیم	(من) دارم می فرستم
/(mă) dă.rim- mi.fe.res.tim/	/(man) dă.ram- mi.fe.res.tam/
(شما) دارید می فرستید	(تو) داری می فرستی
/(šo.mă) dă.rid- mi.fe.res.tid/	/(to) dă.ri- mi.fe.res.ti/
(آنها) دارند می فرستند	(او/آن) دارد می فرستد
/(ăn.hă) dă.rand- mi.fe.res.tand/	/(u/ ăn) dă.rad- mi.fe.res.tad/

248

Simple Past	
ماضی مطلق (گذشته ساده)	
(ما) فرستادیم	(من) فرستادم
/(mă) fe.res.tă.dim/	/(man) fe.res.tă.dam/
(شما) فرستادید	(تو) فرستادی
/(šo.mă) fe.res.tă.did/	/(to) fe.res.tă.di/
(آنها) فرستادند	(او/آن) فرستاد
/(ăn.hă) fe.res.tă.dand/	/(u/ ăn) fe.res.tăd/

Imperfect Indicative	
ماضی استمراری	
(ما) می فرستادیم	(من) می فرستادم
/(mă) mi.fe.res.tă.dim/	/(man) mi.fe.res.tă.dam/
(شما) می فرستادید	(تو) می فرستادی
/(šo.mă) mi.fe.res.tă.did/	/(to) mi.fe.res.tă.di/
(آنها) می فرستادند	(او/آن) می فرستاد
/(ăn.hă) mi.fe.res.tă.dand/	/(u/ ăn) mi.fe.res.tăd/

Present Perfect	
ماضی نقلی	
(ما) فرستاده ایم	(من) فرستاده ام
/(mă) fe.res.tă.de.im/	/(man) fe.res.tă.de.am/
(شما) فرستاده اید	(تو) فرستاده ای
/(šo.mă) fe.res.tă.de.id/	/(to) fe.res.tă.de.i/
(آنها) فرستاده اند	(او/آن) فرستاده است
/(ăn.hă) fe.res.tă.de.and/	/(u/ ăn) fe.res.tă.de- ast/

Past Perfect	
ماضی بعید	
(ما) فرستاده بودیم	(من) فرستاده بودم
/(mă) fe.res.tă.de- bu.dim/	/(man) fe.res.tă.de- bu.dam/
(شما) فرستاده بودید	(تو) فرستاده بودی
/(šo.mă) fe.res.tă.de- bu.did/	/(to) fe.res.tă.de- bu.di/
(آنها) فرستاده بودند	(او/آن) فرستاده بود
/(ăn.hă) fe.res.tă.de- bu.dand/	/(u/ ăn) fe.res.tă.de- bud/

Past Subjunctive	
ماضی التزامی	
(ما) فرستاده باشیم /(mă) fe.res.tă.de- bă.šim/	(من) فرستاده باشم /(man) fe.res.tă.de- bă.šam/
(شما) فرستاده باشید /(šo.mă) fe.res.tă.de- bă.šid/	(تو) فرستاده باشی /(to) fe.res.tă.de- bă.ši/
(آنها) فرستاده باشند /(ăn.hă) fe.res.tă.de- bă.šand/	(او/آن) فرستاده باشد /(u/ ăn) fe.res.tă.de- bă.šad/

Past Progressive	
ماضی مستمر(در جریان)	
(ما) داشتیم می فرستادیم /(mă) dăš.tim- mi.fe.res.tă.dim/	(من) داشتم می فرستادم /(man) dăš.tam- mi.fe.res.tă.dam/
(شما) داشتید می فرستادید /(šo.mă) dăš.tid- mi.fe.res.tă.did/	(تو) داشتی می فرستادی /(to) dăš.ti- mi.fe.res.tă.di/
(آنها) داشتند می فرستادند /(ăn.hă) dăš.tand- mi.fe.res.tă.dand/	(او/آن) داشت می فرستاد /(u/ ăn) dăšt- mi.fe.res.tăd/

Simple Future	
مستقبل (آینده ساده)	
(ما) خواهیم فرستاد /(mă) kă.him- fe.res.tăd/	(من) خواهم فرستاد /(man) kă.ham- fe.res.tăd/
(شما) خواهید فرستاد /(šo.mă) kă.hid- fe.res.tăd/	(تو) خواهی فرستاد /(to) kă.hi- fe.res.tăd/
(آنها) خواهند فرستاد /(ăn.hă) kă.hand- fe.res.tăd/	(او/آن) خواهد فرستاد /(u/ ăn) kă.had- fe.res.tăd/

Command	
امر	
بفرستید! /be.fe.res.tid/	بفرست! /be.fe.rest/

to sew

دوختَن

/duǩ.tan/

Plural	Singular
Simple Present	
مضارع اخباری(حال ساده)	
(ما) می دوزیم	(من) می دوزم
/(mǎ) mi.du.zim/	/(man) mi.du.zam/
(شما) می دوزید	(تو) می دوزی
/(šo.mǎ) mi.du.zid/	/(to) mi.du.zi/
(آنها) می دوزند	(او/آن) می دوزد
/(ǎn.hǎ) mi.du.zand/	/(u/ ǎn) mi.du.zad/
Present Subjunctive	
مضارع التزامی	
(ما) بدوزیم	(من) بدوزم
/(mǎ) be.du.zim/	/(man) be.du.zam/
(شما) بدوزید	(تو) بدوزی
/(šo.mǎ) be.du.zid/	/(to) be.du.zi/
(آنها) بدوزند	(او/آن) بدوزد
/(ǎn.hǎ) be.du.zand/	/(u/ ǎn) be.du.zad/
Present Progressive	
مضارع مستمر(در جریان)	
(ما) داریم می دوزیم	(من) دارم می دوزم
/(mǎ) dǎ.rim- mi.du.zim/	/(man) dǎ.ram- mi.du.zam/
(شما) دارید می دوزید	(تو) داری می دوزی
/(šo.mǎ) dǎ.rid- mi.du.zid/	/(to) dǎ.ri- mi.du.zi/
(آنها) دارند می دوزند	(او/آن) دارد می دوزد
/(ǎn.hǎ) dǎ.rand- mi.du.zand/	/(u/ ǎn) dǎ.rad- mi.du.zad/

251

Simple Past	
ماضی مطلق (گذشته ساده)	
(ما) دوختیم	(من) دوختم
/(mǎ) duǩ.tim/	/(man) duǩ.tam/
(شما) دوختید	(تو) دوختی
/(šo.mǎ) duǩ.tid/	/(to) duǩ.ti/
(آنها) دوختند	(او/آن) دوخت
/(ǎn.hǎ) duǩ.tand/	/(u/ ǎn) duǩt/

Imperfect Indicative	
ماضی استمراری	
(ما) می دوختیم	(من) می دوختم
/(mǎ) mi.duǩ.tim/	/(man) mi.duǩ.tam/
(شما) می دوختید	(تو) می دوختی
/(šo.mǎ) mi.duǩ.tid/	/(to) mi.duǩ.ti/
(آنها) می دوختند	(او/آن) می دوخت
/(ǎn.hǎ) mi.duǩ.tand/	/(u/ ǎn) mi.duǩt/

Present Perfect	
ماضی نقلی	
(ما) دوخته ایم	(من) دوخته ام
/(mǎ) duǩ.te.im/	/(man) duǩ.te.am/
(شما) دوخته اید	(تو) دوخته ای
/(šo.mǎ) duǩ.te.id/	/(to) duǩ.te.i/
(آنها) دوخته اند	(او/آن) دوخته است
/(ǎn.hǎ) duǩ.te.and/	/(u/ ǎn) duǩ.te- ast/

Past Perfect	
ماضی بعید	
(ما) دوخته بودیم	(من) دوخته بودم
/(mǎ) duǩ.te- bu.dim/	/(man) duǩ.te- bu.dam/
(شما) دوخته بودید	(تو) دوخته بودی
/(šo.mǎ) duǩ.te- bu.did/	/(to) duǩ.te- bu.di/
(آنها) دوخته بودند	(او/آن) دوخته بود
/(ǎn.hǎ) duǩ.te- bu.dand/	/(u/ ǎn) duǩ.te- bud/

Past Subjunctive	
ماضی التزامی	
(ما) دوخته باشیم	(من) دوخته باشم
/(mă) duǩ.te- bă.šim/	/(man) duǩ.te- bă.šam/
(شما) دوخته باشید	(تو) دوخته باشی
/(šo.mă) duǩ.te- bă.šid/	/(to) duǩ.te- bă.ši/
(آنها) دوخته باشند	(او/آن) دوخته باشد
/(ăn.hă) duǩ.te- bă.šand/	/(u/ ăn) duǩ.te- bă.šad/

Past Progressive	
ماضی مستمر(در جریان)	
(ما) داشتیم می دوختیم	(من) داشتم می دوختم
/(mă) dăš.tim- mi.duǩ.tim/	/(man) dăš.tam- mi.duǩ.tam/
(شما) داشتید می دوختید	(تو) داشتی می دوختی
/(šo.mă) dăš.tid- mi.duǩ.tid/	/(to) dăš.ti- mi.duǩ.ti/
(آنها) داشتند می دوختند	(او/آن) داشت می دوخت
/(ăn.hă) dăš.tand- mi.duǩ.tand/	/(u/ ăn) dăšt- mi.duǩt/

Simple Future	
مستقبل (آینده ساده)	
(ما) خواهیم دوخت	(من) خواهم دوخت
/(mă) ǩă.him- duǩt/	/(man) ǩă.ham- duǩt/
(شما) خواهید دوخت	(تو) خواهی دوخت
/(šo.mă) ǩă.hid- duǩt/	/(to) ǩă.hi- duǩt/
(آنها) خواهند دوخت	(او/آن) خواهد دوخت
/(ăn.hă) ǩă.hand- duǩt/	/(u/ ăn) ǩă.had- duǩt/

Command	
امر	
بدوزید!	بدوز!
/be.du.zid/	/be.duz/

253

to show

نِمودَن

/ne.mu.dan/

Plural	Singular
Simple Present مضارع اخباری(حال ساده)	
(ما) می نماییم /(mǎ) mi.na.mǎ.yim/	(من) می نمایم /(man) mi.na.mǎ.yam/
(شما) می نمایید /(šo.mǎ) mi.na.mǎ.yid/	(تو) می نمایی /(to) mi.na.mǎ.yi/
(آنها) می نمایند /(ǎn.hǎ) mi.na.mǎ.yand/	(او/آن) می نماید /(u/ ǎn) mi.na.mǎ.yad/
Present Subjunctive مضارع التزامی	
(ما) بنماییم /(mǎ) be.na.mǎ.yim/	(من) بنمایم /(man) be.na.mǎ.yam/
(شما) بنمایید /(šo.mǎ) be.na.mǎ.yid/	(تو) بنمایی /(to) be.na.mǎ.yi/
(آنها) بنمایند /(ǎn.hǎ) be.na.mǎ.yand/	(او/آن) بنماید /(u/ ǎn) be.na.mǎ.yad/
Present Progressive مضارع مستمر(در جریان)	
(ما) داریم می نماییم /(mǎ) dǎ.rim- mi.na.mǎ.yim/	(من) دارم می نمایم /(man) dǎ.ram- mi.na.mǎ.yam/
(شما) دارید می نمایید /(šo.mǎ) dǎ.rid- mi.na.mǎ.yid/	(تو) داری می نمایی /(to) dǎ.ri- mi.na.mǎ.yi/
(آنها) دارند می نمایند /(ǎn.hǎ) dǎ.rand- mi.na.mǎ.yand/	(او/آن) دارد می نماید /(u/ ǎn) dǎ.rad- mi.na.mǎ.yad/

	Simple Past
	ماضی مطلق (گذشته ساده)
(ما) نمودیم	(من) نمودم
/(mǎ) ne.mu.dim/	/(man) ne.mu.dam/
(شما) نمودید	(تو) نمودی
/(šo.mǎ) ne.mu.did/	/(to) ne.mu.di/
(آنها) نمودند	(او/آن) نمود
/(ǎn.hǎ) ne.mu.dand/	/(u/ ǎn) ne.mud/

	Imperfect Indicative
	ماضی استمراری
(ما) می نمودیم	(من) می نمودم
/(mǎ) mi.ne.mu.dim/	/(man) mi.ne.mu.dam/
(شما) می نمودید	(تو) می نمودی
/(šo.mǎ) mi.ne.mu.did/	/(to) mi.ne.mu.di/
(آنها) می نمودند	(او/آن) می نمود
/(ǎn.hǎ) mi.ne.mu.dand/	/(u/ ǎn) mi.ne.mud/

	Present Perfect
	ماضی نقلی
(ما) نموده ایم	(من) نموده ام
/(mǎ) ne.mu.de.im/	/(man) ne.mu.de.am/
(شما) نموده اید	(تو) نموده ای
/(šo.mǎ) ne.mu.de.id/	/(to) ne.mu.de.i/
(آنها) نموده اند	(او/آن) نموده است
/(ǎn.hǎ) ne.mu.de.and/	/(u/ ǎn) ne.mu.de- ast/

	Past Perfect
	ماضی بعید
(ما) نموده بودیم	(من) نموده بودم
/(mǎ) ne.mu.de- bu.dim/	/(man) ne.mu.de- bu.dam/
(شما) نموده بودید	(تو) نموده بودی
/(šo.mǎ) ne.mu.de- bu.did/	/(to) ne.mu.de- bu.di/
(آنها) نموده بودند	(او/آن) نموده بود
/(ǎn.hǎ) ne.mu.de- bu.dand/	/(u/ ǎn) ne.mu.de- bud/

255

Past Subjunctive	
ماضی التزامی	
(ما) نموده باشیم	(من) نموده باشم
/(mă) ne.mu.de- bă.šim/	/(man) ne.mu.de- bă.šam/
(شما) نموده باشید	(تو) نموده باشی
/(šo.mă) ne.mu.de- bă.šid/	/(to) ne.mu.de- bă.ši/
(آنها) نموده باشند	(او/آن) نموده باشد
/(ăn.hă) ne.mu.de- bă.šand/	/(u/ ăn) ne.mu.de- bă.šad/

Past Progressive	
ماضی مستمر(در جریان)	
(ما) داشتیم می نمودیم	(من) داشتم می نمودم
/(mă) dăš.tim- mi.ne.mu.dim/	/(man) dăš.tam- mi.ne.mu.dam/
(شما) داشتید می نمودید	(تو) داشتی می نمودی
/(šo.mă) dăš.tid- mi.ne.mu.did/	/(to) dăš.ti- mi.ne.mu.di/
(آنها) داشتند می نمودند	(او/آن) داشت می نمود
/(ăn.hă) dăš.tand- mi.ne.mu.dand/	/(u/ ăn) dăšt- mi.ne.mud/

Simple Future	
مستقبل (آینده ساده)	
(ما) خواهیم نمود	(من) خواهم نمود
/(mă) kă.him- ne.mud/	/(man) kă.ham- ne.mud/
(شما) خواهید نمود	(تو) خواهی نمود
/(šo.mă) kă.hid- ne.mud/	/(to) kă.hi- ne.mud/
(آنها) خواهند نمود	(او/آن) خواهد نمود
/(ăn.hă) kă.hand- ne.mud/	/(u/ ăn) kă.had- ne.mud/

Command	
امر	
بنمایید!	بنمای!
/be.na.mă.yid/	/be.na.măy/

to sit

نِشَستَن

/ne.šas.tan/

Plural	Singular
Simple Present <div dir="rtl">مضارع اخباری(حال ساده)</div>	
<div dir="rtl">(ما) می نشینیم</div> /(mǎ) mi.ne.ši.nim/	<div dir="rtl">(من) می نشینم</div> /(man) mi.ne.ši.nam/
<div dir="rtl">(شما) می نشینید</div> /(šo.mǎ) mi.ne.ši.nid/	<div dir="rtl">(تو) می نشینی</div> /(to) mi.ne.ši.ni/
<div dir="rtl">(آنها) می نشینند</div> /(ǎn.hǎ) mi.ne.ši.nand/	<div dir="rtl">(او/آن) می نشیند</div> /(u/ ǎn) mi.ne.ši.nad/

Plural	Singular
Present Subjunctive <div dir="rtl">مضارع التزامی</div>	
<div dir="rtl">(ما) بنشینیم</div> /(mǎ) be.ne.ši.nim/	<div dir="rtl">(من) بنشینم</div> /(man) be.ne.ši.nam/
<div dir="rtl">(شما) بنشینید</div> /(šo.mǎ) be.ne.ši.nid/	<div dir="rtl">(تو) بنشینی</div> /(to) be.ne.ši.ni/
<div dir="rtl">(آنها) بنشینند</div> /(ǎn.hǎ) be.ne.ši.nand/	<div dir="rtl">(او/آن) بنشیند</div> /(u/ ǎn) be.ne.ši.nad/

Plural	Singular
Present Progressive <div dir="rtl">مضارع مستمر(در جریان)</div>	
<div dir="rtl">(ما) داریم می نشینیم</div> /(mǎ) dǎ.rim- mi.ne.ši.nim/	<div dir="rtl">(من) دارم می نشینم</div> /(man) dǎ.ram- mi.ne.ši.nam/
<div dir="rtl">(شما) دارید می نشینید</div> /(šo.mǎ) dǎ.rid- mi.ne.ši.nid/	<div dir="rtl">(تو) داری می نشینی</div> /(to) dǎ.ri- mi.ne.ši.ni/
<div dir="rtl">(آنها) دارند می نشینند</div> /(ǎn.hǎ) dǎ.rand- mi.ne.ši.nand/	<div dir="rtl">(او/آن) دارد می نشیند</div> /(u/ ǎn) dǎ.rad- mi.ne.ši.nad/

	Simple Past	
	ماضی مطلق (گذشته ساده)	
(ما) نشستیم		(من) نشستم
/(mă) ne.šas.tim/		/(man) ne.šas.tam/
(شما) نشستید		(تو) نشستی
/(šo.mă) ne.šas.tid/		/(to) ne.šas.ti/
(آنها) نشستند		(او/آن) نشست
/(ăn.hă) ne.šas.tand/		/(u/ ăn) ne.šast/

	Imperfect Indicative	
	ماضی استمراری	
(ما) می نشستیم		(من) می نشستم
/(mă) mi.ne.šas.tim/		/(man) mi.ne.šas.tam/
(شما) می نشستید		(تو) می نشستی
/(šo.mă) mi.ne.šas.tid/		/(to) mi.ne.šas.ti/
(آنها) می نشستند		(او/آن) می نشست
/(ăn.hă) mi.ne.šas.tand/		/(u/ ăn) mi.ne.šast/

	Present Perfect	
	ماضی نقلی	
(ما) نشسته ایم		(من) نشسته ام
/(mă) ne.šas.te.im/		/(man) ne.šas.te.am/
(شما) نشسته اید		(تو) نشسته ای
/(šo.mă) ne.šas.te.id/		/(to) ne.šas.te.i/
(آنها) نشسته اند		(او/آن) نشسته است
/(ăn.hă) ne.šas.te.and/		/(u/ ăn) ne.šas.te- ast/

	Past Perfect	
	ماضی بعید	
(ما) نشسته بودیم		(من) نشسته بودم
/(mă) ne.šas.te- bu.dim/		/(man) ne.šas.te- bu.dam/
(شما) نشسته بودید		(تو) نشسته بودی
/(šo.mă) ne.šas.te- bu.did/		/(to) ne.šas.te- bu.di/
(آنها) نشسته بودند		(او/آن) نشسته بود
/(ăn.hă) ne.šas.te- bu.dand/		/(u/ ăn) ne.šas.te- bud/

Past Subjunctive
ماضی التزامی

(ما) نشسته باشیم	(من) نشسته باشم
/(mă) ne.šas.te- bă.šim/	/(man) ne.šas.te- bă.šam/
(شما) نشسته باشید	(تو) نشسته باشی
/(šo.mă) ne.šas.te- bă.šid/	/(to) ne.šas.te- bă.ši/
(آنها) نشسته باشند	(او/آن) نشسته باشد
/(ăn.hă) ne.šas.te- bă.šand/	/(u/ ăn) ne.šas.te- bă.šad/

Past Progressive
ماضی مستمر(در جریان)

(ما) داشتیم می نشستیم	(من) داشتم می نشستم
/(mă) dăš.tim- mi.ne.šas.tim/	/(man) dăš.tam- mi.ne.šas.tam/
(شما) داشتید می نشستید	(تو) داشتی می نشستی
/(šo.mă) dăš.tid- mi.ne.šas.tid/	/(to) dăš.ti- mi.ne.šas.ti/
(آنها) داشتند می نشستند	(او/آن) داشت می نشست
/(ăn.hă) dăš.tand- mi.ne.šas.tand/	/(u/ ăn) dăšt- mi.ne.šast/

Simple Future
مستقبل (آینده ساده)

(ما) خواهیم نشست	(من) خواهم نشست
/(mă) ǩă.him- ne.šast/	/(man) ǩă.ham- ne.šast/
(شما) خواهید نشست	(تو) خواهی نشست
/(šo.mă) ǩă.hid- ne.šast/	/(to) ǩă.hi- ne.šast/
(آنها) خواهند نشست	(او/آن) خواهد نشست
/(ăn.hă) ǩă.hand- ne.šast/	/(u/ ăn) ǩă.had- ne.šast/

Command
امر

بنشینید!	بنشین!
/be.ne.ši.nid/	/be.ne.šin/

259

to sleep

خُفتَن

/ǩof.tan/

Plural	Singular
Simple Present مضارع اخباری(حال ساده)	
(ما) می خوابیم /(mǎ) mi.ǩǎ.bim/	(من) می خوابم /(man) mi.ǩǎ.bam/
(شما) می خوابید /(šo.mǎ) mi.ǩǎ.bid/	(تو) می خوابی /(to) mi.ǩǎ.bi/
(آنها) می خوابند /(ǎn.hǎ) mi.ǩǎ.band/	(او/ آن) می خوابد /(u/ ǎn) mi.ǩǎ.bad/
Present Subjunctive مضارع التزامی	
(ما) بخوابیم /(mǎ) be.ǩǎ.bim/	(من) بخوابم /(man) be.ǩǎ.bam/
(شما) بخوابید /(šo.mǎ) be.ǩǎ.bid/	(تو) بخوابی /(to) be.ǩǎ.bi/
(آنها) بخوابند /(ǎn.hǎ) be.ǩǎ.band/	(او/ آن) بخوابد /(u/ ǎn) be.ǩǎ.bad/
Present Progressive مضارع مستمر(در جریان)	
(ما) داریم می خوابیم /(mǎ) dǎ.rim- mi.ǩǎ.bim/	(من) دارم می خوابم /(man) dǎ.ram- mi.ǩǎ.bam/
(شما) دارید می خوابید /(šo.mǎ) dǎ.rid- mi.ǩǎ.bid/	(تو) داری می خوابی /(to) dǎ.ri- mi.ǩǎ.bi/
(آنها) دارند می خوابند /(ǎn.hǎ) dǎ.rand- mi.ǩǎ.band/	(او/ آن) دارد می خوابد /(u/ ǎn) dǎ.rad- mi.ǩǎ.bad/

<table>
<tr><td colspan="2" align="center">**Simple Past**
ماضی مطلق (گذشته ساده)</td></tr>
<tr><td align="center">(ما) خفتیم
/(mǎ) ǩof.tim/</td><td align="center">(من) خفتم
/(man) ǩof.tam/</td></tr>
<tr><td align="center">(شما) خفتید
/(šo.mǎ) ǩof.tid/</td><td align="center">(تو) خفتی
/(to) ǩof.ti/</td></tr>
<tr><td align="center">(آنها) خفتند
/(ǎn.hǎ) ǩof.tand/</td><td align="center">(او/آن) خفت
/(u/ ǎn) ǩoft/</td></tr>
</table>

<table>
<tr><td colspan="2" align="center">**Imperfect Indicative**
ماضی استمراری</td></tr>
<tr><td align="center">(ما) می خفتیم
/(mǎ) mi.ǩof.tim/</td><td align="center">(من) می خفتم
/(man) mi.ǩof.tam/</td></tr>
<tr><td align="center">(شما) می خفتید
/(šo.mǎ) mi.ǩof.tid/</td><td align="center">(تو) می خفتی
/(to) mi.ǩof.ti/</td></tr>
<tr><td align="center">(آنها) می خفتند
/(ǎn.hǎ) mi.ǩof.tand/</td><td align="center">(او/آن) می خفت
/(u/ ǎn) mi.ǩoft/</td></tr>
</table>

<table>
<tr><td colspan="2" align="center">**Present Perfect**
ماضی نقلی</td></tr>
<tr><td align="center">(ما) خفته ایم
/(mǎ) ǩof.te.im/</td><td align="center">(من) خفته ام
/(man) ǩof.te.am/</td></tr>
<tr><td align="center">(شما) خفته اید
/(šo.mǎ) ǩof.te.id/</td><td align="center">(تو) خفته ای
/(to) ǩof.te.i/</td></tr>
<tr><td align="center">(آنها) خفته اند
/(ǎn.hǎ) ǩof.te.and/</td><td align="center">(او/آن) خفته است
/(u/ ǎn) ǩof.te- ast/</td></tr>
</table>

<table>
<tr><td colspan="2" align="center">**Past Perfect**
ماضی بعید</td></tr>
<tr><td align="center">(ما) خفته بودیم
/(mǎ) ǩof.te- bu.dim/</td><td align="center">(من) خفته بودم
/(man) ǩof.te- bu.dam/</td></tr>
<tr><td align="center">(شما) خفته بودید
/(šo.mǎ) ǩof.te- bu.did/</td><td align="center">(تو) خفته بودی
/(to) ǩof.te- bu.di/</td></tr>
<tr><td align="center">(آنها) خفته بودند
/(ǎn.hǎ) ǩof.te- bu.dand/</td><td align="center">(او/آن) خفته بود
/(u/ ǎn) ǩof.te- bud/</td></tr>
</table>

	Past Subjunctive
ماضی التزامی	
(ما) خفته باشیم	(من) خفته باشم
/(mă) ǩof.te- bă.šim/	/(man) ǩof.te- bă.šam/
(شما) خفته باشید	(تو) خفته باشی
/(šo.mă) ǩof.te- bă.šid/	/(to) ǩof.te- bă.ši/
(آنها) خفته باشند	(او/آن) خفته باشد
/(ăn.hă) ǩof.te- bă.šand/	/(u/ ăn) ǩof.te- bă.šad/

	Past Progressive
ماضی مستمر(در جریان)	
(ما) داشتیم می خفتیم	(من) داشتم می خفتم
/(mă) dăš.tim- mi.ǩof.tim/	/(man) dăš.tam- mi.ǩof.tam/
(شما) داشتید می خفتید	(تو) داشتی می خفتی
/(šo.mă) dăš.tid- mi.ǩof.tid/	/(to) dăš.ti- mi.ǩof.ti/
(آنها) داشتند می خفتند	(او/آن) داشت می خفت
/(ăn.hă) dăš.tand- mi.ǩof.tand/	/(u/ ăn) dăšt- mi.ǩoft/

	Simple Future
مستقبل (آینده ساده)	
(ما) خواهیم خفت	(من) خواهم خفت
/(mă) ǩă.him- ǩoft/	/(man) ǩă.ham- ǩoft/
(شما) خواهید خفت	(تو) خواهی خفت
/(šo.mă) ǩă.hid- ǩoft/	/(to) ǩă.hi- ǩoft/
(آنها) خواهند خفت	(او/آن) خواهد خفت
/(ăn.hă) ǩă.hand- ǩoft/	/(u/ ăn) ǩă.had- ǩoft/

	Command
امر	
بخوابید!	بخواب!
/be.ǩă.bid/	/be.ǩăb/

to stand

ایستادَن

/is.tă.dan/

Plural	Singular
Simple Present مضارع اخباری(حال ساده)	
(ما) می ایستیم /(mă) mi.is.tim/	(من) می ایستم /(man) mi.is.tam/
(شما) می ایستید /(šo.mă) mi.is.tid/	(تو) می ایستی /(to) mi.is.ti/
(آنها) می ایستند /(ăn.hă) mi.is.tand/	(او/آن) می ایستد /(u/ ăn) mi.is.tad/
Present Subjunctive مضارع التزامی	
(ما) بایستیم /(mă) be.is.tim/	(من) بایستم /(man) be.is.tam/
(شما) بایستید /(šo.mă) be.is.tid/	(تو) بایستی /(to) be.is.ti/
(آنها) بایستند /(ăn.hă) be.is.tand/	(او/آن) بایستد /(u/ ăn) be.is.tad/
Present Progressive مضارع مستمر(در جریان)	
(ما) داریم می ایستیم /(mă) dă.rim- mi.is.tim/	(من) دارم می ایستم /(man) dă.ram- mi.is.tam/
(شما) دارید می ایستید /(šo.mă) dă.rid- mi.is.tid/	(تو) داری می ایستی /(to) dă.ri- mi.is.ti/
(آنها) دارند می ایستند /(ăn.hă) dă.rand- mi.is.tand/	(او/آن) دارد می ایستد /(u/ ăn) dă.rad- mi.is.tad/

Simple Past
ماضی مطلق (گذشته ساده)

(ما) ایستادیم /(mǎ) is.tǎ.dim/	(من) ایستادم /(man) is.tǎ.dam/
(شما) ایستادید /(šo.mǎ) is.tǎ.did/	(تو) ایستادی /(to) is.tǎ.di/
(آنها) ایستادند /(ǎn.hǎ) is.tǎ.dand/	(او/ آن) ایستاد /(u/ ǎn) is.tǎd/

Imperfect Indicative
ماضی استمراری

(ما) می ایستادیم /(mǎ) mi.is.tǎ.dim/	(من) می ایستادم /(man) mi.is.tǎ.dam/
(شما) می ایستادید /(šo.mǎ) mi.is.tǎ.did/	(تو) می ایستادی /(to) mi.is.tǎ.di/
(آنها) می ایستادند /(ǎn.hǎ) mi.is.tǎ.dand/	(او/ آن) می ایستاد /(u/ ǎn) mi.is.tǎd/

Present Perfect
ماضی نقلی

(ما) ایستاده ایم /(mǎ) is.tǎ.de.im/	(من) ایستاده ام /(man) is.tǎ.de.am/
(شما) ایستاده اید /(šo.mǎ) is.tǎ.de.id/	(تو) ایستاده ای /(to) is.tǎ.de.i/
(آنها) ایستاده اند /(ǎn.hǎ) is.tǎ.de.and/	(او/ آن) ایستاده است /(u/ ǎn) is.tǎ.de- ast/

Past Perfect
ماضی بعید

(ما) ایستاده بودیم /(mǎ) is.tǎ.de- bu.dim/	(من) ایستاده بودم /(man) is.tǎ.de- bu.dam/
(شما) ایستاده بودید /(šo.mǎ) is.tǎ.de- bu.did/	(تو) ایستاده بودی /(to) is.tǎ.de- bu.di/
(آنها) ایستاده بودند /(ǎn.hǎ) is.tǎ.de- bu.dand/	(او/ آن) ایستاده بود /(u/ ǎn) is.tǎ.de- bud/

264

Past Subjunctive
ماضی التزامی

(ما) ایستاده باشیم	(من) ایستاده باشم
/(mă) is.tă.de- bă.šim/	/(man) is.tă.de- bă.šam/
(شما) ایستاده باشید	(تو) ایستاده باشی
/(šo.mă) is.tă.de- bă.šid/	/(to) is.tă.de- bă.ši/
(آنها) ایستاده باشند	(او/آن) ایستاده باشد
/(ăn.hă) is.tă.de- bă.šand/	/(u/ ăn) is.tă.de- bă.šad/

Past Progressive
ماضی مستمر(در جریان)

(ما) داشتیم می ایستادیم	(من) داشتم می ایستادم
/(mă) dăš.tim- mi.is.tă.dim/	/(man) dăš.tam- mi.is.tă.dam/
(شما) داشتید می ایستادید	(تو) داشتی می ایستادی
/(šo.mă) dăš.tid- mi.is.tă.did/	/(to) dăš.ti- mi.is.tă.di/
(آنها) داشتند می ایستادند	(او/آن) داشت می ایستاد
/(ăn.hă) dăš.tand- mi.is.tă.dand/	/(u/ ăn) dăšt- mi.is.tăd/

Simple Future
مستقبل (آینده ساده)

(ما) خواهیم ایستاد	(من) خواهم ایستاد
/(mă) kă.him- is.tăd/	/(man) kă.ham- is.tăd/
(شما) خواهید ایستاد	(تو) خواهی ایستاد
/(šo.mă) kă.hid- is.tăd/	/(to) kă.hi- is.tăd/
(آنها) خواهند ایستاد	(او/آن) خواهد ایستاد
/(ăn.hă) kă.hand- is.tăd/	/(u/ ăn) kă.had- is.tăd/

Command
امر

بایستید!	بایست!
/be.is.tid/	/be.ist/

265

to steal

رُبودَن

/ro.bu.dan/

Plural	Singular
Simple Present مضارع اخباری(حال ساده)	
(ما) می ربابیم /(mă) mi.ro.bă.yim/	(من) می ربایم /(man) mi.ro.bă.yam/
(شما) می ربابید /(šo.mă) mi.ro.bă.yid/	(تو) می ربایی /(to) mi.ro.bă.yi/
(آنها) می ربایند /(ăn.hă) mi.ro.bă.yand/	(او/آن) می رباید /(u/ ăn) mi.ro.bă.yad/
Present Subjunctive مضارع التزامی	
(ما) بربابیم /(mă) be.ro.bă.yim/	(من) بربایم /(man) be.ro.bă.yam/
(شما) بربابید /(šo.mă) be.ro.bă.yid/	(تو) بربایی /(to) be.ro.bă.yi/
(آنها) بربایند /(ăn.hă) be.ro.bă.yand/	(او/آن) برباید /(u/ ăn) be.ro.bă.yad/
Present Progressive مضارع مستمر(در جریان)	
(ما) داریم می ربابیم /(mă) dă.rim- mi.ro.bă.yim/	(من) دارم می ربایم /(man) dă.ram- mi.ro.bă.yam/
(شما) دارید می ربابید /(šo.mă) dă.rid- mi.ro.bă.yid/	(تو) داری می ربایی /(to) dă.ri- mi.ro.bă.yi/
(آنها) دارند می ربایند /(ăn.hă) dă.rand- mi.ro.bă.yand/	(او/آن) دارد می رباید /(u/ ăn) dă.rad- mi.ro.bă.yad/

Simple Past	
ماضی مطلق (گذشته ساده)	
(ما) ربودیم	(من) ربودم
/(mǎ) ro.bu.dim/	/(man) ro.bu.dam/
(شما) ربودید	(تو) ربودی
/(šo.mǎ) ro.bu.did/	/(to) ro.bu.di/
(آنها) ربودند	(او/آن) ربود
/(ǎn.hǎ) ro.bu.dand/	/(u/ ǎn) ro.bud/

Imperfect Indicative	
ماضی استمراری	
(ما) می ربودیم	(من) می ربودم
/(mǎ) mi.ro.bu.dim/	/(man) mi.ro.bu.dam/
(شما) می ربودید	(تو) می ربودی
/(šo.mǎ) mi.ro.bu.did/	/(to) mi.ro.bu.di/
(آنها) می ربودند	(او/آن) می ربود
/(ǎn.hǎ) mi.ro.bu.dand/	/(u/ ǎn) mi.ro.bud/

Present Perfect	
ماضی نقلی	
(ما) ربوده ایم	(من) ربوده ام
/(mǎ) ro.bu.de.im/	/(man) ro.bu.de.am/
(شما) ربوده اید	(تو) ربوده ای
/(šo.mǎ) ro.bu.de.id/	/(to) ro.bu.de.i/
(آنها) ربوده اند	(او/آن) ربوده است
/(ǎn.hǎ) ro.bu.de.and/	/(u/ ǎn) ro.bu.de- ast/

Past Perfect	
ماضی بعید	
(ما) ربوده بودیم	(من) ربوده بودم
/(mǎ) ro.bu.de- bu.dim/	/(man) ro.bu.de- bu.dam/
(شما) ربوده بودید	(تو) ربوده بودی
/(šo.mǎ) ro.bu.de- bu.did/	/(to) ro.bu.de- bu.di/
(آنها) ربوده بودند	(او/آن) ربوده بود
/(ǎn.hǎ) ro.bu.de- bu.dand/	/(u/ ǎn) ro.bu.de- bud/

<table>
<tr><td colspan="2" align="center">**Past Subjunctive**
ماضی التزامی</td></tr>
<tr>
<td align="center">(ما) ربوده باشیم
/(mǎ) ro.bu.de- bǎ.šim/</td>
<td align="center">(من) ربوده باشم
/(man) ro.bu.de- bǎ.šam/</td>
</tr>
<tr>
<td align="center">(شما) ربوده باشید
/(šo.mǎ) ro.bu.de- bǎ.šid/</td>
<td align="center">(تو) ربوده باشی
/(to) ro.bu.de- bǎ.ši/</td>
</tr>
<tr>
<td align="center">(آنها) ربوده باشند
/(ǎn.hǎ) ro.bu.de- bǎ.šand/</td>
<td align="center">(او/آن) ربوده باشد
/(u/ ǎn) ro.bu.de- bǎ.šad/</td>
</tr>
</table>

<table>
<tr><td colspan="2" align="center">**Past Progressive**
ماضی مستمر(در جریان)</td></tr>
<tr>
<td align="center">(ما) داشتیم می ربودیم
/(mǎ) dǎš.tim- mi.ro.bu.dim/</td>
<td align="center">(من) داشتم می ربودم
/(man) dǎš.tam- mi.ro.bu.dam/</td>
</tr>
<tr>
<td align="center">(شما) داشتید می ربودید
/(šo.mǎ) dǎš.tid- mi.ro.bu.did/</td>
<td align="center">(تو) داشتی می ربودی
/(to) dǎš.ti- mi.ro.bu.di/</td>
</tr>
<tr>
<td align="center">(آنها) داشتند می ربودند
/(ǎn.hǎ) dǎš.tand- mi.ro.bu.dand/</td>
<td align="center">(او/آن) داشت می ربود
/(u/ ǎn) dǎšt- mi.ro.bud/</td>
</tr>
</table>

<table>
<tr><td colspan="2" align="center">**Simple Future**
مستقبل (آینده ساده)</td></tr>
<tr>
<td align="center">(ما) خواهیم ربود
/(mǎ) kǎ.him- ro.bud/</td>
<td align="center">(من) خواهم ربود
/(man) kǎ.ham- ro.bud/</td>
</tr>
<tr>
<td align="center">(شما) خواهید ربود
/(šo.mǎ) kǎ.hid- ro.bud/</td>
<td align="center">(تو) خواهی ربود
/(to) kǎ.hi- ro.bud/</td>
</tr>
<tr>
<td align="center">(آنها) خواهند ربود
/(ǎn.hǎ) kǎ.hand- ro.bud/</td>
<td align="center">(او/آن) خواهد ربود
/(u/ ǎn) kǎ.had- ro.bud/</td>
</tr>
</table>

<table>
<tr><td colspan="2" align="center">**Command**
امر</td></tr>
<tr>
<td align="center">بربایید!
/be.ro.bǎ.yid/</td>
<td align="center">بربای!
/be.ro.bǎy/</td>
</tr>
</table>

to stimulate

بَرآنگیختَن

/bar.an.giǩ.tan/

Plural	Singular
Simple Present مضارع اخباری(حال ساده)	
(ما) بر می انگیزیم /(mǎ) bar.mi.an.gi.zim/	(من) بر می انگیزم /(man) bar.mi.an.gi.zam/
(شما) بر می انگیزید /(šo.mǎ) bar.mi.an.gi.zid/	(تو) بر می انگیزی /(to) bar.mi.an.gi.zi/
(آنها) بر می انگیزند /(ǎn.hǎ) bar.mi.an.gi.zand/	(او/آن) بر می انگیزد /(u/ ǎn) bar.mi.an.gi.zad/
Present Subjunctive مضارع التزامی	
(ما) بر بینگیزیم /(mǎ) bar.bi.yan.gi.zim/	(من) بر بینگیزم /(man) bar.bi.yan.gi.zam/
(شما) بر بینگیزید /(šo.mǎ) bar.bi.yan.gi.zid/	(تو) بر بینگیزی /(to) bar.bi.yan.gi.zi/
(آنها) بر بینگیزند /(ǎn.hǎ) bar.bi.yan.gi.zand/	(او/آن) بر بینگیزد /(u/ ǎn) bar.bi.yan.gi.zad/
Present Progressive مضارع مستمر(در جریان)	
(ما) داریم بر می انگیزیم /(mǎ) dǎ.rim- bar.mi.an.gi.zim/	(من) دارم بر می انگیزم /(man) dǎ.ram- bar.mi.an.gi.zam/
(شما) دارید بر می انگیزید /(šo.mǎ) dǎ.rid- bar.mi.an.gi.zid/	(تو) داری بر می انگیزی /(to) dǎ.ri- bar.mi.an.gi.zi/
(آنها) دارند بر می انگیزند /(ǎn.hǎ) dǎ.rand- bar.mi.an.gi.zand/	(او/آن) دارد بر می انگیزد /(u/ ǎn) dǎ.rad- bar.mi.an.gi.zad/

Simple Past
ماضی مطلق (گذشته ساده)

(ما) بر انگیختیم	(من) بر انگیختم
/(mǎ) bar.an.giǩ.tim/	/(man) bar.an.giǩ.tam/
(شما) بر انگیختید	(تو) بر انگیختی
/(šo.mǎ) bar.an.giǩ.tid/	/(to) bar.an.giǩ.ti/
(آنها) بر انگیختند	(او/آن) بر انگیخت
/(ǎn.hǎ) bar.an.giǩ.tand/	/(u/ ǎn) bar.an.giǩt/

Imperfect Indicative
ماضی استمراری

(ما) بر می انگیختیم	(من) بر می انگیختم
/(mǎ) bar.mi.an.giǩ.tim/	/(man) bar.mi.an.giǩ.tam/
(شما) بر می انگیختید	(تو) بر می انگیختی
/(šo.mǎ) bar.mi.an.giǩ.tid/	/(to) bar.mi.an.giǩ.ti/
(آنها) بر می انگیختند	(او/آن) بر می انگیخت
/(ǎn.hǎ) bar.mi.an.giǩ.tand/	/(u/ ǎn) bar.mi.an.giǩt/

Present Perfect
ماضی نقلی

(ما) بر انگیخته ایم	(من) بر انگیخته ام
/(mǎ) bar.an.giǩ.te.im/	/(man) bar.an.giǩ.te.am/
(شما) بر انگیخته اید	(تو) بر انگیخته ای
/(šo.mǎ) bar.an.giǩ.te.id/	/(to) bar.an.giǩ.te.i/
(آنها) بر انگیخته اند	(او/آن) بر انگیخته است
/(ǎn.hǎ) bar.an.giǩ.te.and/	/(u/ ǎn) bar.an.giǩ.te- ast/

Past Perfect
ماضی بعید

(ما) بر انگیخته بودیم	(من) بر انگیخته بودم
/(mǎ) bar.an.giǩ.te- bu.dim/	/(man) bar.an.giǩ.te- bu.dam/
(شما) بر انگیخته بودید	(تو) بر انگیخته بودی
/(šo.mǎ) bar.an.giǩ.te- bu.did/	/(to) bar.an.giǩ.te- bu.di/
(آنها) بر انگیخته بودند	(او/آن) بر انگیخته بود
/(ǎn.hǎ) bar.an.giǩ.te- bu.dand/	/(u/ ǎn) bar.an.giǩ.te- bud/

<table>
<tr><td colspan="2" align="center">**Past Subjunctive**
ماضی التزامی</td></tr>
<tr>
<td align="center">(ما) بر انگیخته باشیم
/(mǎ) bar.an.giǩ.te- bǎ.šim/</td>
<td align="center">(من) بر انگیخته باشم
/(man) bar.an.giǩ.te- bǎ.šam/</td>
</tr>
<tr>
<td align="center">(شما) بر انگیخته باشید
/(šo.mǎ) bar.an.giǩ.te- bǎ.šid/</td>
<td align="center">(تو) بر انگیخته باشی
/(to) bar.an.giǩ.te- bǎ.ši/</td>
</tr>
<tr>
<td align="center">(آنها) بر انگیخته باشند
/(ǎn.hǎ) bar.an.giǩ.te- bǎ.šand/</td>
<td align="center">(او/آن) بر انگیخته باشد
/(u/ ǎn) bar.an.giǩ.te- bǎ.šad/</td>
</tr>
</table>

<table>
<tr><td colspan="2" align="center">**Past Progressive**
ماضی مستمر(در جریان)</td></tr>
<tr>
<td align="center">(ما) داشتیم بر می انگیختیم
/(mǎ) dǎš.tim- bar.mi.an.giǩ.tim/</td>
<td align="center">(من) داشتم بر می انگیختم
/(man) dǎš.tam- bar.mi.an.giǩ.tam/</td>
</tr>
<tr>
<td align="center">(شما) داشتید بر می انگیختید
/(šo.mǎ) dǎš.tid- bar.mi.an.giǩ.tid/</td>
<td align="center">(تو) داشتی بر می انگیختی
/(to) dǎš.ti- bar.mi.an.giǩ.ti/</td>
</tr>
<tr>
<td align="center">(آنها) داشتند بر می انگیختند
/(ǎn.hǎ) dǎš.tand- bar.mi.an.giǩ.tand/</td>
<td align="center">(او/آن) داشت بر می انگیخت
/(u/ ǎn) dǎšt- bar.mi.an.giǩt/</td>
</tr>
</table>

<table>
<tr><td colspan="2" align="center">**Simple Future**
مستقبل (آینده ساده)</td></tr>
<tr>
<td align="center">(ما) برخواهیم انگیخت
/(mǎ) bar.ǩǎ.him- an.giǩt/</td>
<td align="center">(من) برخواهم انگیخت
/(man) bar.ǩǎ.ham- an.giǩt/</td>
</tr>
<tr>
<td align="center">(شما) برخواهید انگیخت
/(šo.mǎ) bar.ǩǎ.hid- an.giǩt/</td>
<td align="center">(تو) برخواهی انگیخت
/(to) bar.ǩǎ.hi- an.giǩt/</td>
</tr>
<tr>
<td align="center">(آنها) برخواهند انگیخت
/(ǎn.hǎ) bar.ǩǎ.hand- an.giǩt/</td>
<td align="center">(او/آن) برخواهد انگیخت
/(u/ ǎn) bar.ǩǎ.had- an.giǩt/</td>
</tr>
</table>

<table>
<tr><td colspan="2" align="center">**Command**
امر</td></tr>
<tr>
<td align="center">بر انگیزید!
/bar.an.gi.zid/</td>
<td align="center">بر انگیز!
/bar.an.giz/</td>
</tr>
</table>

271

to stir

هَم زَدَن

/ham- za.dan/

Plural	Singular
Simple Present مضارع اخباری(حال ساده)	
(ما) هم می زنیم /(mǎ) ham- mi.za.nim/	(من) هم می زنم /(man) ham- mi.za.nam/
(شما) هم می زنید /(šo.mǎ) ham- mi.za.nid/	(تو) هم می زنی /(to) ham- mi.za.ni/
(آنها) هم می زنند /(ǎn.hǎ) ham- mi.za.nand/	(او/آن) هم می زند /(u/ ǎn) ham- mi.za.nad/
Present Subjunctive مضارع التزامی	
(ما) هم بزنیم /(mǎ) ham- be.za.nim/	(من) هم بزنم /(man) ham- be.za.nam/
(شما) هم بزنید /(šo.mǎ) ham- be.za.nid/	(تو) هم بزنی /(to) ham- be.za.ni/
(آنها) هم بزنند /(ǎn.hǎ) ham- be.za.nand/	(او/آن) هم بزند /(u/ ǎn) ham- be.za.nad/
Present Progressive مضارع مستمر(در جریان)	
(ما) داریم هم می زنیم /(mǎ) dǎ.rim- ham- mi.za.nim/	(من) دارم هم می زنم /(man) dǎ.ram- ham- mi.za.nam/
(شما) دارید هم می زنید /(šo.mǎ) dǎ.rid- ham- mi.za.nid/	(تو) داری هم می زنی /(to) dǎ.ri- ham- mi.za.ni/
(آنها) دارند هم می زنند /(ǎn.hǎ) dǎ.rand- ham- mi.za.nand/	(او/آن) دارد هم می زند /(u/ ǎn) dǎ.rad- ham- mi.za.nad/

Simple Past	
ماضی مطلق (گذشته ساده)	
(ما) هم زدیم	(من) هم زدم
/(mǎ) ham- za.dim/	/(man) ham- za.dam/
(شما) هم زدید	(تو) هم زدی
/(šo.mǎ) ham- za.did/	/(to) ham- za.di/
(آنها) هم زدند	(او/آن) هم زد
/(ǎn.hǎ) ham- za.dand/	/(u/ ǎn) ham- zad/

Imperfect Indicative	
ماضی استمراری	
(ما) هم می زدیم	(من) هم می زدم
/(mǎ) ham- mi.za.dim/	/(man) ham- mi.za.dam/
(شما) هم می زدید	(تو) هم می زدی
/(šo.mǎ) ham- mi.za.did/	/(to) ham- mi.za.di/
(آنها) هم می زدند	(او/آن) هم می زد
/(ǎn.hǎ) ham- mi.za.dand/	/(u/ ǎn) ham- mi.zad/

Present Perfect	
ماضی نقلی	
(ما) هم زده ایم	(من) هم زده ام
/(mǎ) ham- za.de.im/	/(man) ham- za.de.am/
(شما) هم زده اید	(تو) هم زده ای
/(šo.mǎ) ham- za.de.id/	/(to) ham- za.de.i/
(آنها) هم زده اند	(او/آن) هم زده است
/(ǎn.hǎ) ham- za.de.and/	/(u/ ǎn) ham- za.de- ast/

Past Perfect	
ماضی بعید	
(ما) هم زده بودیم	(من) هم زده بودم
/(mǎ) ham- za.de- bu.dim/	/(man) ham- za.de- bu.dam/
(شما) هم زده بودید	(تو) هم زده بودی
/(šo.mǎ) ham- za.de- bu.did/	/(to) ham- za.de- bu.di/
(آنها) هم زده بودند	(او/آن) هم زده بود
/(ǎn.hǎ) ham- za.de- bu.dand/	/(u/ ǎn) ham- za.de- bud/

Past Subjunctive	
ماضی التزامی	
(ما) هم زده باشیم	(من) هم زده باشم
/(mă) ham- za.de- bă.šim/	/(man) ham- za.de- bă.šam/
(شما) هم زده باشید	(تو) هم زده باشی
/(šo.mă) ham- za.de- bă.šid/	/(to) ham- za.de- bă.ši/
(آنها) هم زده باشند	(او/آن) هم زده باشد
/(ăn.hă) ham- za.de- bă.šand/	/(u/ ăn) ham- za.de- bă.šad/

Past Progressive	
ماضی مستمر (در جریان)	
(ما) داشتیم هم می زدیم	(من) داشتم هم می زدم
/(mă) dăš.tim- ham- mi.za.dim/	/(man) dăš.tam- ham- mi.za.dam/
(شما) داشتید هم می زدید	(تو) داشتی هم می زدی
/(šo.mă) dăš.tid- ham- mi.za.did/	/(to) dăš.ti- ham- mi.za.di/
(آنها) داشتند هم می زدند	(او/آن) داشت هم می زد
/(ăn.hă) dăš.tand- ham- mi.za.dand/	/(u/ ăn) dăšt- ham- mi.zad/

Simple Future	
مستقبل (آینده ساده)	
(ما) هم خواهیم زد	(من) هم خواهم زد
/(mă) ham- xă.him- zad/	/(man) ham- xă.ham- zad/
(شما) هم خواهید زد	(تو) هم خواهی زد
/(šo.mă) ham- xă.hid- zad/	/(to) ham- xă.hi- zad/
(آنها) هم خواهند زد	(او/آن) هم خواهد زد
/(ăn.hă) ham- xă.hand- zad/	/(u/ ăn) ham- xă.had- zad/

Command	
امر	
هم بزنید!	هم بزن!
/ham- be.za.nid/	/ham- be.zan/

274

to tell

گُفتَن

/gof.tan/

Plural	Singular
Simple Present	
مضارع اخباری(حال ساده)	
(ما) می گوییم	(من) می گویم
/(mǎ) mi.gu.yim/	/(man) mi.gu.yam/
(شما) می گویید	(تو) می گویی
/(šo.mǎ) mi.gu.yid/	/(to) mi.gu.yi/
(آنها) می گویند	(او/آن) می گوید
/(ǎn.hǎ) mi.gu.yand/	/(u/ ǎn) mi.gu.yad/
Present Subjunctive	
مضارع التزامی	
(ما) بگوییم	(من) بگویم
/(mǎ) be.gu.yim/	/(man) be.gu.yam/
(شما) بگویید	(تو) بگویی
/(šo.mǎ) be.gu.yid/	/(to) be.gu.yi/
(آنها) بگویند	(او/آن) بگوید
/(ǎn.hǎ) be.gu.yand/	/(u/ ǎn) be.gu.yad/
Present Progressive	
مضارع مستمر(در جریان)	
(ما) داریم می گوییم	(من) دارم می گویم
/(mǎ) dǎ.rim- mi.gu.yim/	/(man) dǎ.ram- mi.gu.yam/
(شما) دارید می گویید	(تو) داری می گویی
/(šo.mǎ) dǎ.rid- mi.gu.yid/	/(to) dǎ.ri- mi.gu.yi/
(آنها) دارند می گویند	(او/آن) دارد می گوید
/(ǎn.hǎ) dǎ.rand- mi.gu.yand/	/(u/ ǎn) dǎ.rad- mi.gu.yad/

Simple Past	
ماضی مطلق (گذشته ساده)	
(ما) گفتیم	(من) گفتم
/(mă) gof.tim/	/(man) gof.tam/
(شما) گفتید	(تو) گفتی
/(šo.mă) gof.tid/	/(to) gof.ti/
(آنها) گفتند	(او/آن) گفت
/(ăn.hă) gof.tand/	/(u/ ăn) goft/

Imperfect Indicative	
ماضی استمراری	
(ما) می گفتیم	(من) می گفتم
/(mă) mi.gof.tim/	/(man) mi.gof.tam/
(شما) می گفتید	(تو) می گفتی
/(šo.mă) mi.gof.tid/	/(to) mi.gof.ti/
(آنها) می گفتند	(او/آن) می گفت
/(ăn.hă) mi.gof.tand/	/(u/ ăn) mi.goft/

Present Perfect	
ماضی نقلی	
(ما) گفته ایم	(من) گفته ام
/(mă) gof.te.im/	/(man) gof.te.am/
(شما) گفته اید	(تو) گفته ای
/(šo.mă) gof.te.id/	/(to) gof.te.i/
(آنها) گفته اند	(او/آن) گفته است
/(ăn.hă) gof.te.and/	/(u/ ăn) gof.te- ast/

Past Perfect	
ماضی بعید	
(ما) گفته بودیم	(من) گفته بودم
/(mă) gof.te- bu.dim/	/(man) gof.te- bu.dam/
(شما) گفته بودید	(تو) گفته بودی
/(šo.mă) gof.te- bu.did/	/(to) gof.te- bu.di/
(آنها) گفته بودند	(او/آن) گفته بود
/(ăn.hă) gof.te- bu.dand/	/(u/ ăn) gof.te- bud/

Past Subjunctive	
ماضی التزامی	
(ما) گفته باشیم	(من) گفته باشم
/(mǎ) gof.te- bǎ.šim/	/(man) gof.te- bǎ.šam/
(شما) گفته باشید	(تو) گفته باشی
/(šo.mǎ) gof.te- bǎ.šid/	/(to) gof.te- bǎ.ši/
(آنها) گفته باشند	(او/آن) گفته باشد
/(ǎn.hǎ) gof.te- bǎ.šand/	/(u/ ǎn) gof.te- bǎ.šad/

Past Progressive	
ماضی مستمر(در جریان)	
(ما) داشتیم می گفتیم	(من) داشتم می گفتم
/(mǎ) dǎš.tim- mi.gof.tim/	/(man) dǎš.tam- mi.gof.tam/
(شما) داشتید می گفتید	(تو) داشتی می گفتی
/(šo.mǎ) dǎš.tid- mi.gof.tid/	/(to) dǎš.ti- mi.gof.ti/
(آنها) داشتند می گفتند	(او/آن) داشت می گفت
/(ǎn.hǎ) dǎš.tand- mi.gof.tand/	/(u/ ǎn) dǎšt- mi.goft/

Simple Future	
مستقبل (آینده ساده)	
(ما) خواهیم گفت	(من) خواهم گفت
/(mǎ) ǩǎ.him- goft/	/(man) ǩǎ.ham- goft/
(شما) خواهید گفت	(تو) خواهی گفت
/(šo.mǎ) ǩǎ.hid- goft/	/(to) ǩǎ.hi- goft/
(آنها) خواهند گفت	(او/آن) خواهد گفت
/(ǎn.hǎ) ǩǎ.hand- goft/	/(u/ ǎn) ǩǎ.had- goft/

Command	
امر	
بگویید!	* بگو!
/be.gu.yid/	/be.gu/

* also: بگوی!

to test

آزمودَن

/ăz.mu.dan/

Plural	Singular
Simple Present	
مضارع اخباری(حال ساده)	
(ما) می آزماییم	(من) می آزمایم
/(mă) mi.ăz.mă.yim/	/(man) mi.ăz.mă.yam/
(شما) می آزمایید	(تو) می آزمایی
/(šo.mă) mi.ăz.mă.yid/	/(to) mi.ăz.mă.yi/
(آنها) می آزمایند	(او/آن) می آزماید
/(ăn.hă) mi.ăz.mă.yand/	/(u/ ăn) mi.ăz.mă.yad/
Present Subjunctive	
مضارع التزامی	
(ما) بیازماییم	(من) بیازمایم
/(mă) bi.yăz.mă.yim/	/(man) bi.yăz.mă.yam/
(شما) بیازمایید	(تو) بیازمایی
/(šo.mă) bi.yăz.mă.yid/	/(to) bi.yăz.mă.yi/
(آنها) بیازمایند	(او/آن) بیازماید
/(ăn.hă) bi.yăz.mă.yand/	/(u/ ăn) bi.yăz.mă.yad/
Present Progressive	
مضارع مستمر(در جریان)	
(ما) داریم می آزماییم	(من) دارم می آزمایم
/(mă) dă.rim- mi.ăz.mă.yim/	/(man) dă.ram- mi.ăz.mă.yam/
(شما) دارید می آزمایید	(تو) داری می آزمایی
/(šo.mă) dă.rid- mi.ăz.mă.yid/	/(to) dă.ri- mi.ăz.mă.yi/
(آنها) دارند می آزمایند	(او/آن) دارد می آزماید
/(ăn.hă) dă.rand- mi.ăz.mă.yand/	/(u/ ăn) dă.rad- mi.ăz.mă.yad/

Simple Past
ماضی مطلق (گذشته ساده)

(ما) آزمودیم	(من) آزمودم
/(mǎ) ǎz.mu.dim/	/(man) ǎz.mu.dam/
(شما) آزمودید	(تو) آزمودی
/(šo.mǎ) ǎz.mu.did/	/(to) ǎz.mu.di/
(آنها) آزمودند	(او/آن) آزمود
/(ǎn.hǎ) ǎz.mu.dand/	/(u/ ǎn) ǎz.mud/

Imperfect Indicative
ماضی استمراری

(ما) می آزمودیم	(من) می آزمودم
/(mǎ) mi.ǎz.mu.dim/	/(man) mi.ǎz.mu.dam/
(شما) می آزمودید	(تو) می آزمودی
/(šo.mǎ) mi.ǎz.mu.did/	/(to) mi.ǎz.mu.di/
(آنها) می آزمودند	(او/آن) می آزمود
/(ǎn.hǎ) mi.ǎz.mu.dand/	/(u/ ǎn) mi.ǎz.mud/

Present Perfect
ماضی نقلی

(ما) آزموده ایم	(من) آزموده ام
/(mǎ) ǎz.mu.de.im/	/(man) ǎz.mu.de.am/
(شما) آزموده اید	(تو) آزموده ای
/(šo.mǎ) ǎz.mu.de.id/	/(to) ǎz.mu.de.i/
(آنها) آزموده اند	(او/آن) آزموده است
/(ǎn.hǎ) ǎz.mu.de.and/	/(u/ ǎn) ǎz.mu.de- ast/

Past Perfect
ماضی بعید

(ما) آزموده بودیم	(من) آزموده بودم
/(mǎ) ǎz.mu.de- bu.dim/	/(man) ǎz.mu.de- bu.dam/
(شما) آزموده بودید	(تو) آزموده بودی
/(šo.mǎ) ǎz.mu.de- bu.did/	/(to) ǎz.mu.de- bu.di/
(آنها) آزموده بودند	(او/آن) آزموده بود
/(ǎn.hǎ) ǎz.mu.de- bu.dand/	/(u/ ǎn) ǎz.mu.de- bud/

Past Subjunctive	
ماضی التزامی	
(ما) آزموده باشیم	(من) آزموده باشم
/(mă) ăz.mu.de- bă.šim/	/(man) ăz.mu.de- bă.šam/
(شما) آزموده باشید	(تو) آزموده باشی
/(šo.mă) ăz.mu.de- bă.šid/	/(to) ăz.mu.de- bă.ši/
(آنها) آزموده باشند	(او/آن) آزموده باشد
/(ăn.hă) ăz.mu.de- bă.šand/	/(u/ ăn) ăz.mu.de- bă.šad/

Past Progressive	
ماضی مستمر(در جریان)	
(ما) داشتیم می آزمودیم	(من) داشتم می آزمودم
/(mă) dăš.tim- mi.ăz.mu.dim/	/(man) dăš.tam- mi.ăz.mu.dam/
(شما) داشتید می آزمودید	(تو) داشتی می آزمودی
/(šo.mă) dăš.tid- mi.ăz.mu.did/	/(to) dăš.ti- mi.ăz.mu.di/
(آنها) داشتند می آزمودند	(او/آن) داشت می آزمود
/(ăn.hă) dăš.tand- mi.ăz.mu.dand/	/(u/ ăn) dăšt- mi.ăz.mud/

Simple Future	
مستقبل (آینده ساده)	
(ما) خواهیم آزمود	(من) خواهم آزمود
/(mă) kă.him- ăz.mud/	/(man) kă.ham- ăz.mud/
(شما) خواهید آزمود	(تو) خواهی آزمود
/(šo.mă) kă.hid- ăz.mud/	/(to) kă.hi- ăz.mud/
(آنها) خواهند آزمود	(او/آن) خواهد آزمود
/(ăn.hă) kă.hand- ăz.mud/	/(u/ ăn) kă.had- ăz.mud/

Command	
امر	
بیاموزید!	بیاموز!
/bi.yă.mu.zid/	/bi.yă.muz/

to traverse

پیمودَن

/pey.mu.dan/

Plural	Singular
Simple Present مضارع اخباری(حال ساده)	
(ما) می پیماییم /(mă) mi.pey.mă.yim/	(من) می پیمایم /(man) mi.pey.mă.yam/
(شما) می پیمایید /(šo.mă) mi.pey.mă.yid/	(تو) می پیمایی /(to) mi.pey.mă.yi/
(آنها) می پیمایند /(ăn.hă) mi.pey.mă.yand/	(او/آن) می پیماید /(u/ ăn) mi.pey.mă.yad/
Present Subjunctive مضارع التزامی	
(ما) بپیماییم /(mă) be.pey.mă.yim/	(من) بپیمایم /(man) be.pey.mă.yam/
(شما) بپیمایید /(šo.mă) be.pey.mă.yid/	(تو) بپیمایی /(to) be.pey.mă.yi/
(آنها) بپیمایند /(ăn.hă) be.pey.mă.yand/	(او/آن) بپیماید /(u/ ăn) be.pey.mă.yad/
Present Progressive مضارع مستمر(در جریان)	
(ما) داریم می پیماییم /(mă) dă.rim- mi.pey.mă.yim/	(من) دارم می پیمایم /(man) dă.ram- mi.pey.mă.yam/
(شما) دارید می پیمایید /(šo.mă) dă.rid- mi.pey.mă.yid/	(تو) داری می پیمایی /(to) dă.ri- mi.pey.mă.yi/
(آنها) دارند می پیمایند /(ăn.hă) dă.rand- mi.pey.mă.yand/	(او/آن) دارد می پیماید /(u/ ăn) dă.rad- mi.pey.mă.yad/

Simple Past
ماضی مطلق (گذشته ساده)

(ما) پیمودیم	(من) پیمودم
/(mǎ) pey.mu.dim/	/(man) pey.mu.dam/
(شما) پیمودید	(تو) پیمودی
/(šo.mǎ) pey.mu.did/	/(to) pey.mu.di/
(آنها) پیمودند	(او/آن) پیمود
/(ǎn.hǎ) pey.mu.dand/	/(u/ ǎn) pey.mud/

Imperfect Indicative
ماضی استمراری

(ما) می پیمودیم	(من) می پیمودم
/(mǎ) mi.pey.mu.dim/	/(man) mi.pey.mu.dam/
(شما) می پیمودید	(تو) می پیمودی
/(šo.mǎ) mi.pey.mu.did/	/(to) mi.pey.mu.di/
(آنها) می پیمودند	(او/آن) می پیمود
/(ǎn.hǎ) mi.pey.mu.dand/	/(u/ ǎn) mi.pey.mud/

Present Perfect
ماضی نقلی

(ما) پیموده ایم	(من) پیموده ام
/(mǎ) pey.mu.de.im/	/(man) pey.mu.de.am/
(شما) پیموده اید	(تو) پیموده ای
/(šo.mǎ) pey.mu.de.id/	/(to) pey.mu.de.i/
(آنها) پیموده اند	(او/آن) پیموده است
/(ǎn.hǎ) pey.mu.de.and/	/(u/ ǎn) pey.mu.de- ast/

Past Perfect
ماضی بعید

(ما) پیموده بودیم	(من) پیموده بودم
/(mǎ) pey.mu.de- bu.dim/	/(man) pey.mu.de- bu.dam/
(شما) پیموده بودید	(تو) پیموده بودی
/(šo.mǎ) pey.mu.de- bu.did/	/(to) pey.mu.de- bu.di/
(آنها) پیموده بودند	(او/آن) پیموده بود
/(ǎn.hǎ) pey.mu.de- bu.dand/	/(u/ ǎn) pey.mu.de- bud/

<table>
<tr><td colspan="2" align="center">**Past Subjunctive**
ماضی التزامی</td></tr>
<tr>
<td align="center">(ما) پیموده باشیم
/(mă) pey.mu.de- bă.šim/</td>
<td align="center">(من) پیموده باشم
/(man) pey.mu.de- bă.šam/</td>
</tr>
<tr>
<td align="center">(شما) پیموده باشید
/(šo.mă) pey.mu.de- bă.šid/</td>
<td align="center">(تو) پیموده باشی
/(to) pey.mu.de- bă.ši/</td>
</tr>
<tr>
<td align="center">(آنها) پیموده باشند
/(ăn.hă) pey.mu.de- bă.šand/</td>
<td align="center">(او/آن) پیموده باشد
/(u/ ăn) pey.mu.de- bă.šad/</td>
</tr>
</table>

<table>
<tr><td colspan="2" align="center">**Past Progressive**
ماضی مستمر(در جریان)</td></tr>
<tr>
<td align="center">(ما) داشتیم می پیمودیم
/(mă) dăš.tim- mi.pey.mu.dim/</td>
<td align="center">(من) داشتم می پیمودم
/(man) dăš.tam- mi.pey.mu.dam/</td>
</tr>
<tr>
<td align="center">(شما) داشتید می پیمودید
/(šo.mă) dăš.tid- mi.pey.mu.did/</td>
<td align="center">(تو) داشتی می پیمودی
/(to) dăš.ti- mi.pey.mu.di/</td>
</tr>
<tr>
<td align="center">(آنها) داشتند می پیمودند
/(ăn.hă) dăš.tand- mi.pey.mu.dand/</td>
<td align="center">(او/آن) داشت می پیمود
/(u/ ăn) dăšt- mi.pey.mud/</td>
</tr>
</table>

<table>
<tr><td colspan="2" align="center">**Simple Future**
مستقبل (آینده ساده)</td></tr>
<tr>
<td align="center">(ما) خواهیم پیمود
/(mă) kă.him- pey.mud/</td>
<td align="center">(من) خواهم پیمود
/(man) kă.ham- pey.mud/</td>
</tr>
<tr>
<td align="center">(شما) خواهید پیمود
/(šo.mă) kă.hid- pey.mud/</td>
<td align="center">(تو) خواهی پیمود
/(to) kă.hi- pey.mud/</td>
</tr>
<tr>
<td align="center">(آنها) خواهند پیمود
/(ăn.hă) kă.hand- pey.mud/</td>
<td align="center">(او/آن) خواهد پیمود
/(u/ ăn) kă.had- pey.mud/</td>
</tr>
</table>

<table>
<tr><td colspan="2" align="center">**Command**
امر</td></tr>
<tr>
<td align="center">بپیمایید!
/be.pey.mă.yid/</td>
<td align="center">بپیمای!
/be.pey.măy/</td>
</tr>
</table>

to understand

دَر یافتَن

/dar.yăf.tan/

Plural	Singular
Simple Present مضارع اخباری(حال ساده)	
(ما) در می یابیم /(mă) dar.mi.yă.bim/	(من) در می یابم /(man) dar.mi.yă.bam/
(شما) در می یابید /(šo.mă) dar.mi.yă.bid/	(تو) در می یابی /(to) dar.mi.yă.bi/
(آنها) در می یابند /(ăn.hă) dar.mi.yă.band/	(او/آن) در می یابد /(u/ ăn) dar.mi.yă.bad/
Present Subjunctive مضارع التزامی	
(ما) در بیابیم /(mă) dar.bi.yă.bim/	(من) در بیابم /(man) dar.bi.yă.bam/
(شما) در بیابید /(šo.mă) dar.bi.yă.bid/	(تو) در بیابی /(to) dar.bi.yă.bi/
(آنها) در بیابند /(ăn.hă) dar.bi.yă.band/	(او/آن) در بیابد /(u/ ăn) dar.bi.yă.bad/
Present Progressive مضارع مستمر(در جریان)	
(ما) داریم در می یابیم /(mă) dă.rim- dar.mi.yă.bim/	(من) دارم در می یابم /(man) dă.ram- dar.mi.yă.bam/
(شما) دارید در می یابید /(šo.mă) dă.rid- dar.mi.yă.bid/	(تو) داری در می یابی /(to) dă.ri- dar.mi.yă.bi/
(آنها) دارند در می یابند /(ăn.hă) dă.rand- dar.mi.yă.band/	(او/آن) دارد در می یابد /(u/ ăn) dă.rad- dar.mi.yă.bad/

Simple Past
ماضی مطلق (گذشته ساده)

(ما) در یافتیم	(من) در یافتم
/(mǎ) dar.yǎf.tim/	/(man) dar.yǎf.tam/
(شما) در یافتید	(تو) در یافتی
/(šo.mǎ) dar.yǎf.tid/	/(to) dar.yǎf.ti/
(آنها) در یافتند	(او/آن) در یافت
/(ǎn.hǎ) dar.yǎf.tand/	/(u/ ǎn) dar.yǎft/

Imperfect Indicative
ماضی استمراری

(ما) در می یافتیم	(من) در می یافتم
/(mǎ) dar.mi.yǎf.tim/	/(man) dar.mi.yǎf.tam/
(شما) در می یافتید	(تو) در می یافتی
/(šo.mǎ) dar.mi.yǎf.tid/	/(to) dar.mi.yǎf.ti/
(آنها) در می یافتند	(او/آن) در می یافت
/(ǎn.hǎ) dar.mi.yǎf.tand/	/(u/ ǎn) dar.mi.yǎft/

Present Perfect
ماضی نقلی

(ما) در یافته ایم	(من) در یافته ام
/(mǎ) dar.yǎf.te.im/	/(man) dar.yǎf.te.am/
(شما) در یافته اید	(تو) در یافته ای
/(šo.mǎ) dar.yǎf.te.id/	/(to) dar.yǎf.te.i/
(آنها) در یافته اند	(او/آن) در یافته است
/(ǎn.hǎ) dar.yǎf.te.and/	/(u/ ǎn) dar.yǎf.te- ast/

Past Perfect
ماضی بعید

(ما) در یافته بودیم	(من) در یافته بودم
/(mǎ) dar.yǎf.te- bu.dim/	/(man) dar.yǎf.te- bu.dam/
(شما) در یافته بودید	(تو) در یافته بودی
/(šo.mǎ) dar.yǎf.te- bu.did/	/(to) dar.yǎf.te- bu.di/
(آنها) در یافته بودند	(او/آن) در یافته بود
/(ǎn.hǎ) dar.yǎf.te- bu.dand/	/(u/ ǎn) dar.yǎf.te- bud/

Past Subjunctive
ماضی التزامی

(ما) در یافته باشیم	(من) در یافته باشم
/(mǎ) dar.yǎf.te- bǎ.šim/	/(man) dar.yǎf.te- bǎ.šam/
(شما) در یافته باشید	(تو) در یافته باشی
/(šo.mǎ) dar.yǎf.te- bǎ.šid/	/(to) dar.yǎf.te- bǎ.ši/
(آنها) در یافته باشند	(او/آن) در یافته باشد
/(ǎn.hǎ) dar.yǎf.te- bǎ.šand/	/(u/ ǎn) dar.yǎf.te- bǎ.šad/

Past Progressive
ماضی مستمر(در جریان)

(ما) داشتیم در می یافتیم	(من) داشتم در می یافتم
/(mǎ) dǎš.tim- dar.mi.yǎf.tim/	/(man) dǎš.tam- dar.mi.yǎf.tam/
(شما) داشتید در می یافتید	(تو) داشتی در می یافتی
/(šo.mǎ) dǎš.tid- dar.mi.yǎf.tid/	/(to) dǎš.ti- dar.mi.yǎf.ti/
(آنها) داشتند در می یافتند	(او/آن) داشت در می یافت
/(ǎn.hǎ) dǎš.tand- dar.mi.yǎf.tand/	/(u/ ǎn) dǎšt- dar.mi.yǎft/

Simple Future
مستقبل (آینده ساده)

(ما) در خواهیم یافت	(من) در خواهم یافت
/(mǎ) dar.ǩǎ.him- yǎft/	/(man) dar.ǩǎ.ham- yǎft/
(شما) در خواهید یافت	(تو) در خواهی یافت
/(šo.mǎ) dar.ǩǎ.hid- yǎft/	/(to) dar.ǩǎ.hi- yǎft/
(آنها) در خواهند یافت	(او/آن) در خواهد یافت
/(ǎn.hǎ) dar.ǩǎ.hand- yǎft/	/(u/ ǎn) dar.ǩǎ.had- yǎft/

Command
امر

* در بیابید!	* در بیاب!
/dar.bi.yǎ.bid/	/dar.bi.yǎb/

* also: در یابید!   در یاب!

286

to want

خواستَن

/kǎs.tan/

Plural	Singular
Simple Present مضارع اخباری(حال ساده)	
(ما) می خواهیم /(mǎ) mi.kǎ.him/	(من) می خواهم /(man) mi.kǎ.ham/
(شما) می خواهید /(šo.mǎ) mi.kǎ.hid/	(تو) می خواهی /(to) mi.kǎ.hi/
(آنها) می خواهند /(ǎn.hǎ) mi.kǎ.hand/	(او/آن) می خواهد /(u/ ǎn) mi.kǎ.had/
Present Subjunctive مضارع التزامی	
(ما) بخواهیم /(mǎ) be.kǎ.him/	(من) بخواهم /(man) be.kǎ.ham/
(شما) بخواهید /(šo.mǎ) be.kǎ.hid/	(تو) بخواهی /(to) be.kǎ.hi/
(آنها) بخواهند /(ǎn.hǎ) be.kǎ.hand/	(او/آن) بخواهد /(u/ ǎn) be.kǎ.had/
Present Progressive مضارع مستمر(در جریان)	
(ما) داریم می خواهیم /(mǎ) dǎ.rim- mi.kǎ.him/	(من) دارم می خواهم /(man) dǎ.ram- mi.kǎ.ham/
(شما) دارید می خواهید /(šo.mǎ) dǎ.rid- mi.kǎ.hid/	(تو) داری می خواهی /(to) dǎ.ri- mi.kǎ.hi/
(آنها) دارند می خواهند /(ǎn.hǎ) dǎ.rand- mi.kǎ.hand/	(او/آن) دارد می خواهد /(u/ ǎn) dǎ.rad- mi.kǎ.had/

Simple Past
ماضی مطلق (گذشته ساده)

(ما) خواستیم	(من) خواستم
/(mă) kăs.tim/	/(man) kăs.tam/
(شما) خواستید	(تو) خواستی
/(šo.mă) kăs.tid/	/(to) kăs.ti/
(آنها) خواستند	(او/آن) خواست
/(ăn.hă) kăs.tand/	/(u/ ăn) kăst/

Imperfect Indicative
ماضی استمراری

(ما) می خواستیم	(من) می خواستم
/(mă) mi.kăs.tim/	/(man) mi.kăs.tam/
(شما) می خواستید	(تو) می خواستی
/(šo.mă) mi.kăs.tid/	/(to) mi.kăs.ti/
(آنها) می خواستند	(او/آن) می خواست
/(ăn.hă) mi.kăs.tand/	/(u/ ăn) mi.kăst/

Present Perfect
ماضی نقلی

(ما) خواسته ایم	(من) خواسته ام
/(mă) kăs.te.im/	/(man) kăs.te.am/
(شما) خواسته اید	(تو) خواسته ای
/(šo.mă) kăs.te.id/	/(to) kăs.te.i/
(آنها) خواسته اند	(او/آن) خواسته است
/(ăn.hă) kăs.te.and/	/(u/ ăn) kăs.te- ast/

Past Perfect
ماضی بعید

(ما) خواسته بودیم	(من) خواسته بودم
/(mă) kăs.te- bu.dim/	/(man) kăs.te- bu.dam/
(شما) خواسته بودید	(تو) خواسته بودی
/(šo.mă) kăs.te- bu.did/	/(to) kăs.te- bu.di/
(آنها) خواسته بودند	(او/آن) خواسته بود
/(ăn.hă) kăs.te- bu.dand/	/(u/ ăn) kăs.te- bud/

288

Past Subjunctive	
ماضی التزامی	
(ما) خواسته باشیم	(من) خواسته باشم
/(mǎ) ǩǎs.te- bǎ.šim/	/(man) ǩǎs.te- bǎ.šam/
(شما) خواسته باشید	(تو) خواسته باشی
/(šo.mǎ) ǩǎs.te- bǎ.šid/	/(to) ǩǎs.te- bǎ.ši/
(آنها) خواسته باشند	(او/آن) خواسته باشد
/(ǎn.hǎ) ǩǎs.te- bǎ.šand/	/(u/ ǎn) ǩǎs.te- bǎ.šad/

Past Progressive	
ماضی مستمر(در جریان)	
(ما) داشتیم می خواستیم	(من) داشتم می خواستم
/(mǎ) dǎš.tim- mi.ǩǎs.tim/	/(man) dǎš.tam- mi.ǩǎs.tam/
(شما) داشتید می خواستید	(تو) داشتی می خواستی
/(šo.mǎ) dǎš.tid- mi.ǩǎs.tid/	/(to) dǎš.ti- mi.ǩǎs.ti/
(آنها) داشتند می خواستند	(او/آن) داشت می خواست
/(ǎn.hǎ) dǎš.tand- mi.ǩǎs.tand/	/(u/ ǎn) dǎšt- mi.ǩǎst/

Simple Future	
مستقبل (آینده ساده)	
(ما) خواهیم خواست	(من) خواهم خواست
/(mǎ) ǩǎ.him- ǩǎst/	/(man) ǩǎ.ham- ǩǎst/
(شما) خواهید خواست	(تو) خواهی خواست
/(šo.mǎ) ǩǎ.hid- ǩǎst/	/(to) ǩǎ.hi- ǩǎst/
(آنها) خواهند خواست	(او/آن) خواهد خواست
/(ǎn.hǎ) ǩǎ.hand- ǩǎst/	/(u/ ǎn) ǩǎ.had- ǩǎst/

Command	
امر	
بخواهید!	بخواه!
/be.ǩǎ.hid/	/be.ǩǎh/

to wash

شُستَن

/šos.tan/

Plural	Singular
Simple Present	
مضارع اخباری(حال ساده)	
(ما) می شوییم /(mǎ) mi.šu.yim/	(من) می شویم /(man) mi.šu.yam/
(شما) می شویید /(šo.mǎ) mi.šu.yid/	(تو) می شویی /(to) mi.šu.yi/
(آنها) می شویند /(ǎn.hǎ) mi.šu.yand/	(او/آن) می شوید /(u/ ǎn) mi.šu.yad/
Present Subjunctive	
مضارع التزامی	
(ما) بشوییم /(mǎ) be.šu.yim/	(من) بشویم /(man) be.šu.yam/
(شما) بشویید /(šo.mǎ) be.šu.yid/	(تو) بشویی /(to) be.šu.yi/
(آنها) بشویند /(ǎn.hǎ) be.šu.yand/	(او/آن) بشوید /(u/ ǎn) be.šu.yad/
Present Progressive	
مضارع مستمر(در جریان)	
(ما) داریم می شوییم /(mǎ) dǎ.rim- mi.šu.yim/	(من) دارم می شویم /(man) dǎ.ram- mi.šu.yam/
(شما) دارید می شویید /(šo.mǎ) dǎ.rid- mi.šu.yid/	(تو) داری می شویی /(to) dǎ.ri- mi.šu.yi/
(آنها) دارند می شویند /(ǎn.hǎ) dǎ.rand- mi.šu.yand/	(او/آن) دارد می شوید /(u/ ǎn) dǎ.rad- mi.šu.yad/

Simple Past
ماضی مطلق (گذشته ساده)

(ما) شستیم	(من) شستم
/(mǎ) šos.tim/	/(man) šos.tam/
(شما) شستید	(تو) شستی
/(šo.mǎ) šos.tid/	/(to) šos.ti/
(آنها) شستند	(او/آن) شست
/(ǎn.hǎ) šos.tand/	/(u/ ǎn) šost/

Imperfect Indicative
ماضی استمراری

(ما) می شستیم	(من) می شستم
/(mǎ) mi.šos.tim/	/(man) mi.šos.tam/
(شما) می شستید	(تو) می شستی
/(šo.mǎ) mi.šos.tid/	/(to) mi.šos.ti/
(آنها) می شستند	(او/آن) می شست
/(ǎn.hǎ) mi.šos.tand/	/(u/ ǎn) mi.šost/

Present Perfect
ماضی نقلی

(ما) شسته ایم	(من) شسته ام
/(mǎ) šos.te.im/	/(man) šos.te.am/
(شما) شسته اید	(تو) شسته ای
/(šo.mǎ) šos.te.id/	/(to) šos.te.i/
(آنها) شسته اند	(او/آن) شسته است
/(ǎn.hǎ) šos.te.and/	/(u/ ǎn) šos.te- ast/

Past Perfect
ماضی بعید

(ما) شسته بودیم	(من) شسته بودم
/(mǎ) šos.te- bu.dim/	/(man) šos.te- bu.dam/
(شما) شسته بودید	(تو) شسته بودی
/(šo.mǎ) šos.te- bu.did/	/(to) šos.te- bu.di/
(آنها) شسته بودند	(او/آن) شسته بود
/(ǎn.hǎ) šos.te- bu.dand/	/(u/ ǎn) šos.te- bud/

Past Subjunctive
ماضی التزامی

(ما) شسته باشیم	(من) شسته باشم
/(mǎ) šos.te- bǎ.šim/	/(man) šos.te- bǎ.šam/
(شما) شسته باشید	(تو) شسته باشی
/(šo.mǎ) šos.te- bǎ.šid/	/(to) šos.te- bǎ.ši/
(آنها) شسته باشند	(او/آن) شسته باشد
/(ǎn.hǎ) šos.te- bǎ.šand/	/(u/ ǎn) šos.te- bǎ.šad/

Past Progressive
ماضی مستمر(در جریان)

(ما) داشتیم می شستیم	(من) داشتم می شستم
/(mǎ) dǎš.tim- mi.šos.tim/	/(man) dǎš.tam- mi.šos.tam/
(شما) داشتید می شستید	(تو) داشتی می شستی
/(šo.mǎ) dǎš.tid- mi.šos.tid/	/(to) dǎš.ti- mi.šos.ti/
(آنها) داشتند می شستند	(او/آن) داشت می شست
/(ǎn.hǎ) dǎš.tand- mi.šos.tand/	/(u/ ǎn) dǎšt- mi.šost/

Simple Future
مستقبل (آینده ساده)

(ما) خواهیم شست	(من) خواهم شست
/(mǎ) ǩǎ.him- šost/	/(man) ǩǎ.ham- šost/
(شما) خواهید شست	(تو) خواهی شست
/(šo.mǎ) ǩǎ.hid- šost/	/(to) ǩǎ.hi- šost/
(آنها) خواهند شست	(او/آن) خواهد شست
/(ǎn.hǎ) ǩǎ.hand- šost/	/(u/ ǎn) ǩǎ.had- šost/

Command
امر

بشویید!	بشوی!
/be.šu.yid/	/be.šuy/

to wear out

فَرسودَن

/far.su.dan/

Plural	Singular
Simple Present مضارع اخباری(حال ساده)	
(ما) می فرساییم /(mǎ) mi.far.sǎ.yim/	(من) می فرسایم /(man) mi.far.sǎ.yam/
(شما) می فرسایید /(šo.mǎ) mi.far.sǎ.yid/	(تو) می فرسایی /(to) mi.far.sǎ.yi/
(آنها) می فرسایند /(ǎn.hǎ) mi.far.sǎ.yand/	(او/آن) می فرساید /(u/ ǎn) mi.far.sǎ.yad/
Present Subjunctive مضارع التزامی	
(ما) بفرساییم /(mǎ) be.far.sǎ.yim/	(من) بفرسایم /(man) be.far.sǎ.yam/
(شما) بفرسایید /(šo.mǎ) be.far.sǎ.yid/	(تو) بفرسایی /(to) be.far.sǎ.yi/
(آنها) بفرسایند /(ǎn.hǎ) be.far.sǎ.yand/	(او/آن) بفرساید /(u/ ǎn) be.far.sǎ.yad/
Present Progressive مضارع مستمر(در جریان)	
(ما) داریم می فرساییم /(mǎ) dǎ.rim- mi.far.sǎ.yim/	(من) دارم می فرسایم /(man) dǎ.ram- mi.far.sǎ.yam/
(شما) دارید می فرسایید /(šo.mǎ) dǎ.rid- mi.far.sǎ.yid/	(تو) داری می فرسایی /(to) dǎ.ri- mi.far.sǎ.yi/
(آنها) دارند می فرسایند /(ǎn.hǎ) dǎ.rand- mi.far.sǎ.yand/	(او/آن) دارد می فرساید /(u/ ǎn) dǎ.rad- mi.far.sǎ.yad/

Simple Past
Simple Past
ماضی مطلق (گذشته ساده)

(ما) فرسودیم	(من) فرسودم
/(mă) far.su.dim/	/(man) far.su.dam/
(شما) فرسودید	(تو) فرسودی
/(šo.mă) far.su.did/	/(to) far.su.di/
(آنها) فرسودند	(او/آن) فرسود
/(ăn.hă) far.su.dand/	/(u/ ăn) far.sud/

Imperfect Indicative
ماضی استمراری

(ما) می فرسودیم	(من) می فرسودم
/(mă) mi.far.su.dim/	/(man) mi.far.su.dam/
(شما) می فرسودید	(تو) می فرسودی
/(šo.mă) mi.far.su.did/	/(to) mi.far.su.di/
(آنها) می فرسودند	(او/آن) می فرسود
/(ăn.hă) mi.far.su.dand/	/(u/ ăn) mi.far.sud/

Present Perfect
ماضی نقلی

(ما) فرسوده ایم	(من) فرسوده ام
/(mă) far.su.de.im/	/(man) far.su.de.am/
(شما) فرسوده اید	(تو) فرسوده ای
/(šo.mă) far.su.de.id/	/(to) far.su.de.i/
(آنها) فرسوده اند	(او/آن) فرسوده است
/(ăn.hă) far.su.de.and/	/(u/ ăn) far.su.de- ast/

Past Perfect
ماضی بعید

(ما) فرسوده بودیم	(من) فرسوده بودم
/(mă) far.su.de- bu.dim/	/(man) far.su.de- bu.dam/
(شما) فرسوده بودید	(تو) فرسوده بودی
/(šo.mă) far.su.de- bu.did/	/(to) far.su.de- bu.di/
(آنها) فرسوده بودند	(او/آن) فرسوده بود
/(ăn.hă) far.su.de- bu.dand/	/(u/ ăn) far.su.de- bud/

Past Subjunctive	
ماضی التزامی	
(ما) فرسوده باشیم	(من) فرسوده باشم
/(mǎ) far.su.de- bǎ.šim/	/(man) far.su.de- bǎ.šam/
(شما) فرسوده باشید	(تو) فرسوده باشی
/(šo.mǎ) far.su.de- bǎ.šid/	/(to) far.su.de- bǎ.ši/
(آنها) فرسوده باشند	(او/ آن) فرسوده باشد
/(ǎn.hǎ) far.su.de- bǎ.šand/	/(u/ ǎn) far.su.de- bǎ.šad/

Past Progressive	
ماضی مستمر(در جریان)	
(ما) داشتیم می فرسودیم	(من) داشتم می فرسودم
/(mǎ) dǎš.tim- mi.far.su.dim/	/(man) dǎš.tam- mi.far.su.dam/
(شما) داشتید می فرسودید	(تو) داشتی می فرسودی
/(šo.mǎ) dǎš.tid- mi.far.su.did/	/(to) dǎš.ti- mi.far.su.di/
(آنها) داشتند می فرسودند	(او/ آن) داشت می فرسود
/(ǎn.hǎ) dǎš.tand- mi.far.su.dand/	/(u/ ǎn) dǎšt- mi.far.sud/

Simple Future	
مستقبل (آینده ساده)	
(ما) خواهیم فرسود	(من) خواهم فرسود
/(mǎ) kǎ.him- far.sud/	/(man) kǎ.ham- far.sud/
(شما) خواهید فرسود	(تو) خواهی فرسود
/(šo.mǎ) kǎ.hid- far.sud/	/(to) kǎ.hi- far.sud/
(آنها) خواهند فرسود	(او/ آن) خواهد فرسود
/(ǎn.hǎ) kǎ.hand- far.sud/	/(u/ ǎn) kǎ.had- far.sud/

Command	
امر	
بفرسایید!	بفرسای!
/be.far.sǎ.yid/	/be.far.sǎy/

to weave

رشتَن

/reš.tan/

Plural	Singular
Simple Present مضارع اخباری(حال ساده)	
(ما) می ریسیم /(mǎ) mi.ri.sim/	(من) می ریسم /(man) mi.ri.sam/
(شما) می ریسید /(šo.mǎ) mi.ri.sid/	(تو) می ریسی /(to) mi.ri.si/
(آنها) می ریسند /(ǎn.hǎ) mi.ri.sand/	(او/آن) می ریسد /(u/ ǎn) mi.ri.sad/
Present Subjunctive مضارع التزامی	
(ما) بریسیم /(mǎ) be.ri.sim/	(من) بریسم /(man) be.ri.sam/
(شما) بریسید /(šo.mǎ) be.ri.sid/	(تو) بریسی /(to) be.ri.si/
(آنها) بریسند /(ǎn.hǎ) be.ri.sand/	(او/آن) بریسد /(u/ ǎn) be.ri.sad/
Present Progressive مضارع مستمر(در جریان)	
(ما) داریم می ریسیم /(mǎ) dǎ.rim- mi.ri.sim/	(من) دارم می ریسم /(man) dǎ.ram- mi.ri.sam/
(شما) دارید می ریسید /(šo.mǎ) dǎ.rid- mi.ri.sid/	(تو) داری می ریسی /(to) dǎ.ri- mi.ri.si/
(آنها) دارند می ریسند /(ǎn.hǎ) dǎ.rand- mi.ri.sand/	(او/آن) دارد می ریسد /(u/ ǎn) dǎ.rad- mi.ri.sad/

296

	Simple Past
	ماضی مطلق (گذشته ساده)
(ما) رشتیم	(من) رشتم
/(mǎ) reš.tim/	/(man) reš.tam/
(شما) رشتید	(تو) رشتی
/(šo.mǎ) reš.tid/	/(to) reš.ti/
(آنها) رشتند	(او/آن) رشت
/(ǎn.hǎ) reš.tand/	/(u/ ǎn) rešt/

	Imperfect Indicative
	ماضی استمراری
(ما) می رشتیم	(من) می رشتم
/(mǎ) mi.reš.tim/	/(man) mi.reš.tam/
(شما) می رشتید	(تو) می رشتی
/(šo.mǎ) mi.reš.tid/	/(to) mi.reš.ti/
(آنها) می رشتند	(او/آن) می رشت
/(ǎn.hǎ) mi.reš.tand/	/(u/ ǎn) mi.rešt/

	Present Perfect
	ماضی نقلی
(ما) رشته ایم	(من) رشته ام
/(mǎ) reš.te.im/	/(man) reš.te.am/
(شما) رشته اید	(تو) رشته ای
/(šo.mǎ) reš.te.id/	/(to) reš.te.i/
(آنها) رشته اند	(او/آن) رشته است
/(ǎn.hǎ) reš.te.and/	/(u/ ǎn) reš.te- ast/

	Past Perfect
	ماضی بعید
(ما) رشته بودیم	(من) رشته بودم
/(mǎ) reš.te- bu.dim/	/(man) reš.te- bu.dam/
(شما) رشته بودید	(تو) رشته بودی
/(šo.mǎ) reš.te- bu.did/	/(to) reš.te- bu.di/
(آنها) رشته بودند	(او/آن) رشته بود
/(ǎn.hǎ) reš.te- bu.dand/	/(u/ ǎn) reš.te- bud/

297

Past Subjunctive	
ماضی التزامی	
(ما) رشته باشیم	(من) رشته باشم
/(mǎ) reš.te- bǎ.šim/	/(man) reš.te- bǎ.šam/
(شما) رشته باشید	(تو) رشته باشی
/(šo.mǎ) reš.te- bǎ.šid/	/(to) reš.te- bǎ.ši/
(آنها) رشته باشند	(او/آن) رشته باشد
/(ǎn.hǎ) reš.te- bǎ.šand/	/(u/ ǎn) reš.te- bǎ.šad/

Past Progressive	
ماضی مستمر(در جریان)	
(ما) داشتیم می رشتیم	(من) داشتم می رشتم
/(mǎ) dǎš.tim- mi.reš.tim/	/(man) dǎš.tam- mi.reš.tam/
(شما) داشتید می رشتید	(تو) داشتی می رشتی
/(šo.mǎ) dǎš.tid- mi.reš.tid/	/(to) dǎš.ti- mi.reš.ti/
(آنها) داشتند می رشتند	(او/آن) داشت می رشت
/(ǎn.hǎ) dǎš.tand- mi.reš.tand/	/(u/ ǎn) dǎšt- mi.rešt/

Simple Future	
مستقبل (آینده ساده)	
(ما) خواهیم رشت	(من) خواهم رشت
/(mǎ) kǎ.him- rešt/	/(man) kǎ.ham- rešt/
(شما) خواهید رشت	(تو) خواهی رشت
/(šo.mǎ) kǎ.hid- rešt/	/(to) kǎ.hi- rešt/
(آنها) خواهند رشت	(او/آن) خواهد رشت
/(ǎn.hǎ) kǎ.hand- rešt/	/(u/ ǎn) kǎ.had- rešt/

Command	
امر	
بریسید!	بریس!
/be.ri.sid/	/be.ris/

298

to write

نِوِشتَن

/ne.veš.tan/

Plural	Singular
Simple Present مضارع اخباری(حال ساده)	
(ما) می نویسیم /(mǎ) mi.ne.vi.sim/	(من) می نویسم /(man) mi.ne.vi.sam/
(شما) می نویسید /(šo.mǎ) mi.ne.vi.sid/	(تو) می نویسی /(to) mi.ne.vi.si/
(آنها) می نویسند /(ǎn.hǎ) mi.ne.vi.sand/	(او/آن) می نویسد /(u/ ǎn) mi.ne.vi.sad/
Present Subjunctive مضارع التزامی	
(ما) بنویسیم /(mǎ) be.ne.vi.sim/	(من) بنویسم /(man) be.ne.vi.sam/
(شما) بنویسید /(šo.mǎ) be.ne.vi.sid/	(تو) بنویسی /(to) be.ne.vi.si/
(آنها) بنویسند /(ǎn.hǎ) be.ne.vi.sand/	(او/آن) بنویسد /(u/ ǎn) be.ne.vi.sad/
Present Progressive مضارع مستمر(در جریان)	
(ما) داریم می نویسیم /(mǎ) dǎ.rim- mi.ne.vi.sim/	(من) دارم می نویسم /(man) dǎ.ram- mi.ne.vi.sam/
(شما) دارید می نویسید /(šo.mǎ) dǎ.rid- mi.ne.vi.sid/	(تو) داری می نویسی /(to) dǎ.ri- mi.ne.vi.si/
(آنها) دارند می نویسند /(ǎn.hǎ) dǎ.rand- mi.ne.vi.sand/	(او/آن) دارد می نویسد /(u/ ǎn) dǎ.rad- mi.ne.vi.sad/

	Simple Past
	ماضی مطلق (گذشته ساده)
(ما) نوشتیم	(من) نوشتم
/(mǎ) ne.veš.tim/	/(man) ne.veš.tam/
(شما) نوشتید	(تو) نوشتی
/(šo.mǎ) ne.veš.tid/	/(to) ne.veš.ti/
(آنها) نوشتند	(او/آن) نوشت
/(ǎn.hǎ) ne.veš.tand/	/(u/ ǎn) ne.vešt/

	Imperfect Indicative
	ماضی استمراری
(ما) می نوشتیم	(من) می نوشتم
/(mǎ) mi.ne.veš.tim/	/(man) mi.ne.veš.tam/
(شما) می نوشتید	(تو) می نوشتی
/(šo.mǎ) mi.ne.veš.tid/	/(to) mi.ne.veš.ti/
(آنها) می نوشتند	(او/آن) می نوشت
/(ǎn.hǎ) mi.ne.veš.tand/	/(u/ ǎn) mi.ne.vešt/

	Present Perfect
	ماضی نقلی
(ما) نوشته ایم	(من) نوشته ام
/(mǎ) ne.veš.te.im/	/(man) ne.veš.te.am/
(شما) نوشته اید	(تو) نوشته ای
/(šo.mǎ) ne.veš.te.id/	/(to) ne.veš.te.i/
(آنها) نوشته اند	(او/آن) نوشته است
/(ǎn.hǎ) ne.veš.te.and/	/(u/ ǎn) ne.veš.te- ast/

	Past Perfect
	ماضی بعید
(ما) نوشته بودیم	(من) نوشته بودم
/(mǎ) ne.veš.te- bu.dim/	/(man) ne.veš.te- bu.dam/
(شما) نوشته بودید	(تو) نوشته بودی
/(šo.mǎ) ne.veš.te- bu.did/	/(to) ne.veš.te- bu.di/
(آنها) نوشته بودند	(او/آن) نوشته بود
/(ǎn.hǎ) ne.veš.te- bu.dand/	/(u/ ǎn) ne.veš.te- bud/

Past Subjunctive	
ماضی التزامی	
(ما) نوشته باشیم	(من) نوشته باشم
/(mă) ne.veš.te- bă.šim/	/(man) ne.veš.te- bă.šam/
(شما) نوشته باشید	(تو) نوشته باشی
/(šo.mă) ne.veš.te- bă.šid/	/(to) ne.veš.te- bă.ši/
(آنها) نوشته باشند	(او/آن) نوشته باشد
/(ăn.hă) ne.veš.te- bă.šand/	/(u/ ăn) ne.veš.te- bă.šad/

Past Progressive	
ماضی مستمر(در جریان)	
(ما) داشتیم می نوشتیم	(من) داشتم می نوشتم
/(mă) dăš.tim- mi.ne.veš.tim/	/(man) dăš.tam- mi.ne.veš.tam/
(شما) داشتید می نوشتید	(تو) داشتی می نوشتی
/(šo.mă) dăš.tid- mi.ne.veš.tid/	/(to) dăš.ti- mi.ne.veš.ti/
(آنها) داشتند می نوشتند	(او/آن) داشت می نوشت
/(ăn.hă) dăš.tand- mi.ne.veš.tand/	/(u/ ăn) dăšt- mi.ne.vešt/

Simple Future	
مستقبل (آینده ساده)	
(ما) خواهیم نوشت	(من) خواهم نوشت
/(mă) kă.him- ne.vešt/	/(man) kă.ham- ne.vešt/
(شما) خواهید نوشت	(تو) خواهی نوشت
/(šo.mă) kă.hid- ne.vešt/	/(to) kă.hi- ne.vešt/
(آنها) خواهند نوشت	(او/آن) خواهد نوشت
/(ăn.hă) kă.hand- ne.vešt/	/(u/ ăn) kă.had- ne.vešt/

Command	
امر	
بنویسید!	بنویس!
/be.ne.vi.sid/	/be.ne.vis/

Regular and Irregular Persian Verbs and their Stems

All Persian verbs in their infinitive form, regardless of being a *regular* or an *irregular* verb end either in: "دن" or "تن".

All verbs have two stems: present and past. The stem of a verb is the part of a verb which usually does not change when the verb is conjugated. Categorizing the *regular* verbs, in order to figure out the present and the past stems is doable, because neither the present nor the past stem in *regular* Persian verbs change. In contrast, identifying the stems in *irregular* Persian verbs is not an easy task since the present stem of the *irregular* verbs changes. Even though, some similar rules may apply to each set of *irregular* verbs, there are always some exceptions to each group which can make the teaching and learning process challenging. The good news is that the number of commonly used *irregular* verbs in the Persian language is limited.

In this part of the book, we will briefly go over the rules for identifying the stems (present and past) in *regular* verbs and then, a table containing the present and the past stems of the 100 *irregular* Persian verbs presented in this book is provided. The table of 100 *irregular* Persian verbs also consists of the synonyms to each verb.

Identifying the Past and Present Stems
in Regular and Irregular Persian Verbs

1- In regular verbs (infinitives) ending in: "تَن" /.tan/

   a) Present stems are formed by eliminating the **"تن"** from the end of the infinitives.

   b) Past stems are formed by eliminating the **"ن"** from the end of the infinitives.

NOTE: Most Persian verbs ending in "تَن" are _irregular_.

- Examples of the verbs in this group:

(definition) معنی	(past stem) بن ماضی	(present stem) بن مضارع	(infinitive) مصدر
to bloom	شِکُفت	شِکُف	شِکُفتَن= شِکُف + تَن /še.kof.tan/
to kill	کُشت	کُش	کُشتَن = کُش + تَن /koš.tan/

2.1- In regular verbs (infinitives) ending in: "دن" /.dan/

a) Present stems are formed by eliminating the "دن" from the end of the infinitives.

b) Past stems are formed by eliminating the "ن" from the end of the infinitives.

- Examples of the verbs in this group:

(definition) معنی	(past stem) بن ماضی	(present stem) بن مضارع	(infinitive) مصدر
to bring	آوَرد	آوَر	آوَردَن= آوَر + دَن /ă.var.dan/
to cover	پوشاند	پوشان	پوشاندَن= پوشان + دَن /pu.šăn.dan/

2.2- In regular verbs (infinitives) ending in: "یدن" /i.dan/

a) Present stems are formed by eliminating the "یدن" from the end of the infinitives.

b) Past stems are formed by eliminating the "ن" from the end of the infinitives.

- Examples of the verbs in this group:

(definition) معنی	(past stem) بن ماضی	(present stem) بن مضارع	(infinitive) مصدر
to ask	پُرسید	پُرس	پُرسیدَن= پُرس + یدَن /por.si.dan/
to dance	رَقصید	رَقص	رَقصیدَن= رَقص + یدَن /rağ.si.dan/

305

3- In Irregular verbs (infinitives) ending either in: "دن" or "تن"

Categorizing this group of verbs in order to identify the present and the past stems is challenging; therefore the following table for the stems of the 100 irregular Persian verbs presented in this book is provided. This table also consists of the synonyms to each verb; the more commonly used equivalent verbs have been identified by an asterisk (*). For example: Consider the verb "آزردن" and its equivalent "آزار دادن *". In this case, "آزار دادن *" is the more commonly used verb in the Persian language.

definition معنی	synonym مترادف	past stem بن ماضی	present stem بن مضارع	infinitive مصدر
to decorate	تزئین کردن * /taz.in- kar.dan/	آراست /ă.răst/	آرای /ă.răy/	آراستن /ă.răs.tan/
to bother	آزار دادن * /ă.zăr- dă.dan/	آزرد /ă.zord/	آزار /ă.zăr/	آزردن /ă.zor.dan/
to test	آزمایش کردن * /ăz.mă.ye	آزمود /ăz.mud/	آزمای /ăz.măy/	آزمودن /ăz.mu.dan/
to rest	استراحت کردن * /es.te.ră.hat- kar.dan/	آسود /ă.sud/	آسای /ă.săy/	آسودن /ă.su.dan/
to be disturbed	آشفته شدن * /ă.šof.te- šo.dan/	آشفت /ă.šoft/	آشوب /ă.šub/	آشفتن /ă.šof.tan/
to create	خلق کردن /ǩalǧ- kar.dan/	آفرید /ă.fa.rid/	آفرین /ă.fa.rin/	آفریدن * /ă.fa.ri.dan/
to pollute	آلوده کردن * /ă.lu.de- kar.dan/	آلود /ă.lud/	آلای /ă.lăy/	آلودن /ă.lu.dan/
to come	نزدیک شدن /naz.dik- šo.dan/	آمد /ă.mad/	آی /ăy/	آمدن * /ă.ma.dan/

306

1.to learn 2.to teach	۱. * یادگرفتن /yǎd- ge.ref.tan/ ۲. * یاد دادن /yǎd- dǎ.dan/	آموخت /ǎ.muǩt/	آموز /ǎ.muz/	آموختن /ǎ.muǩ.tan/
to blend	* قاطی کردن /ǧǎ.ti- kar.dan/	آمیخت /ǎ.miǩt/	آمیز /ǎ.miz/	آمیختن /ǎ.miǩ.tan/
to hang	* آویزان کردن /ǎ.vi.zǎn- kar.dan/	آویخت /ǎ.viǩt/	آویز /ǎ.viz/	آویختن /ǎ.viǩ.tan/
to fall	سقوط کردن /so.ǧut- kar.dan/	افتاد /of.tǎd/	افت /oft/	* افتادن /of.tǎ.dan/
to raise (a flag)	افراختن /af.rǎǩ.tan/	افراشت /af.rǎšt/	افراز /af.rǎz/	* افراشتن /af.rǎš.tan/
to kindle	* روشن کردن /ro.šan- kar.dan/	افروخت /af.ruǩt/	افروز /af.ruz/	افروختن /af.ruǩ.tan/
to add	* اضافه کردن /e.zǎ.fe- kar.dan/	افزود /af.zud/	افزای /af.zǎy/	افزودن /af.zu.dan/
to pile up	* جمع کردن /jam'- kar.dan/	انباشت /an.bǎšt/	انبار /an.bǎr/	انباشتن /an.bǎš.tan/
to drop	پرتاب کردن /par.tǎb- kar.dan/	انداخت /an.dǎǩt/	انداز /an.dǎz/	* انداختن /an.dǎǩ.tan/
to save, to store	* پس انداز کردن /pas.an.dǎz- kar.dan/	اندوخت /an.duǩt/	اندوز /an.duz/	اندوختن /an.duǩ.tan/
to stand	برپا خاستن /bar.pǎ- ǩas.tan/	ایستاد /is.tǎd/	ایست /ist/	* ایستادن /is.tǎ.dan/
to lose	بازنده شدن /bǎ.zan.de- šo.dan/	باخت /bǎǩt/	باز /bǎz/	* باختن /bǎǩ.tan/
to prevent	* جلوگیری کردن /je.lo.gi.ri- kar.dan/	بازداشت /bǎz.dǎšt/	بازدار /bǎz.dǎr/	بازداشتن /bǎz.dǎš.tan/
to retell	* بازگو کردن /bǎz.gu- kar.dan/	بازگفت /bǎz.goft/	بازگوی /bǎz.guy/	بازگفتن /bǎz.gof.tan/

to forgive	بخشیدن * /baǩ.ši.dan/	بخشود /baǩ.šud/	بخشای /baǩ.šǎy/	بخشودن /baǩ.šu.dan/
to overthrow	سرنگون کردن /sar.ne.gun- kar.dan/	برانداخت /bar.an.dǎǩt/	برانداز /bar.an.dǎz/	برانداختن * /bar.an.dǎǩ.tan/
to stimulate	دگرگون کردن * /de.gar.gun- kar.dan/	برانگیخت /bar.an.giǩt/	برانگیز /bar.an.giz/	برانگیختن /bar.an.giǩ.tan/
to rise	بلند شدن * /bo.land- šo.dan/	برخاست /bar.ǩǎst/	برخیز /bar.ǩiz/	برخاستن /bar.ǩǎs.tan/
to pick up	بلند کردن /bo.land- kar.dan/	برداشت /bar.dǎšt/	بردار /bar.dǎr/	برداشتن * /bar.dǎš.tan/
to come back	باز گشتن /bǎz.gaš.tan/	برگشت /bar.gašt/	برگرد /bar.gard/	برگشتن * /bar.gaš.tan/
to select	انتخاب کردن * /en.te.ǩǎb- kar.dan/	برگزید /bar.go.zid/	برگزین /bar.go.zin/	برگزیدن /bar.go.zi.dan/
to close	مسدود کردن /mas.dud- kar.dan/	بست /bast/	بند /band/	بستن * /bas.tan/
to be	وجود داشتن /vo.jud- dǎš.tan/	بود /bud/	باش /bǎ/	بودن * /bu.dan/
to refine	تصفیه کردن * /tas.fi.ye- kar.dan/	پالود /pǎ.lud/	پالای /pǎ.lǎy/	پالودن /pǎ.lu.dan/
to cook	پخت و پز کردن /poǩ.to.paz- kardan/	پخت /poǩt/	پز /paz/	پختن * /poǩ.tan/
to accept	قبول کردن * /ğa.bul- kar.dan/	پذیرفت /pa.zi.roft/	پذیر /pa.zir/	پذیرفتن /pa.zi.rof.tan/
to pay	پرداخت کردن * /par.dǎǩt- kar.dan/	پرداخت /par.dǎǩt/	پرداز /par.dǎz/	پرداختن /par.dǎǩ.tan/
to deem	خیال کردن * /ǩi.yǎl- kar.dan/	پنداشت /pen.dǎšt/	پندار /pen.dǎr/	پنداشتن /pen.dǎš.tan/
to groom	مرتّب کردن * /mo.rat.tab- kar.dan/	پیراست /pi.rǎst/	پیرای /pi.rǎy/	پیراستن /pi.rǎs.tan/

to traverse	طی کردن *	پیمود	پیمای	پیمودن
	/tey- kar.dan/	/pey.mud/	/pey.mǎy/	/pey.mu.dan/
to join	همراه شدن *	پیوست	پیوند	پیوستن
	/ham.rǎh- šo.dan/	/pey.vast/	/pey.vand/	/pey.vas.tan/
to gallop	چهار نعل رفتن	تاخت	تاز	تاختن *
	/ča.hǎr- na'l- raf.tan/	/tǎkt/	/tǎz/	/tǎk.tan/
to braid	بافتن *	تافت	تاب	تافتن
	/bǎf.tan/	/tǎft/	/tǎb/	/tǎf.tan/
to be able to	قادر بودن	توانست	توان	توانستن *
	/ğǎ.der- bu.dan/	/ta.vǎ.nest/	/ta.vǎn/	/ta.vǎ.nes.tan/
to leap	جهیدن *	جَست	جَه	جَستن
	/ja.hi.dan/	/jast/	/jah/	/jas.tan/
to seek	جستجو کردن *	جُست	جوی	جُستن
	/jos.te.ju- kar.dan/	/jost/	/juy/	/jos.tan/
to pick (a flower), to cut (w/ scissors)	قطع کردن	چید	چین	چیدن *
	/ğat'- kar.dan/	/čid/	/čin/	/či.dan/
to sleep	خوابیدن *	خُفت	خواب	خفتن
	/kǎ.bi.dan/	/koft/	/kǎb/	/kof.tan/
to want	طلب کردن	خواست	خواه	خواستن *
	/ta.lab- kar.dan/	/kǎst/	/kǎh/	/kǎs.tan/
to give	ارزانی کردن	داد	ده	دادن *
	/ar.zǎ.ni- kar.dan/	/dǎd/	/deh/	/dǎ.dan/
to have	مالک بودن	داشت	دار	داشتن *
	/mǎ.lek- bu.dan/	/dǎšt/	/dǎr/	/dǎš.tan/
to know	آگاه بودن	دانست	دان	دانستن *
	/ǎ.gǎh- bu.dan/	/dǎ.nest/	/dǎn/	/dǎ.nes.tan/
to understand	درک کردن *	دریافت	دریاب	دریافتن
	/dark- kar.dan/	/dar.yǎft/	/dar.yǎb/	/dar.yǎf.tan/
to sew	خیّاطی کردن	دوخت	دوز	دوختن *
	/kay.yǎ.ti- kar.dan/	/dukt/	/duz/	/duk.tan/

to see	تماشا کردن /ta.mǎ.šǎ- kar.dan/	دید /did/	بین /be.bin/	* دیدن /di.dan/
to steal	* دزدیدن /doz.di.dan/	ربود /ro.bud/	ربای /ro.bǎy/	ربودن /ro.bu.dan/
to weave	* ریسیدن /ri.si.dan/	رشت /rešt/	ریس /ris/	رشتن /reš.tan/
to go	دور شدن /dur- šo.dan/	رفت /raft/	رو /ro/	* رَفتن /raf.tan/
to pour, to spill	جاری کردن /jǎ.ri- kar.dan/	ریخت /rikt/	ریز /riz/	* ریختن /rik.tan/
to hit, to play (a musical instrument)	نواختن /na.vǎk.tan/	زد /zad/	زن /zan/	* زدن /za.dan/
to erase	* پاک کردن /pǎk- kar.dan/	زدود /zo.dud/	زدای /zo.dǎy/	زدودن /zo.du.dan/
to live	* زندگی کردن /zen.de.gi- kar.dan/	زیست /zist/	زی /zi/	زیستن /zis.tan/
to build	درست کردن /do.rost- kar.dan/	ساخت /sǎkt/	ساز /sǎz/	* ساختن /sǎk.tan/
to entrust	واگذار کردن /vǎ.go.zǎr- kar.dan/	سپرد /se.pord/	سپار /se.pǎr/	* سپردن /se.por.dan/
to praise	* ستایش کردن /se.tǎ.yeš- kar.dan/	ستود /se.tud/	ستای /se.tǎy/	ستودن /se.tu.dan/
to compose	* شعر گفتن /še'r- gof.tan/	سرود /so.rud/	سرای /so.rǎy/	سرودن /so.ru.dan/
to burn	آتش گرفتن /ǎ.taš- ge.ref.tan/	سوخت /sukt/	سوز /suz/	* سوختن /suk.tan/
to hurry	* شتاب کردن /še.tǎb- kar.dan/	شتافت /še.tǎft/	شتاب /še.tǎb/	شتافتن /še.tǎf.tan/
to become	گشتن /gaš.tan/	شد /šod/	شو /šo/	* شدن /šo.dan/

	Meaning	Past	Pres Stem	Inf
to wash	شستشو دادن /šos.te.šu- dă.dan/	شست /šost/	شوی /šuy/	* شستن /šos.tan/
to break	خرد کردن /ǩord- kar.dan/	شکست /še.kast/	شکن /še.kan/	* شکستن /še.kas.tan/
to count	حساب کردن /he.săb- kar.dan/	شمرد /še.mord/	شمار /šo.măr/	* شمردن /še.mor.dan/
to get to know	آشنا شدن /ă.še.nă- šo.dan/	شناخت /še.năkt/	شناس /še.năs/	* شناختن /še.năǩ.tan/
to hear	گوش دادن /guš- dă.dan/	شنید /še.nid/	شنو /še.no/	* شنیدن /še.ni.dan/
to send	روانه کردن /ra.vă.ne- kar.dan/	فرستاد /fe.res.tăd/	فرست /fe.rest/	* فرستادن /fe.res.tă.dan/
to wear out	* فرسوده شدن /far.su.de- šo.dan/	فرسود /far.sud/	فرسای /far.săy/	فرسودن /far.su.dan/
to order	* فرمان دادن /far.măn- dă.dan/	فرمود /far.mud/	فرمای /far.măy/	فرمودن /far.mu.dan/
to sell	به فروش رساندن /be- fo.ruš- re.săn.dan/	فروخت /fo.ruǩt/	فروش /fo.ruš/	* فروختن /fo.ruǩ.tan/
to seduce	* فریب دادن /fa.rib- dă.dan/	فریفت /fa.rift/	فریب /fa.rib/	فریفتن /fa.rif.tan/
to plant	کشت و زرع کردن /keš.to.zar'- kar.dan/	کاشت /kăšt/	کار /kăr/	* کاشتن /kăš.tan/
to do	انجام دادن /an.jăm- dă.dan/	کرد /kard/	کن /kon/	* کردن /kar.dan/
to fuse	* داغ کردن /dăǧ- kar.dan/	گداخت /go.dăǩt/	گداز /go.dăz/	گداختن /go.dăǩ.tan/
to put	نهادن /na.hă.dan/	گذاشت /go.zăšt/	گذار /go.zăr/	* گذاشتن /go.zăš.tan/
to pass	عبور کردن /'o.bur- kar.dan/	گذشت /go.zašt/	گذر /go.zar/	* گذشتن /go.zaš.tan/

to catch	قاپیدن /ğă.pi.dan/	گرفت /ge.reft/	گیر /gir/	* گرفتن /ge.ref.tan/
to escape	* فرار کردن /fa.răr- kar.dan/	گریخت /go.riǩt/	گریز /go.riz/	گریختن /go.riǩ.tan/
to cry	* گریه کردن /ger.ye- kar.dan/	گریست /ge.rist/	گری /gery/	گریستن /ge.ris.tan/
to choose	* انتخاب کردن /en.te.ǩăb- kar.dan/	گزید /go.zid/	گزین /go.zin/	گزیدن /go.zi.dan/
to come apart	* پاره کردن /pă.re- kar.dan/	گسیخت /go.siǩt/	گسل /go.sal/	گسیختن /go.siǩ.tan/
to search	جستجو کردن /jos.te.ju- kar.dan/	گشت /gašt/	گرد /gard/	* گشتن /gaš.tan/
to open	* باز کردن /băz- kar.dan/	گشود /go.šud/	گشای /go.šăy/	گشودن /go.šu.dan/
to tell	حرف زدن /harf- za.dan/	گفت /goft/	گوی /guy/	* گفتن /gof.tan/
to die	جان دادن /jăn- dă.dan/	مرد /mord/	میر /mir/	* مردن /mor.dan/
to sit	قرار گرفتن /ğa.răr- ge.ref.tan/	نشست /ne.šast/	نشین /ne.šin/	* نشستن /ne.šas.tan/
to inscribe	* نوشتن /ne.veš.tan/	نگاشت /ne.găšt/	نگار /ne.găr/	نگاشتن /ne.găš.tan/
to look	* نگاه کردن /ne.găh- kar.dan/	نگریست /ne.ga.rist/	نگر /ne.gar/	نگریستن /ne.ga.ris.tan/
to show	* نشان دادن /ne.šăn- dă.dan/	نمود /ne.mud/	نمای /ne.măy/	نمودن /ne.mu.dan/
to play (a musical instrument)	* زدن /za.dan/	نواخت /na.văǩt/	نواز /na.văz/	نواختن /na.văǩ.tan/
to write	نگاشتن /ne.găš.tan/	نوشت /ne.vešt/	نویس /ne.vis/	* نوشتن /ne.veš.tan/

to place	گذاشتن *	نهاد	نه	نهادن
	/go.zăš.tan/	/na.hăd/	/neh/	/na.hă.dan/
to stir	مخلوط کردن	هم زد	هم زن	هم زدن *
	/maǩ.lut- kar.dan/	/ham- zad/	/ham- zan/	/ham- za.dan/
to find	پیدا کردن *	یافت	یاب	یافتن
	/pey.dă- kar.dan/	/yăft/	/yăb/	/yăf.tan/

Similar Titles

100
Persian Verbs
(Fully Conjugated in the Most Common Tenses)
ISBN : 978-1939099099

1000 +
Most Useful
Persian Verbs
ISBN : 978-1939099181

To Learn More About BAHAR BOOKS

Please Visit the Website :

www.baharbooks.com

Bahar Books

Made in the USA
Lexington, KY
31 May 2018